ULTIMATE X-MEN

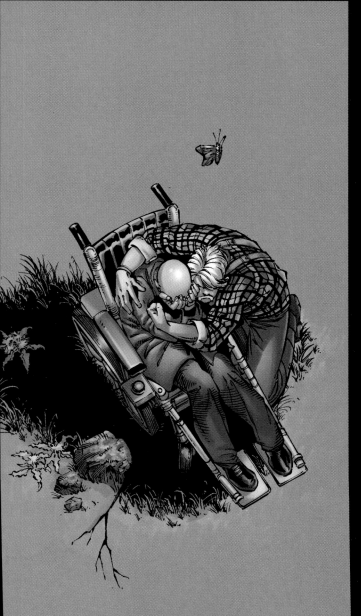

Story
Mark Millar
Chuck Austen

Pencils
Adam Kubert
Chris Bachalo
Esad Ribic

Inks
Livesay
Danny Miki
Chris Bachalo

Colors
J. D. Smith
Dave Stewart

Letters
Sharpefont
Chris Eliopoulos

Cover
Adam Kubert &
Richard Isanove

Assistant Editor
Pete Franco

Associate Editors
Brian Smith
C. B. Cebulski

Editors
Mark Powers
Ralph Macchio

Editor in Chief
Joe Quesada

President
Bill Jemas

WORLD
TOUR

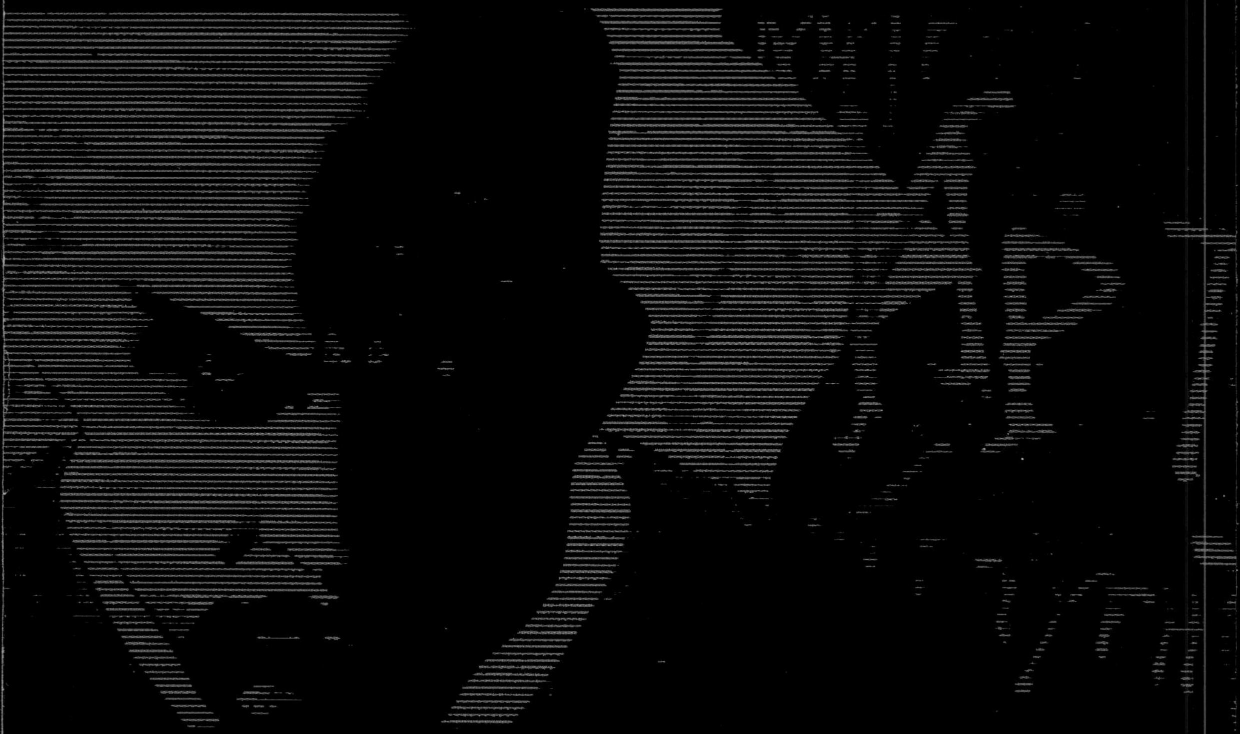

ULTIMATE X-MEN VOL. 3: WORLD TOUR. Contains material originally published in magazine form as ULTIMATE X-MEN #13-20 . First printing 2002. ISBN# 0-7851-0961-7. Published by MARVEL COMICS, a division of MARVEL ENTERTAINMENT GROUP, INC. OFFICE OF PUBLICATION: 10 East 40th Street, New York, NY 10016. Copyright © 2002 Marvel Characters, Inc. All rights reserved. $17.99 per copy in the U.S. and $29.00 in Canada (GST #R127032852); Canadian Agreement #40668537.   All characters featured in this issue and the distinctive names and likenesses thereof, and all related indicia are trademarks of Marvel Characters, Inc.   No similarity between any of the names, characters, persons, and/or institutions in this magazine with those of any living or dead person or institution is intended, and any such similarity which may exist is purely coincidental. **Printed in Canada.** STAN LEE, Chairman Emeritus. For information regarding advertising in Marvel Comics or on Marvel.com, please contact Russell Brown, Executive Vice President, Consumer Products, Promotions and Media Sales at 212-576-8561 or rbrown@marvel.com

10 9 8 7 6 5 4 3 2 1

ULTIMATE X MEN

It Doesn't Have to be This Way

Millar Kubert Miki

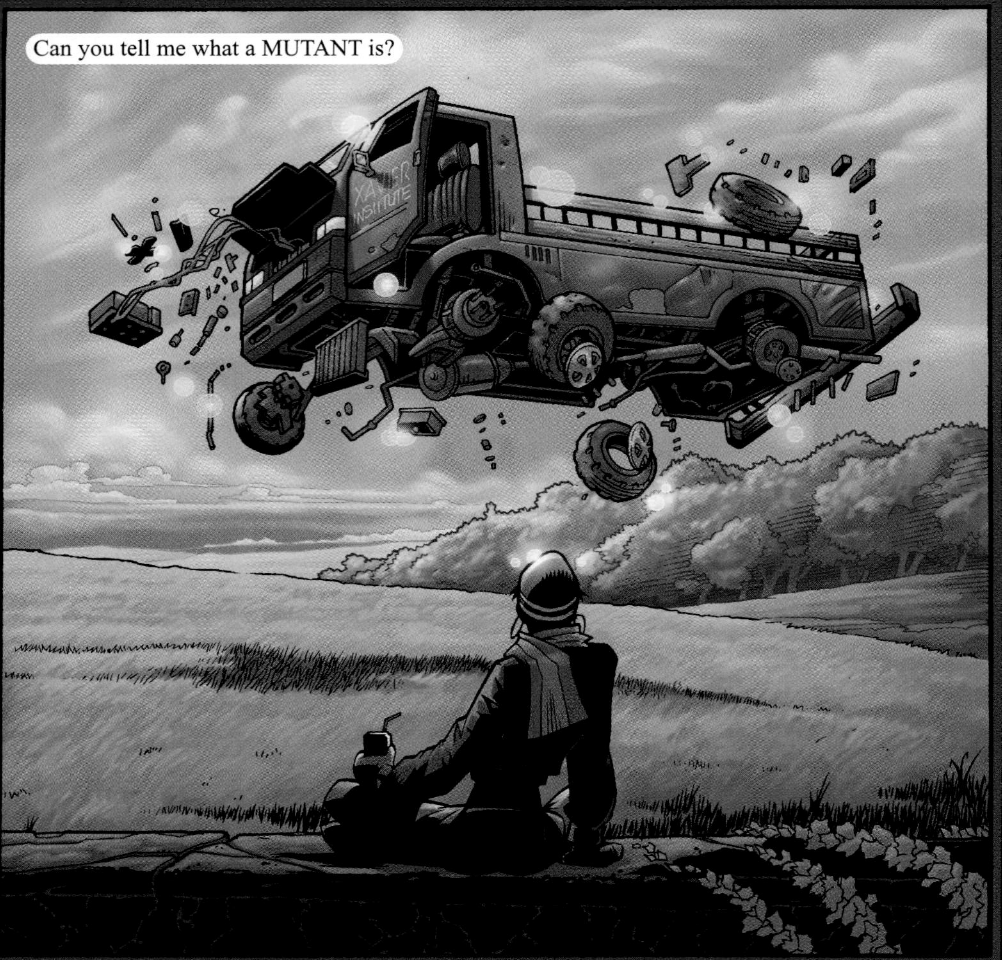
Can you tell me what a MUTANT is?
XAVIER INSTITUTE

Eliopoulos Stewart Smith Macchio Quesada Jemas

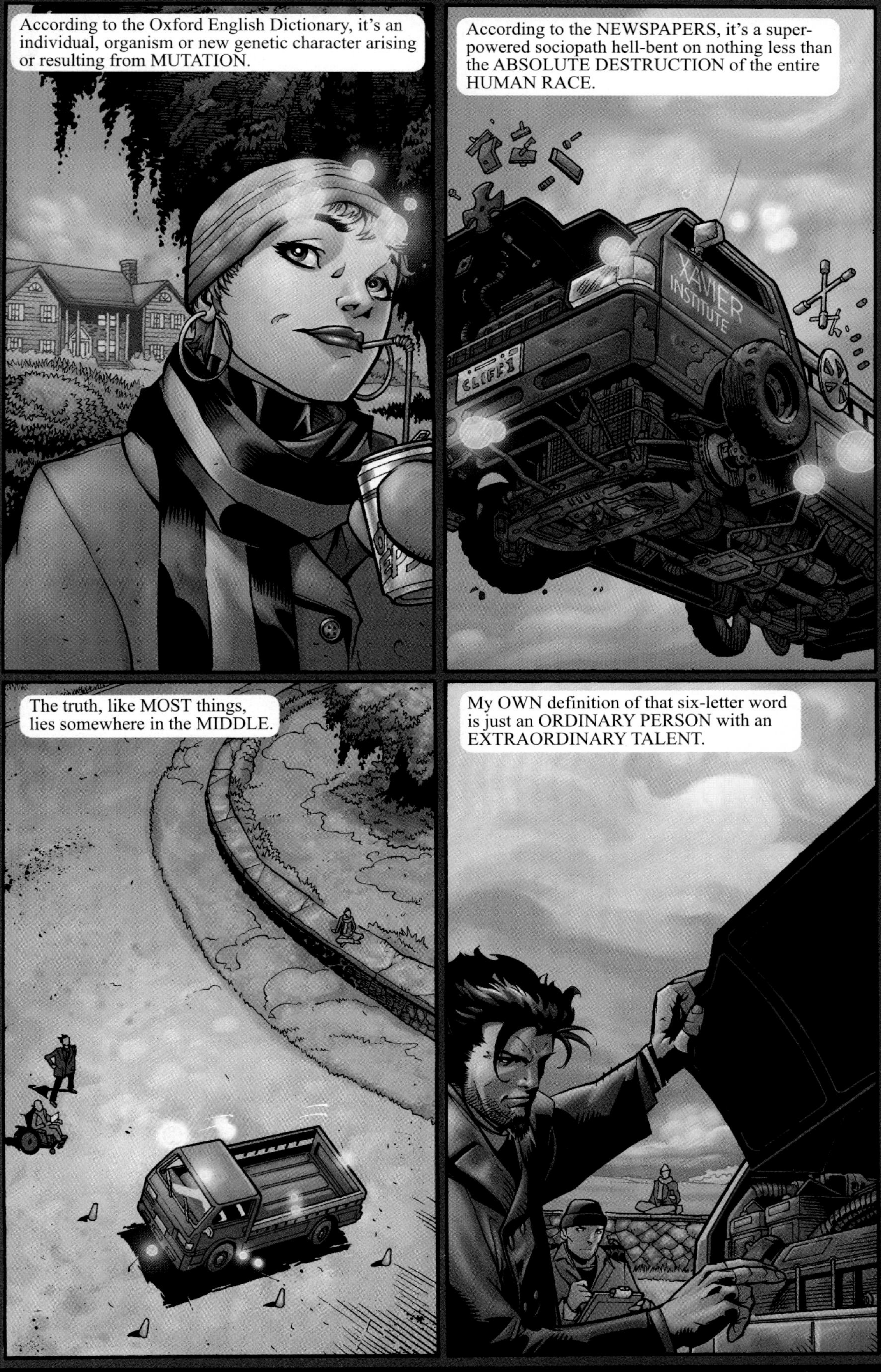
According to the Oxford English Dictionary, it's an individual, organism or new genetic character arising or resulting from MUTATION.
According to the NEWSPAPERS, it's a super-powered sociopath hell-bent on nothing less than the ABSOLUTE DESTRUCTION of the entire HUMAN RACE.
XAVIER INSTITUTE
CLIFF1
The truth, like MOST things, lies somewhere in the MIDDLE.
My OWN definition of that six-letter word is just an ORDINARY PERSON with an EXTRAORDINARY TALENT.

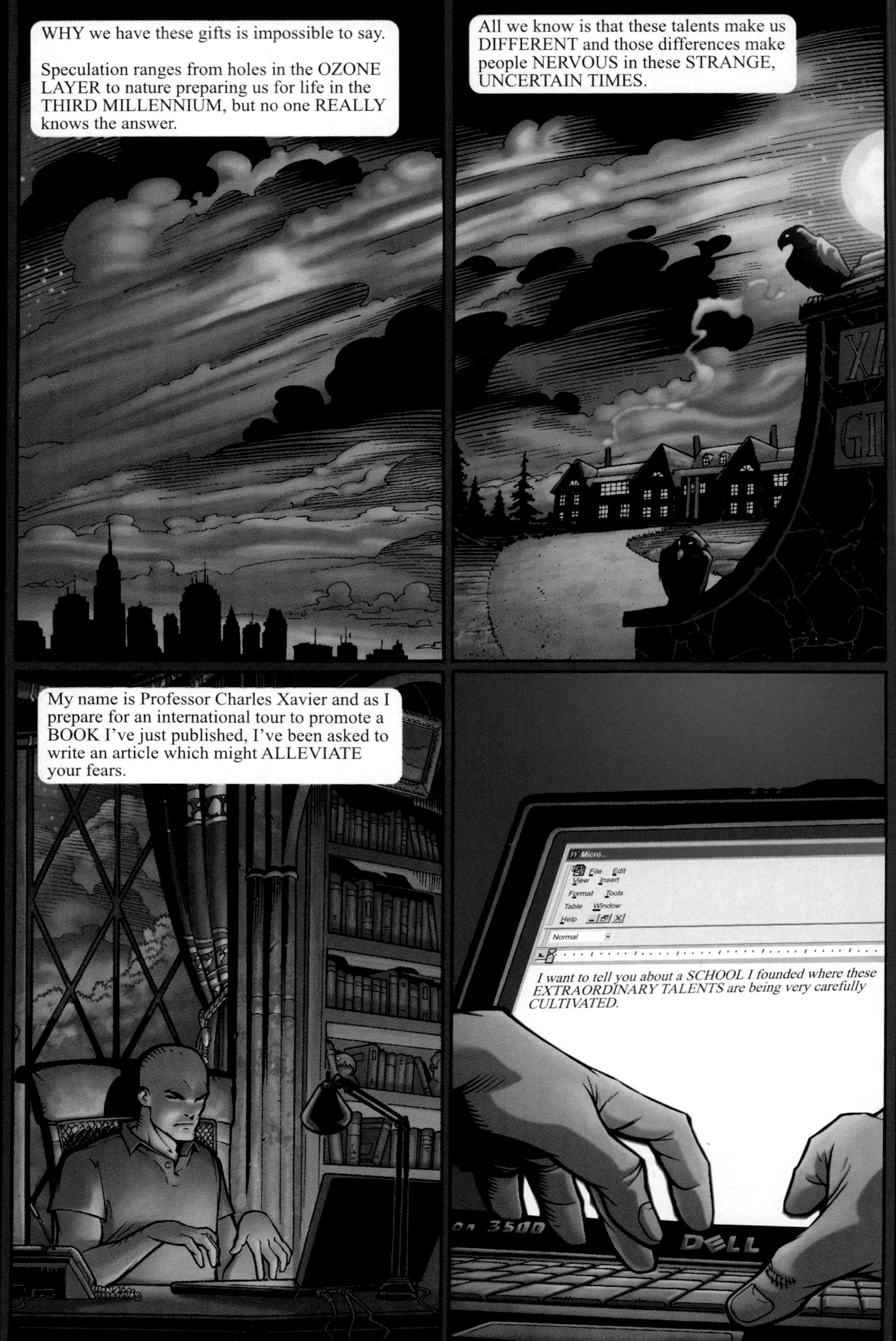
WHY we have these gifts is impossible to say.
Speculation ranges from holes in the OZONE LAYER to nature preparing us for life in the THIRD MILLENNIUM, but no one REALLY knows the answer.
All we know is that these talents make us DIFFERENT and those differences make people NERVOUS in these STRANGE, UNCERTAIN TIMES.
My name is Professor Charles Xavier and as I prepare for an international tour to promote a BOOK I've just published, I've been asked to write an article which might ALLEVIATE your fears.
Micro...
File Edit View Insert Format Tools Table Window Help
Normal
I want to tell you about a SCHOOL I founded where these EXTRAORDINARY TALENTS are being very carefully CULTIVATED.
DELL

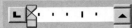

Personally, I've never understood why individuals who exhibit MUTANT abilities are regarded with suspicion when every other form of excellence is LAUDED by society.

Are songwriters persecuted for the power of their LYRICS? Are Quarterbacks hounded for the accuracy of their ARMS?

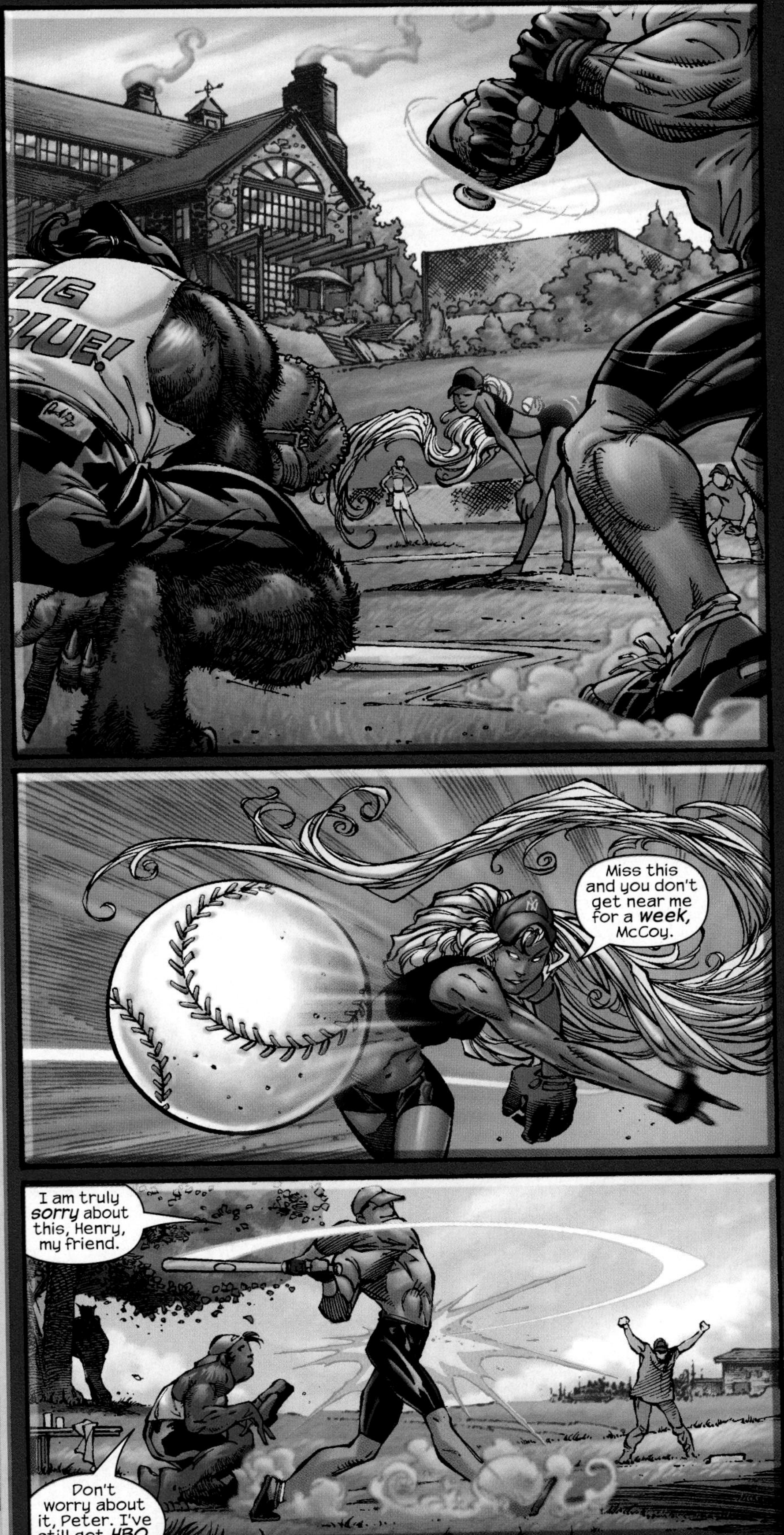

Miss this and you don't get near me for a *week*, McCoy.
I am truly *sorry* about this, Henry, my friend.
Don't worry about it, Peter. I've still got *HBO*.

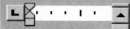

Of course, I don't mean to diminish the BIOLOGY of the situation when ninety-eight percent of all known mutants test positive for the X-FACTOR gene…

But aren't we all slaves to our inherited genetics?

After all, some say MUSIC runs in families…

…and others are clearly born with an aptitude for SPORT.

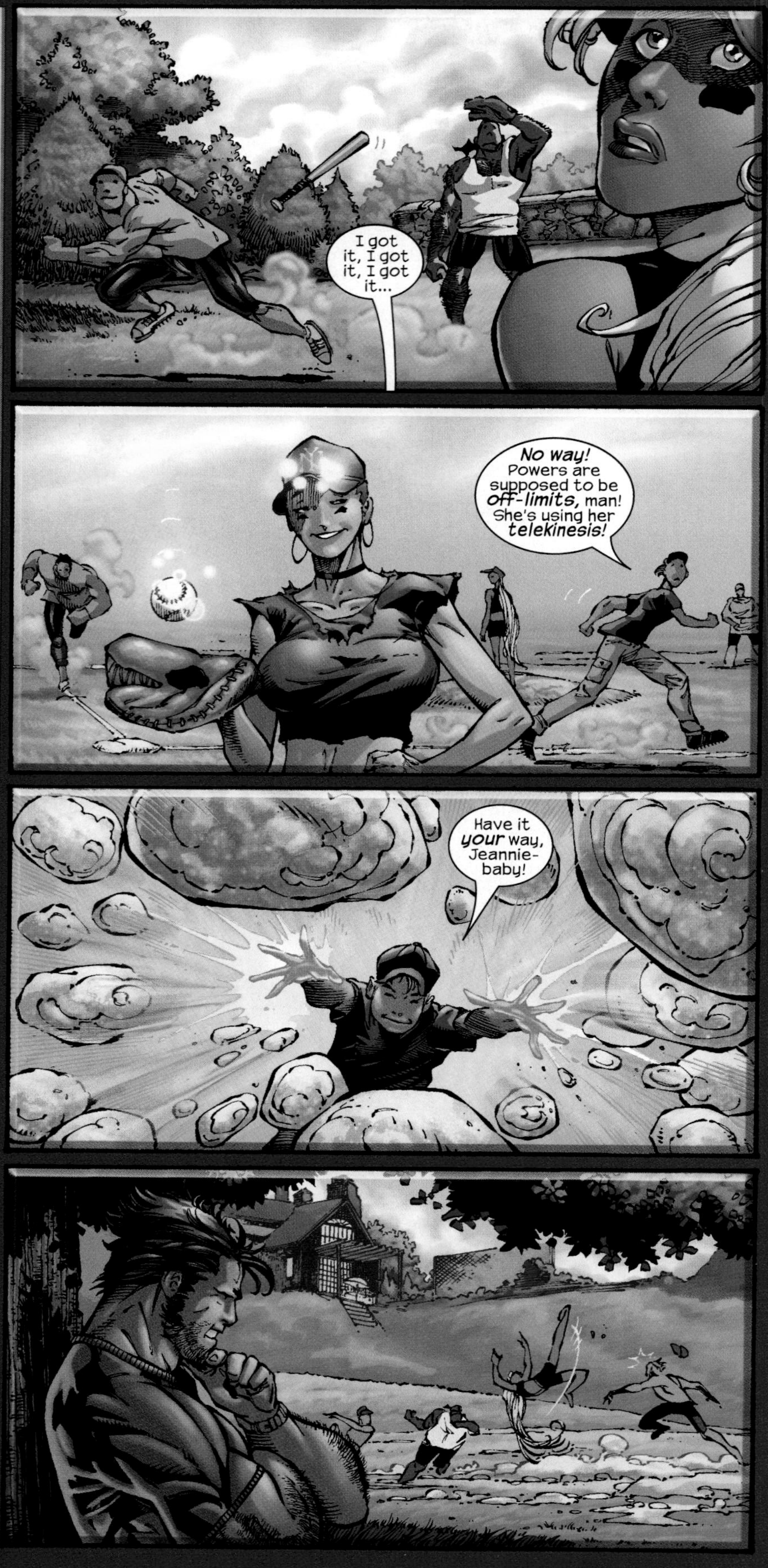

I got it, I got it, I got it...
No way! Powers are supposed to be off-limits, man! She's using her telekinesis!
Have it your way, Jeannie-baby!

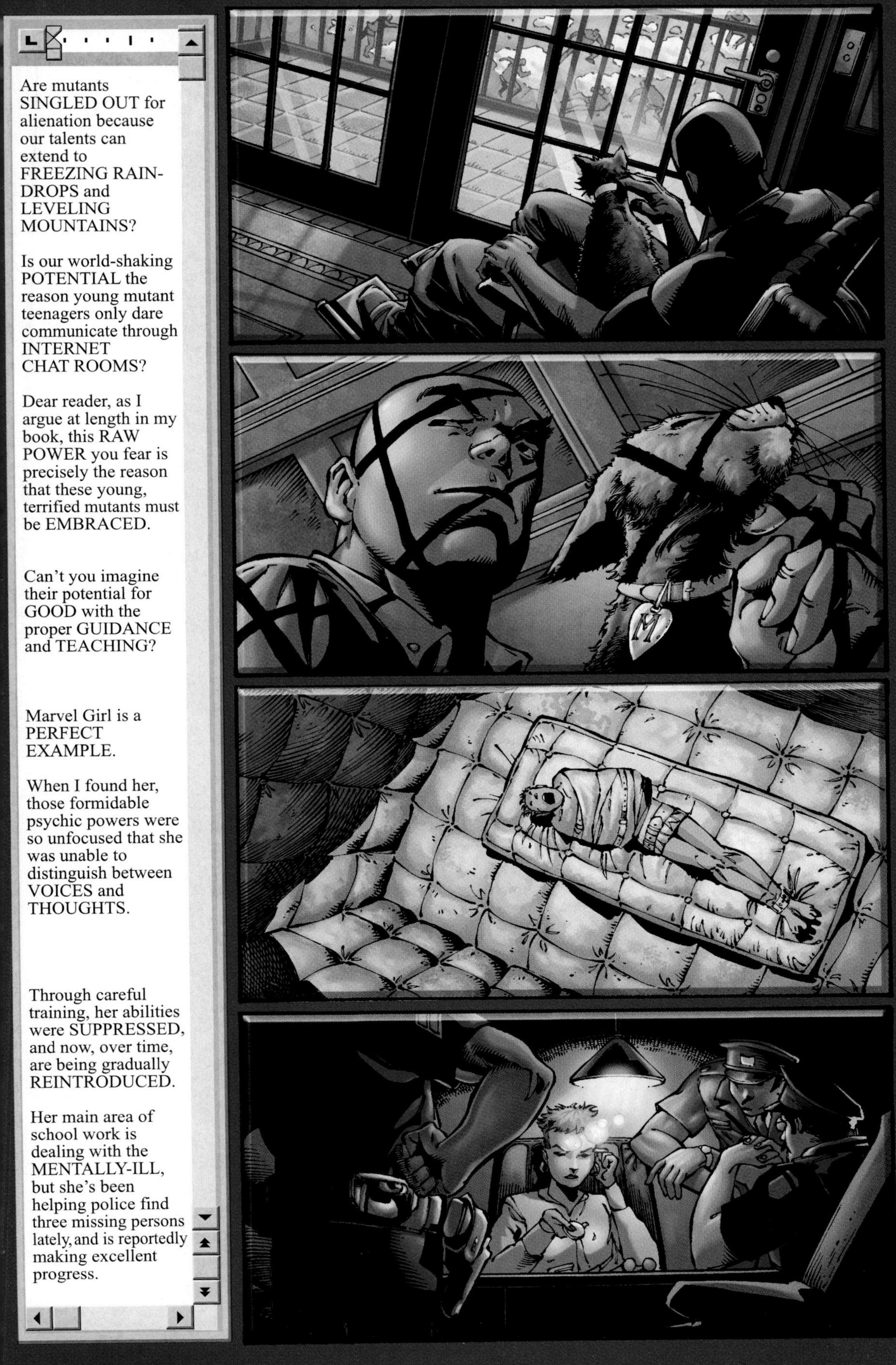
Are mutants SINGLED OUT for alienation because our talents can extend to FREEZING RAIN-DROPS and LEVELING MOUNTAINS?
Is our world-shaking POTENTIAL the reason young mutant teenagers only dare communicate through INTERNET CHAT ROOMS?
Dear reader, as I argue at length in my book, this RAW POWER you fear is precisely the reason that these young, terrified mutants must be EMBRACED.
Can't you imagine their potential for GOOD with the proper GUIDANCE and TEACHING?
Marvel Girl is a PERFECT EXAMPLE.
When I found her, those formidable psychic powers were so unfocused that she was unable to distinguish between VOICES and THOUGHTS.
Through careful training, her abilities were SUPPRESSED, and now, over time, are being gradually REINTRODUCED.
Her main area of school work is dealing with the MENTALLY-ILL, but she's been helping police find three missing persons lately, and is reportedly making excellent progress.
M

Storm is ANOTHER young student who has blossomed in the short time she's been following my PROGRAM.

An illegal Moroccan immigrant with almost no formal schooling, she's currently in the middle of a telepathic JOINT-DIPLOMA in both HORTICULTURE and ECONOMICS.

Last week, she used her atmospheric manipulation to reinvigorate a recession-hit FARMING COMMMUNITY and achieved a well-deserved A-PLUS for APPLIED USE of her ABILITIES.

Of course, there's more to education than TRADITIONAL ACADEMICS. My syllabus specializes in pop-culture, conversation and the arts of SELF-DEFENSE too.

Cyclops, for example, might have very poor grades, but his leadership skills are EXCEPTIONAL in our virtual reality COMBAT CLASSES.

Twice a week, between CHEMISTRY and HUMOR, I ask him to utilize these gifts and do something DANGEROUS with groups of UNDER-PRIVILEGED YOUNGSTERS.

As a orphan HIMSELF, I know he appreciates the importance of a solid and dependable ROLE MODEL.

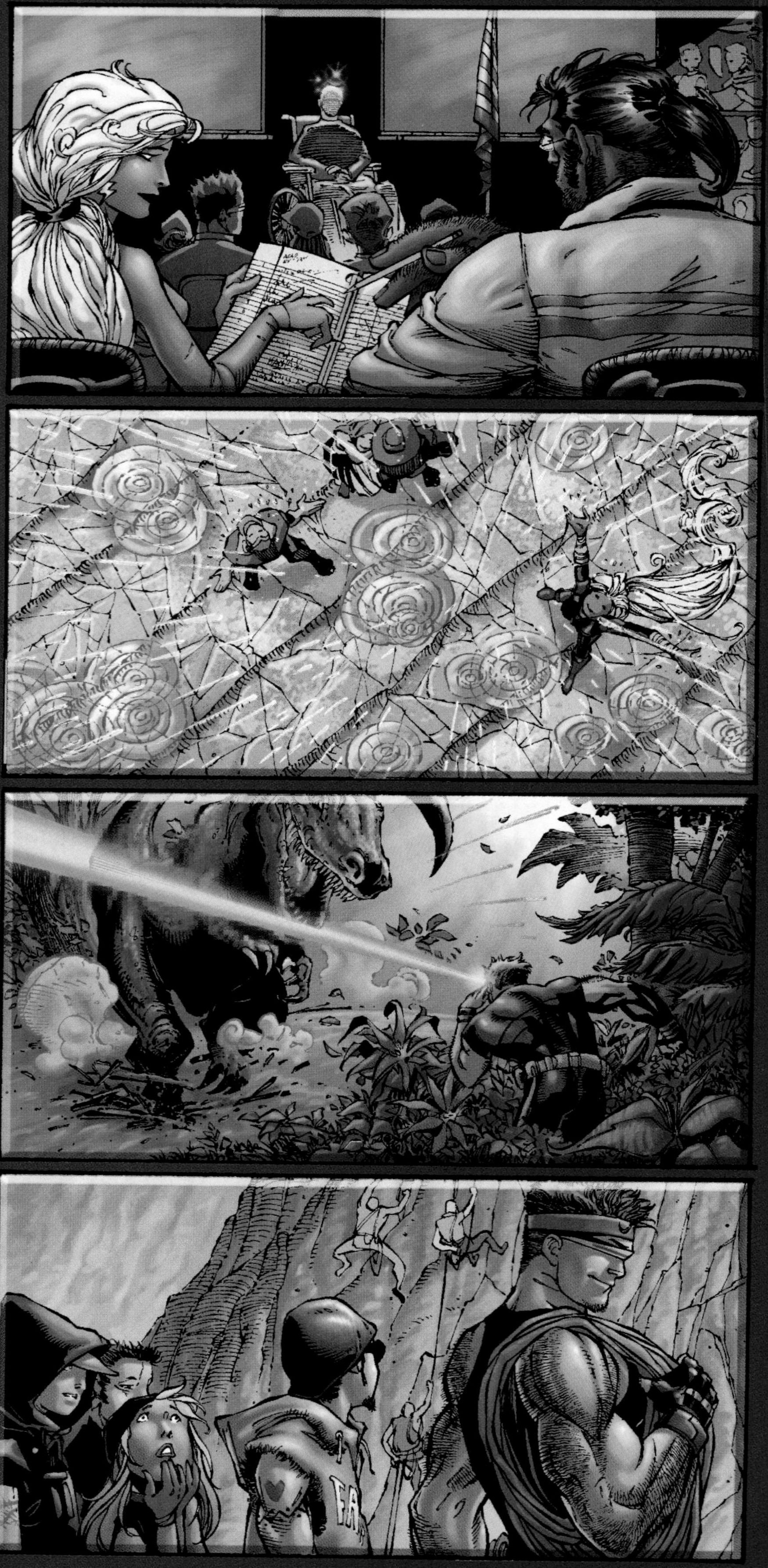

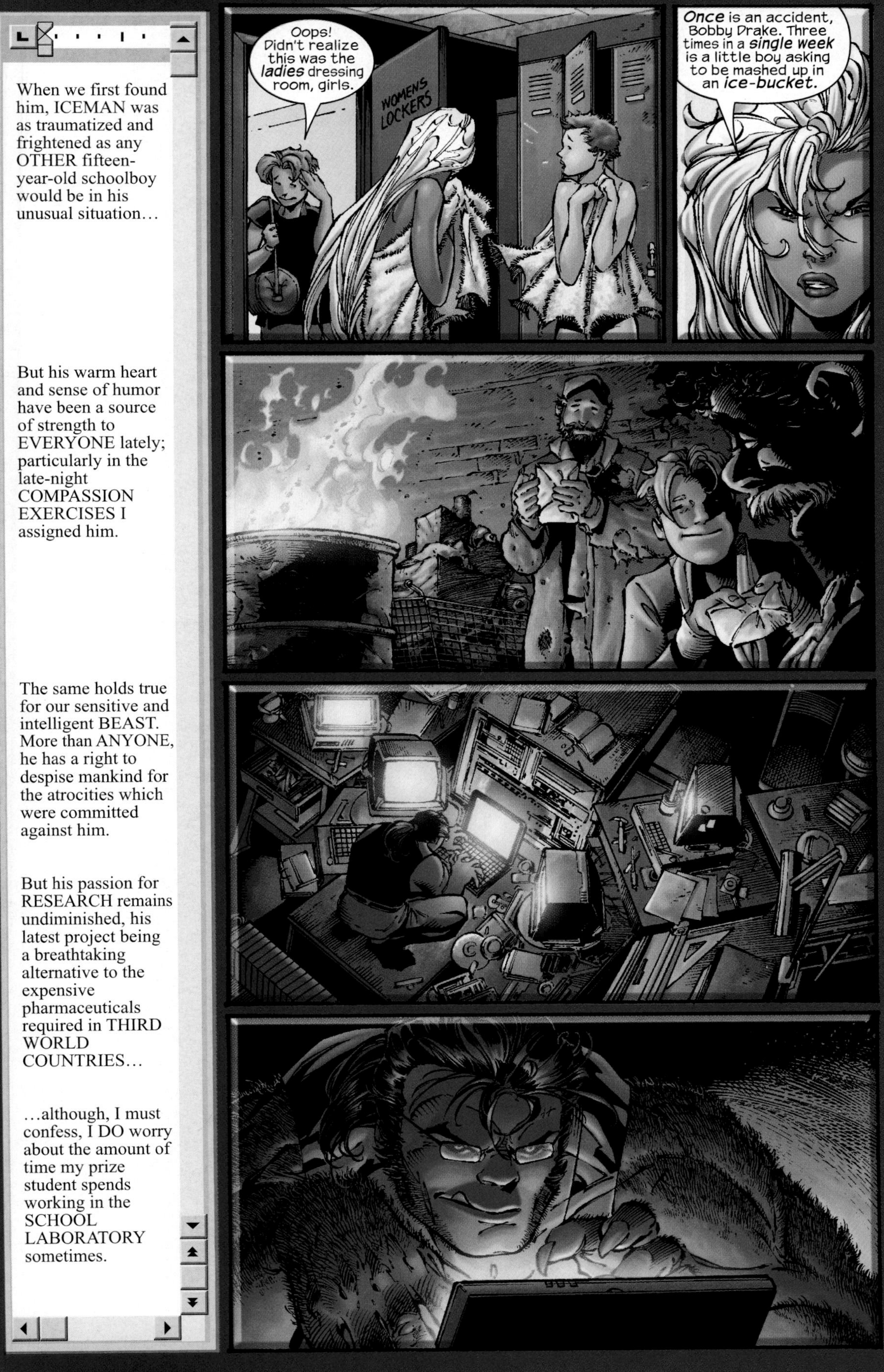
When we first found him, ICEMAN was as traumatized and frightened as any OTHER fifteen-year-old schoolboy would be in his unusual situation…
Oops! Didn't realize this was the *ladies* dressing room, girls.
WOMEN'S LOCKERS
Once is an accident, Bobby Drake. Three times in a *single week* is a little boy asking to be mashed up in an *ice-bucket.*
But his warm heart and sense of humor have been a source of strength to EVERYONE lately; particularly in the late-night COMPASSION EXERCISES I assigned him.
The same holds true for our sensitive and intelligent BEAST. More than ANYONE, he has a right to despise mankind for the atrocities which were committed against him.
But his passion for RESEARCH remains undiminished, his latest project being a breathtaking alternative to the expensive pharmaceuticals required in THIRD WORLD COUNTRIES…
…although, I must confess, I DO worry about the amount of time my prize student spends working in the SCHOOL LABORATORY sometimes.

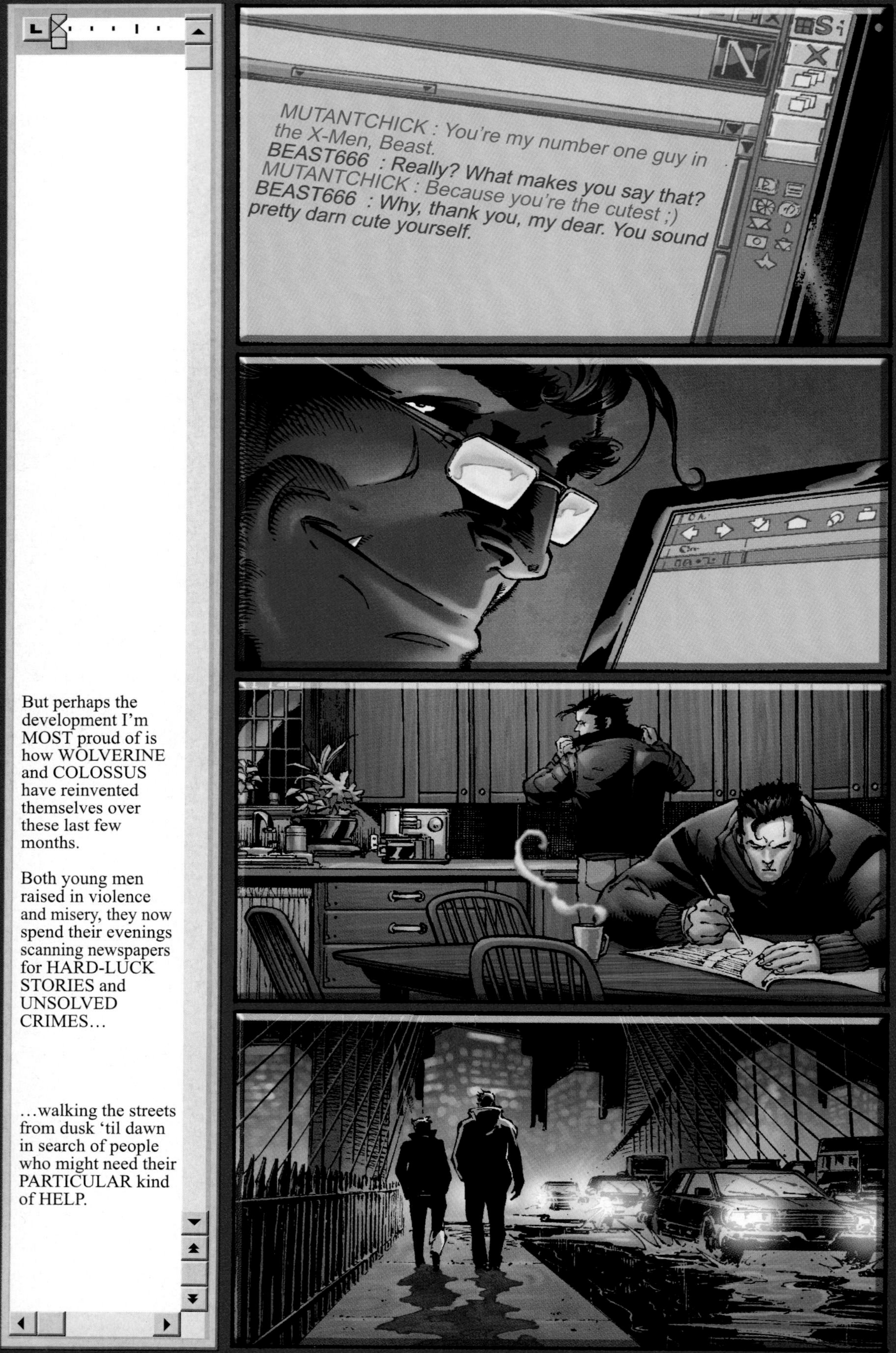
MUTANTCHICK : You're my number one guy in the X-Men, Beast.
BEAST666 : Really? What makes you say that?
MUTANTCHICK : Because you're the cutest ;)
BEAST666 : Why, thank you, my dear. You sound pretty darn cute yourself.
But perhaps the development I'm MOST proud of is how WOLVERINE and COLOSSUS have reinvented themselves over these last few months.
Both young men raised in violence and misery, they now spend their evenings scanning newspapers for HARD-LUCK STORIES and UNSOLVED CRIMES…
…walking the streets from dusk 'til dawn in search of people who might need their PARTICULAR kind of HELP.

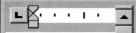

Of course, it would be NAÏVE to suggest that the MUTANT INFLUENCE is always an ENTIRELY positive one.

It's understandable that people are afraid when they see their homo-sapien children declare themselves X-FACTOR POSITIVE or hear the lyrics to their ANTI-HUMAN SONGS.

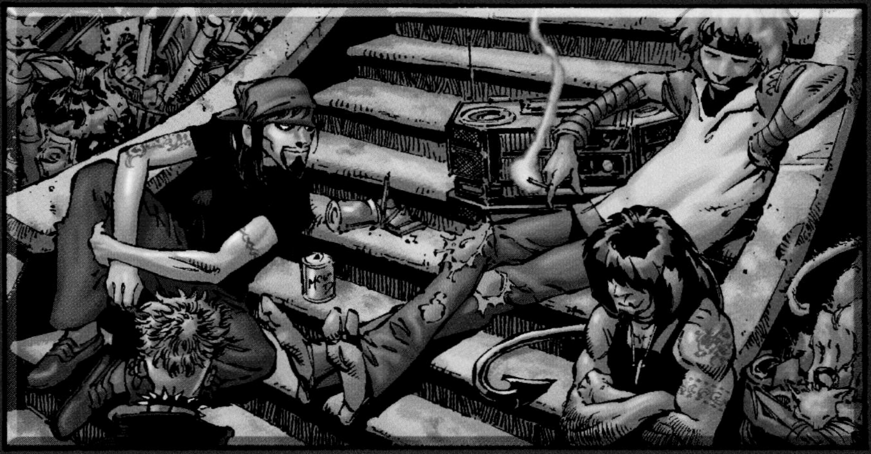

Spike Lee's upcoming MAGNETO bio-pic clearly isn't going to help matters,nor is Professor Bolivar Trask's popular theory that mutants have cruelty HARD-WIRED into our GENES.

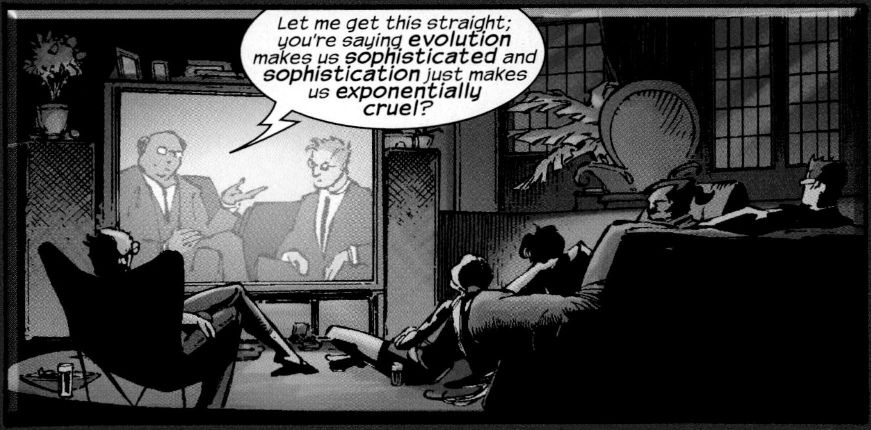
Let me get this straight; you're saying evolution makes us sophisticated and sophistication just makes us exponentially cruel?

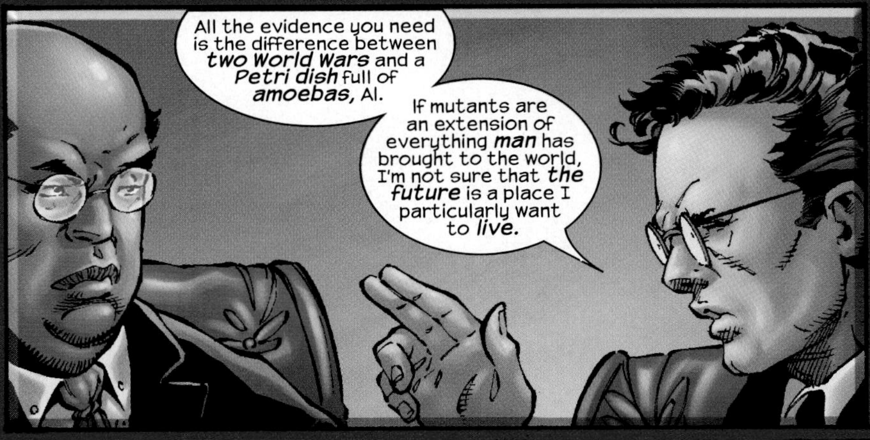
All the evidence you need is the difference between two World Wars and a Petri dish full of amoebas, Al.
If mutants are an extension of everything man has brought to the world, I'm not sure that the future is a place I particularly want to live.

It's a VERY COMPELLING ARGUMENT…

…particularly in light of The Brotherhood of Mutants' re-emergence as a political force and what they did to the Japanese FINANCIAL DISTRICT last week.

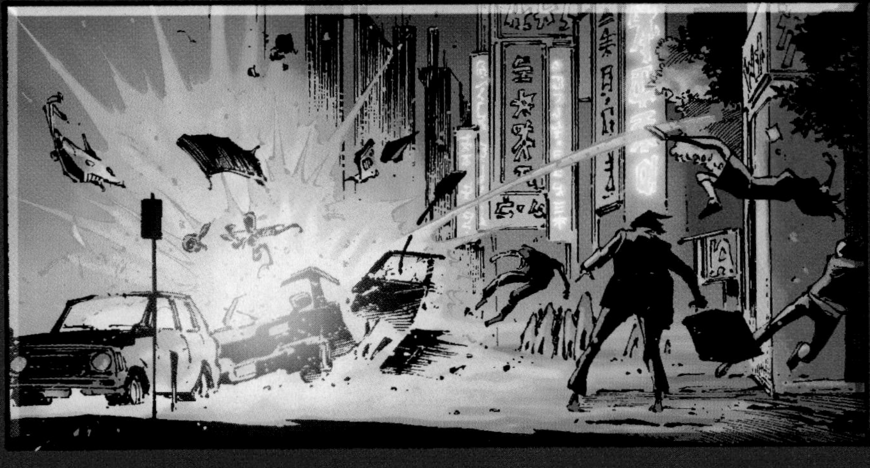

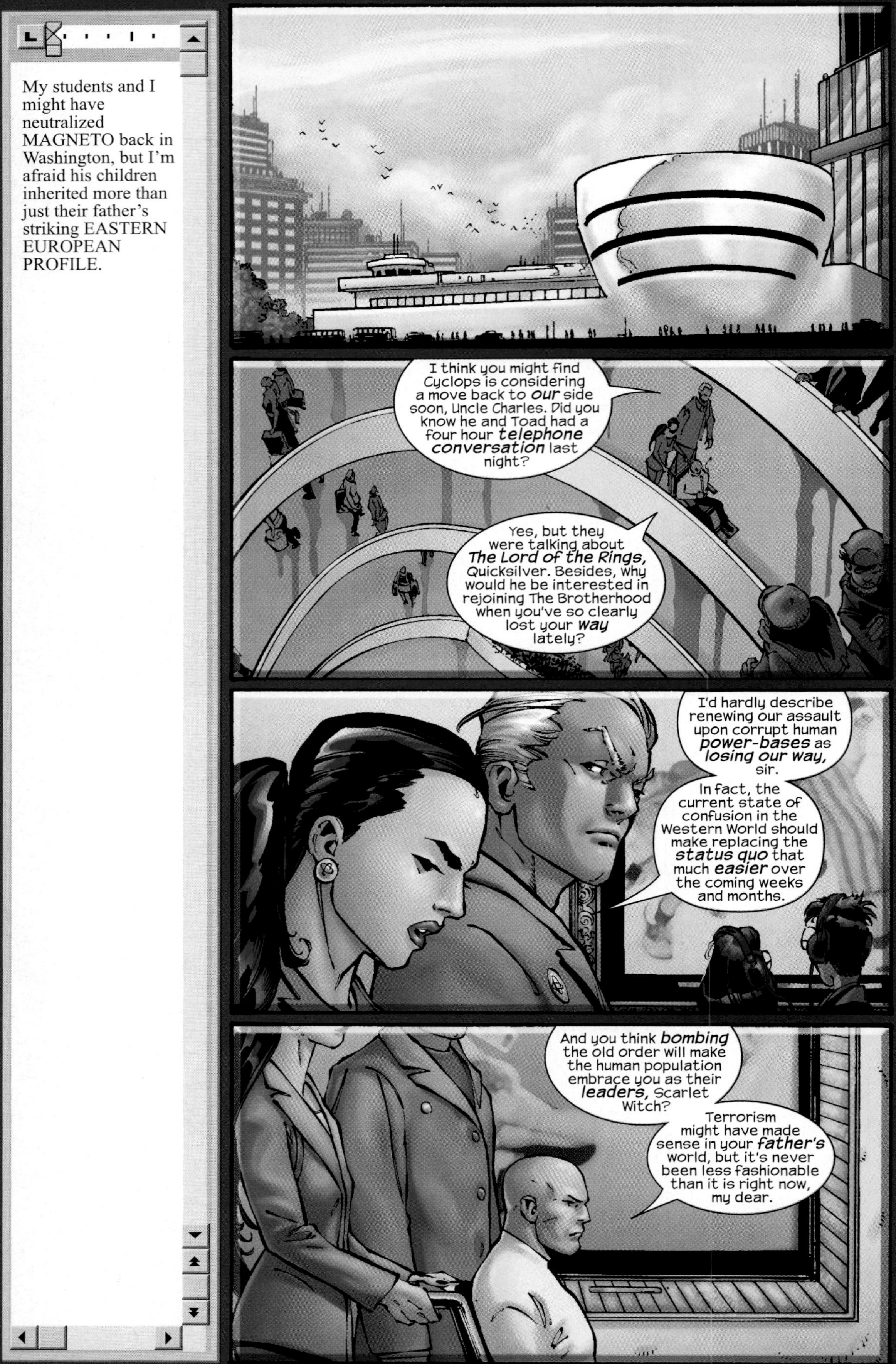
My students and I might have neutralized MAGNETO back in Washington, but I'm afraid his children inherited more than just their father's striking EASTERN EUROPEAN PROFILE.
I think you might find Cyclops is considering a move back to our side soon, Uncle Charles. Did you know he and Toad had a four hour telephone conversation last night?
Yes, but they were talking about The Lord of the Rings, Quicksilver. Besides, why would he be interested in rejoining The Brotherhood when you've so clearly lost your way lately?
I'd hardly describe renewing our assault upon corrupt human power-bases as losing our way, sir.
In fact, the current state of confusion in the Western World should make replacing the status quo that much easier over the coming weeks and months.
And you think bombing the old order will make the human population embrace you as their leaders, Scarlet Witch?
Terrorism might have made sense in your father's world, but it's never been less fashionable than it is right now, my dear.

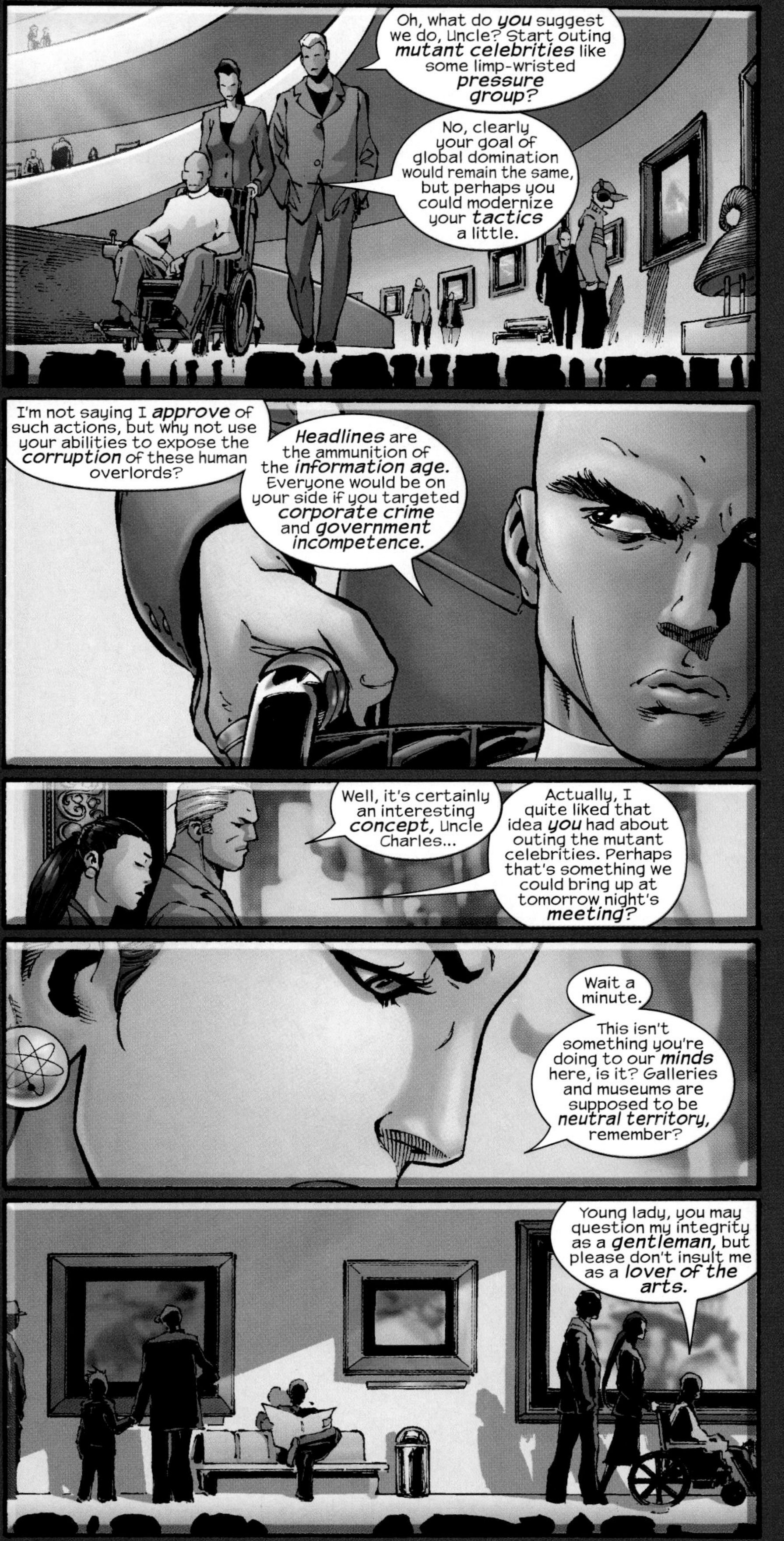
Oh, what do *you* suggest we do, Uncle? Start outing *mutant celebrities* like some limp-wristed *pressure group?*
No, clearly your goal of global domination would remain the same, but perhaps you could modernize your *tactics* a little.
I'm not saying I *approve* of such actions, but why not use your abilities to expose the *corruption* of these human overlords?
Headlines are the ammunition of the *information age.* Everyone would be on your side if you targeted *corporate crime* and *government incompetence.*
Well, it's certainly an interesting *concept,* Uncle Charles...
Actually, I quite liked that idea *you* had about outing the mutant celebrities. Perhaps that's something we could bring up at tomorrow night's *meeting?*
Wait a minute.
This isn't something you're doing to our *minds* here, is it? Galleries and museums are supposed to be *neutral territory,* remember?
Young lady, you may question my integrity as a *gentleman,* but please don't insult me as a *lover of the arts.*

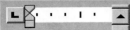

Some people ask why we don't just WAGE WAR on The Brotherhood, but that's such an old-fashioned, IMPERIALISTIC solution to the problem…

As we look around the world today, it's clear that violence breeds nothing but FURTHER violence.

IDEAS are the only way to change the world and, as a teacher, I feel it's my responsibility to PROVE it.

I've always thought it must take a very special kind of person to work with the *severely handicapped.*

Then again, they say the *teachers* gain as much from the experience as the *children.* What do *you* think, Peter?

I can't say I've really given the matter much *thought,* Professor.

Do you recognize the gentleman in the tan jacket playing with the little Down's Syndrome twins over there, young man?

Can you tell me where you might have seen his face *before?*

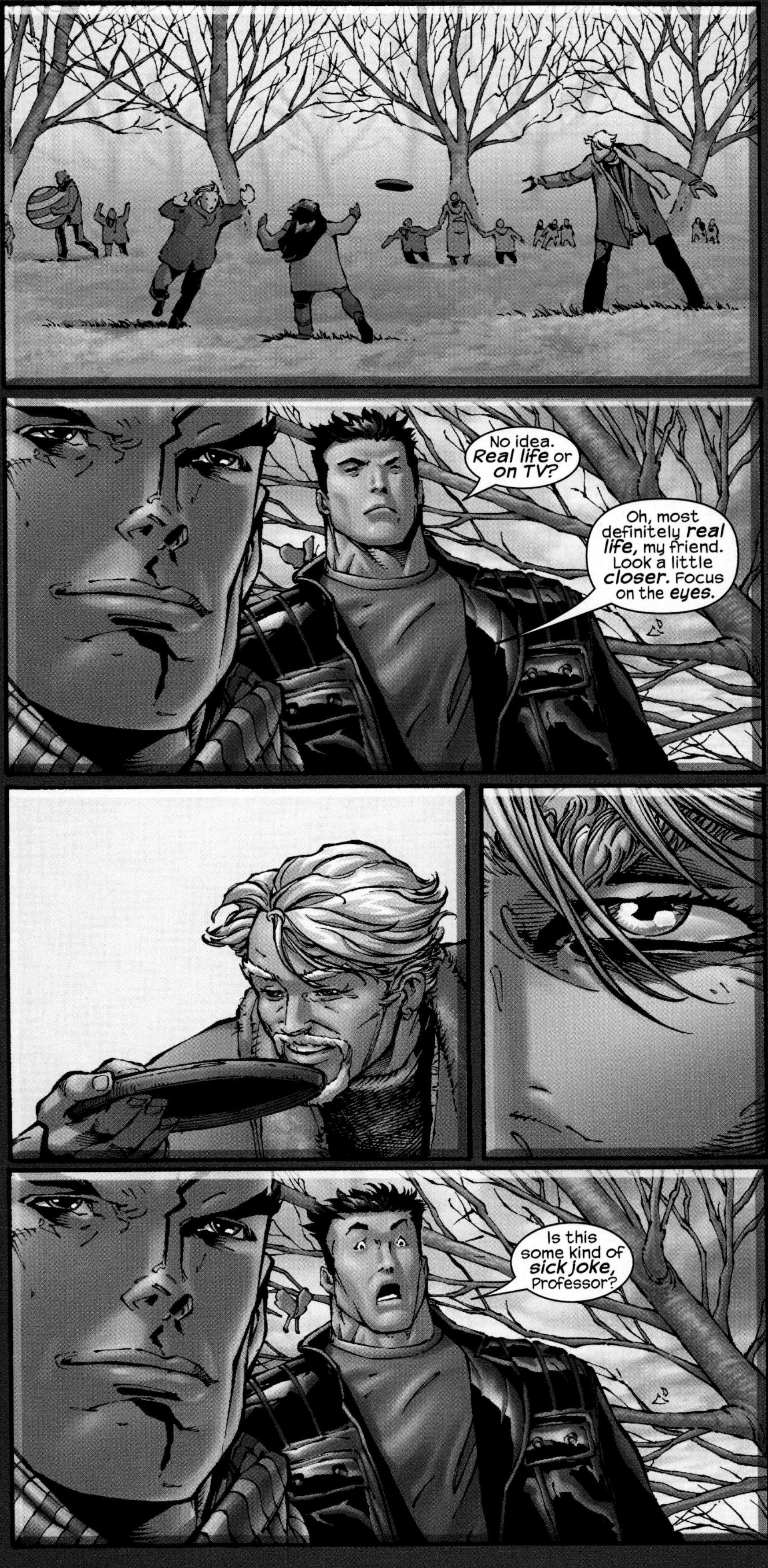
No idea. Real life or on TV?
Oh, most definitely real life, my friend. Look a little closer. Focus on the eyes.
Is this some kind of sick joke, Professor?

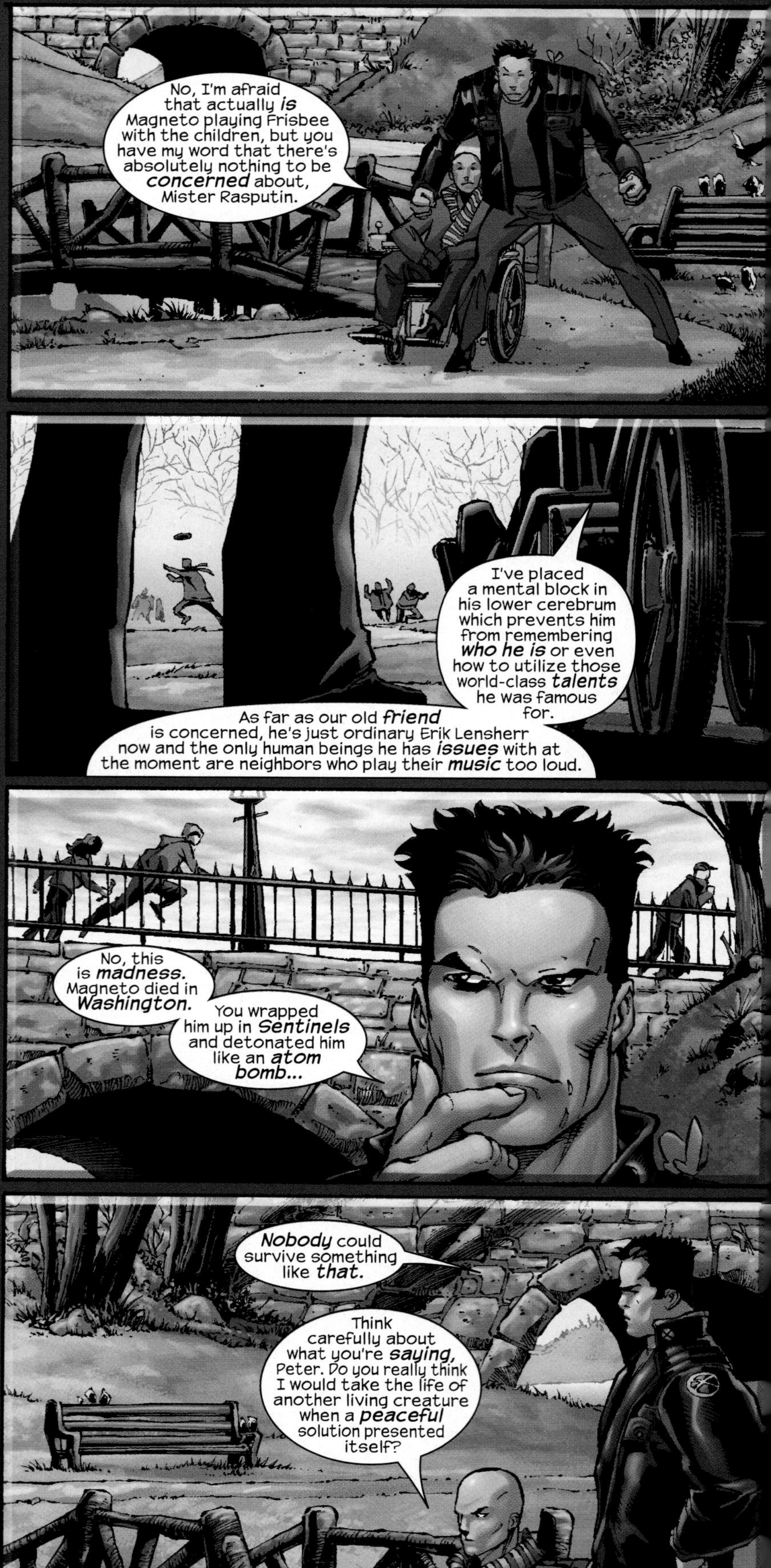
No, I'm afraid that actually is Magneto playing Frisbee with the children, but you have my word that there's absolutely nothing to be concerned about, Mister Rasputin.
I've placed a mental block in his lower cerebrum which prevents him from remembering who he is or even how to utilize those world-class talents he was famous for.
As far as our old friend is concerned, he's just ordinary Erik Lensherr now and the only human beings he has issues with at the moment are neighbors who play their music too loud.
No, this is madness. Magneto died in Washington.
You wrapped him up in Sentinels and detonated him like an atom bomb...
Nobody could survive something like that.
Think carefully about what you're saying, Peter. Do you really think I would take the life of another living creature when a peaceful solution presented itself?

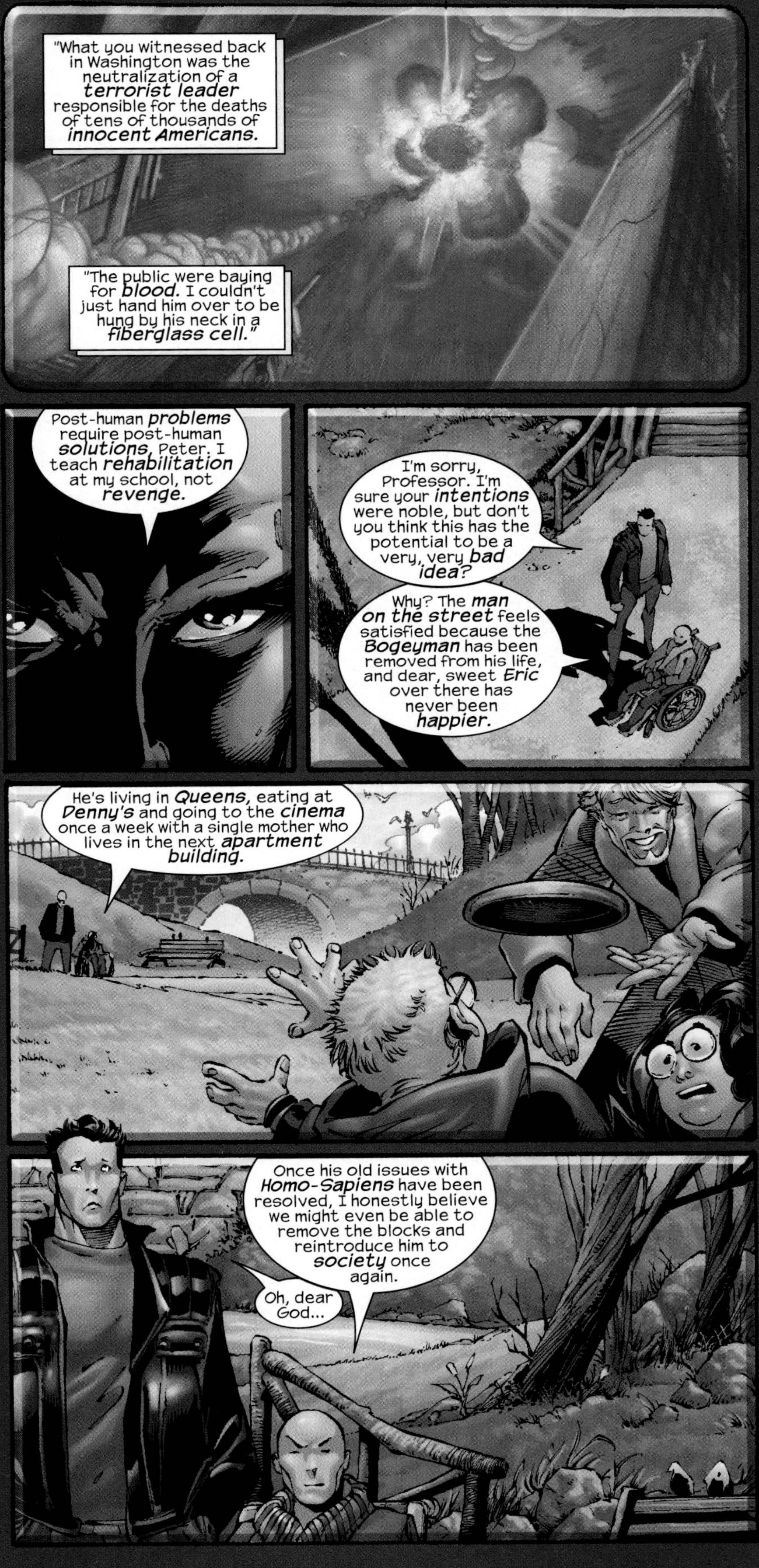
"What you witnessed back in Washington was the neutralization of a terrorist leader responsible for the deaths of tens of thousands of innocent Americans.
"The public were baying for blood. I couldn't just hand him over to be hung by his neck in a fiberglass cell."
Post-human problems require post-human solutions, Peter. I teach rehabilitation at my school, not revenge.
I'm sorry, Professor. I'm sure your intentions were noble, but don't you think this has the potential to be a very, very bad idea?
Why? The man on the street feels satisfied because the Bogeyman has been removed from his life, and dear, sweet Eric over there has never been happier.
He's living in Queens, eating at Denny's and going to the cinema once a week with a single mother who lives in the next apartment building.
Once his old issues with Homo-Sapiens have been resolved, I honestly believe we might even be able to remove the blocks and reintroduce him to society once again.
Oh, dear God...

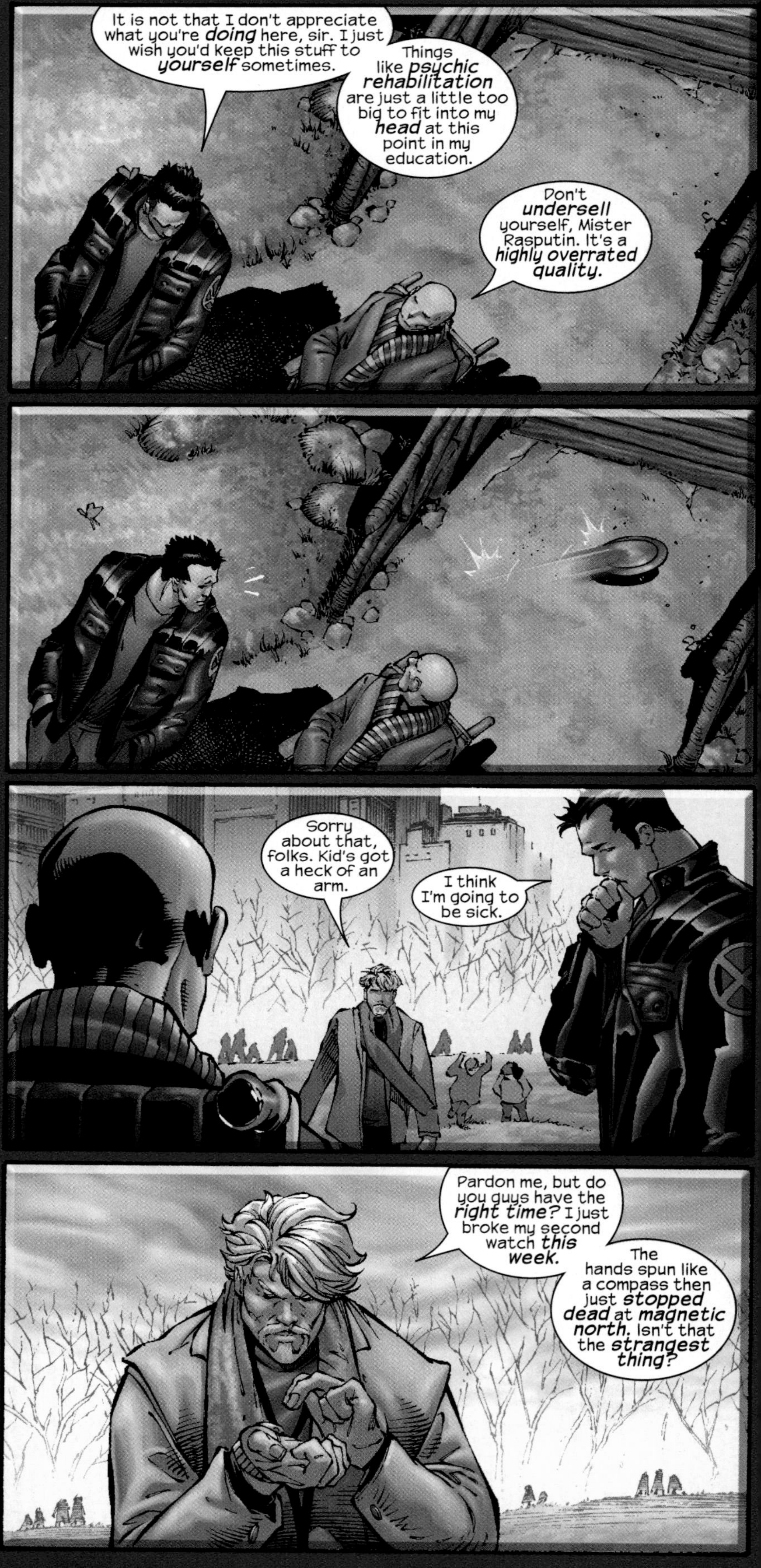
It is not that I don't appreciate what you're *doing* here, sir. I just wish you'd keep this stuff to *yourself* sometimes.
Things like *psychic rehabilitation* are just a little too big to fit into my *head* at this point in my education.
Don't *undersell* yourself, Mister Rasputin. It's a *highly overrated quality.*
Sorry about that, folks. Kid's got a heck of an arm.
I think I'm going to be sick.
Pardon me, but do you guys have the *right time?* I just broke my second watch *this week.*
The hands spun like a compass then just *stopped dead* at *magnetic north.* Isn't that the *strangest thing?*

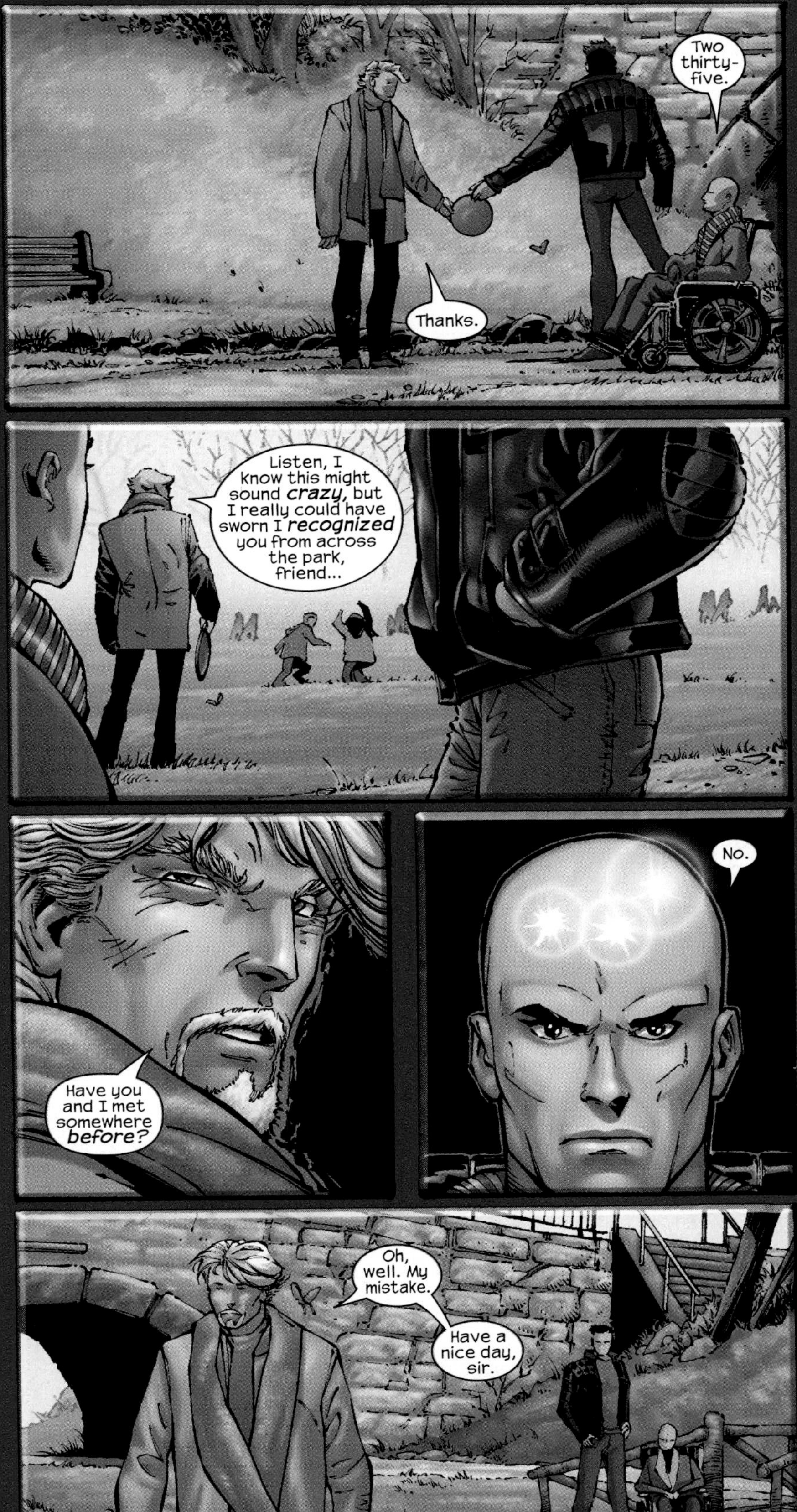
Two thirty-five.
Thanks.
Listen, I know this might sound *crazy*, but I really could have sworn I *recognized* you from across the park, friend...
Have you and I met somewhere *before*?
No.
Oh, well. My mistake.
Have a nice day, sir.

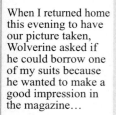

When I returned home this evening to have our picture taken, Wolverine asked if he could borrow one of my suits because he wanted to make a good impression in the magazine…

Cyclops was on the telephone to Toad, laughing about how Storm had caused a tiny thunderstorm in Iceman's large intestine for some reason. I must remember to ask about that later.

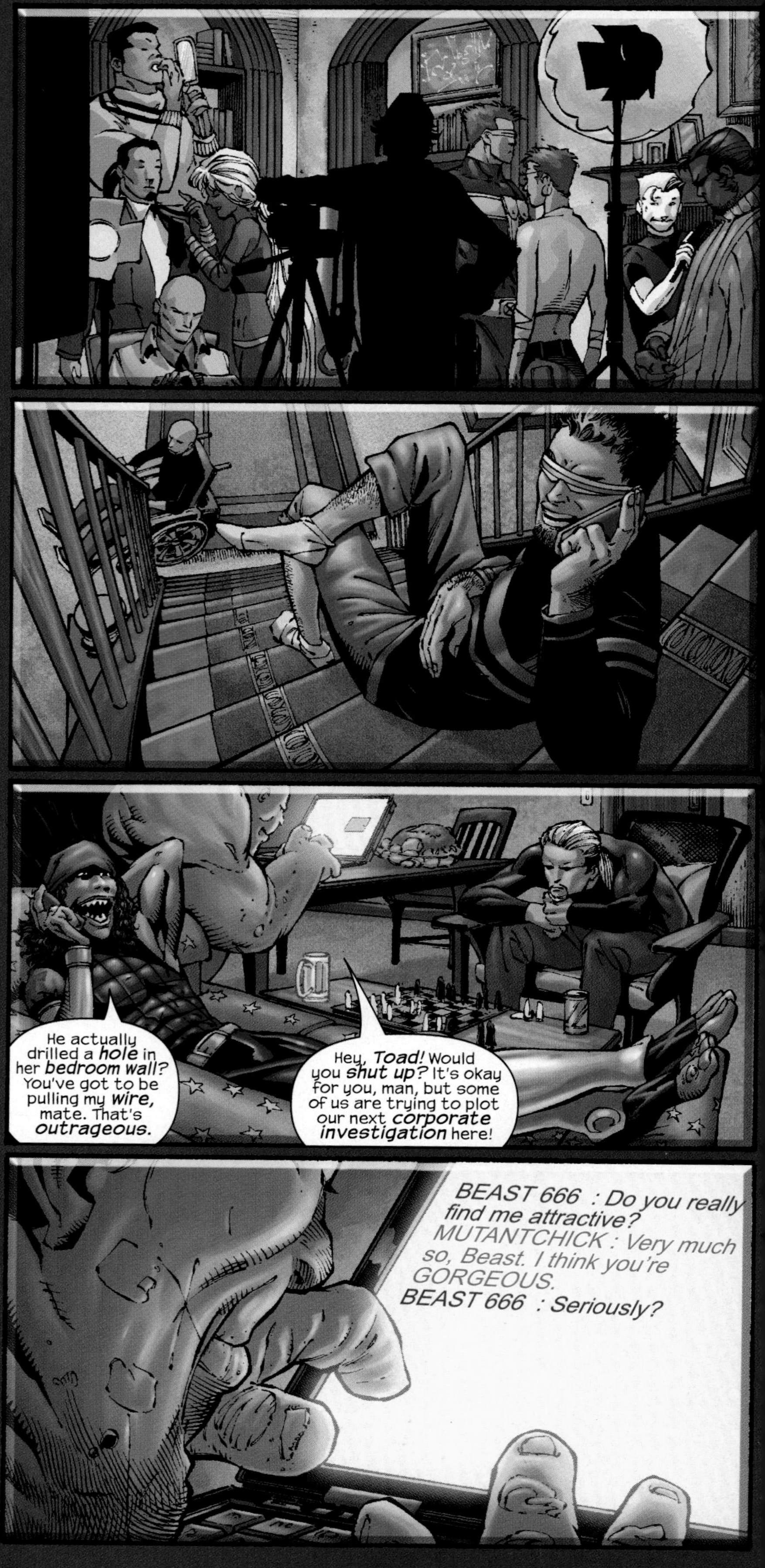
He actually drilled a *hole* in her *bedroom wall*? You've got to be pulling my *wire*, mate. That's *outrageous.*
Hey, *Toad!* Would you *shut up?* It's okay for you, man, but some of us are trying to plot our next *corporate investigation* here!
BEAST 666 : Do you really find me attractive?
MUTANTCHICK : Very much so, Beast. I think you're GORGEOUS.
BEAST 666 : Seriously?

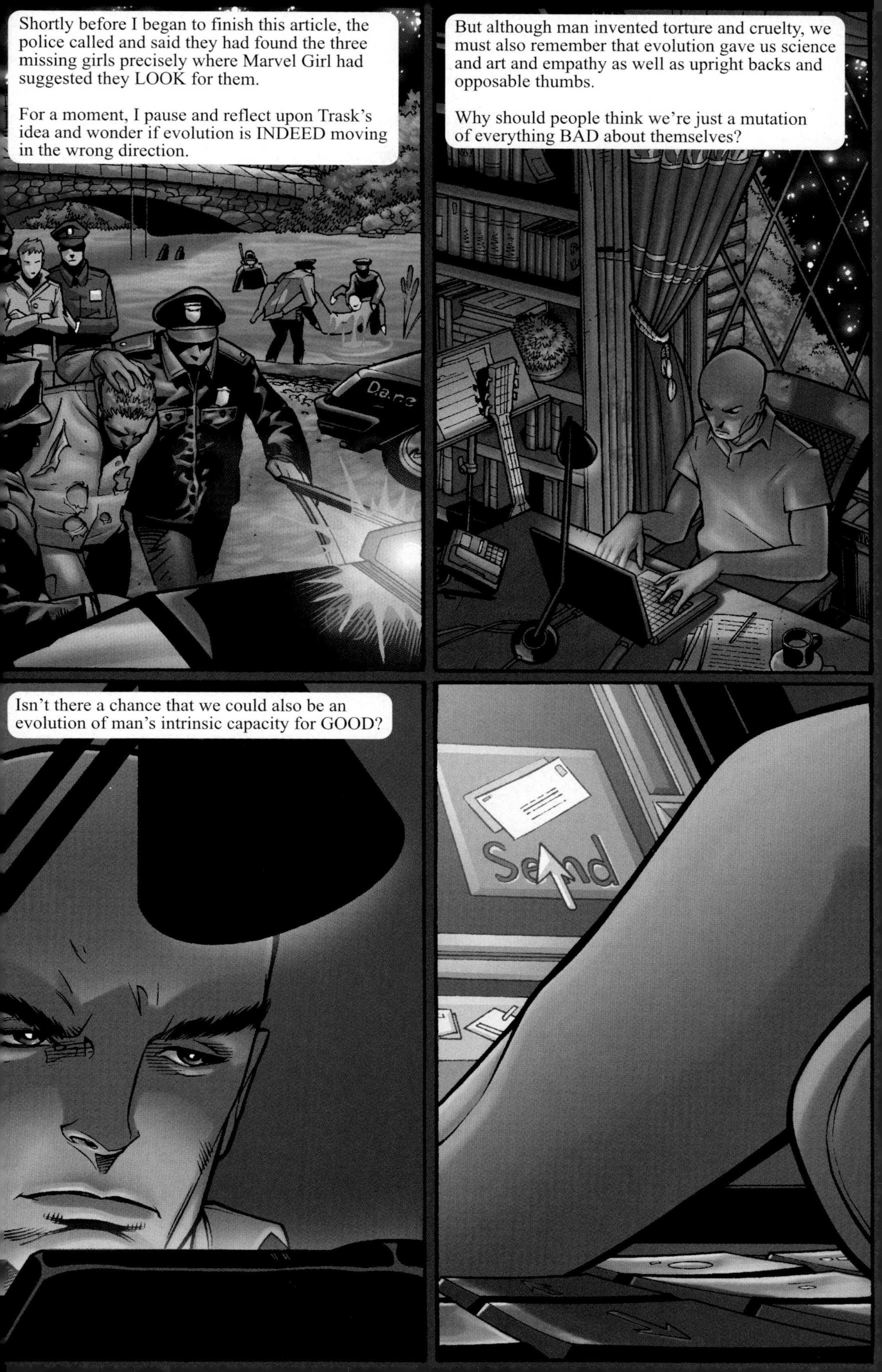
Shortly before I began to finish this article, the police called and said they had found the three missing girls precisely where Marvel Girl had suggested they LOOK for them.
For a moment, I pause and reflect upon Trask's idea and wonder if evolution is INDEED moving in the wrong direction.
Da.ne
But although man invented torture and cruelty, we must also remember that evolution gave us science and art and empathy as well as upright backs and opposable thumbs.
Why should people think we're just a mutation of everything BAD about themselves?
Isn't there a chance that we could also be an evolution of man's intrinsic capacity for GOOD?
Send

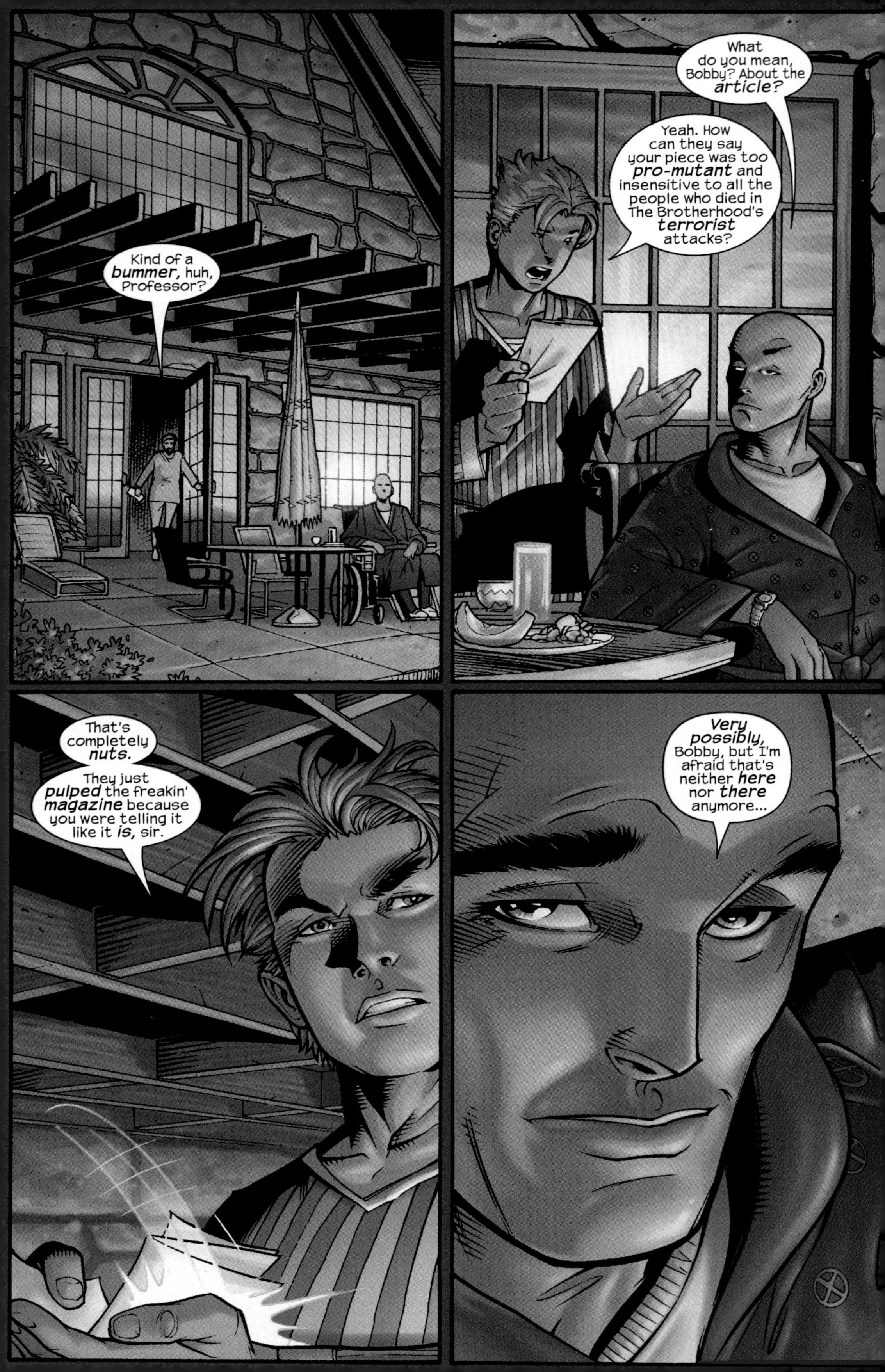
Kind of a bummer, huh, Professor?
What do you mean, Bobby? About the article?
Yeah. How can they say your piece was too pro-mutant and insensitive to all the people who died in The Brotherhood's terrorist attacks?
That's completely nuts.
They just pulped the freakin' magazine because you were telling it like it is, sir.
Very possibly, Bobby, but I'm afraid that's neither here nor there anymore...

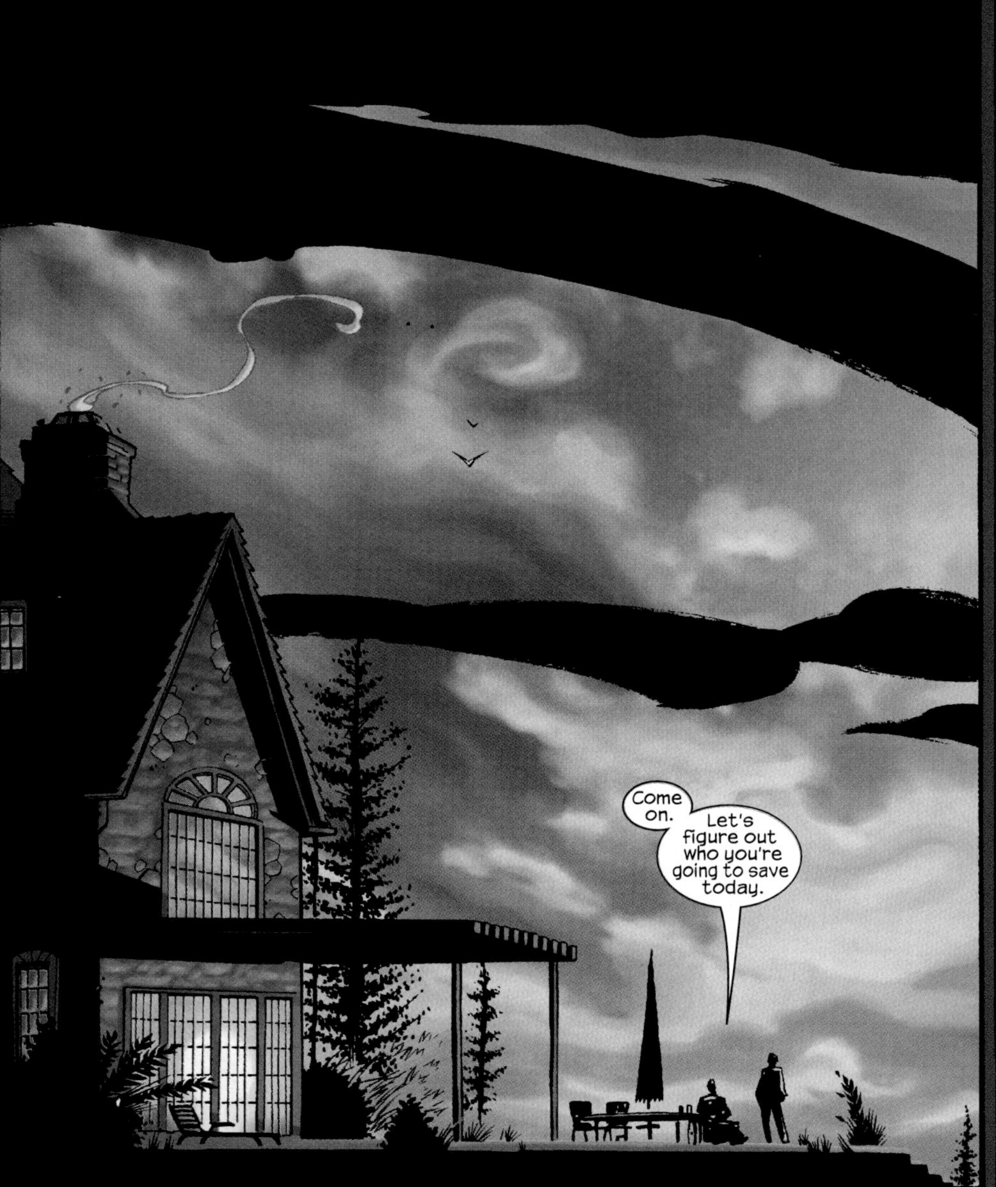
Come on.
Let's figure out who you're going to save today.

Millar Kubert Miki

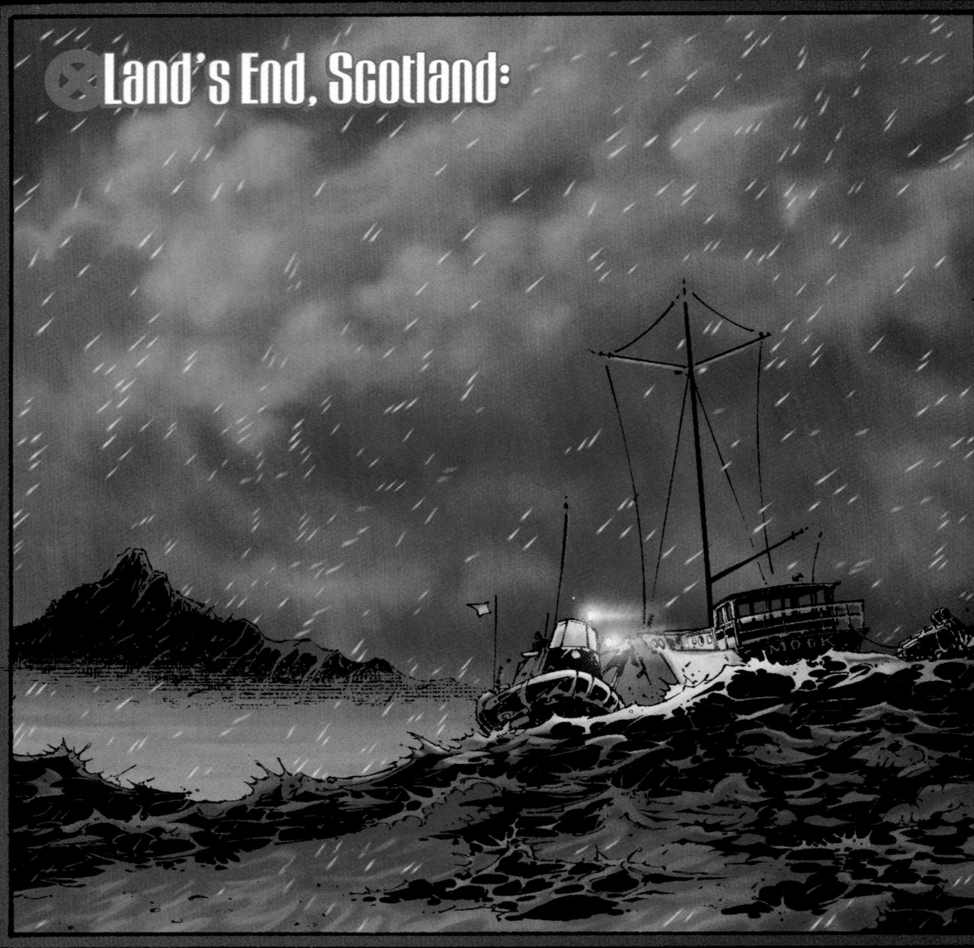
Land's End, Scotland:

Eliopoulos Stewart Smith Macchio Quesada Jemas

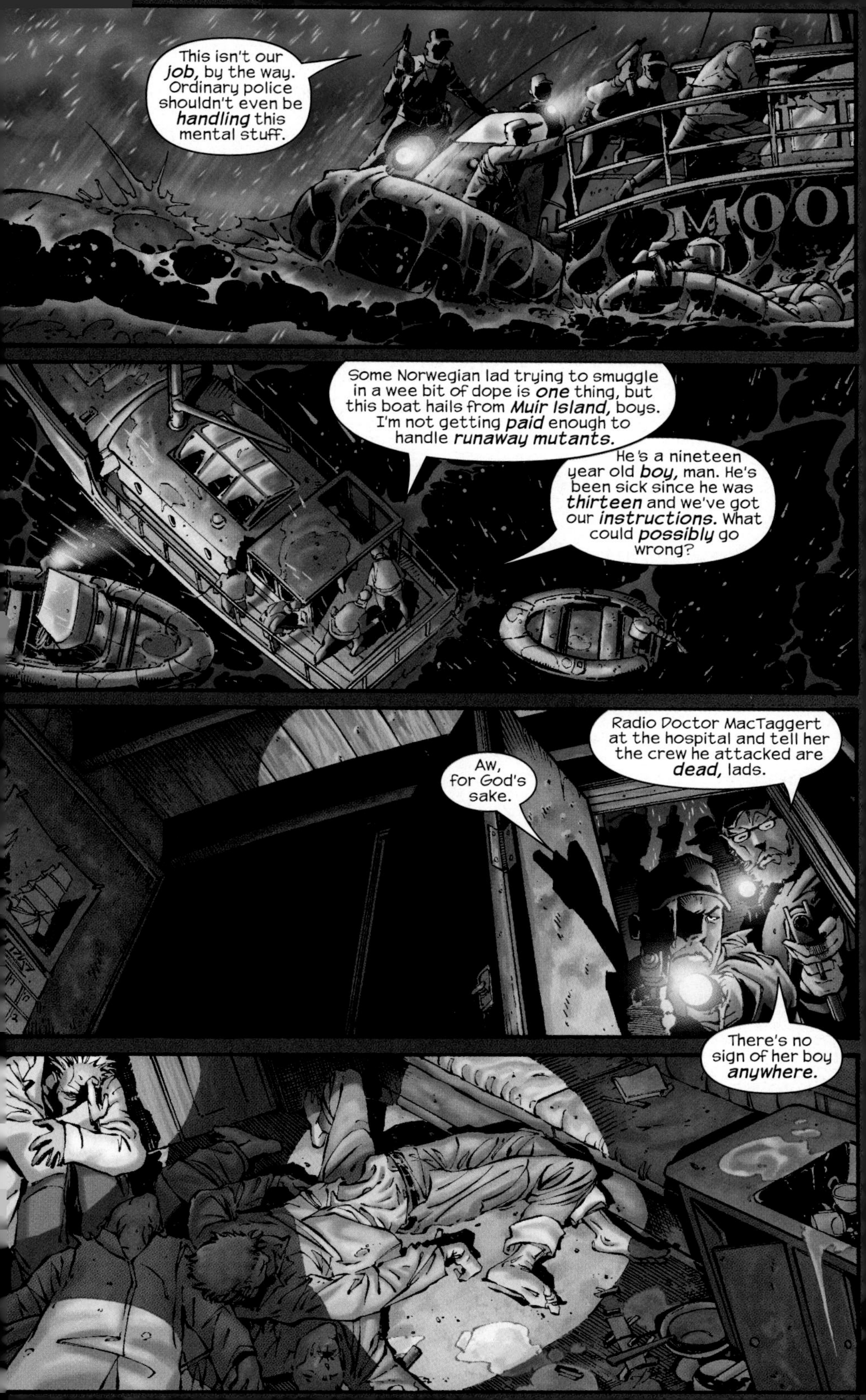
This isn't our job, by the way. Ordinary police shouldn't even be handling this mental stuff.
MOO
Some Norwegian lad trying to smuggle in a wee bit of dope is one thing, but this boat hails from Muir Island, boys. I'm not getting paid enough to handle runaway mutants.
He's a nineteen year old boy, man. He's been sick since he was thirteen and we've got our instructions. What could possibly go wrong?
Radio Doctor MacTaggert at the hospital and tell her the crew he attacked are dead, lads.
Aw, for God's sake.
There's no sign of her boy anywhere.

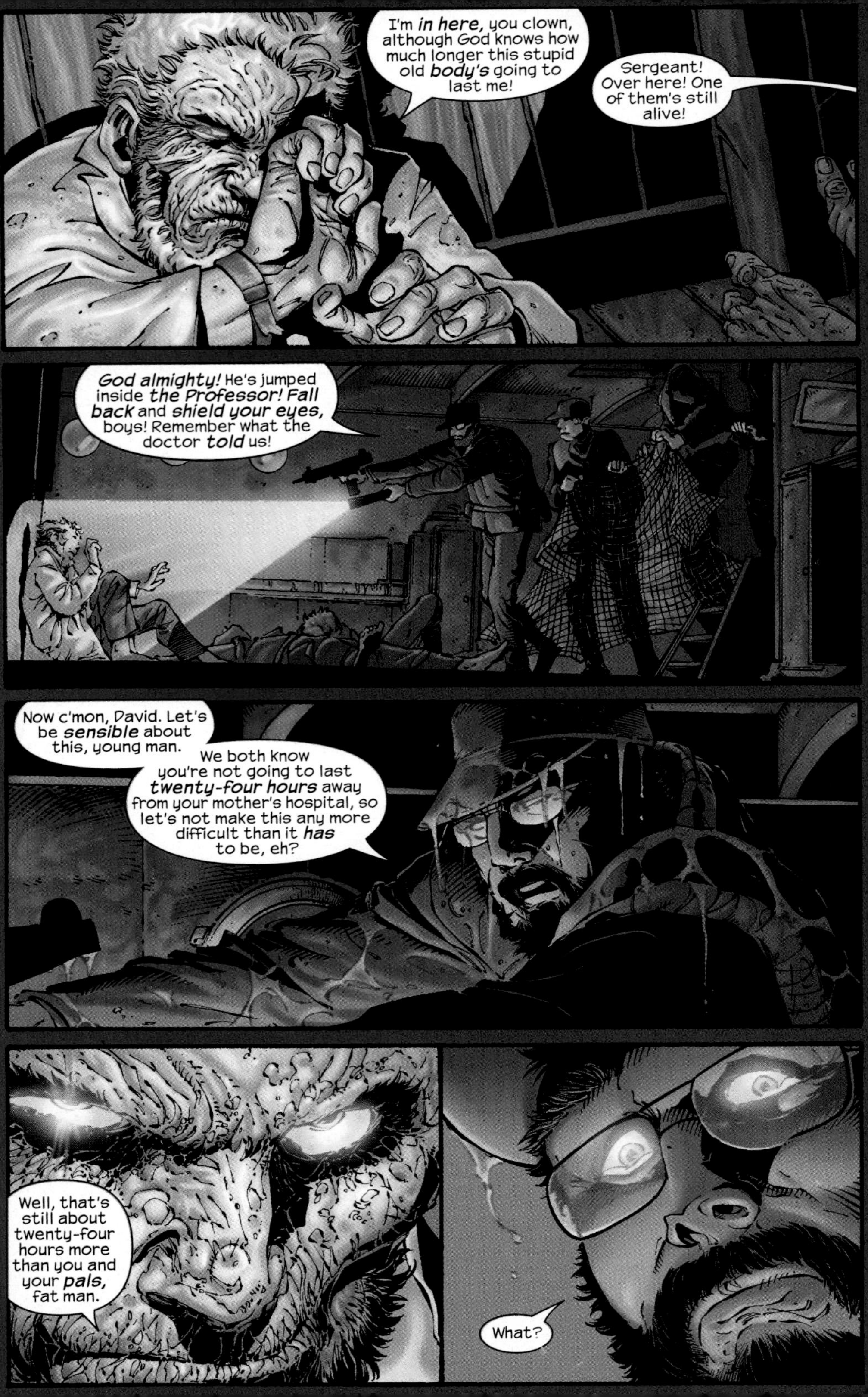

I'm in here, you clown, although God knows how much longer this stupid old body's going to last me!
Sergeant! Over here! One of them's still alive!
God almighty! He's jumped inside the Professor! Fall back and shield your eyes, boys! Remember what the doctor told us!
Now c'mon, David. Let's be sensible about this, young man.
We both know you're not going to last twenty-four hours away from your mother's hospital, so let's not make this any more difficult than it has to be, eh?
Well, that's still about twenty-four hours more than you and your pals, fat man.
What?

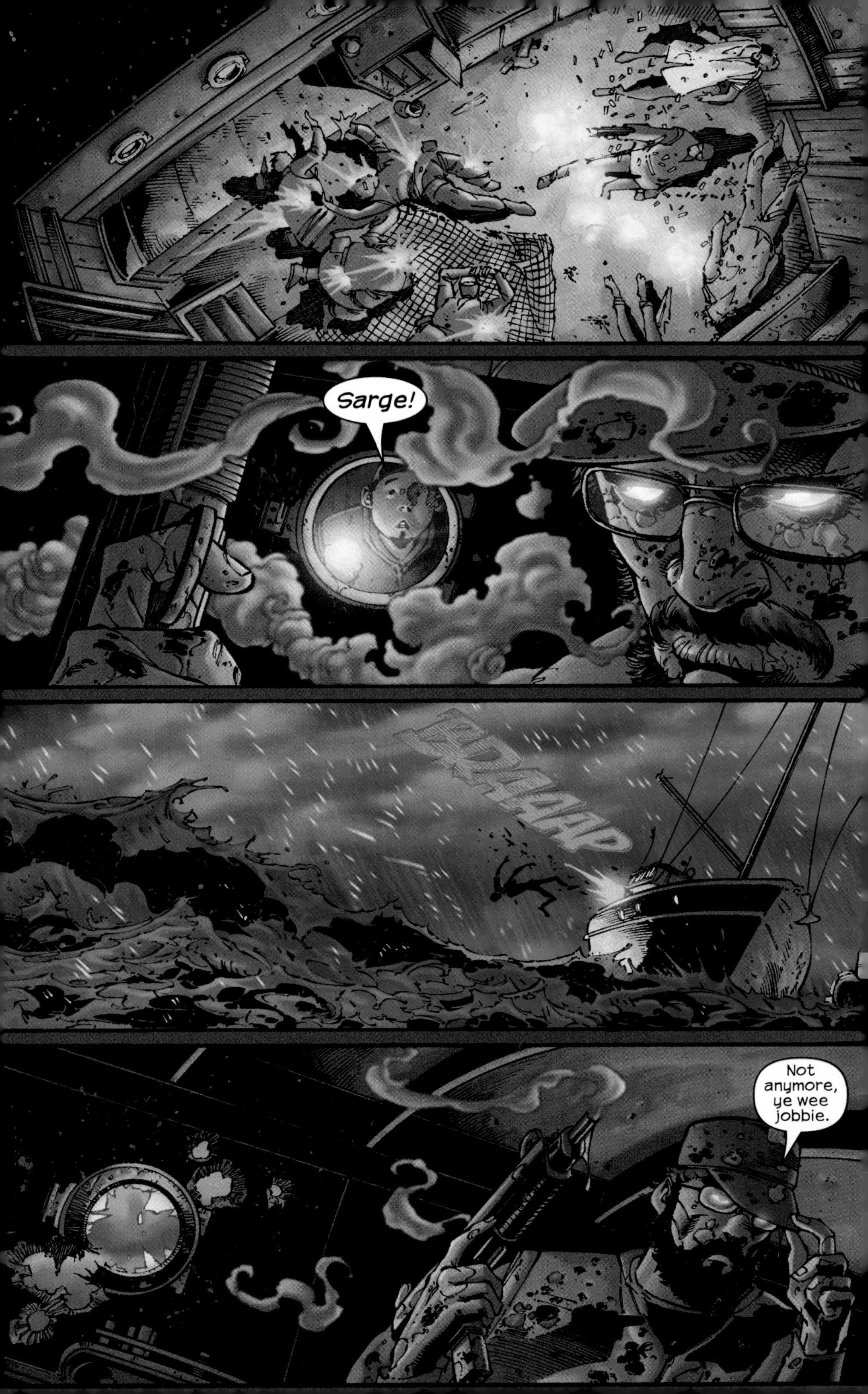
Sarge!
Not anymore, ye wee jobbie.

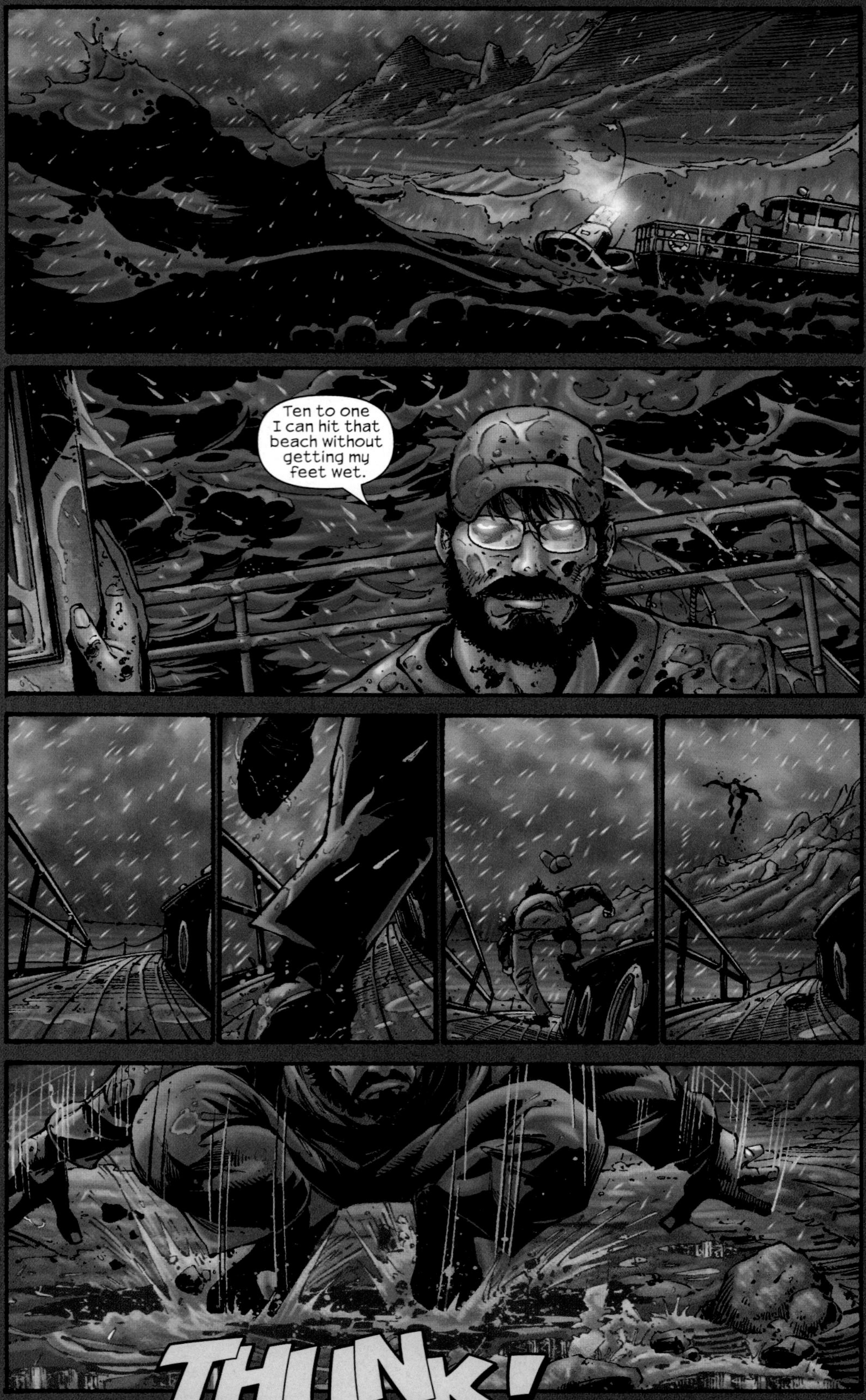
Ten to one I can hit that beach without getting my feet wet.
THUNK!

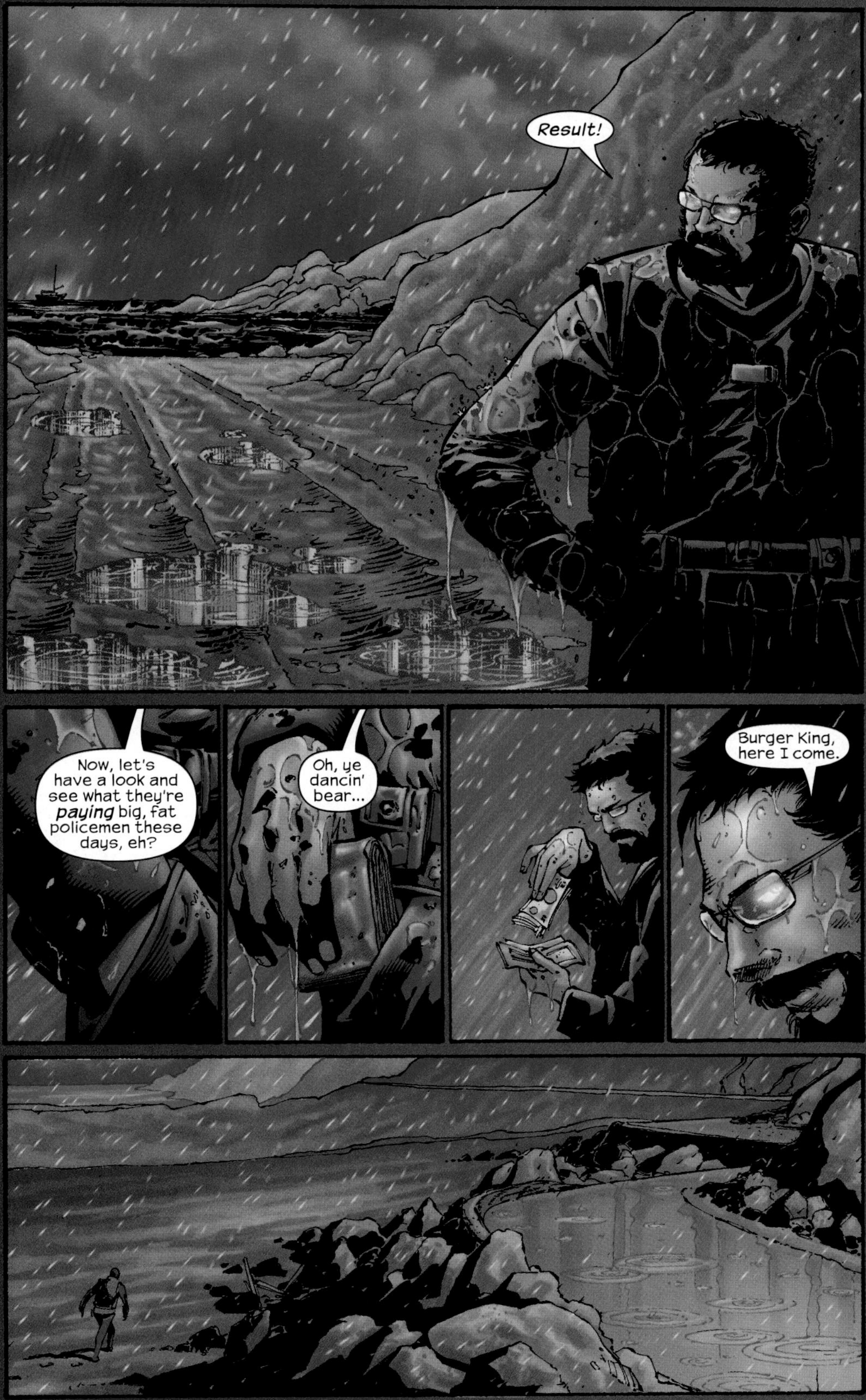
Result!
Now, let's have a look and see what they're *paying* big, fat policemen these days, eh?
Oh, ye dancin' bear...
Burger King, here I come.

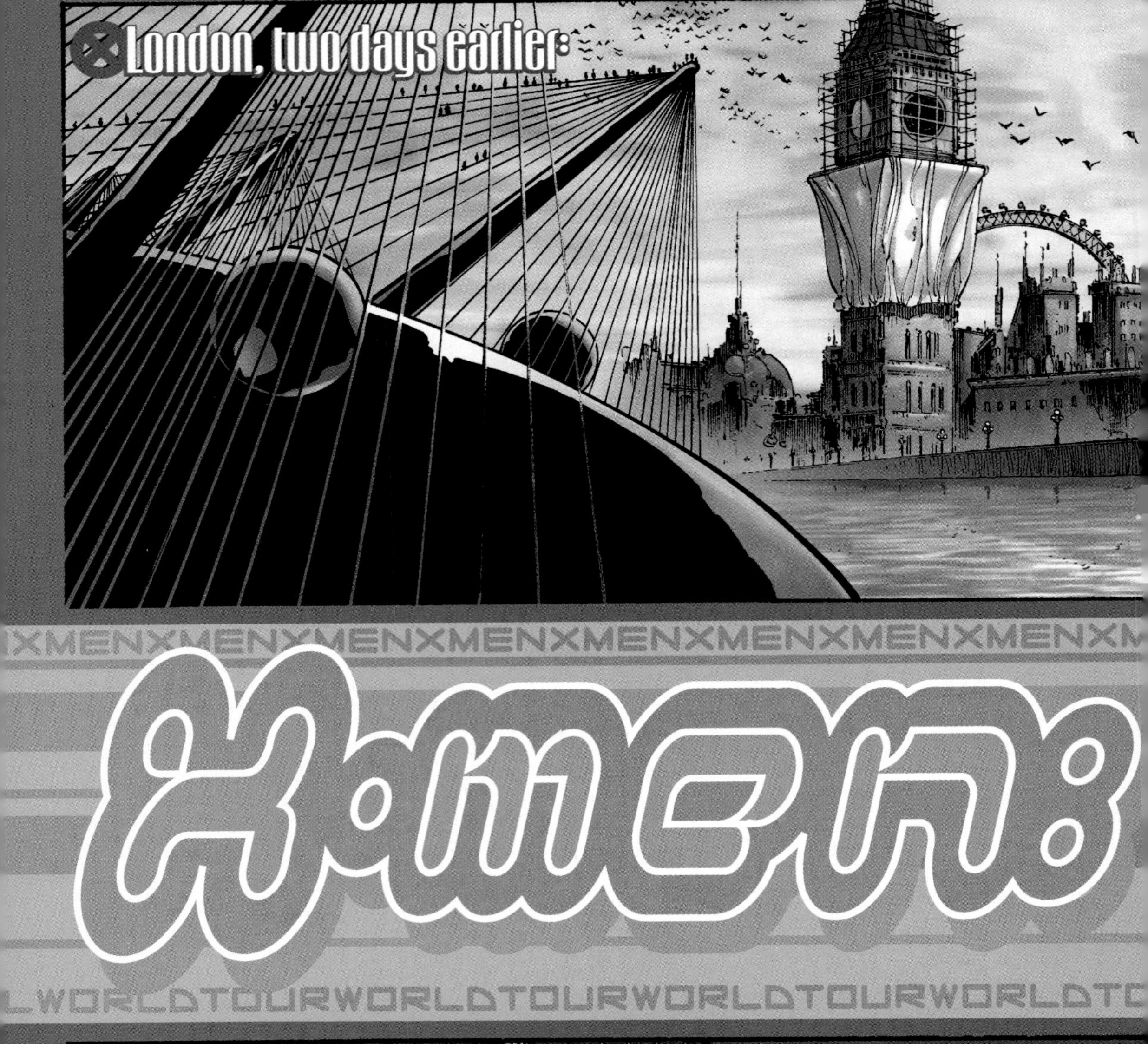
London, two days earlier:

XMENXMENXMENXMENXMENXMENX

WORLDTOURWORLDTOURWORLDTO

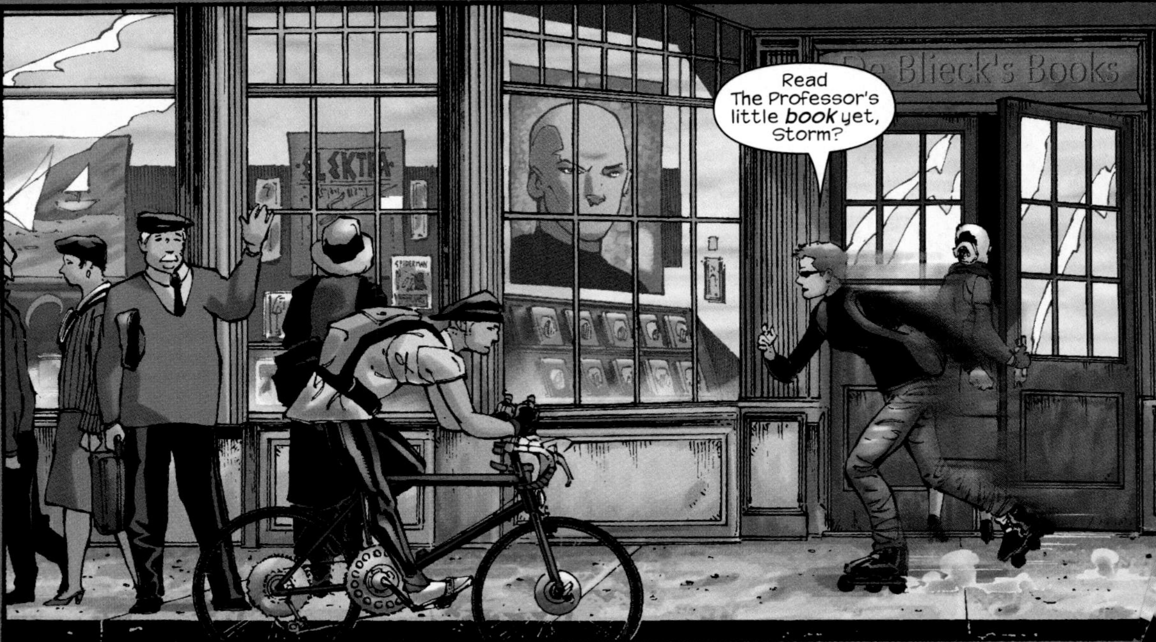
De Blieck's Books
ELEKTRA
Read The Professor's little *book* yet, Storm?

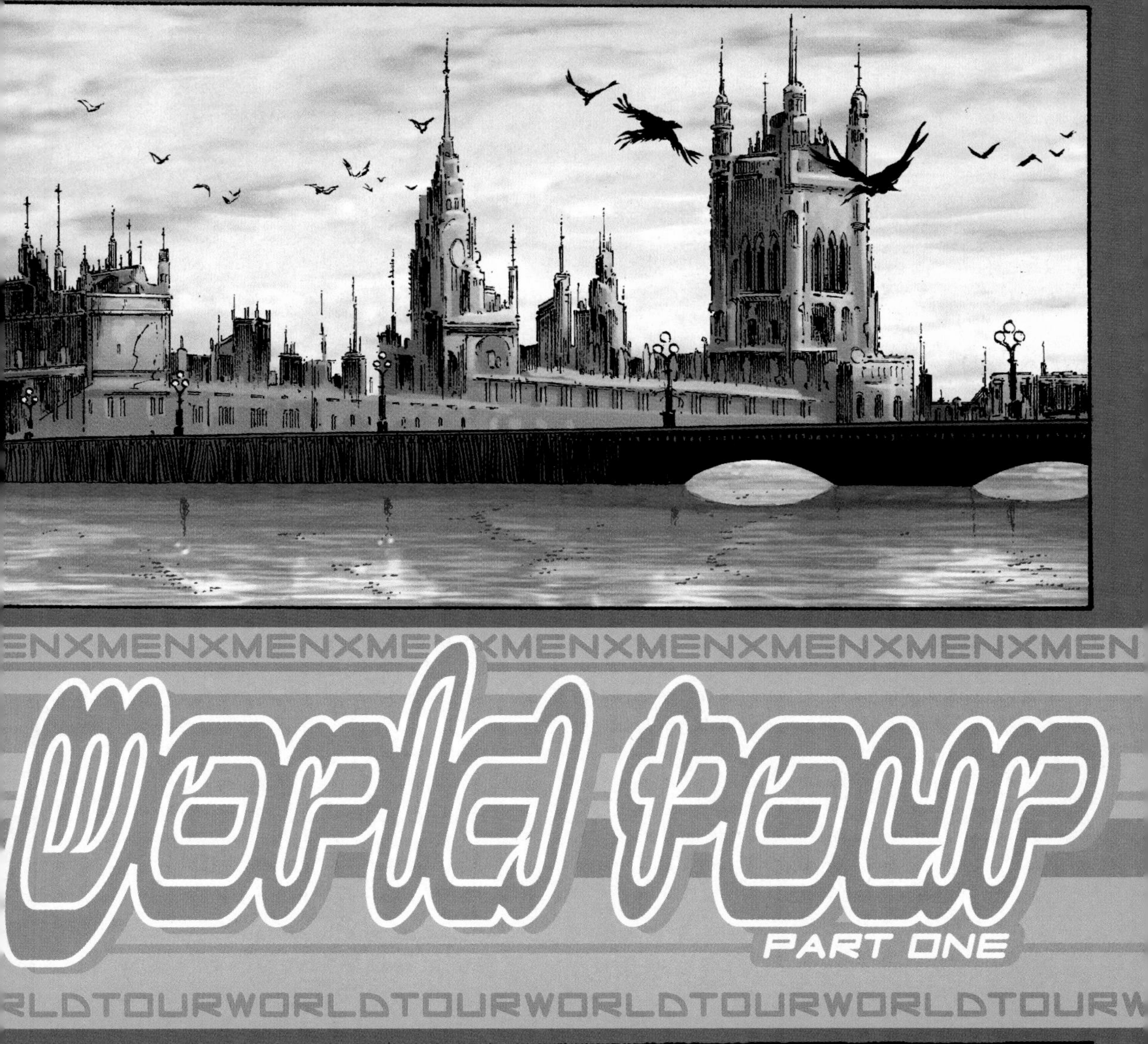

World Tour

PART ONE

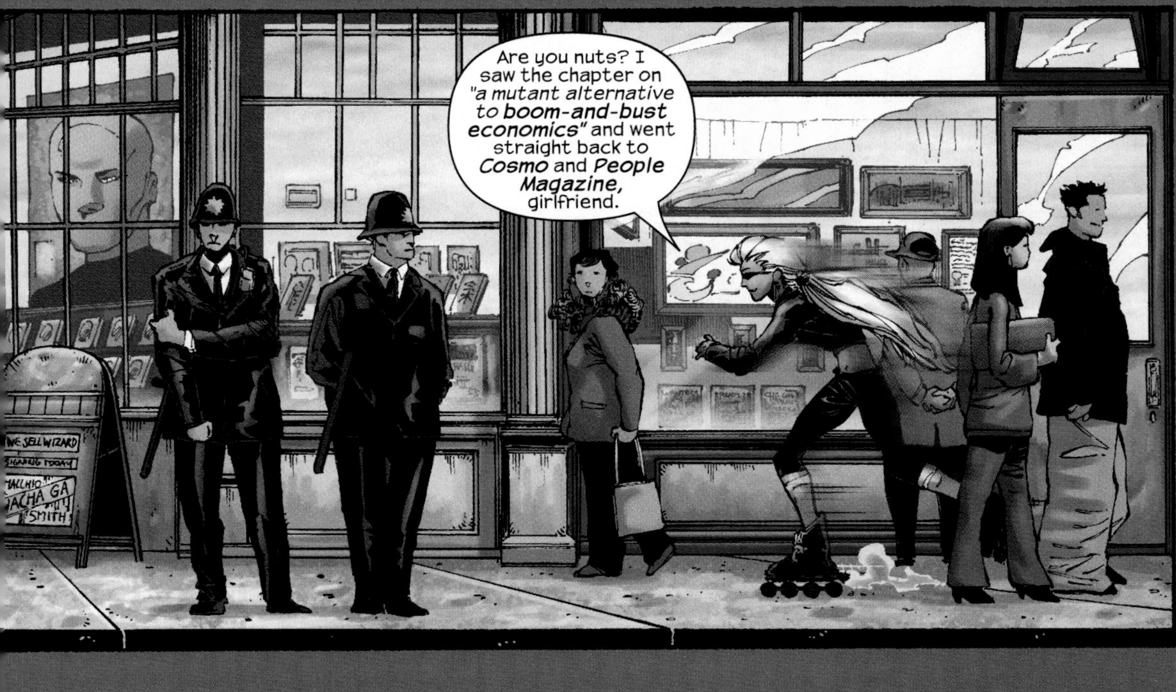

Are you nuts? I saw the chapter on *"a mutant alternative to **boom-and-bust economics**"* and went straight back to ***Cosmo*** and ***People Magazine,*** girlfriend.
WE SELL WIZARD

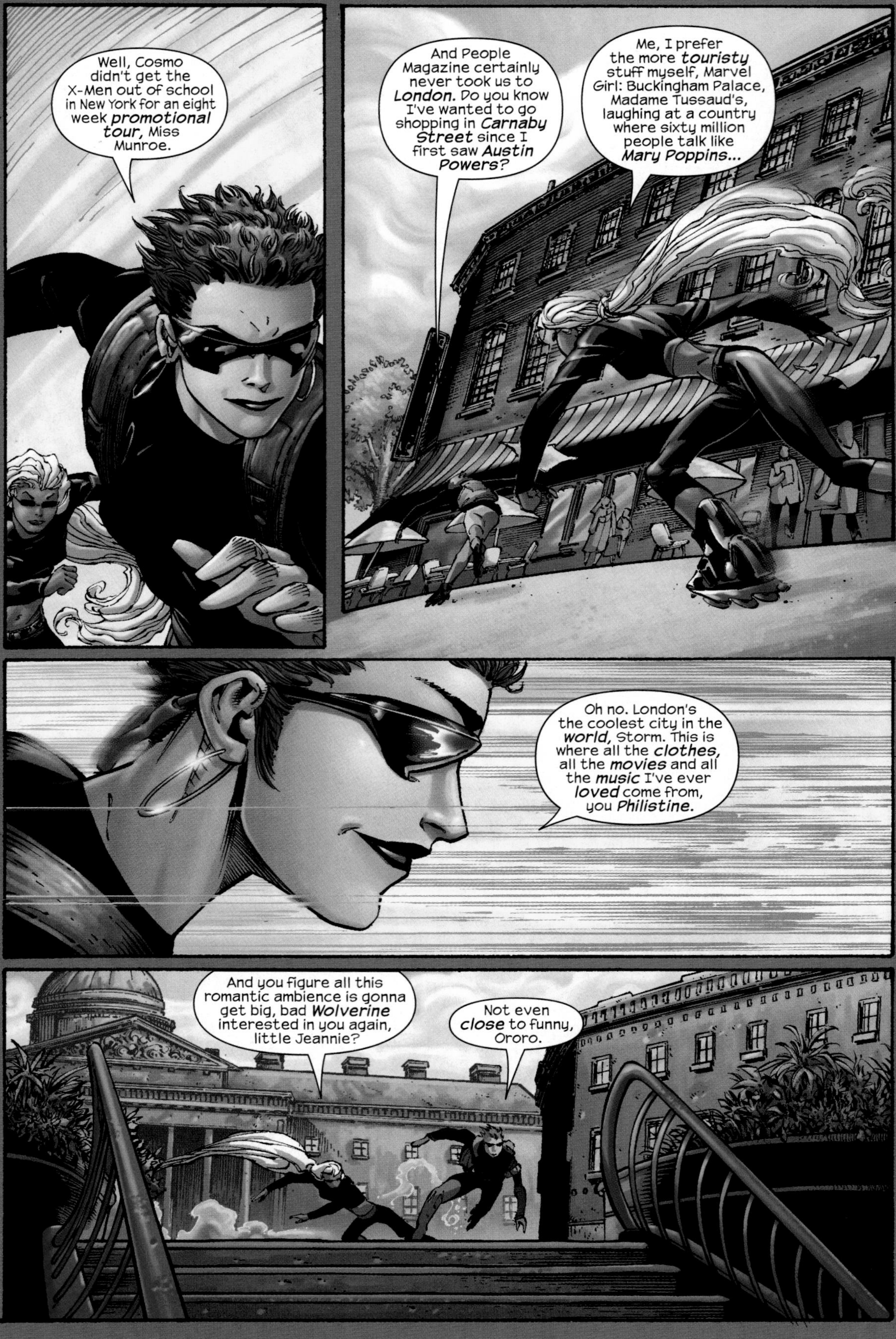
Well, Cosmo didn't get the X-Men out of school in New York for an eight week *promotional tour,* Miss Munroe.
And People Magazine certainly never took us to *London.* Do you know I've wanted to go shopping in *Carnaby Street* since I first saw *Austin Powers*?
Me, I prefer the more *touristy* stuff myself, Marvel Girl: Buckingham Palace, Madame Tussaud's, laughing at a country where sixty million people talk like *Mary Poppins...*
Oh no. London's the coolest city in the *world,* Storm. This is where all the *clothes,* all the *movies* and all the *music* I've ever *loved* come from, you *Philistine.*
And you figure all this romantic ambience is gonna get big, bad *Wolverine* interested in you again, little Jeannie?
Not even *close* to funny, Ororo.

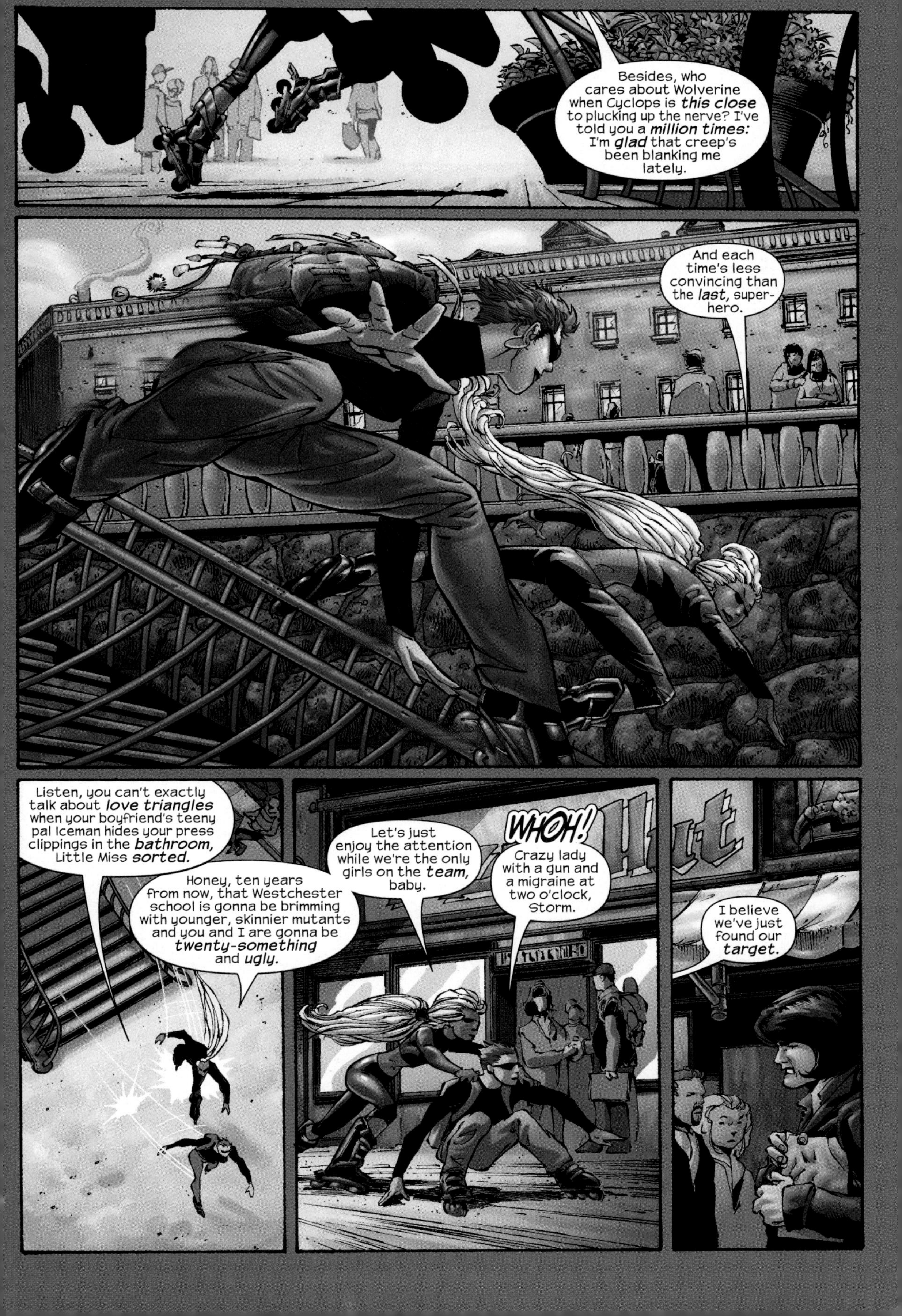

Besides, who cares about Wolverine when Cyclops is ***this close*** to plucking up the nerve? I've told you a ***million times:*** I'm ***glad*** that creep's been blanking me lately.
And each time's less convincing than the ***last,*** super-hero.
Listen, you can't exactly talk about ***love triangles*** when your boyfriend's teeny pal Iceman hides your press clippings in the ***bathroom,*** Little Miss ***sorted.***
Honey, ten years from now, that Westchester school is gonna be brimming with younger, skinnier mutants and you and I are gonna be ***twenty-something*** and ***ugly.***
Let's just enjoy the attention while we're the only girls on the ***team,*** baby.
WHOH!
Crazy lady with a gun and a migraine at two o'clock, Storm.
I believe we've just found our ***target.***

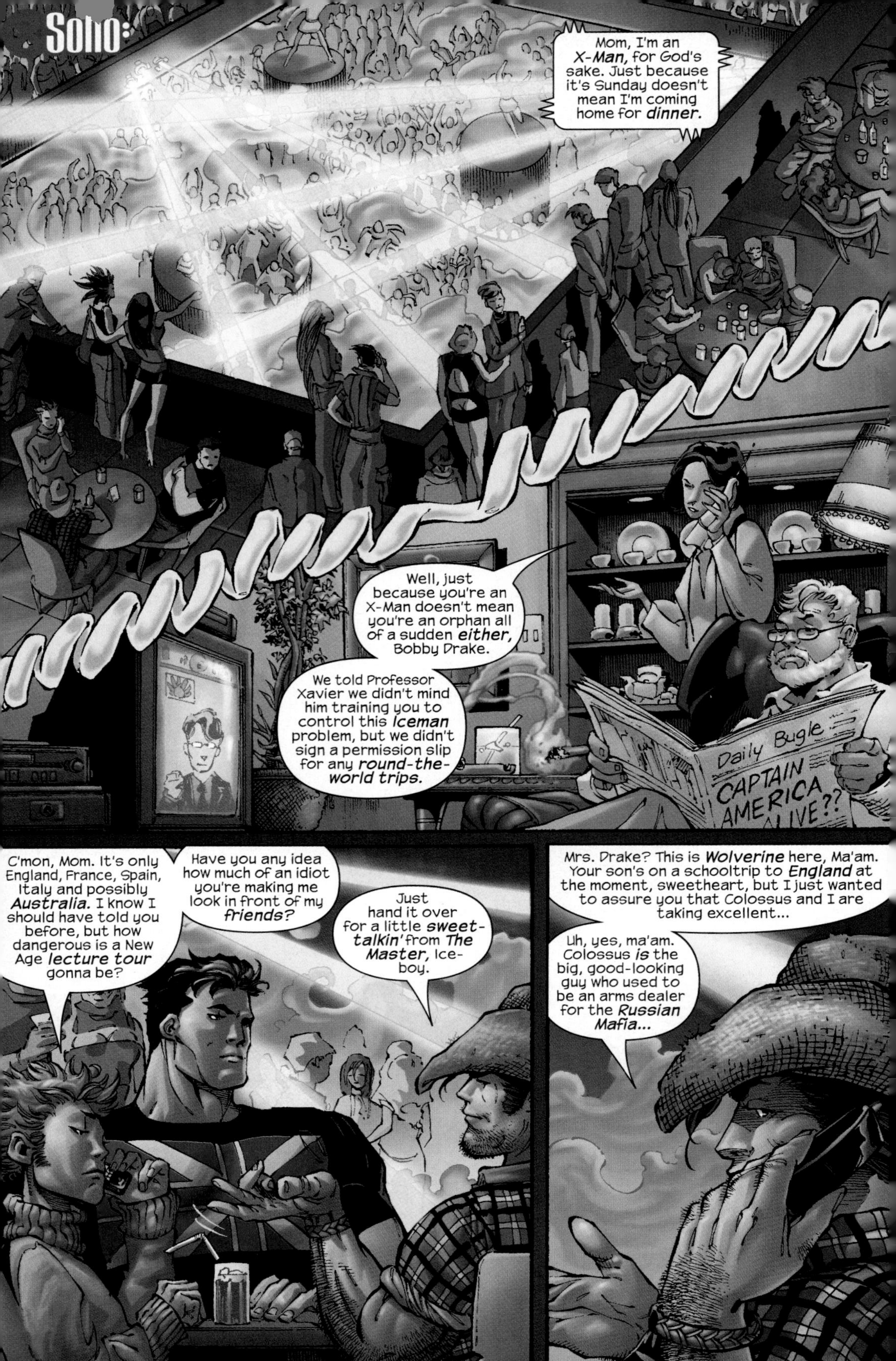
Soho:
Mom, I'm an X-Man, for God's sake. Just because it's Sunday doesn't mean I'm coming home for dinner.
Well, just because you're an X-Man doesn't mean you're an orphan all of a sudden either, Bobby Drake.
We told Professor Xavier we didn't mind him training you to control this Iceman problem, but we didn't sign a permission slip for any round-the-world trips.
Daily Bugle
CAPTAIN AMERICA ALIVE??
C'mon, Mom. It's only England, France, Spain, Italy and possibly Australia. I know I should have told you before, but how dangerous is a New Age lecture tour gonna be?
Have you any idea how much of an idiot you're making me look in front of my friends?
Just hand it over for a little sweet-talkin' from The Master, Ice-boy.
Mrs. Drake? This is Wolverine here, Ma'am. Your son's on a schooltrip to England at the moment, sweetheart, but I just wanted to assure you that Colossus and I are taking excellent...
Uh, yes, ma'am. Colossus is the big, good-looking guy who used to be an arms dealer for the Russian Mafia...

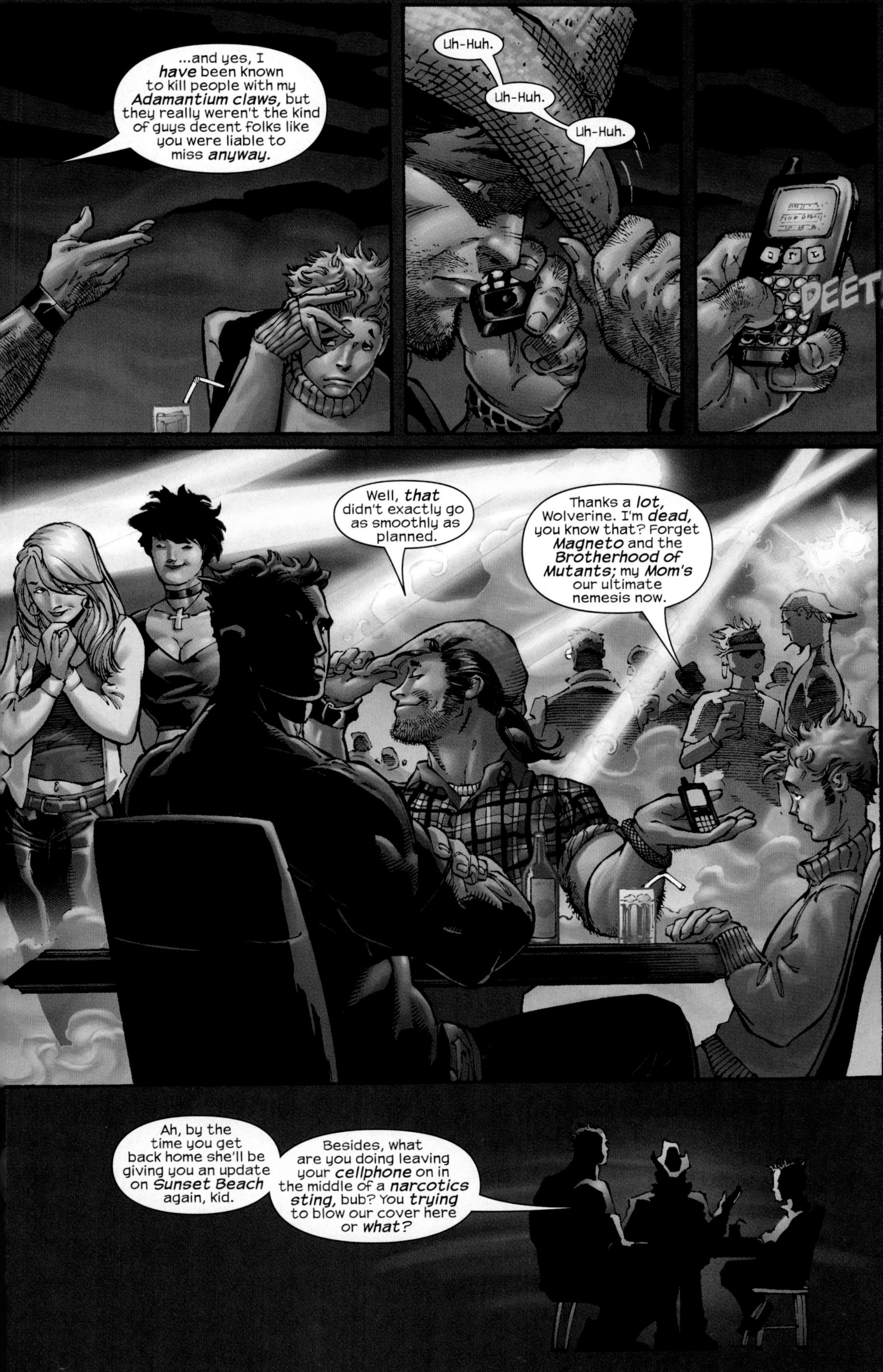
...and yes, I have been known to kill people with my Adamantium claws, but they really weren't the kind of guys decent folks like you were liable to miss anyway.
Uh-Huh.
Uh-Huh.
Uh-Huh.
DEET!
Well, that didn't exactly go as smoothly as planned.
Thanks a lot, Wolverine. I'm dead, you know that? Forget Magneto and the Brotherhood of Mutants; my Mom's our ultimate nemesis now.
Ah, by the time you get back home she'll be giving you an update on Sunset Beach again, kid.
Besides, what are you doing leaving your cellphone on in the middle of a narcotics sting, bub? You trying to blow our cover here or what?

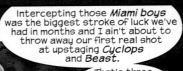

Intercepting those *Miami boys* was the biggest stroke of luck we've had in months and I ain't about to throw away our first real shot at upstaging *Cyclops* and *Beast*.

That's three assignments in a row they've wiped the floor with us and I ain't looking stupid for a *fourth* time. *Right*, Colossus?

Right.

Now look sharp and leave the talking to *the professional*, gentlemen. We're now entering the world of covert operations where Wolverine *reigns supreme*.

Good God.

Do these sodding Americans know the *meaning* of *inconspicuous?*

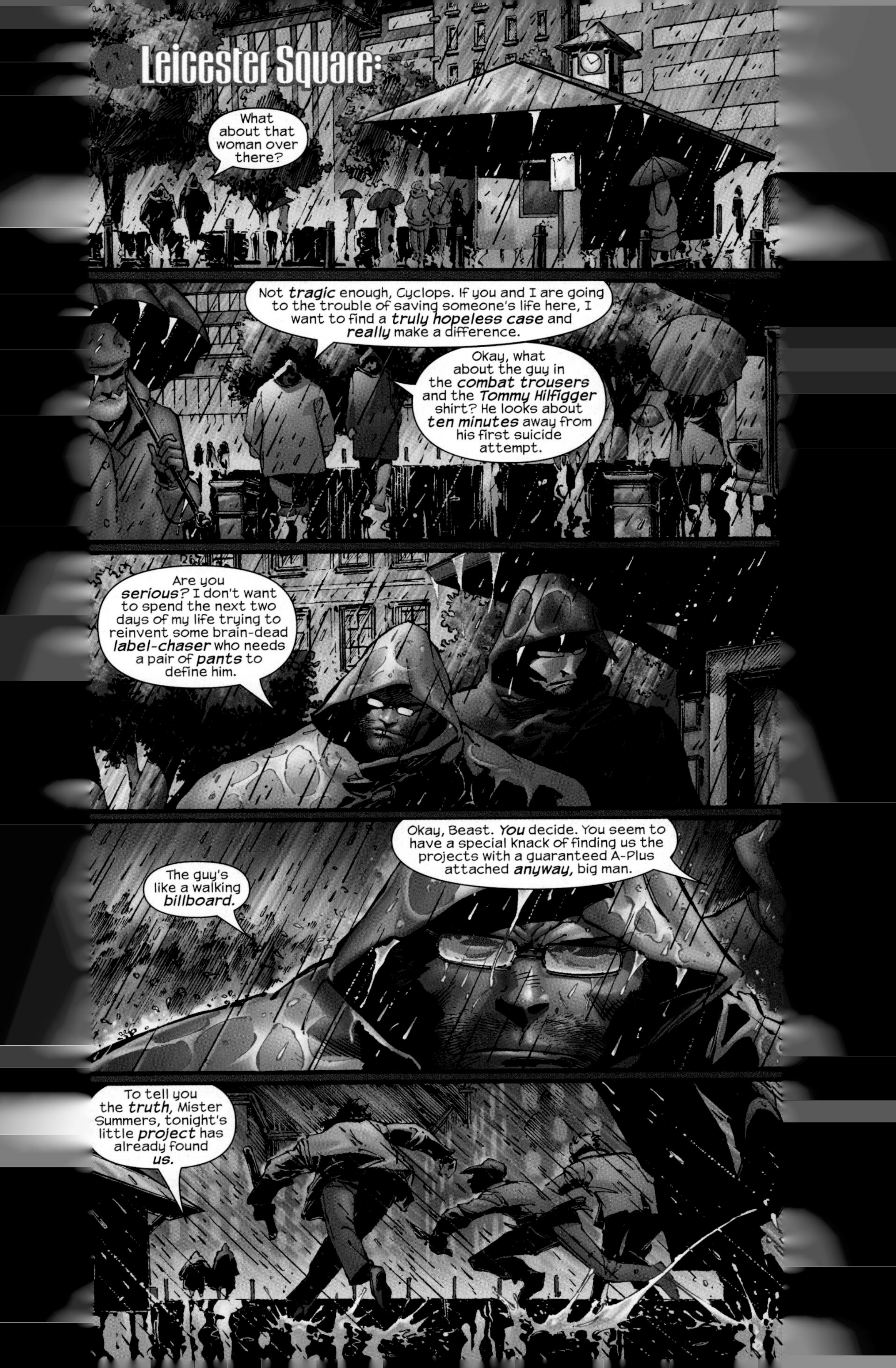
Leicester Square:
What about that woman over there?
Not tragic enough, Cyclops. If you and I are going to the trouble of saving someone's life here, I want to find a truly hopeless case and really make a difference.
Okay, what about the guy in the combat trousers and the Tommy Hilfigger shirt? He looks about ten minutes away from his first suicide attempt.
Are you serious? I don't want to spend the next two days of my life trying to reinvent some brain-dead label-chaser who needs a pair of pants to define him.
The guy's like a walking billboard.
Okay, Beast. You decide. You seem to have a special knack of finding us the projects with a guaranteed A-Plus attached anyway, big man.
To tell you the truth, Mister Summers, tonight's little project has already found us.

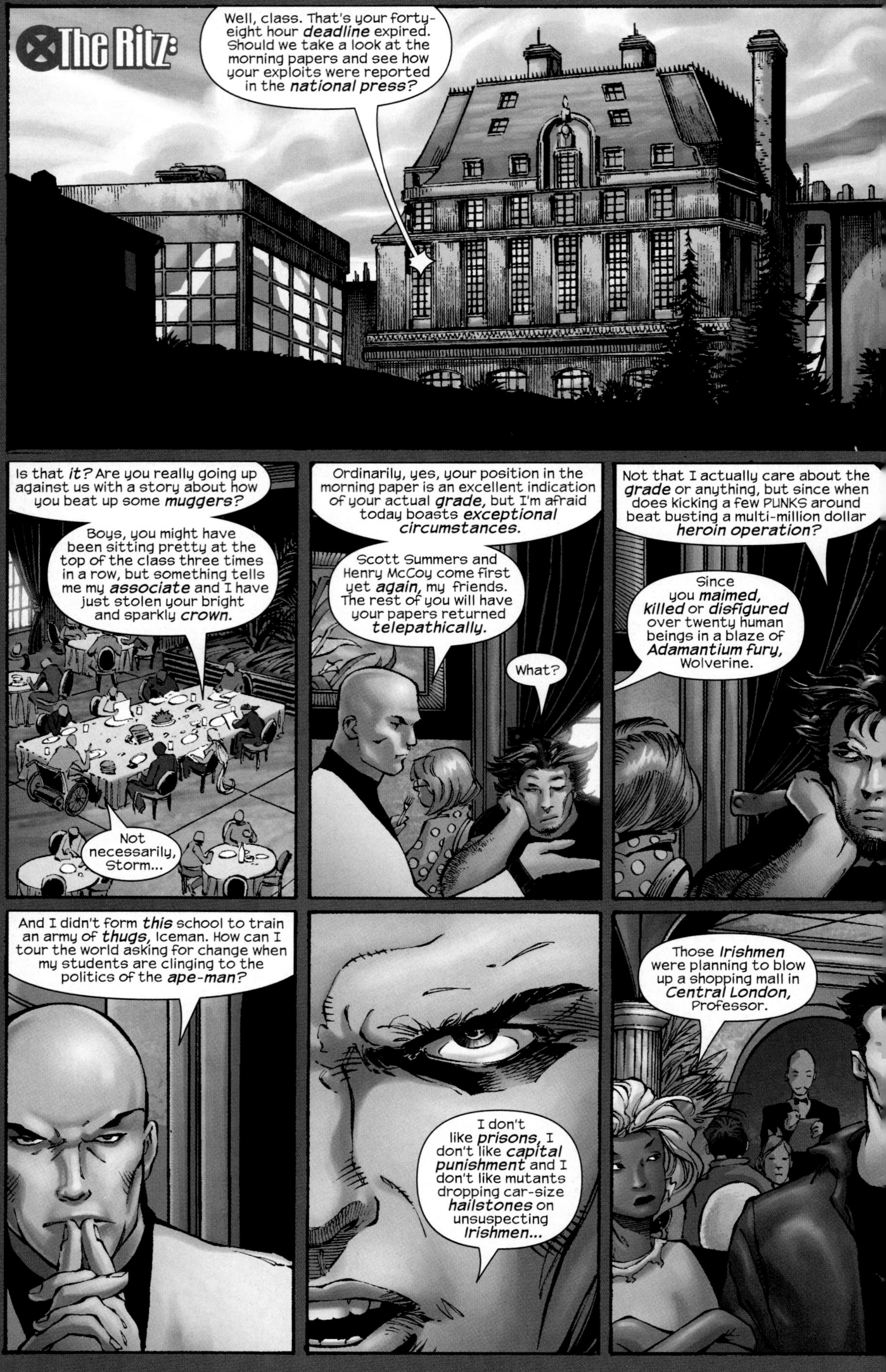

The Ritz:
Well, class. That's your forty-eight hour deadline expired. Should we take a look at the morning papers and see how your exploits were reported in the national press?
Is that it? Are you really going up against us with a story about how you beat up some muggers?
Boys, you might have been sitting pretty at the top of the class three times in a row, but something tells me my associate and I have just stolen your bright and sparkly crown.
Not necessarily, Storm...
Ordinarily, yes, your position in the morning paper is an excellent indication of your actual grade, but I'm afraid today boasts exceptional circumstances.
Scott Summers and Henry McCoy come first yet again, my friends. The rest of you will have your papers returned telepathically.
What?
Not that I actually care about the grade or anything, but since when does kicking a few PUNKS around beat busting a multi-million dollar heroin operation?
Since you maimed, killed or disfigured over twenty human beings in a blaze of Adamantium fury, Wolverine.
And I didn't form this school to train an army of thugs, Iceman. How can I tour the world asking for change when my students are clinging to the politics of the ape-man?
I don't like prisons, I don't like capital punishment and I don't like mutants dropping car-size hailstones on unsuspecting Irishmen...
Those Irishmen were planning to blow up a shopping mall in Central London, Professor.

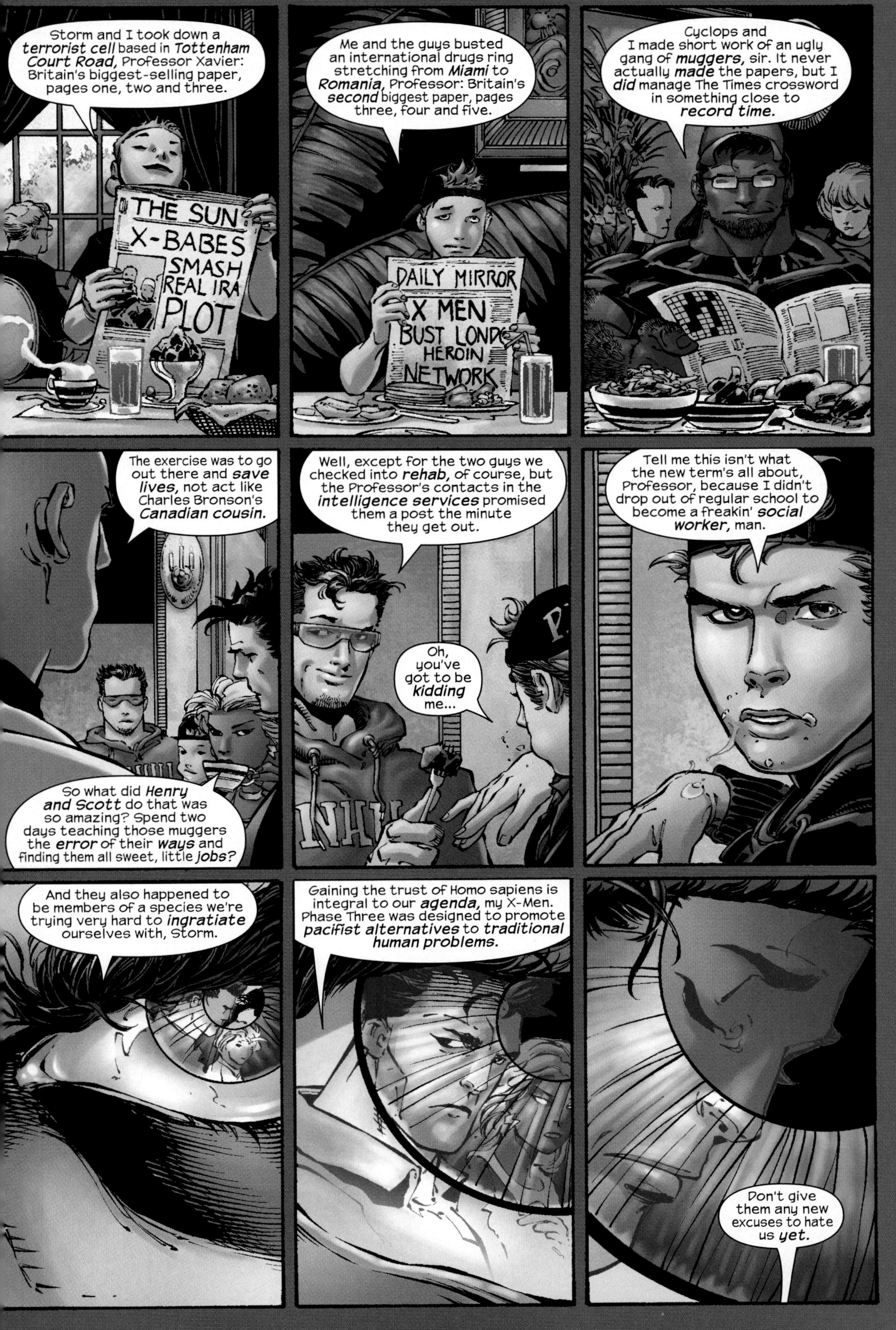
Storm and I took down a terrorist cell based in Tottenham Court Road, Professor Xavier: Britain's biggest-selling paper, pages one, two and three.
THE SUN
X-BABES SMASH REAL IRA PLOT
Me and the guys busted an international drugs ring stretching from Miami to Romania, Professor: Britain's second biggest paper, pages three, four and five.
DAILY MIRROR
X MEN BUST LONDO HEROIN NETWORK
Cyclops and I made short work of an ugly gang of muggers, sir. It never actually made the papers, but I did manage The Times crossword in something close to record time.
The exercise was to go out there and save lives, not act like Charles Bronson's Canadian cousin.
So what did Henry and Scott do that was so amazing? Spend two days teaching those muggers the error of their ways and finding them all sweet, little jobs?
Well, except for the two guys we checked into rehab, of course, but the Professor's contacts in the intelligence services promised them a post the minute they get out.
Oh, you've got to be kidding me...
Tell me this isn't what the new term's all about, Professor, because I didn't drop out of regular school to become a freakin' social worker, man.
And they also happened to be members of a species we're trying very hard to ingratiate ourselves with, Storm.
Gaining the trust of Homo sapiens is integral to our agenda, my X-Men. Phase Three was designed to promote pacifist alternatives to traditional human problems.
Don't give them any new excuses to hate us yet.

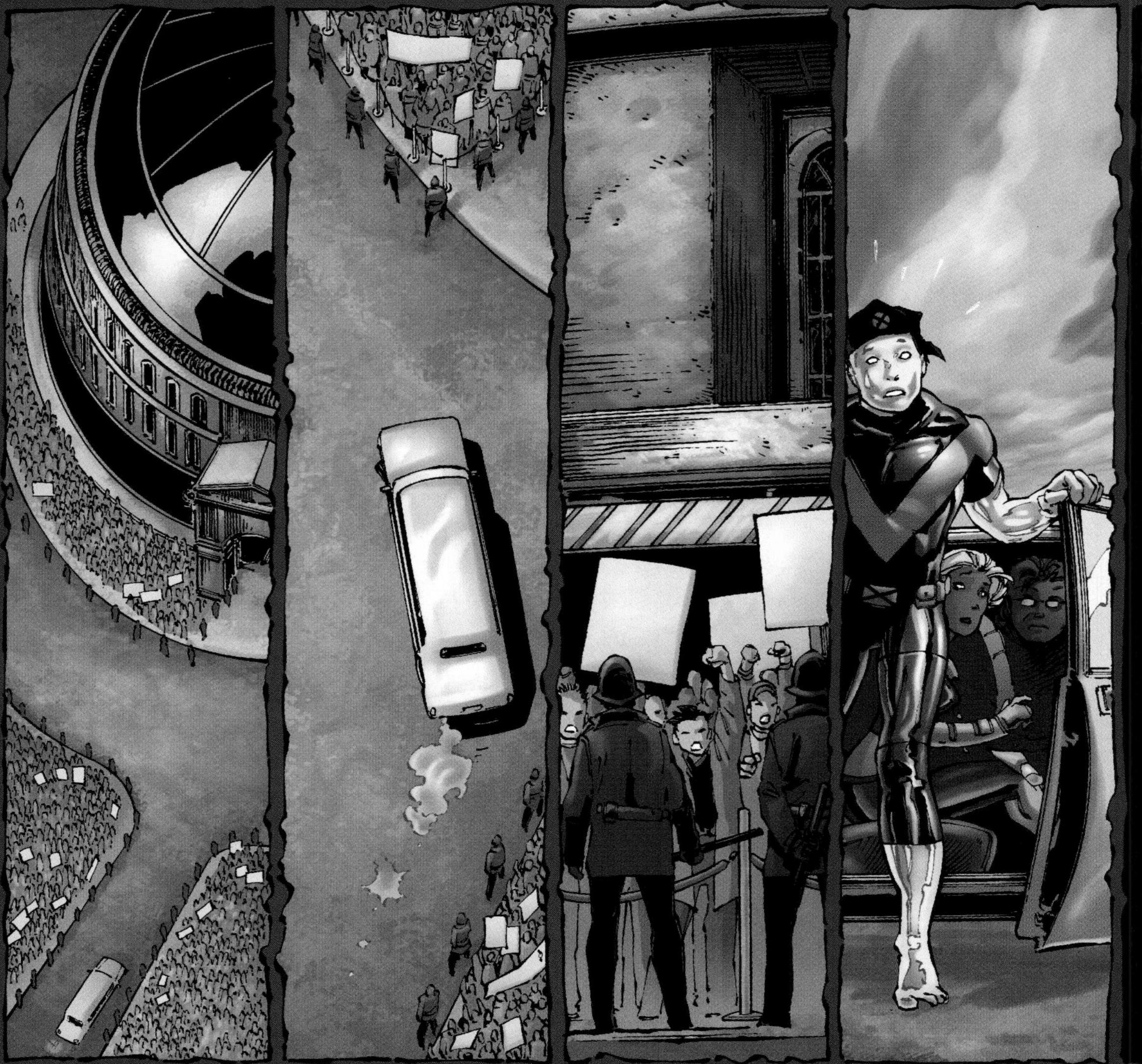
"Professor Xavier, on behalf of the audience, I'd just like to thank you for that inspirational lecture and open the floor up to the thousands of believers in the *audience,* sir.
"Is there anyone out there who'd like to ask the leader of the X-Men a *question?"*
"Hi, Professor. I was just curious how these X-Men operations are *funded,* sir. Is it true you use your psychic powers to manipulate *stocks* and *shares?"*
"No, the cars, the planes and my secret New York school are all paid for out of my *inheritance,* young man.
"It's true I play the *stock market,* but I'd never use my powers for anything as tawdry as *personal financial gain."*
"Did you really mean it when you said you don't have to be a *mutant* to be an *X-Man?"*

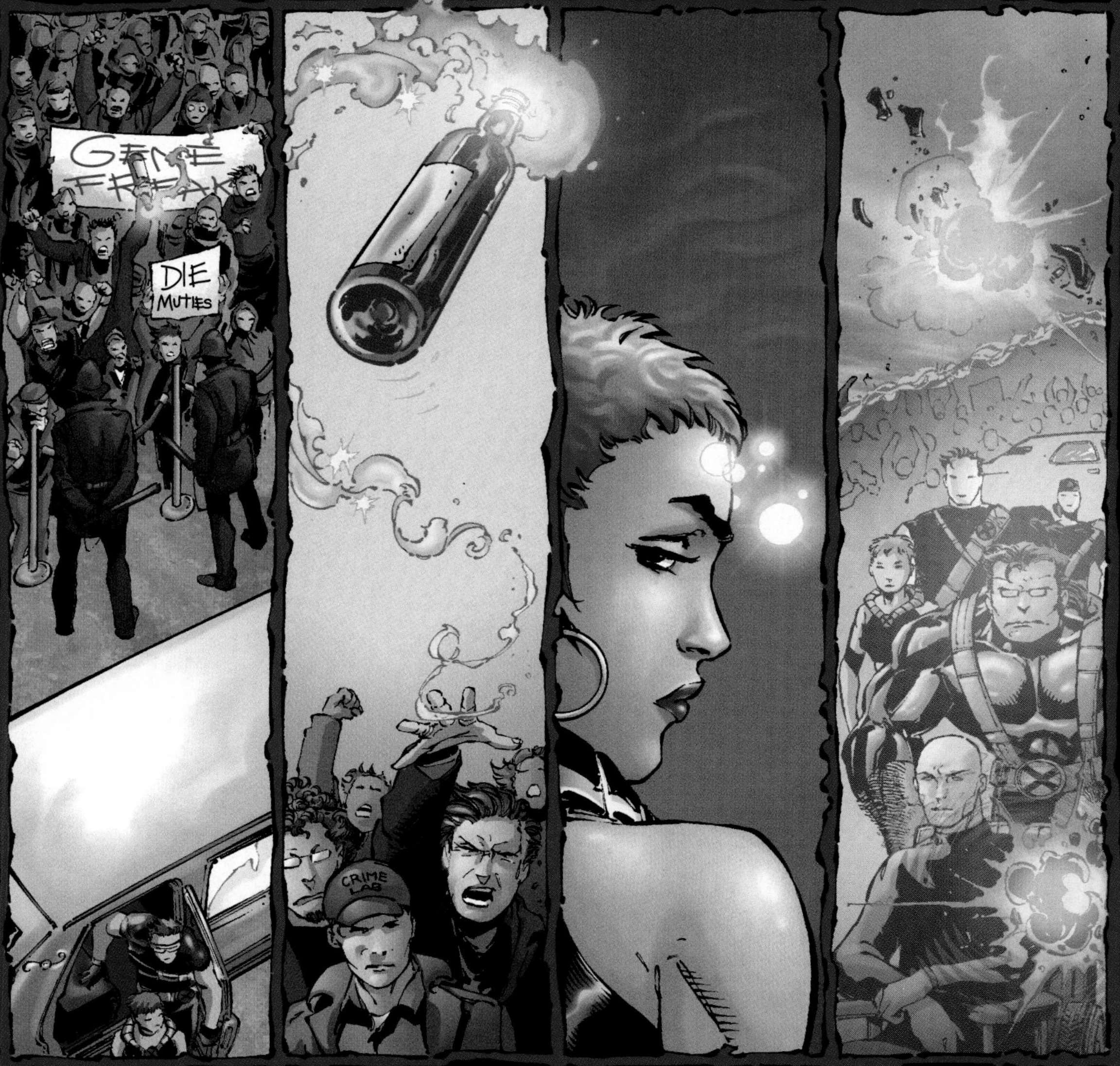
GENE FREAK
DIE MUTIES
CRIME LAB
"Of course. The ideas outlined in the book are a manifesto for man and mutant-kind to live in *harmony.*
"An intelligent person doesn't have to be *x-factor positive* to put on a uniform and head out there to make a difference in their *neighborhood.*"
"What about this rumor that there's a *second* school you've started, Professor Xavier? An island off the coast of *Europe* even your *pupils* don't know about?
"Is it true what they say on the Internet about a school where you're training less *socially acceptable* mutants?"
"I'm afraid I'm not in the *habit* of responding to *Internet speculation,* Miss. Next question, please."
"Professor Xavier! Do the scenes which greeted you and your students outside the Hall tonight ever make you *resentful* of the human race?

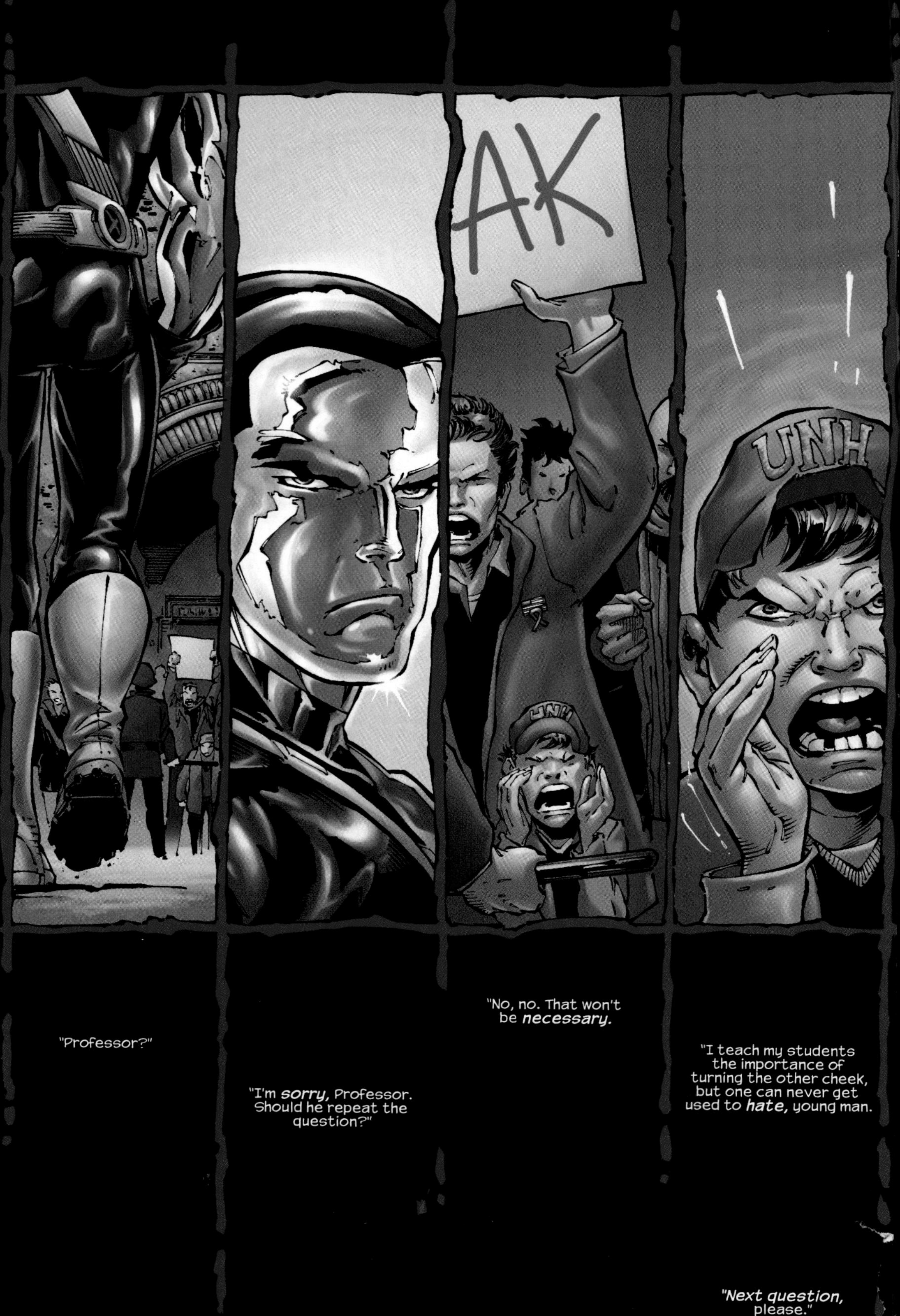
AK
UNH
UNH
"Professor?"
"I'm *sorry,* Professor. Should he repeat the question?"
"No, no. That won't be *necessary.*
"I teach my students the importance of turning the other cheek, but one can never get used to *hate,* young man.
"Next question, please."

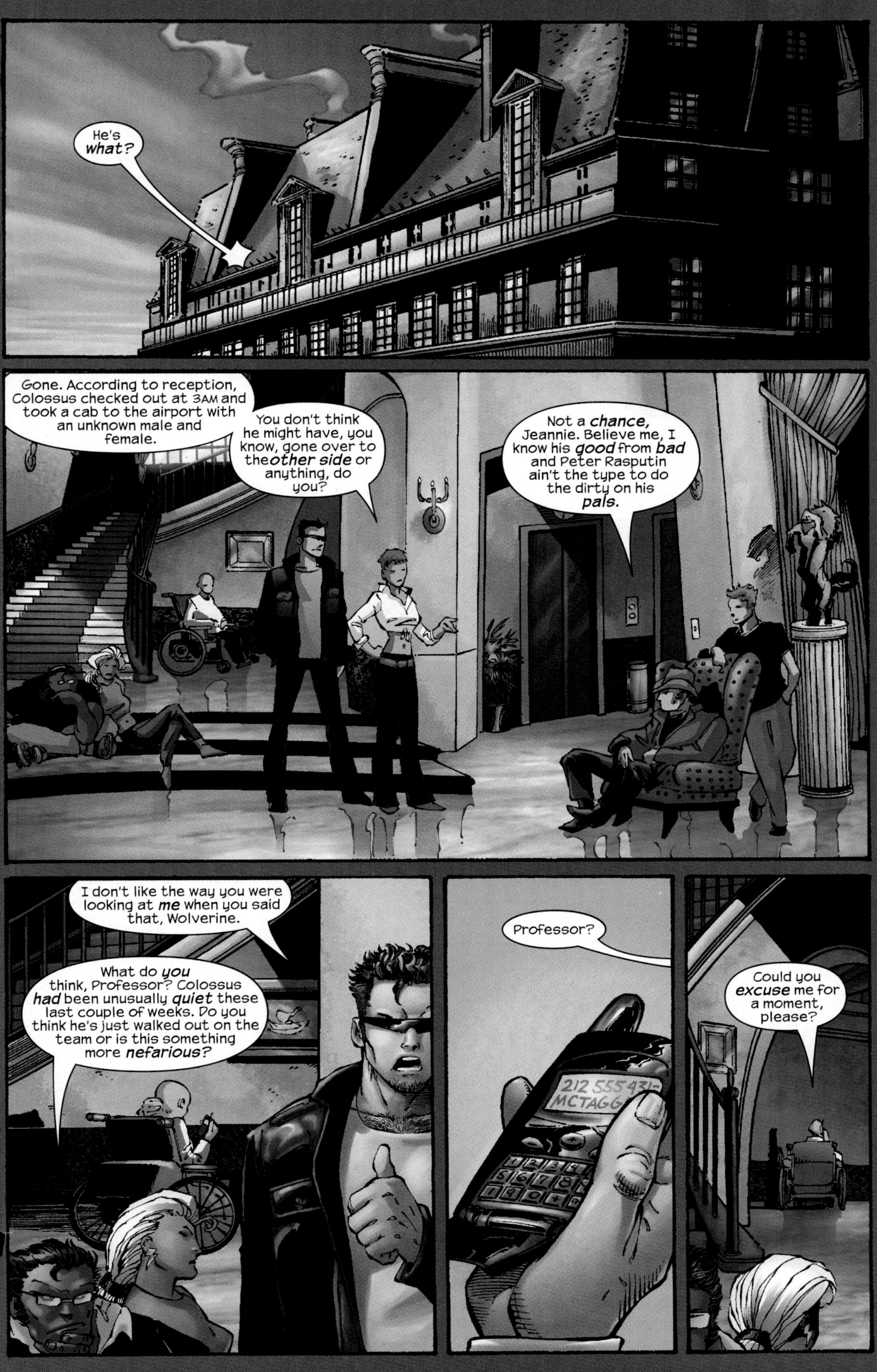
He's what?
Gone. According to reception, Colossus checked out at 3AM and took a cab to the airport with an unknown male and female.
You don't think he might have, you know, gone over to the other side or anything, do you?
Not a chance, Jeannie. Believe me, I know his good from bad and Peter Rasputin ain't the type to do the dirty on his pals.
I don't like the way you were looking at me when you said that, Wolverine.
What do you think, Professor? Colossus had been unusually quiet these last couple of weeks. Do you think he's just walked out on the team or is this something more nefarious?
Professor?
212 55543
MCTAGG
Could you excuse me for a moment, please?

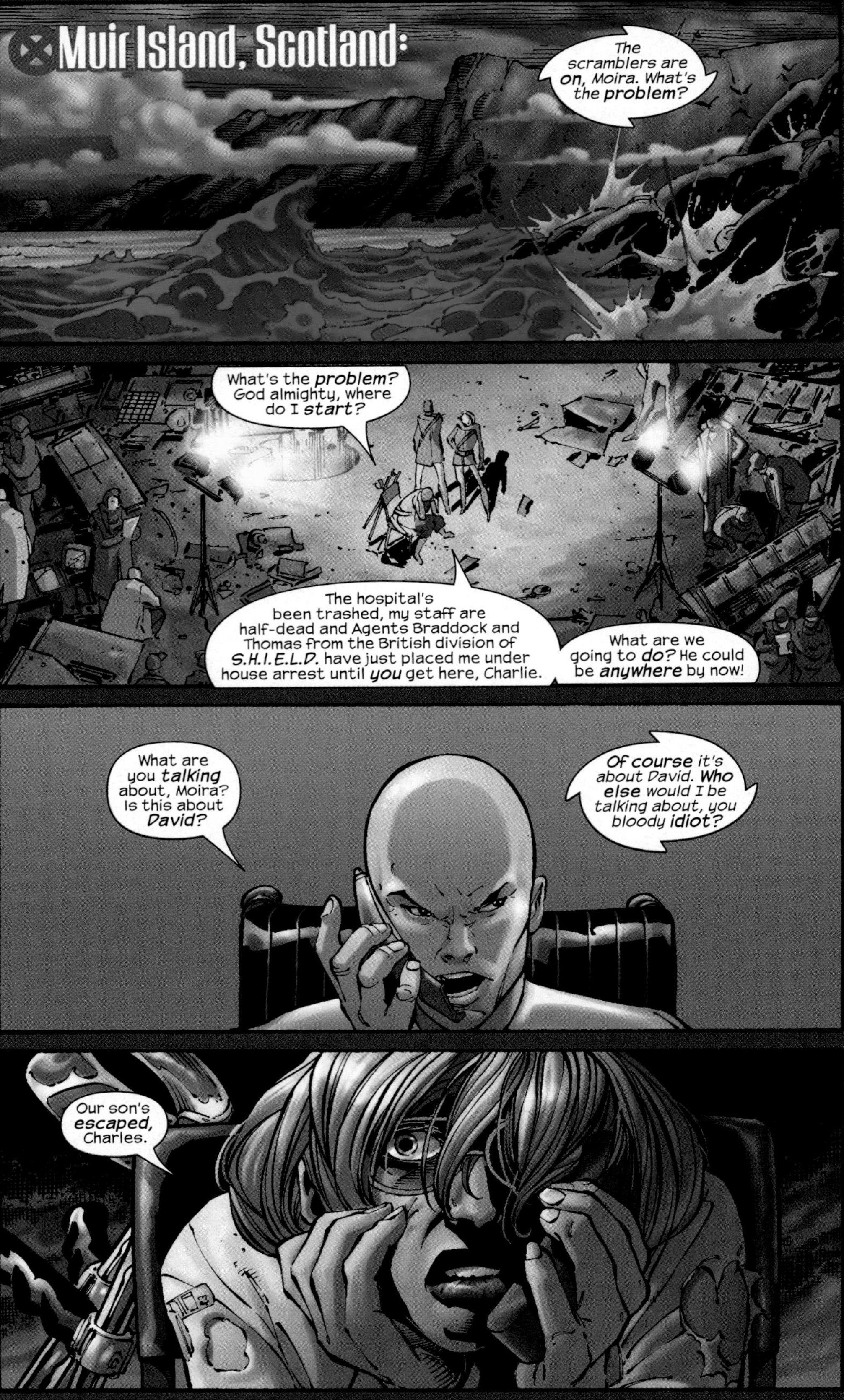
Muir Island, Scotland:
The scramblers are on, Moira. What's the problem?
What's the problem? God almighty, where do I start?
The hospital's been trashed, my staff are half-dead and Agents Braddock and Thomas from the British division of S.H.I.E.L.D. have just placed me under house arrest until you get here, Charlie.
What are we going to do? He could be anywhere by now!
What are you talking about, Moira? Is this about David?
Of course it's about David. Who else would I be talking about, you bloody idiot?
Our son's escaped, Charles.

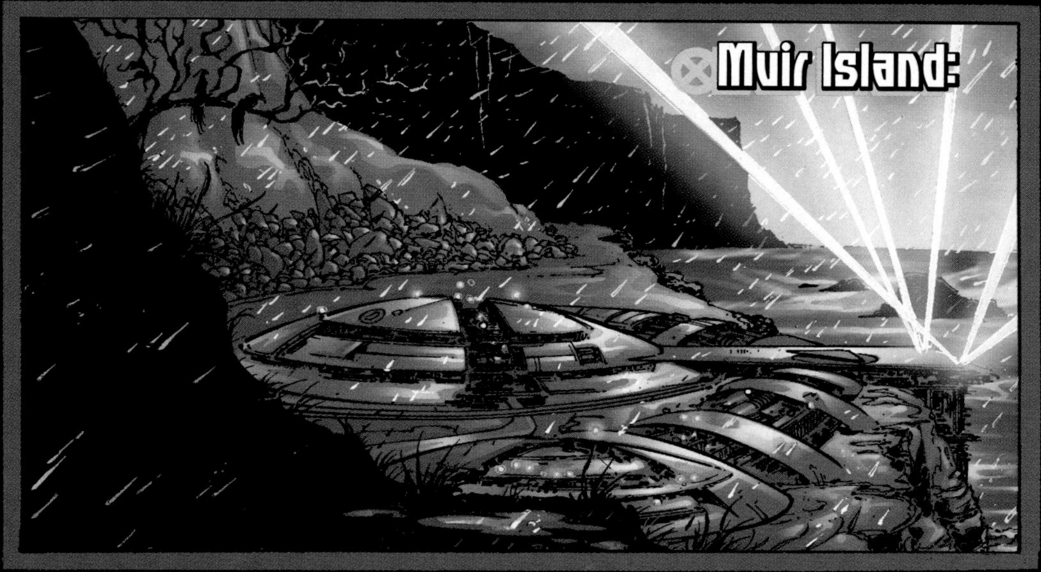
Muir Island:

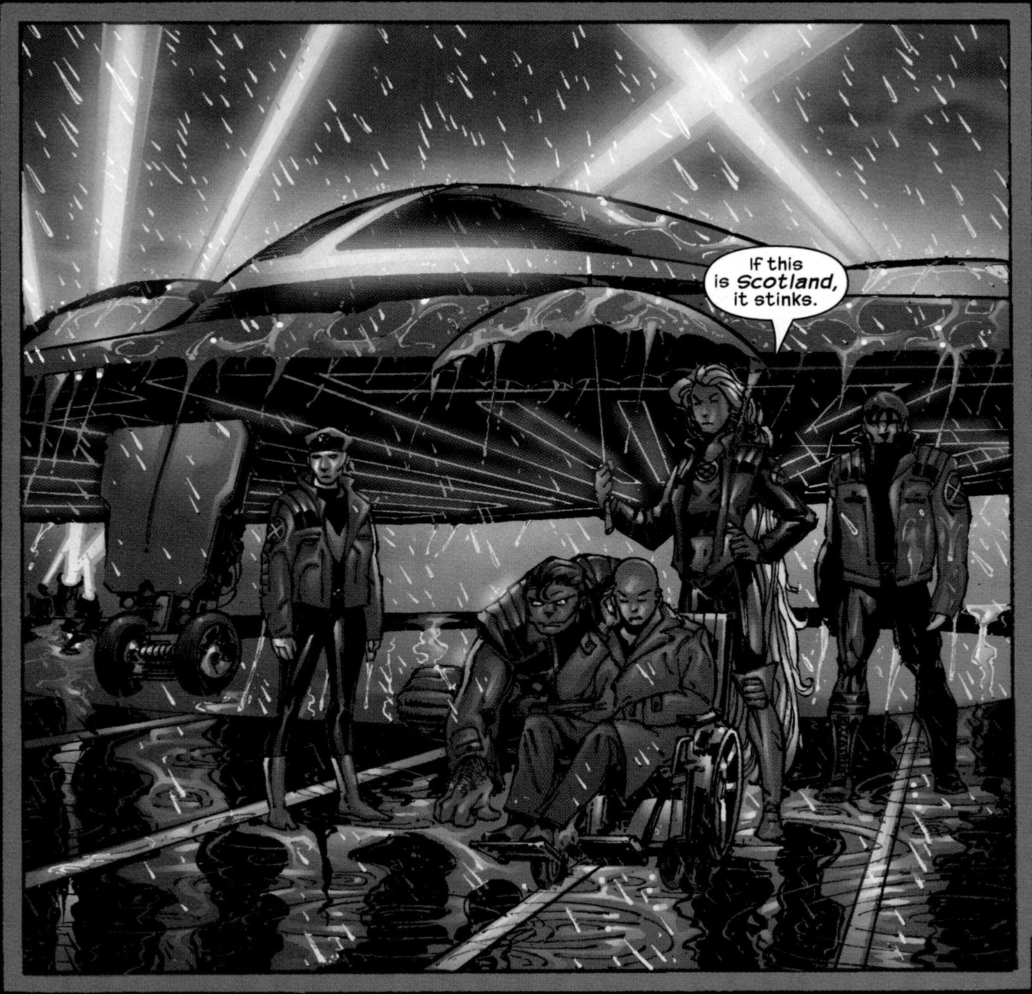
If this is *Scotland,* it stinks.

Mark Millar story Adam Kubert pencils Danny Miki inks
J.D. Smith colors Chris Eliopoulos letters C.B. Cebulski associate editor Brian Smith associate edito
Ralph Macchio editor Joe Quesada editor in chief Bill Jemas president & inspiration

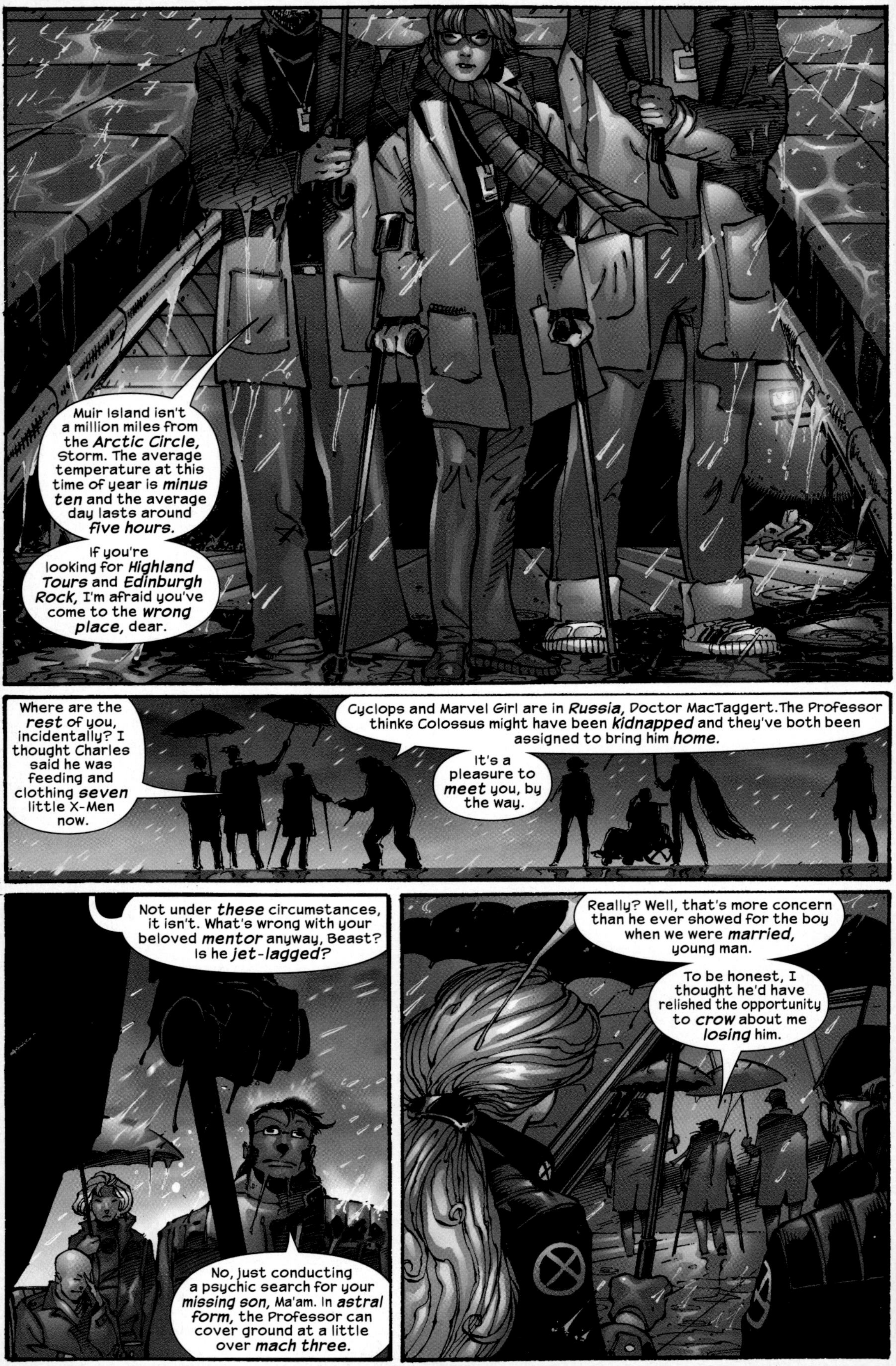
Muir Island isn't a million miles from the *Arctic Circle,* Storm. The average temperature at this time of year is *minus ten* and the average day lasts around *five hours.*
If you're looking for *Highland Tours* and *Edinburgh Rock,* I'm afraid you've come to the *wrong place,* dear.
Where are the *rest* of you, incidentally? I thought Charles said he was feeding and clothing *seven* little X-Men now.
Cyclops and Marvel Girl are in *Russia,* Doctor MacTaggert. The Professor thinks Colossus might have been *kidnapped* and they've both been assigned to bring him *home.*
It's a pleasure to *meet* you, by the way.
Not under *these* circumstances, it isn't. What's wrong with your beloved *mentor* anyway, Beast? Is he *jet-lagged?*
No, just conducting a psychic search for your *missing son,* Ma'am. In *astral form,* the Professor can cover ground at a little over *mach three.*
Really? Well, that's more concern than he ever showed for the boy when we were *married,* young man.
To be honest, I thought he'd have relished the opportunity to *crow* about me *losing* him.

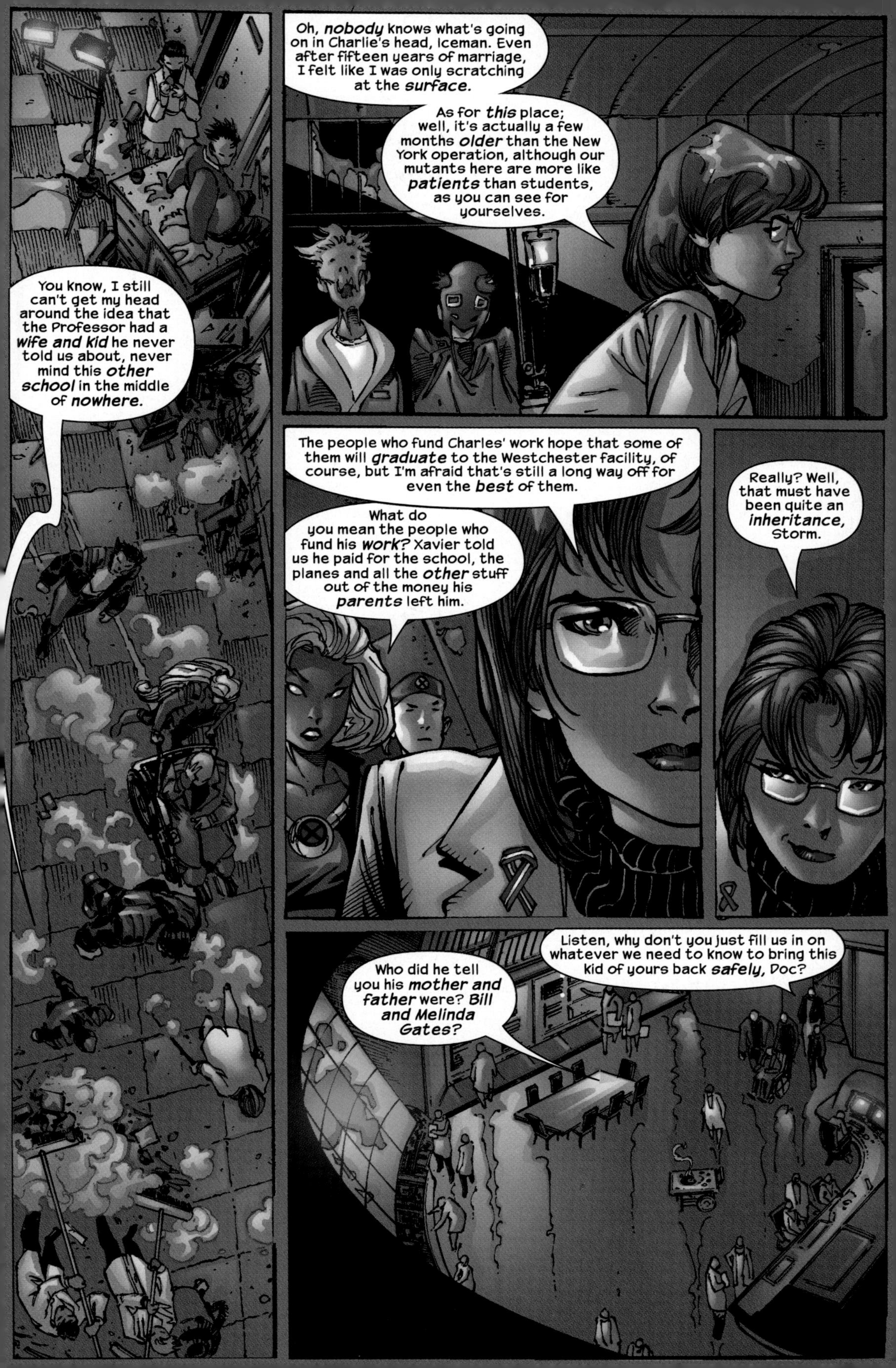
Oh, nobody knows what's going on in Charlie's head, Iceman. Even after fifteen years of marriage, I felt like I was only scratching at the surface.
As for this place; well, it's actually a few months older than the New York operation, although our mutants here are more like patients than students, as you can see for yourselves.
You know, I still can't get my head around the idea that the Professor had a wife and kid he never told us about, never mind this other school in the middle of nowhere.
The people who fund Charles' work hope that some of them will graduate to the Westchester facility, of course, but I'm afraid that's still a long way off for even the best of them.
What do you mean the people who fund his work? Xavier told us he paid for the school, the planes and all the other stuff out of the money his parents left him.
Really? Well, that must have been quite an inheritance, Storm.
Listen, why don't you just fill us in on whatever we need to know to bring this kid of yours back safely, Doc?
Who did he tell you his mother and father were? Bill and Melinda Gates?

"What can I *say*, Wolverine? David was just your typical, little *boy* when Charles and I were together-- average size, average intellect, a devoted *Glasgow Rangers* fan."

"Of course, we always *knew* he was carrying the X-gene, but his powers didn't actually manifest until the day after his father *left* and our lives were thrown into *turmoil*."

"As far as we could ascertain, David had a very limited control of the matter around his person, but even the *slightest* use of these abilities had a devastating effect on his physical body."

"My son would have been dead in a *week* if we hadn't kept him sedated on *Haloperidol* all these years and locked him in a lab where we could monitor him carefully."

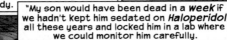

"Why he started to convulse again last night, I still can't say, but I doubt it's a coincidence that his *father* was back in Britain with his nice, little *surrogate family*."

"Unfortunately, this convulsion turned out to be the *fatal* one and he'd have died right there on the operating table if he hadn't jumped into poor Isobel MacLinden."

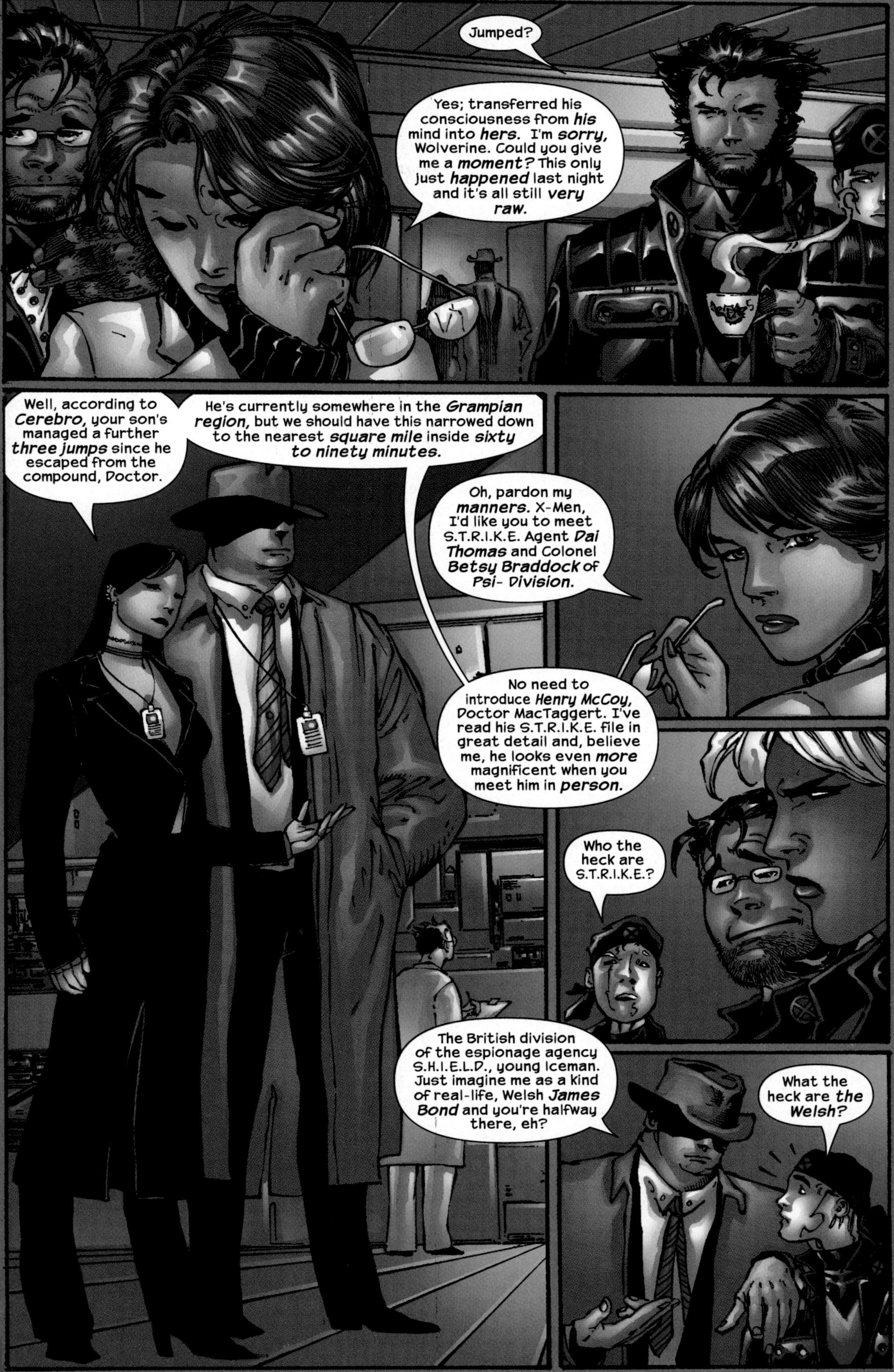
Jumped?
Yes; transferred his consciousness from *his* mind into *hers*. I'm *sorry,* Wolverine. Could you give me a *moment?* This only just *happened* last night and it's all still *very raw*.
Well, according to *Cerebro,* your son's managed a further *three jumps* since he escaped from the compound, Doctor.
He's currently somewhere in the *Grampian region,* but we should have this narrowed down to the nearest *square mile* inside *sixty to ninety minutes.*
Oh, pardon my *manners.* X-Men, I'd like you to meet S.T.R.I.K.E. Agent *Dai Thomas* and Colonel *Betsy Braddock* of *Psi- Division.*
No need to introduce *Henry McCoy,* Doctor MacTaggert. I've read his S.T.R.I.K.E. file in great detail and, believe me, he looks even *more* magnificent when you meet him in *person.*
Who the heck are S.T.R.I.K.E.?
The British division of the espionage agency S.H.I.E.L.D., young Iceman. Just imagine me as a kind of real-life, Welsh *James Bond* and you're halfway there, eh?
What the heck are *the Welsh?*

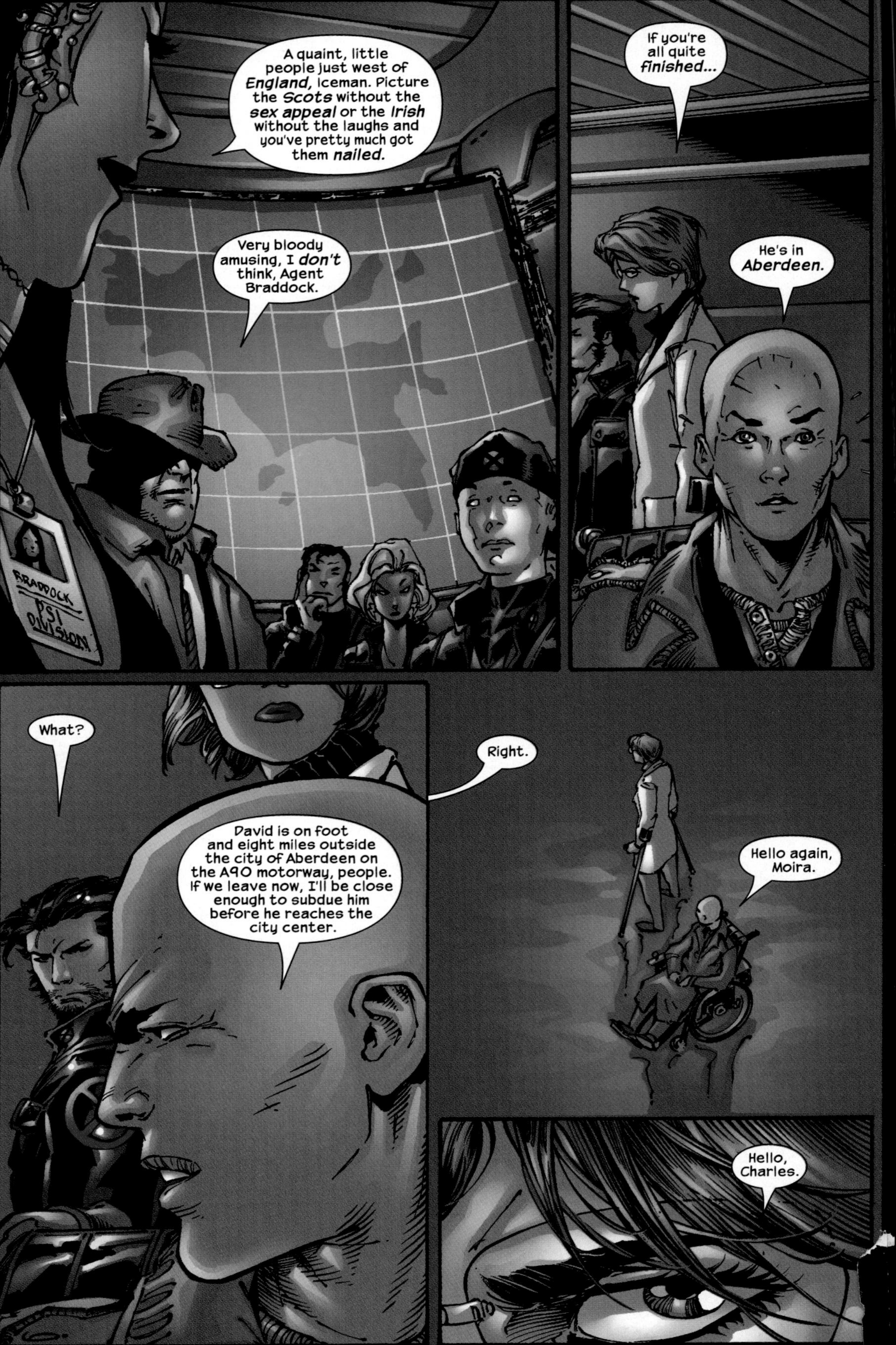
A quaint, little people just west of England, Iceman. Picture the Scots without the sex appeal or the Irish without the laughs and you've pretty much got them nailed.
Very bloody amusing, I don't think, Agent Braddock.
BRADDOCK PSI DIVISION
If you're all quite finished...
He's in Aberdeen.
What?
Right.
David is on foot and eight miles outside the city of Aberdeen on the A90 motorway, people. If we leave now, I'll be close enough to subdue him before he reaches the city center.
Hello again, Moira.
Hello, Charles.

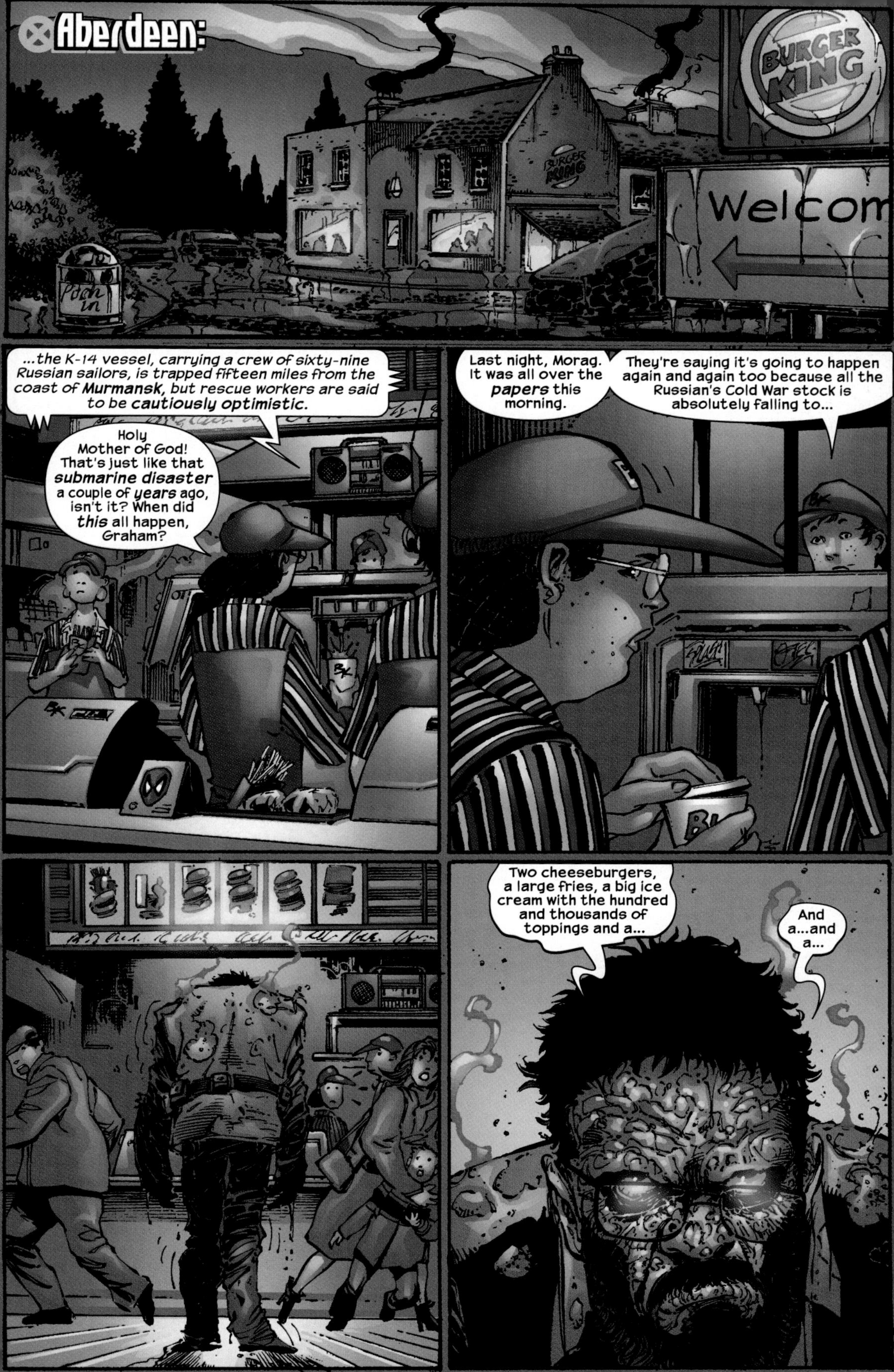
Aberdeen:
BURGER KING
Welcom
...the K-14 vessel, carrying a crew of sixty-nine Russian sailors, is trapped fifteen miles from the coast of Murmansk, but rescue workers are said to be cautiously optimistic.
Holy Mother of God! That's just like that submarine disaster a couple of years ago, isn't it? When did this all happen, Graham?
Last night, Morag. It was all over the papers this morning.
They're saying it's going to happen again and again too because all the Russian's Cold War stock is absolutely falling to...
Two cheeseburgers, a large fries, a big ice cream with the hundred and thousands of toppings and a...
And a...and a...

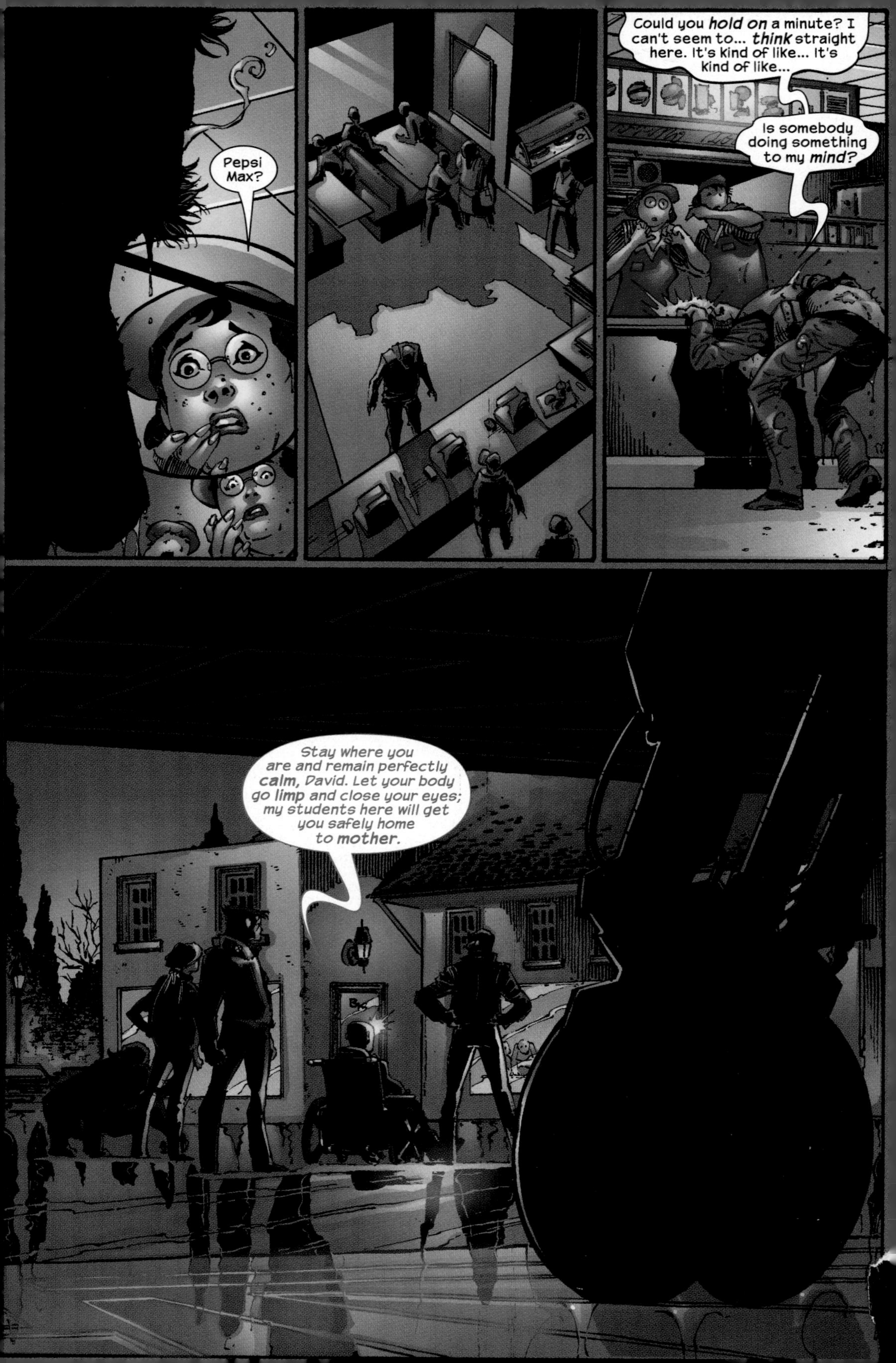

Pepsi Max?
Could you **hold on** a minute? I can't seem to... **think** straight here. It's kind of like... It's kind of like...
Is somebody doing something to my *mind*?
Stay where you are and remain perfectly **calm**, David. Let your body go **limp** and close your eyes; my students here will get you safely home to **mother**.

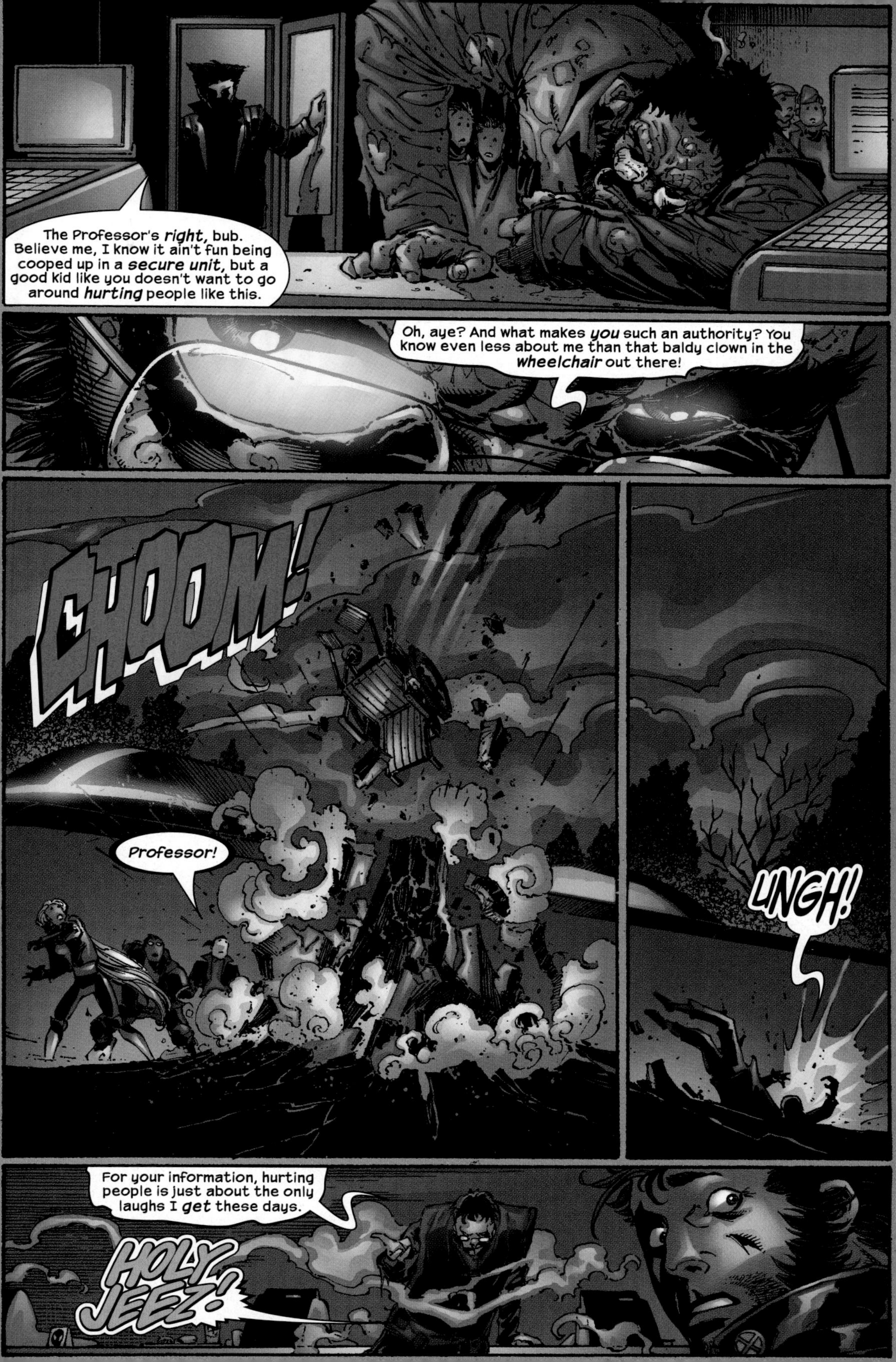
The Professor's *right*, bub. Believe me, I know it ain't fun being cooped up in a *secure unit*, but a good kid like you doesn't want to go around *hurting* people like this.
Oh, aye? And what makes *you* such an authority? You know even less about me than that baldy clown in the *wheelchair* out there!
CHOOM!
Professor!
UNGH!
For your information, hurting people is just about the only laughs I *get* these days.
HOLY JEEZ!

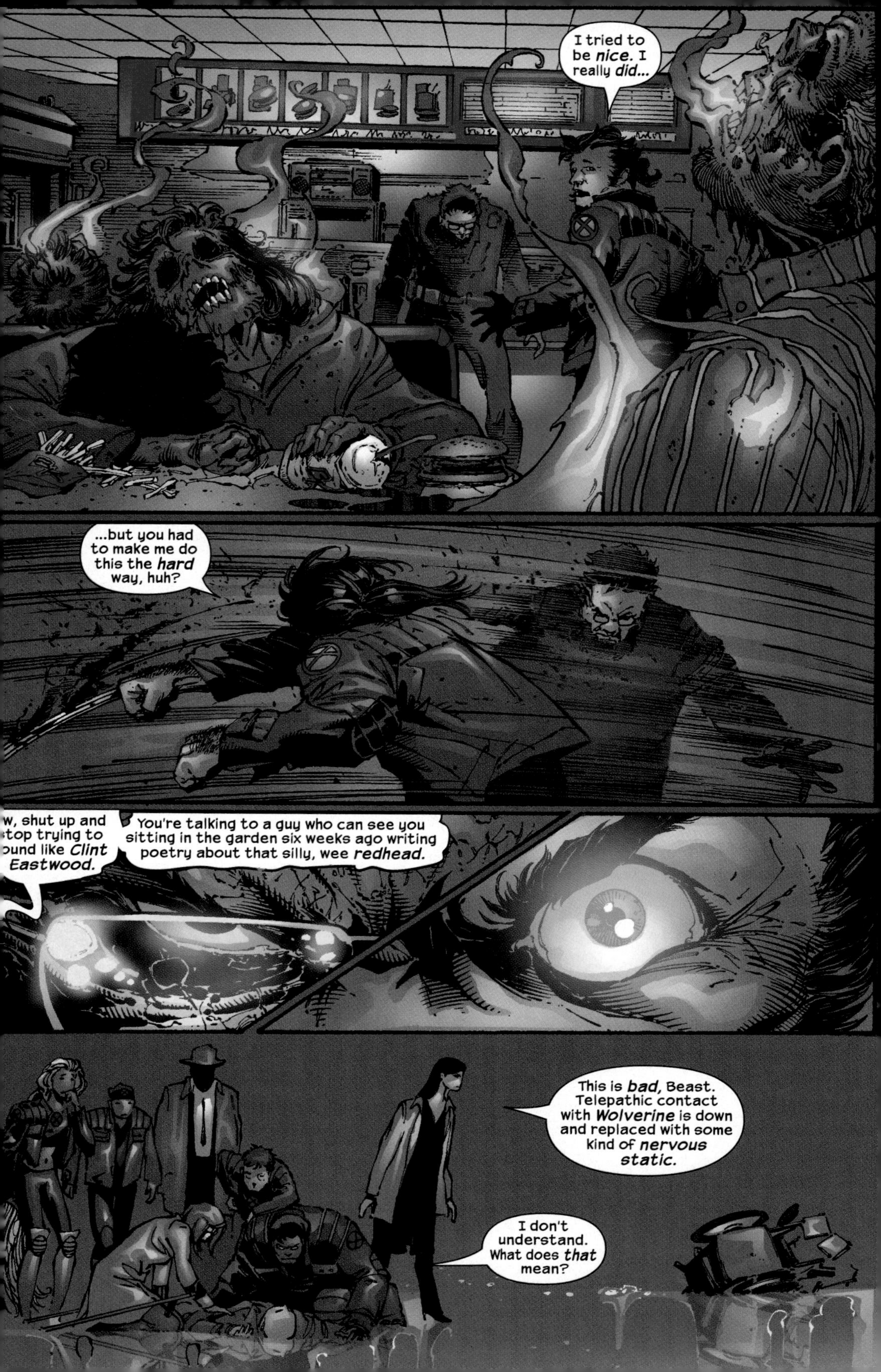

I tried to be *nice*. I really *did*...
...but you had to make me do this the *hard* way, huh?
w, shut up and top trying to ound like *Clint Eastwood*.
You're talking to a guy who can see you sitting in the garden six weeks ago writing poetry about that silly, wee *redhead*.
This is *bad*, Beast. Telepathic contact with *Wolverine* is down and replaced with some kind of *nervous static*.
I don't understand. What does *that* mean?

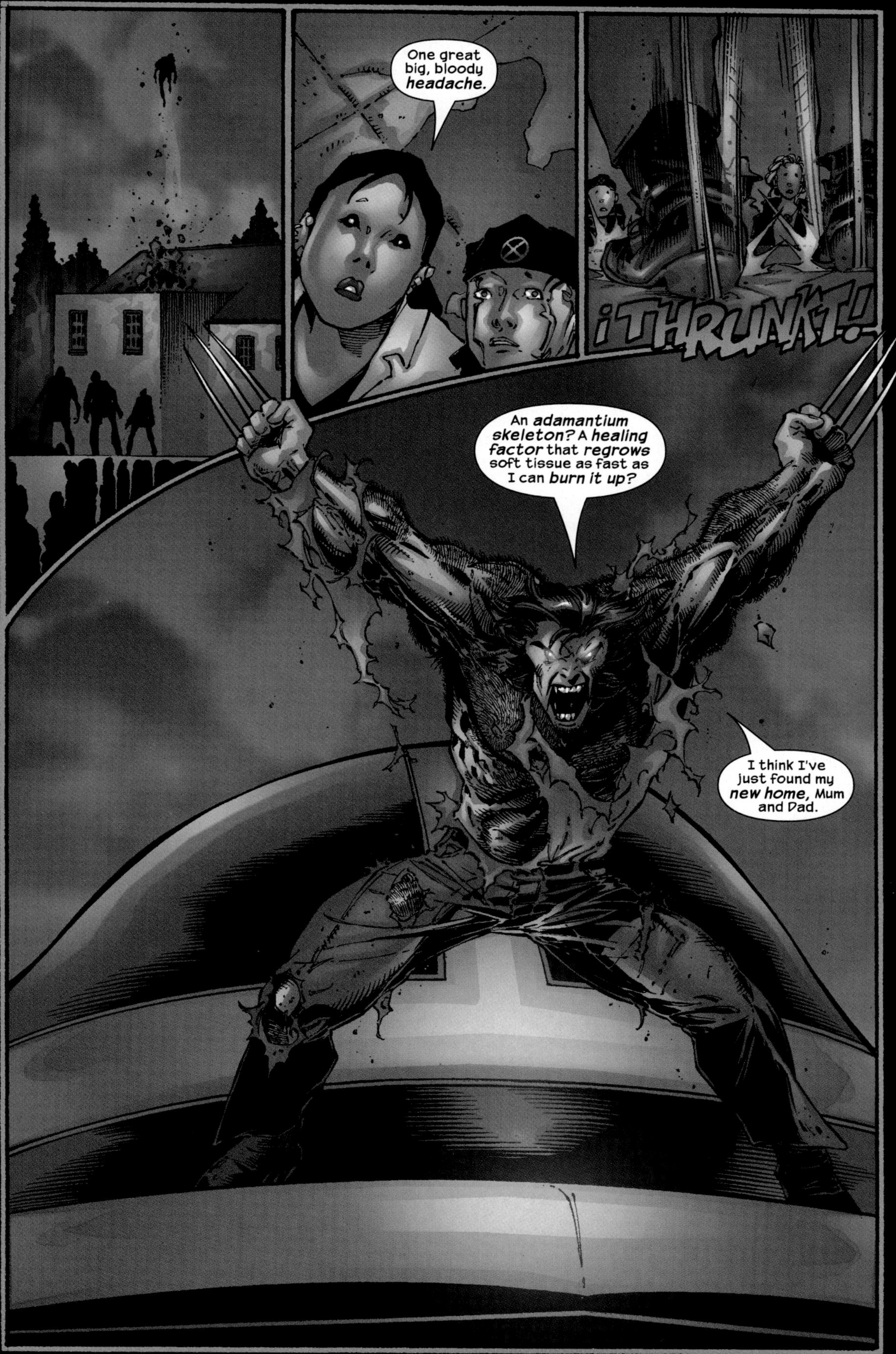
One great big, bloody headache.
¡THRUNKT!
An adamantium skeleton? A healing factor that regrows soft tissue as fast as I can burn it up?
I think I've just found my new home, Mum and Dad.

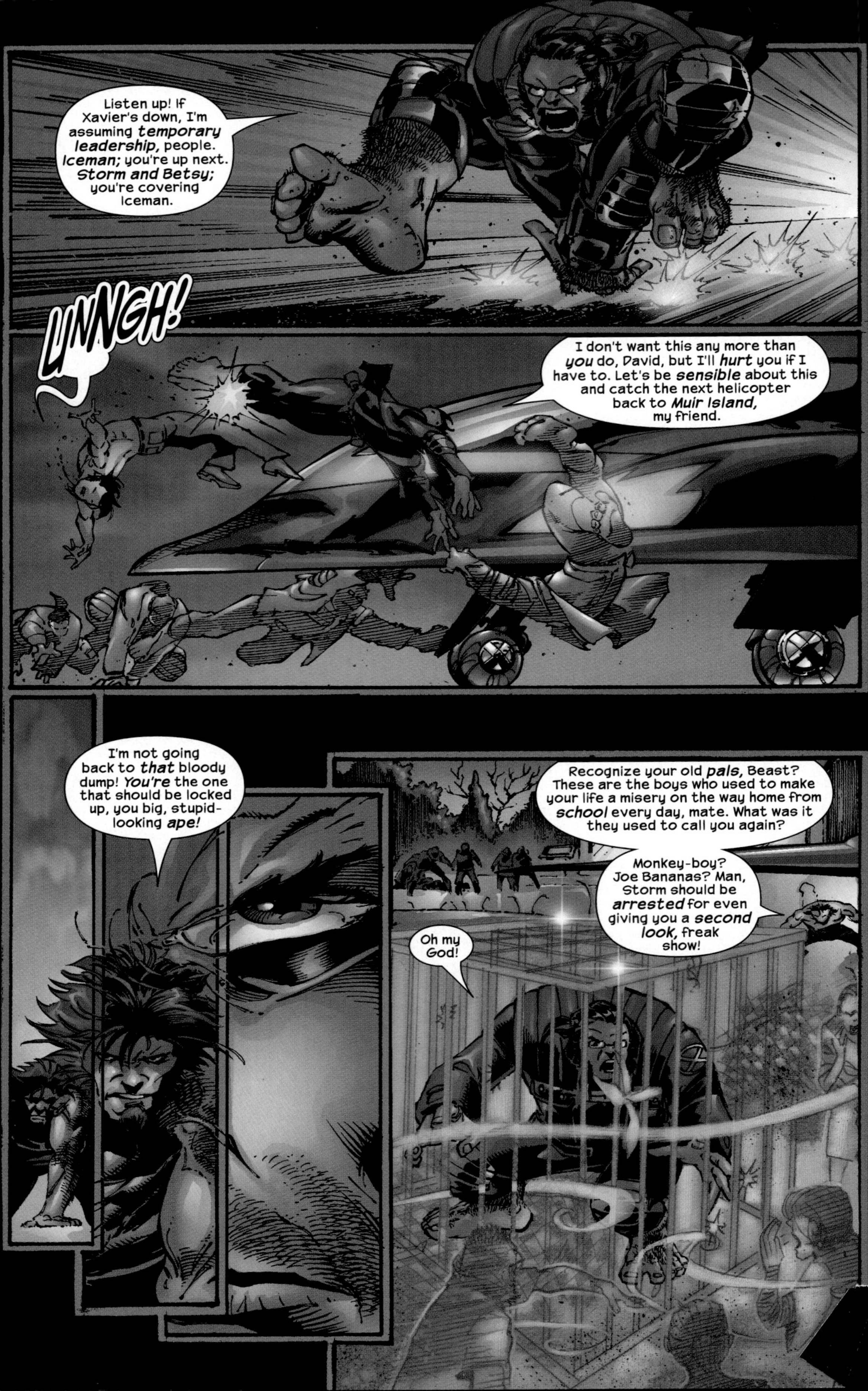
Listen up! If Xavier's down, I'm assuming *temporary leadership,* people. *Iceman;* you're up next. *Storm and Betsy;* you're covering Iceman.
UNNGH!
I don't want this any more than *you* do, David, but I'll *hurt* you if I have to. Let's be *sensible* about this and catch the next helicopter back to *Muir Island,* my friend.
I'm not going back to *that* bloody dump! *You're* the one that should be locked up, you big, stupid-looking *ape!*
Recognize your old *pals,* Beast? These are the boys who used to make your life a misery on the way home from *school* every day, mate. What was it they used to call you again?
Monkey-boy? Joe Bananas? Man, Storm should be *arrested* for even giving you a *second look,* freak show!
Oh my God!

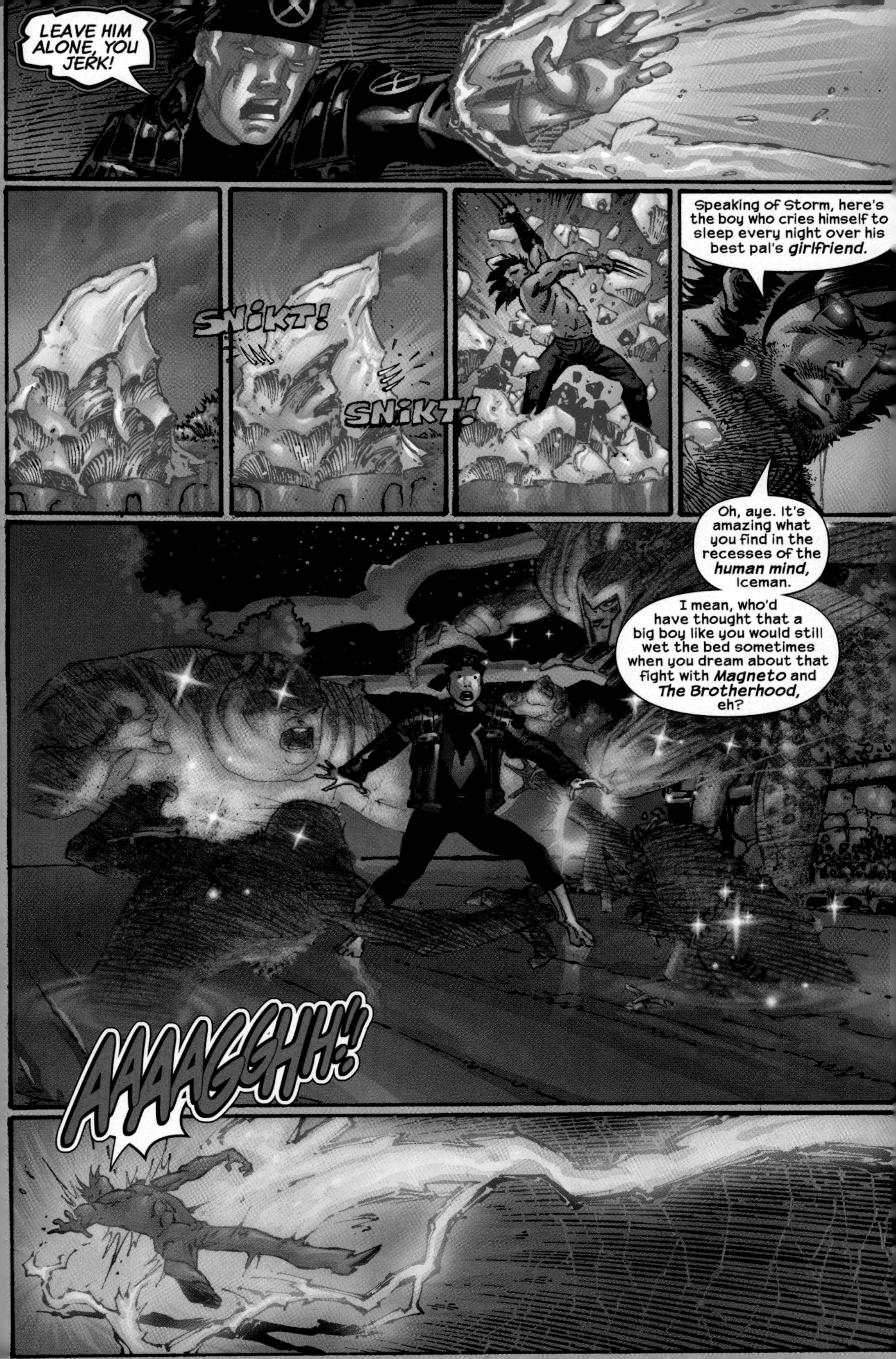
LEAVE HIM ALONE, YOU JERK!
SNIKT!
SNIKT!
Speaking of Storm, here's the boy who cries himself to sleep every night over his best pal's *girlfriend.*
Oh, aye. It's amazing what you find in the recesses of the *human mind,* Iceman.
I mean, who'd have thought that a big boy like you would still wet the bed sometimes when you dream about that fight with *Magneto* and *The Brotherhood,* eh?
AAAAGGHH!!

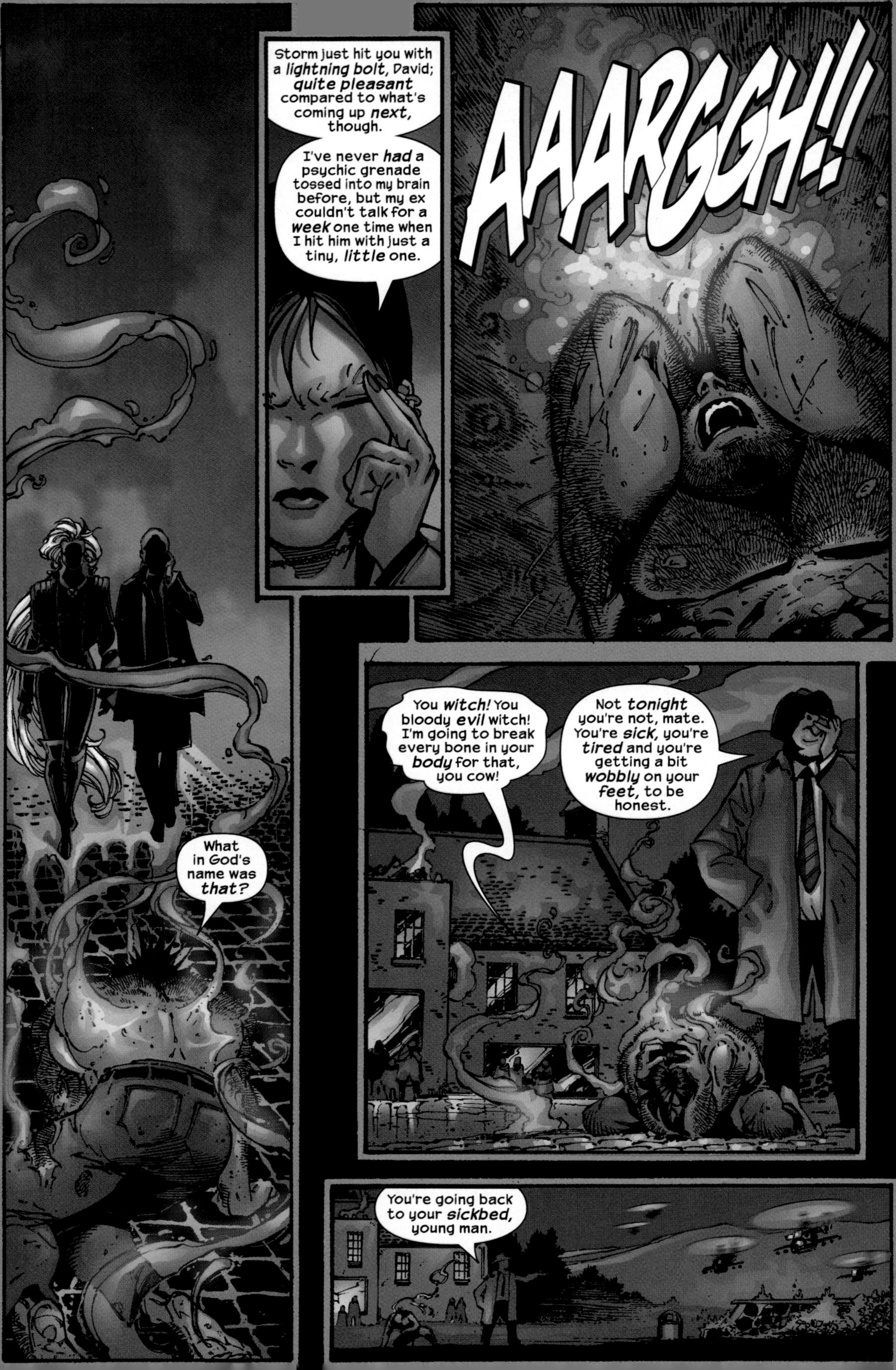
Storm just hit you with a *lightning bolt*, David; *quite pleasant* compared to what's coming up *next*, though.
I've never *had* a psychic grenade tossed into my brain before, but my ex couldn't talk for a *week* one time when I hit him with just a tiny, *little* one.
AAARGGH!!
What in God's name was *that*?
You *witch!* You bloody *evil* witch! I'm going to break every bone in your *body* for that, you cow!
Not *tonight* you're not, mate. You're *sick*, you're *tired* and you're getting a bit *wobbly* on your *feet*, to be honest.
You're going back to your *sickbed*, young man.

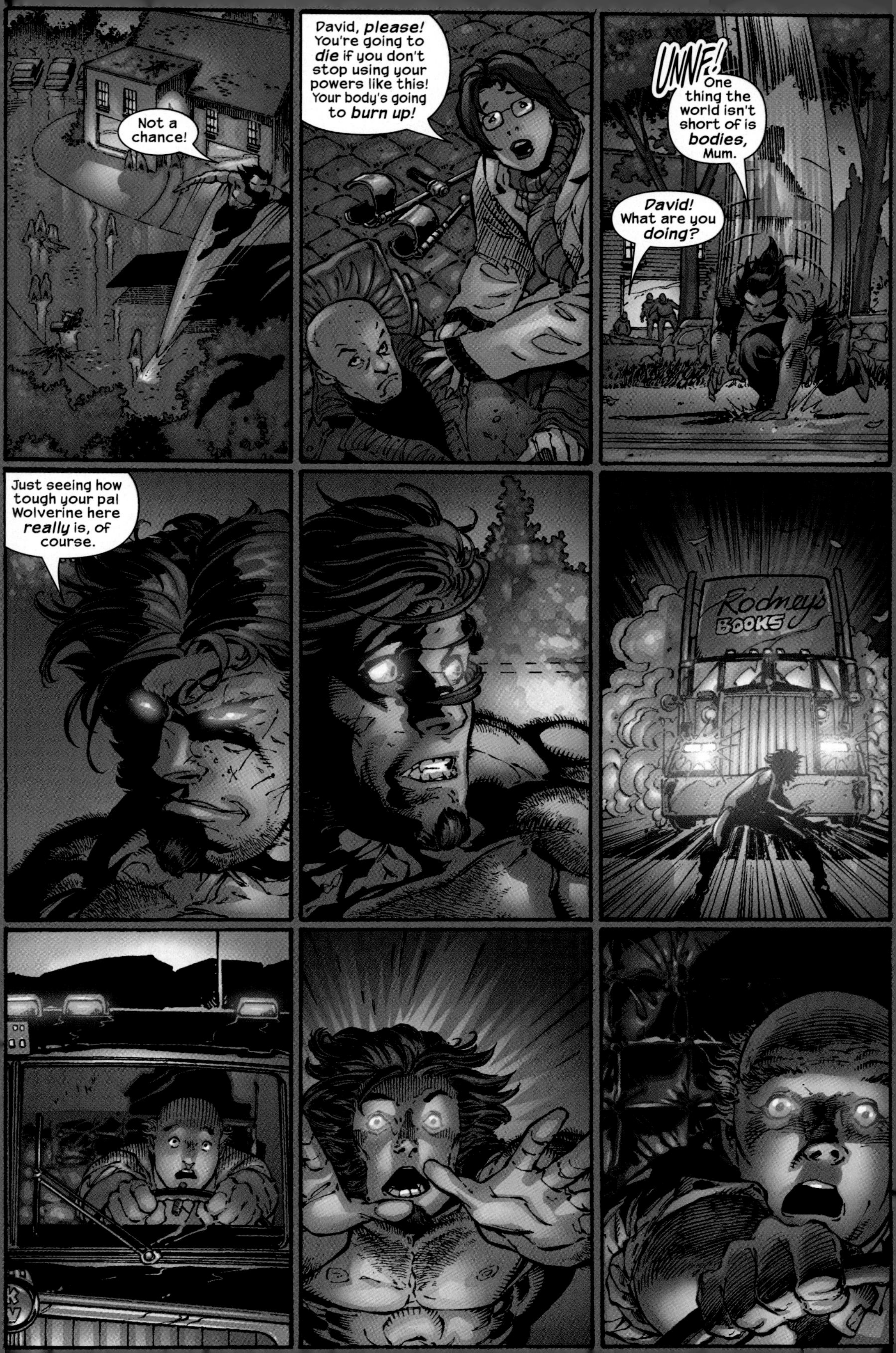
Not a chance!
David, please! You're going to die if you don't stop using your powers like this! Your body's going to burn up!
UNNF!
One thing the world isn't short of is bodies, Mum.
David! What are you doing?
Just seeing how tough your pal Wolverine here really is, of course.
Rodney's BOOKS

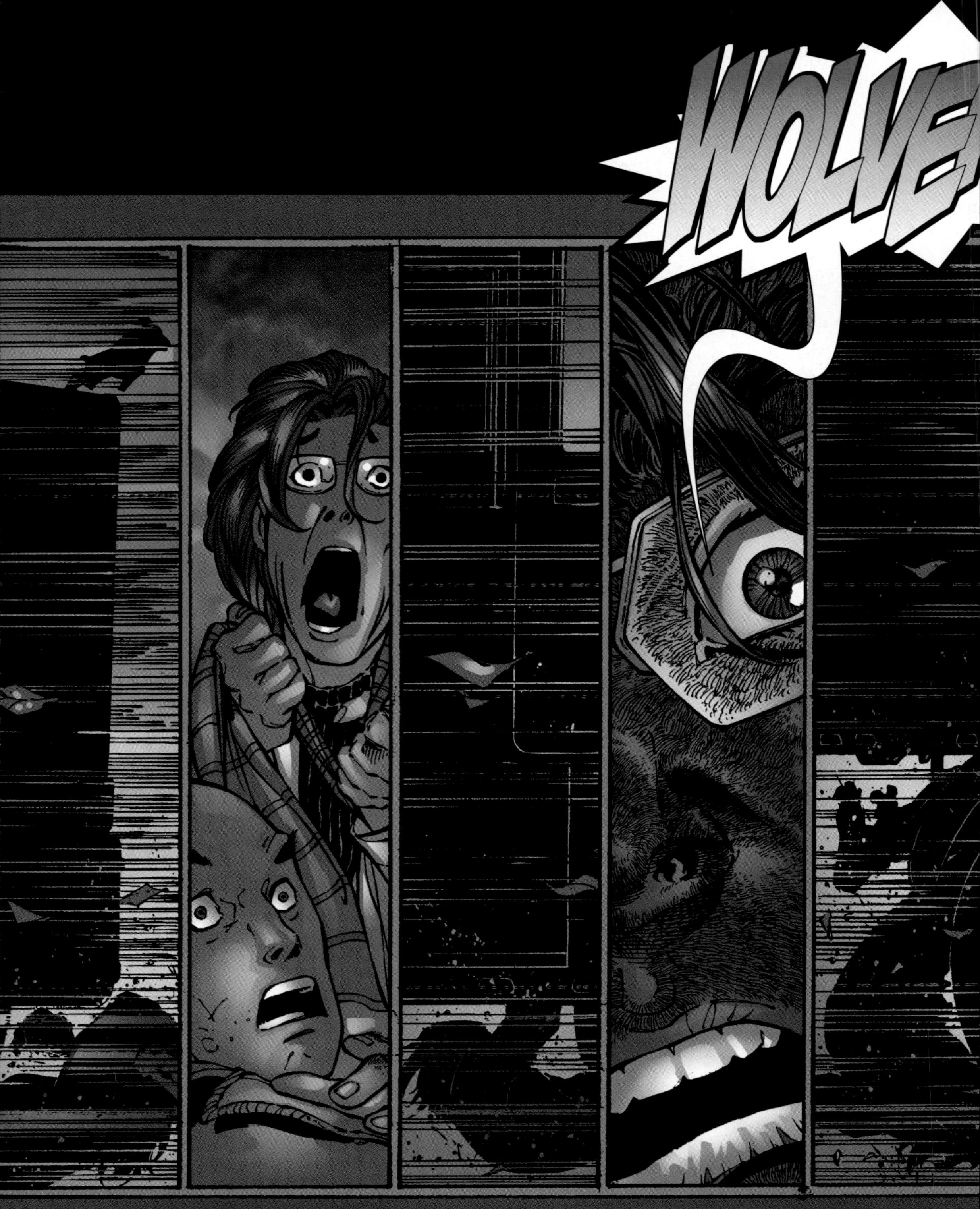
WOLVE

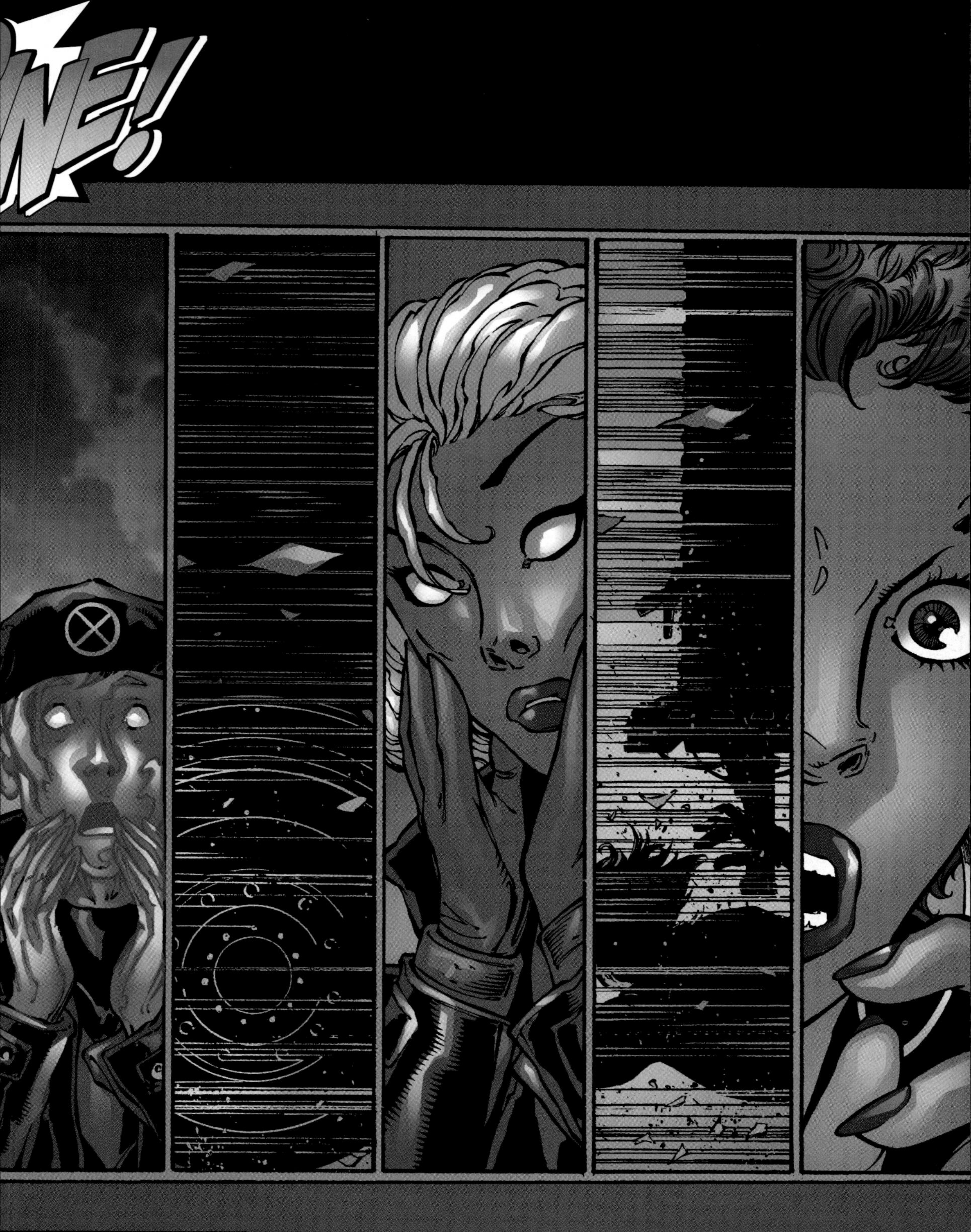

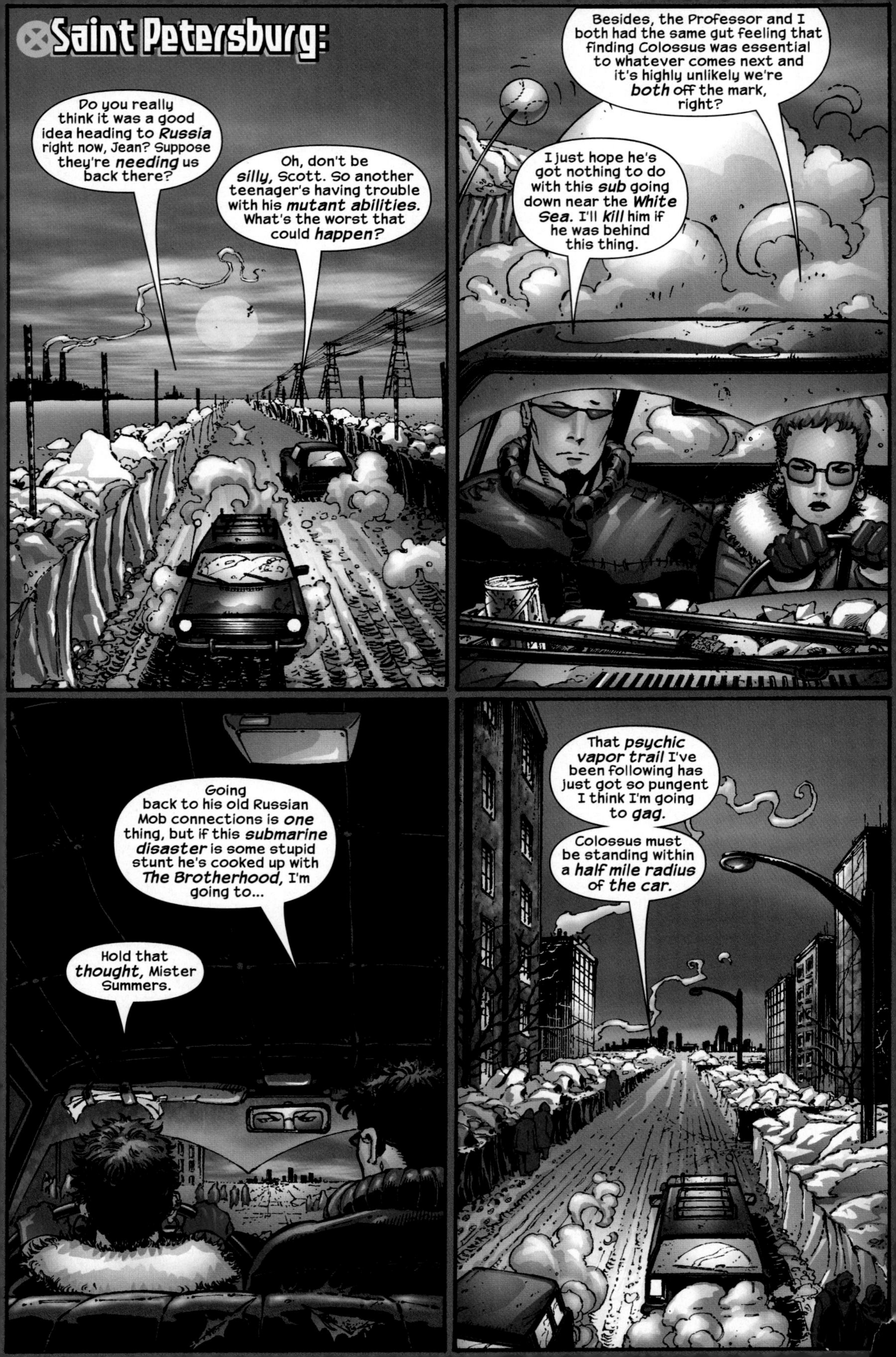

Saint Petersburg:
Do you really think it was a good idea heading to Russia right now, Jean? Suppose they're needing us back there?
Oh, don't be silly, Scott. So another teenager's having trouble with his mutant abilities. What's the worst that could happen?
Besides, the Professor and I both had the same gut feeling that finding Colossus was essential to whatever comes next and it's highly unlikely we're both off the mark, right?
I just hope he's got nothing to do with this sub going down near the White Sea. I'll kill him if he was behind this thing.
Going back to his old Russian Mob connections is one thing, but if this submarine disaster is some stupid stunt he's cooked up with The Brotherhood, I'm going to...
Hold that thought, Mister Summers.
That psychic vapor trail I've been following has just got so pungent I think I'm going to gag.
Colossus must be standing within a half mile radius of the car.

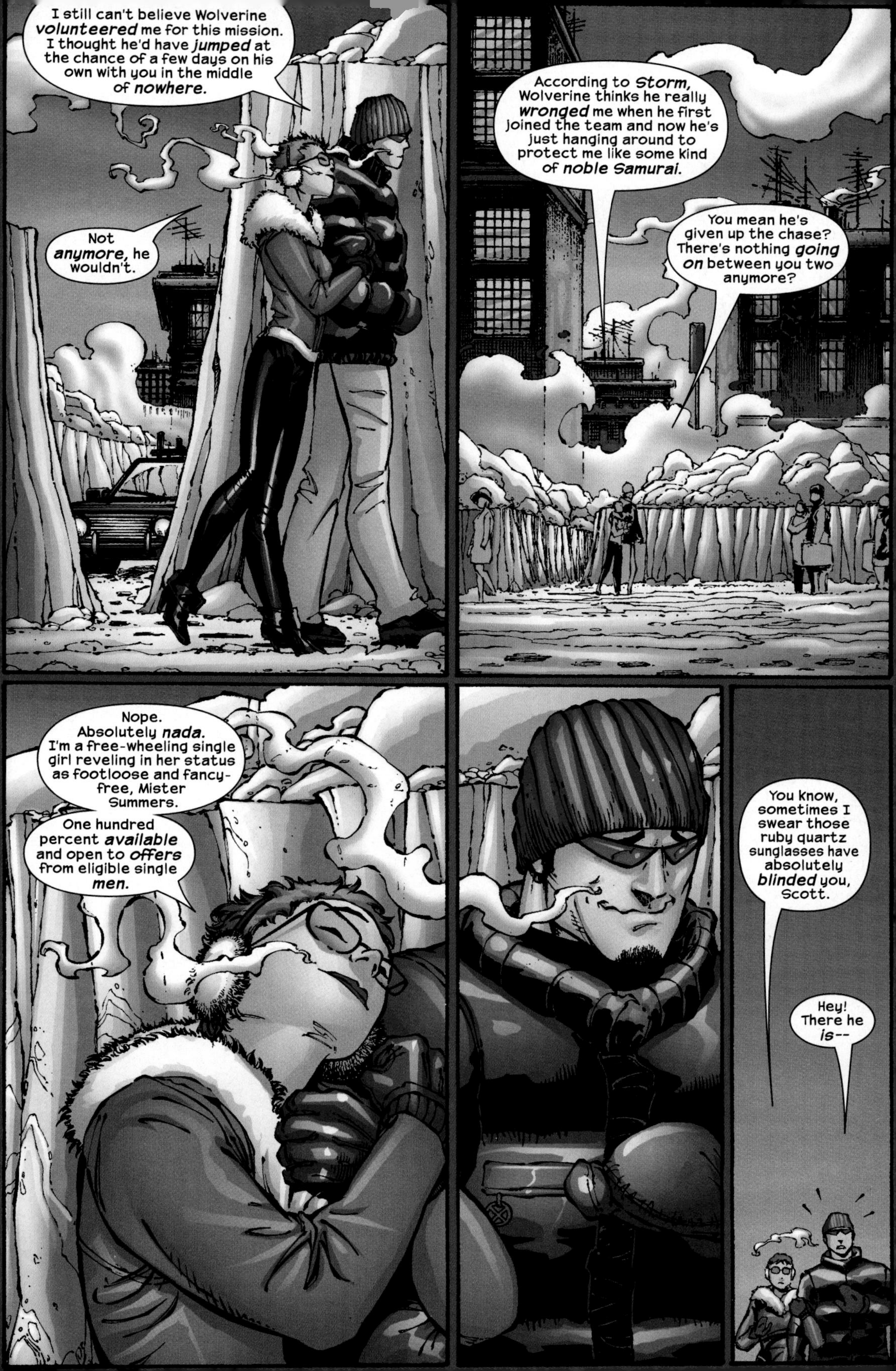
I still can't believe Wolverine volunteered me for this mission. I thought he'd have jumped at the chance of a few days on his own with you in the middle of nowhere.
Not anymore, he wouldn't.
According to Storm, Wolverine thinks he really wronged me when he first joined the team and now he's just hanging around to protect me like some kind of noble Samurai.
You mean he's given up the chase? There's nothing going on between you two anymore?
Nope. Absolutely nada. I'm a free-wheeling single girl reveling in her status as footloose and fancy-free, Mister Summers.
One hundred percent available and open to offers from eligible single men.
You know, sometimes I swear those ruby quartz sunglasses have absolutely blinded you, Scott.
Hey! There he is--

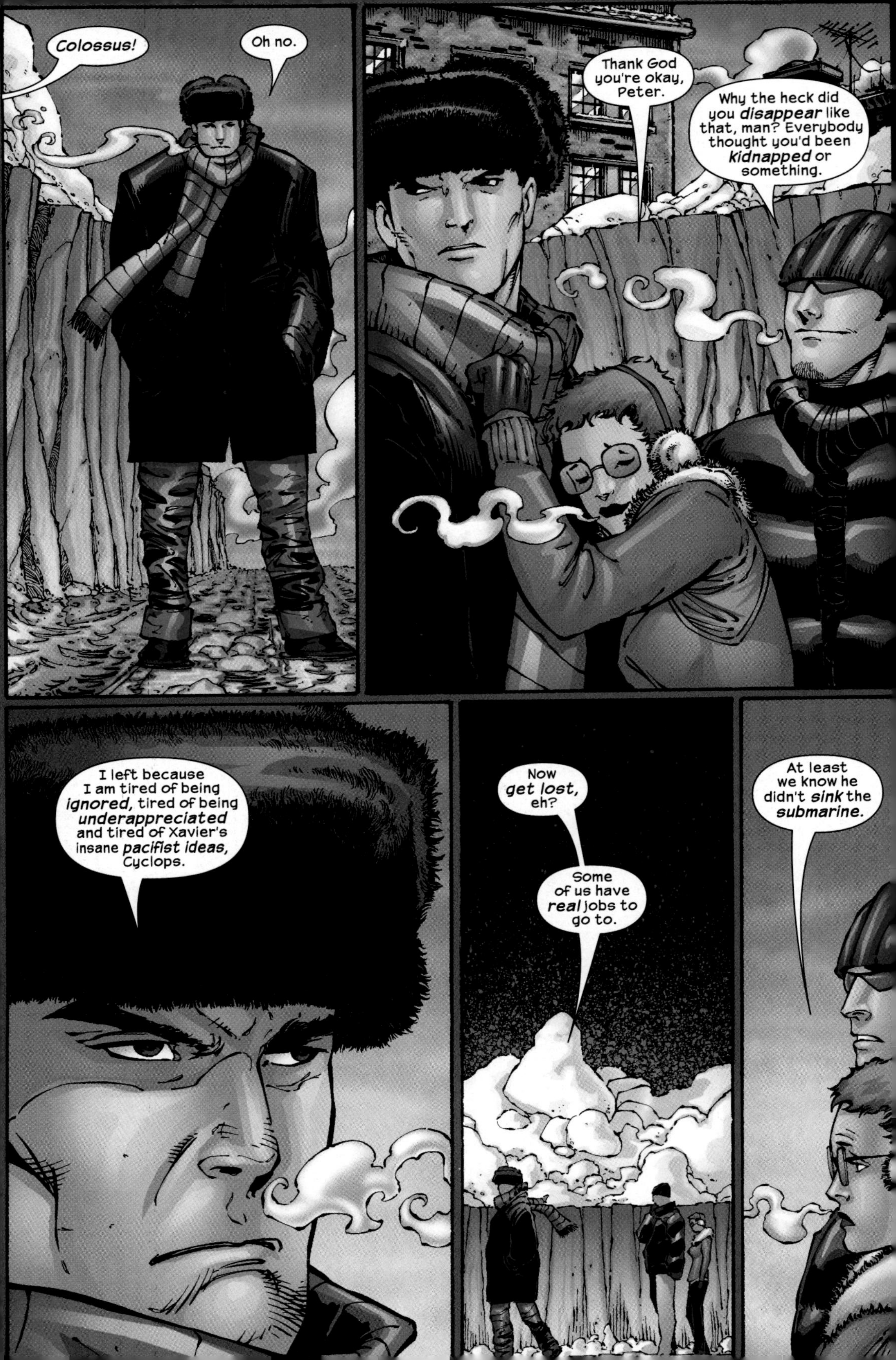
Colossus!
Oh no.
Thank God you're okay, Peter.
Why the heck did you disappear like that, man? Everybody thought you'd been kidnapped or something.
I left because I am tired of being ignored, tired of being underappreciated and tired of Xavier's insane pacifist ideas, Cyclops.
Now get lost, eh?
Some of us have real jobs to go to.
At least we know he didn't sink the submarine.

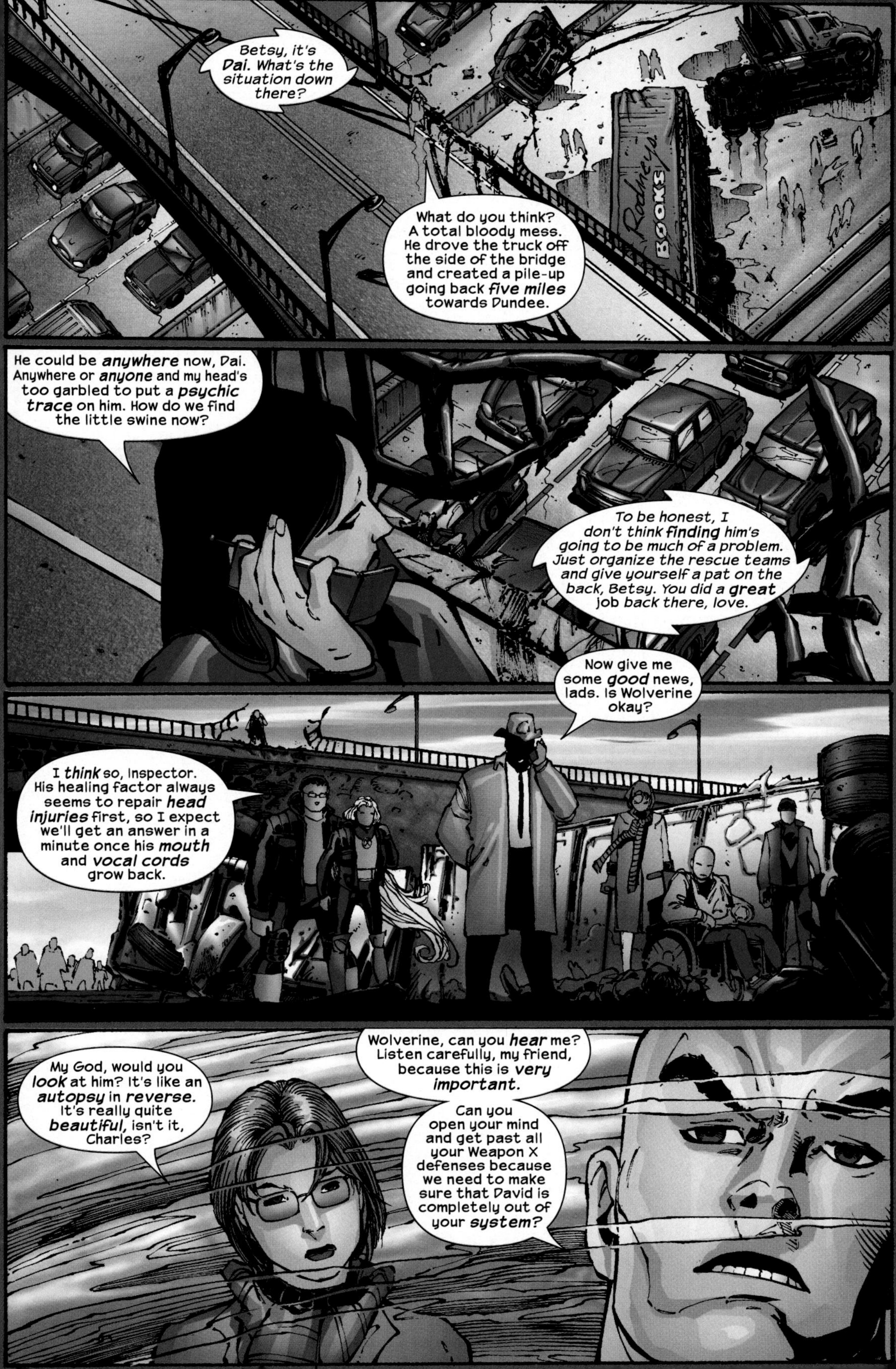
Betsy, it's Dai. What's the situation down there?
What do you think? A total bloody mess. He drove the truck off the side of the bridge and created a pile-up going back five miles towards Dundee.
Rodney's BOOKS
He could be anywhere now, Dai. Anywhere or anyone and my head's too garbled to put a psychic trace on him. How do we find the little swine now?
To be honest, I don't think finding him's going to be much of a problem. Just organize the rescue teams and give yourself a pat on the back, Betsy. You did a great job back there, love.
Now give me some good news, lads. Is Wolverine okay?
I think so, Inspector. His healing factor always seems to repair head injuries first, so I expect we'll get an answer in a minute once his mouth and vocal cords grow back.
My God, would you look at him? It's like an autopsy in reverse. It's really quite beautiful, isn't it, Charles?
Wolverine, can you hear me? Listen carefully, my friend, because this is very important.
Can you open your mind and get past all your Weapon X defenses because we need to make sure that David is completely out of your system?

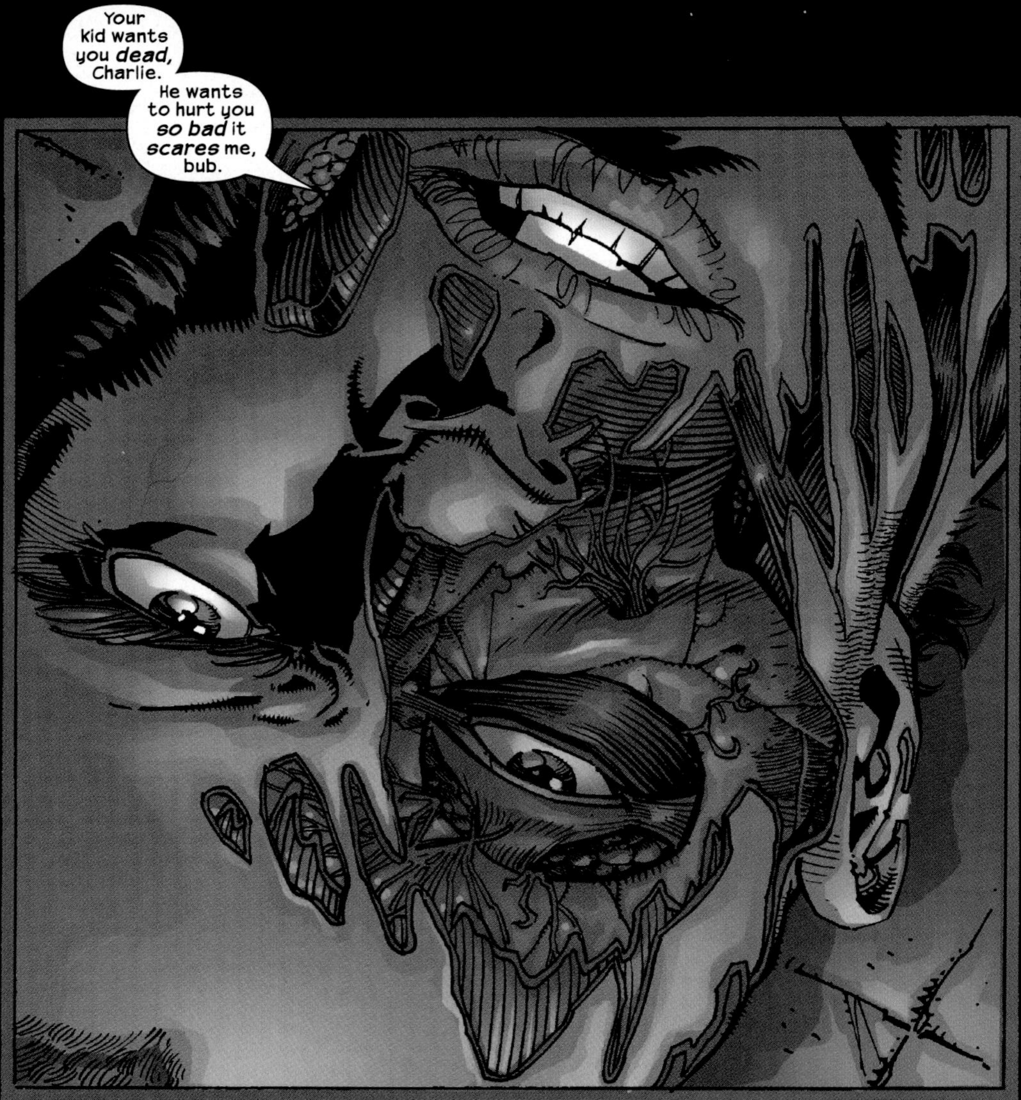
Your kid wants you *dead,* Charlie.
He wants to hurt you *so bad* it *scares* me, bub.

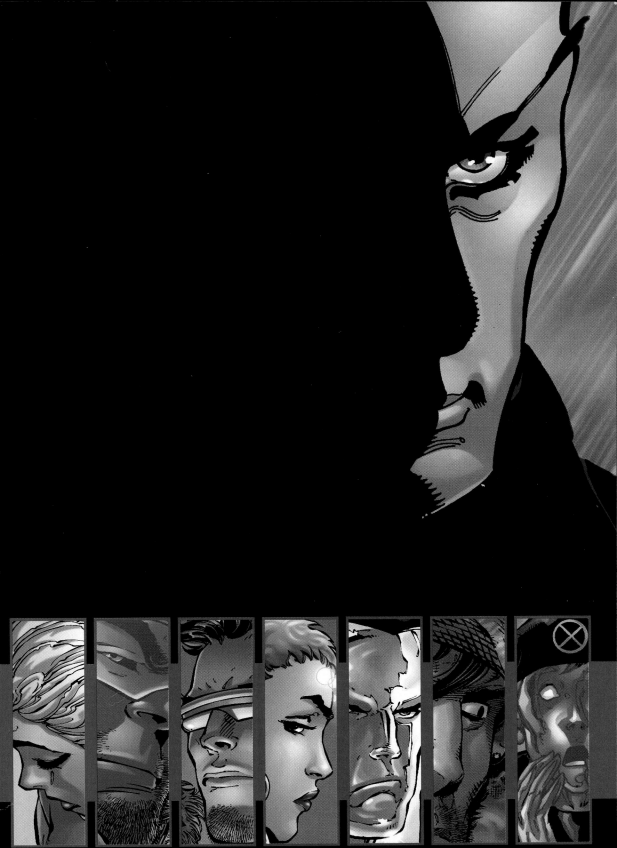

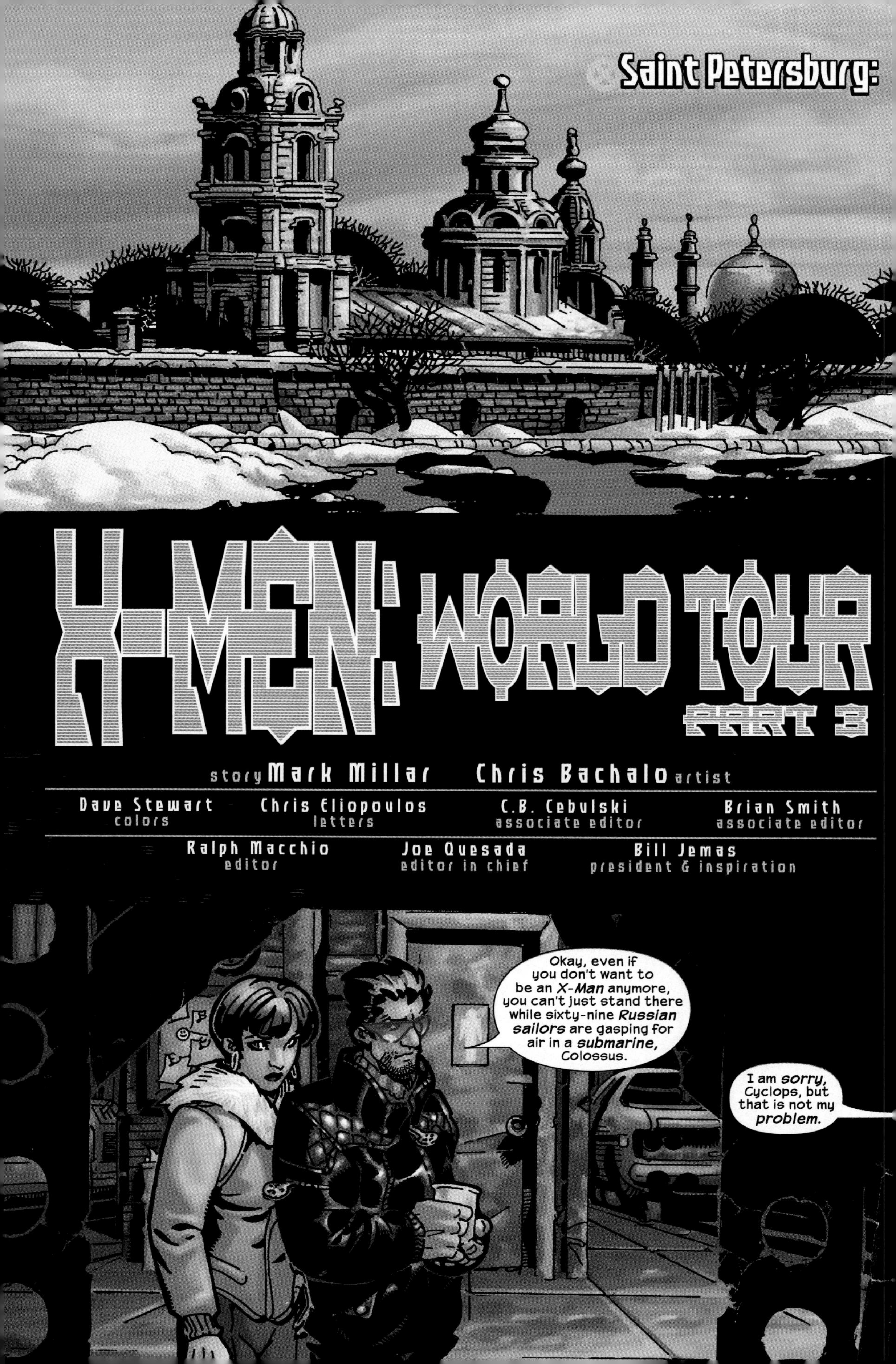
Saint Petersburg:
X-MEN: WORLD TOUR
PART 3
story Mark Millar
Chris Bachalo artist
Dave Stewart colors
Chris Eliopoulos letters
C.B. Cebulski associate editor
Brian Smith associate editor
Ralph Macchio editor
Joe Quesada editor in chief
Bill Jemas president & inspiration
Okay, even if you don't want to be an X-Man anymore, you can't just stand there while sixty-nine Russian sailors are gasping for air in a submarine, Colossus.
I am sorry, Cyclops, but that is not my problem.

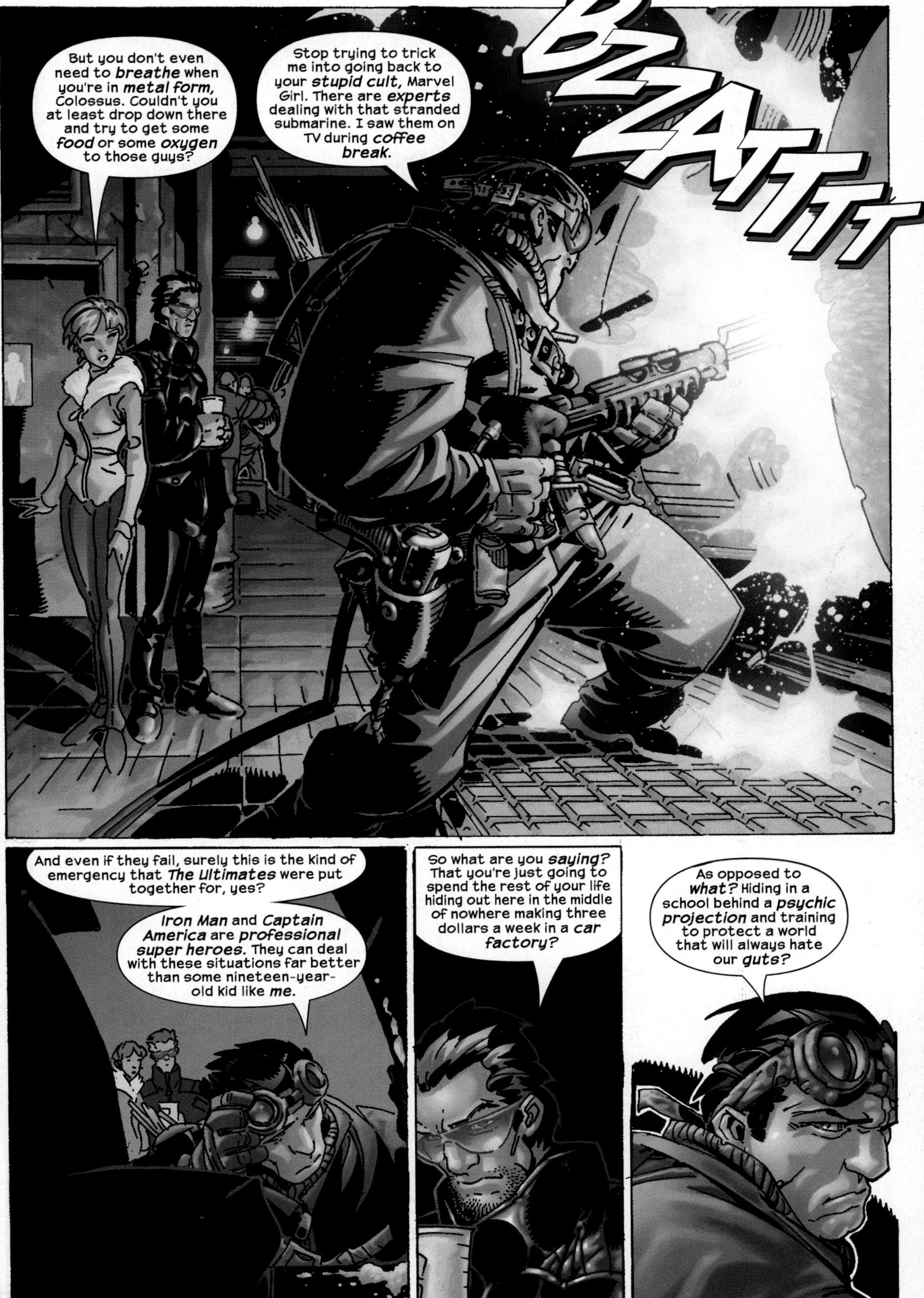

But you don't even need to breathe when you're in metal form, Colossus. Couldn't you at least drop down there and try to get some food or some oxygen to those guys?
Stop trying to trick me into going back to your stupid cult, Marvel Girl. There are experts dealing with that stranded submarine. I saw them on TV during coffee break.
BZZATTTT
And even if they fail, surely this is the kind of emergency that The Ultimates were put together for, yes?
Iron Man and Captain America are professional super heroes. They can deal with these situations far better than some nineteen-year-old kid like me.
So what are you saying? That you're just going to spend the rest of your life hiding out here in the middle of nowhere making three dollars a week in a car factory?
As opposed to what? Hiding in a school behind a psychic projection and training to protect a world that will always hate our guts?

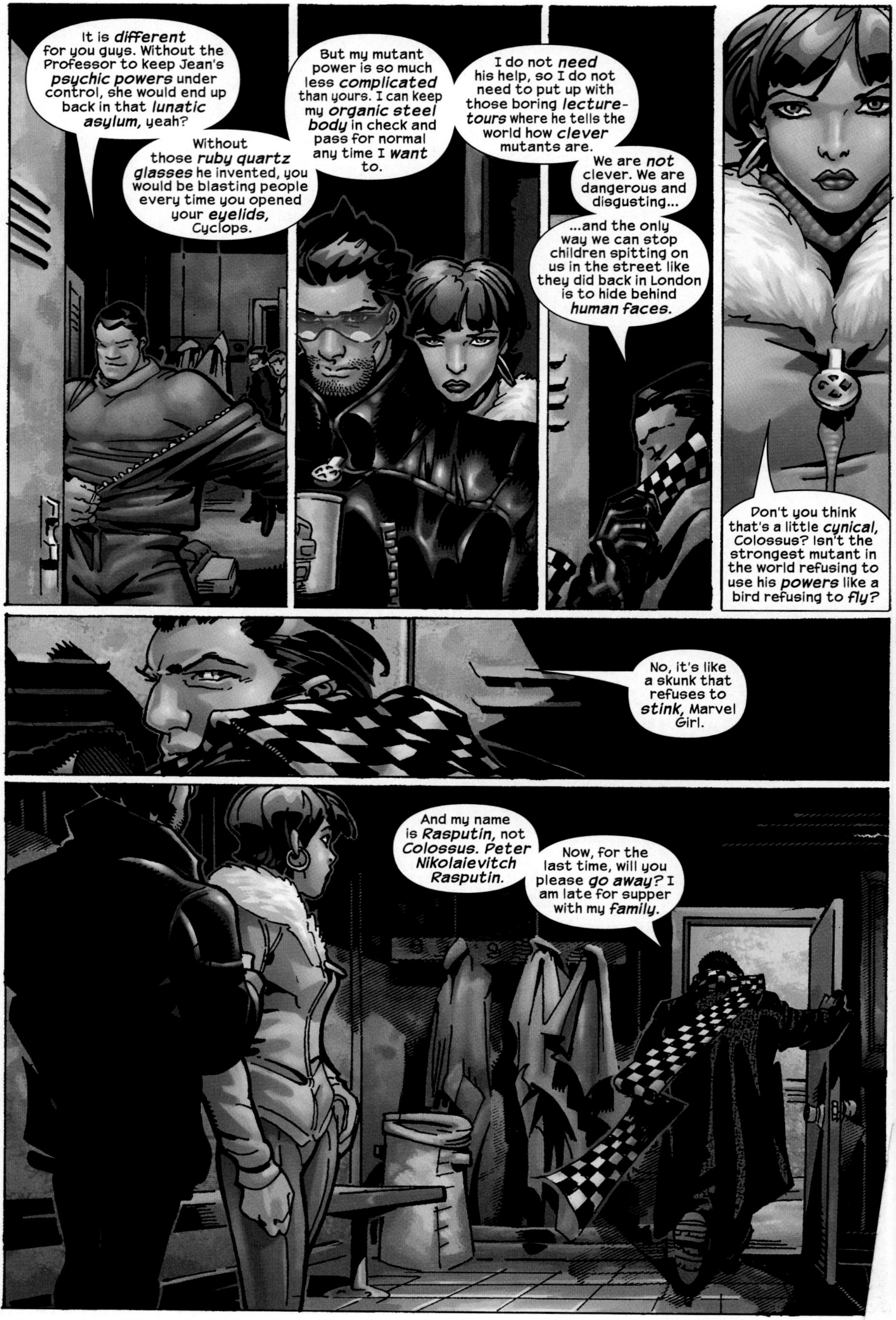
It is different for you guys. Without the Professor to keep Jean's psychic powers under control, she would end up back in that lunatic asylum, yeah?
Without those ruby quartz glasses he invented, you would be blasting people every time you opened your eyelids, Cyclops.
But my mutant power is so much less complicated than yours. I can keep my organic steel body in check and pass for normal any time I want to.
I do not need his help, so I do not need to put up with those boring lecture-tours where he tells the world how clever mutants are.
We are not clever. We are dangerous and disgusting...
...and the only way we can stop children spitting on us in the street like they did back in London is to hide behind human faces.
Don't you think that's a little cynical, Colossus? Isn't the strongest mutant in the world refusing to use his powers like a bird refusing to fly?
No, it's like a skunk that refuses to stink, Marvel Girl.
And my name is Rasputin, not Colossus. Peter Nikolaievitch Rasputin.
Now, for the last time, will you please go away? I am late for supper with my family.

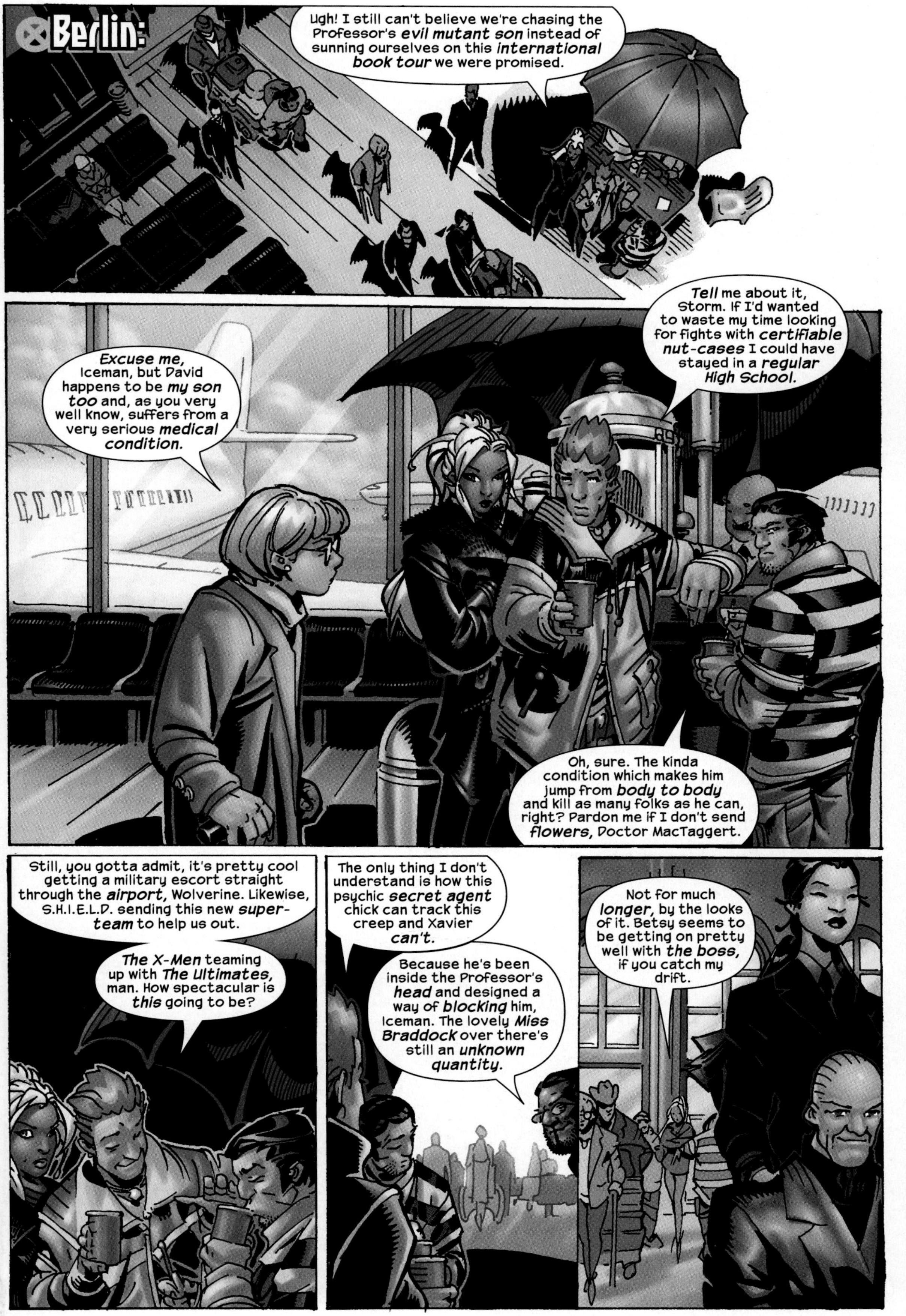
Berlin:
Ugh! I still can't believe we're chasing the Professor's evil mutant son instead of sunning ourselves on this international book tour we were promised.
Excuse me, Iceman, but David happens to be my son too and, as you very well know, suffers from a very serious medical condition.
Tell me about it, Storm. If I'd wanted to waste my time looking for fights with certifiable nut-cases I could have stayed in a regular High School.
Oh, sure. The kinda condition which makes him jump from body to body and kill as many folks as he can, right? Pardon me if I don't send flowers, Doctor MacTaggert.
Still, you gotta admit, it's pretty cool getting a military escort straight through the airport, Wolverine. Likewise, S.H.I.E.L.D. sending this new super-team to help us out.
The X-Men teaming up with The Ultimates, man. How spectacular is this going to be?
The only thing I don't understand is how this psychic secret agent chick can track this creep and Xavier can't.
Because he's been inside the Professor's head and designed a way of blocking him, Iceman. The lovely Miss Braddock over there's still an unknown quantity.
Not for much longer, by the looks of it. Betsy seems to be getting on pretty well with the boss, if you catch my drift.

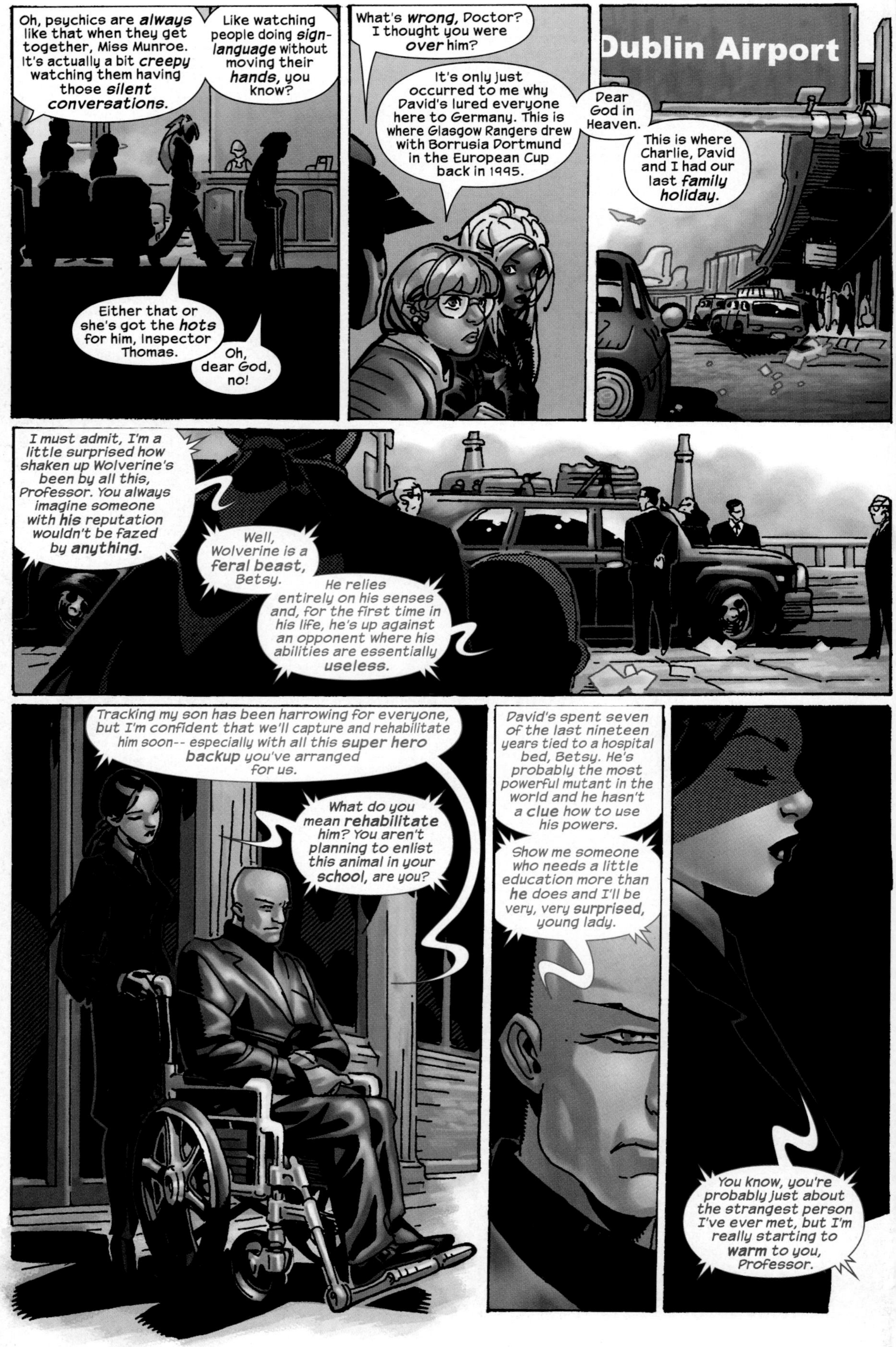
Oh, psychics are always like that when they get together, Miss Munroe. It's actually a bit creepy watching them having those silent conversations.
Like watching people doing sign-language without moving their hands, you know?
Either that or she's got the hots for him, Inspector Thomas.
Oh, dear God, no!
What's wrong, Doctor? I thought you were over him?
It's only just occurred to me why David's lured everyone here to Germany. This is where Glasgow Rangers drew with Borrusia Dortmund in the European Cup back in 1995.
Dublin Airport
Dear God in Heaven.
This is where Charlie, David and I had our last family holiday.
I must admit, I'm a little surprised how shaken up Wolverine's been by all this, Professor. You always imagine someone with his reputation wouldn't be fazed by anything.
Well, Wolverine is a feral beast, Betsy.
He relies entirely on his senses and, for the first time in his life, he's up against an opponent where his abilities are essentially useless.
Tracking my son has been harrowing for everyone, but I'm confident that we'll capture and rehabilitate him soon-- especially with all this super hero backup you've arranged for us.
What do you mean rehabilitate him? You aren't planning to enlist this animal in your school, are you?
David's spent seven of the last nineteen years tied to a hospital bed, Betsy. He's probably the most powerful mutant in the world and he hasn't a clue how to use his powers.
Show me someone who needs a little education more than he does and I'll be very, very surprised, young lady.
You know, you're probably just about the strangest person I've ever met, but I'm really starting to warm to you, Professor.

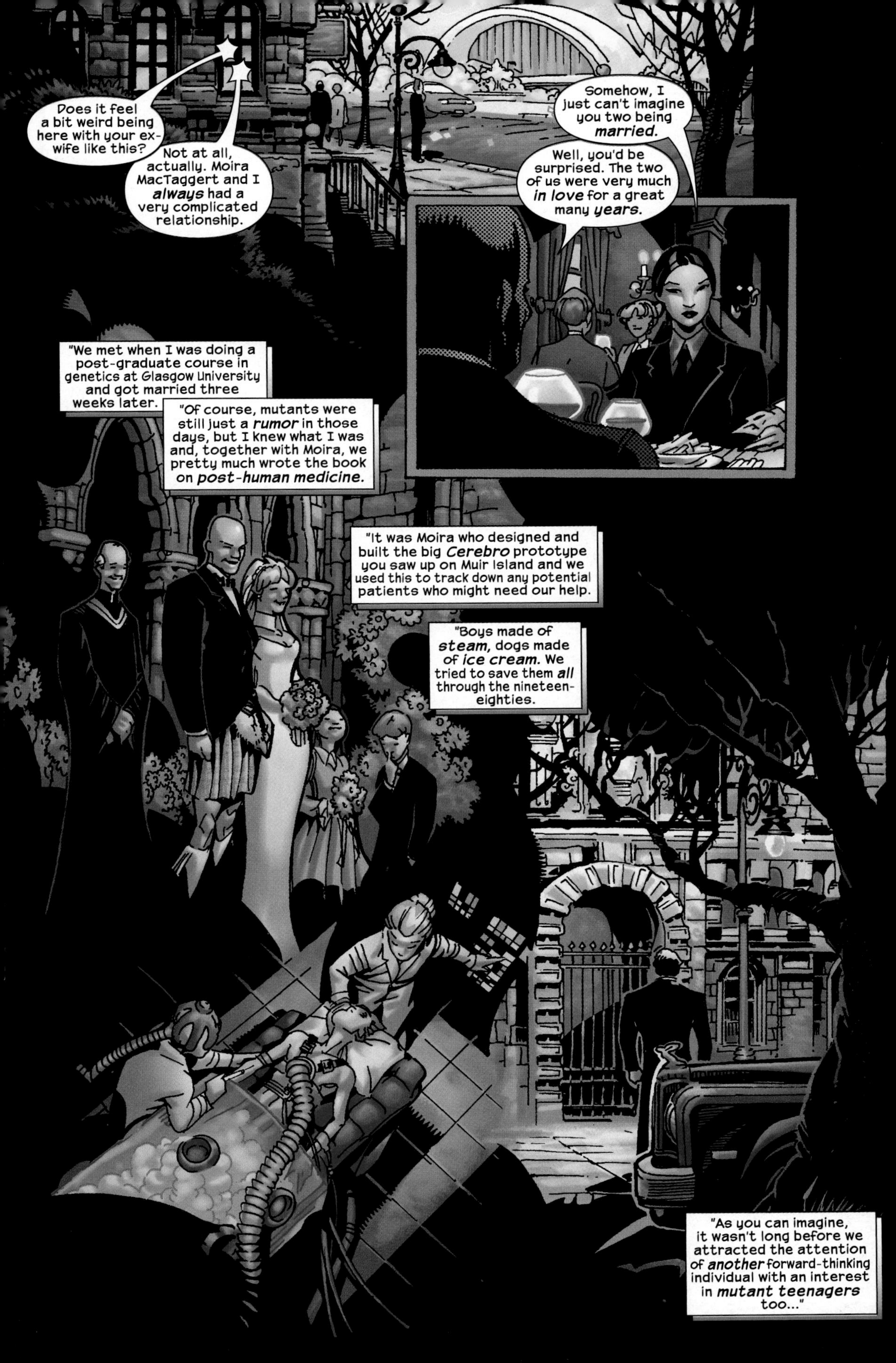
Does it feel a bit weird being here with your ex-wife like this?
Not at all, actually. Moira MacTaggert and I *always* had a very complicated relationship.
Somehow, I just can't imagine you two being *married*.
Well, you'd be surprised. The two of us were very much *in love* for a great many *years*.
"We met when I was doing a post-graduate course in genetics at Glasgow University and got married three weeks later.
"Of course, mutants were still just a *rumor* in those days, but I knew what I was and, together with Moira, we pretty much wrote the book on *post-human medicine.*
"It was Moira who designed and built the big *Cerebro* prototype you saw up on Muir Island and we used this to track down any potential patients who might need our help.
"Boys made of *steam*, dogs made of *ice cream.* We tried to save them *all* through the nineteen-eighties.
"As you can imagine, it wasn't long before we attracted the attention of *another* forward-thinking individual with an interest in *mutant teenagers* too..."

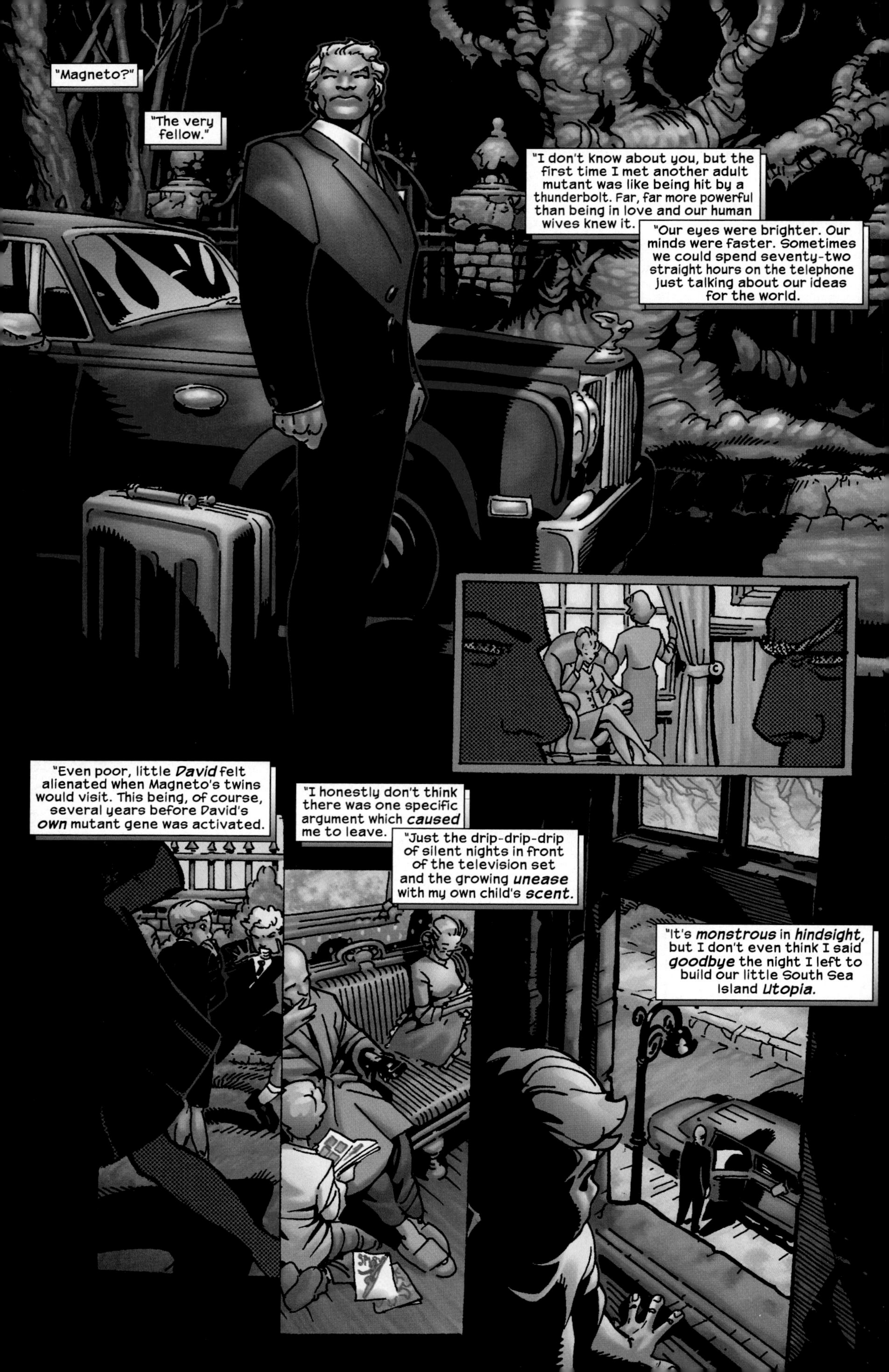
"Magneto?"
"The very fellow."
"I don't know about you, but the first time I met another adult mutant was like being hit by a thunderbolt. Far, far more powerful than being in love and our human wives knew it.
"Our eyes were brighter. Our minds were faster. Sometimes we could spend seventy-two straight hours on the telephone just talking about our ideas for the world.
"Even poor, little David felt alienated when Magneto's twins would visit. This being, of course, several years before David's own mutant gene was activated.
"I honestly don't think there was one specific argument which caused me to leave.
"Just the drip-drip-drip of silent nights in front of the television set and the growing unease with my own child's scent.
"It's monstrous in hindsight, but I don't even think I said goodbye the night I left to build our little South Sea Island Utopia.

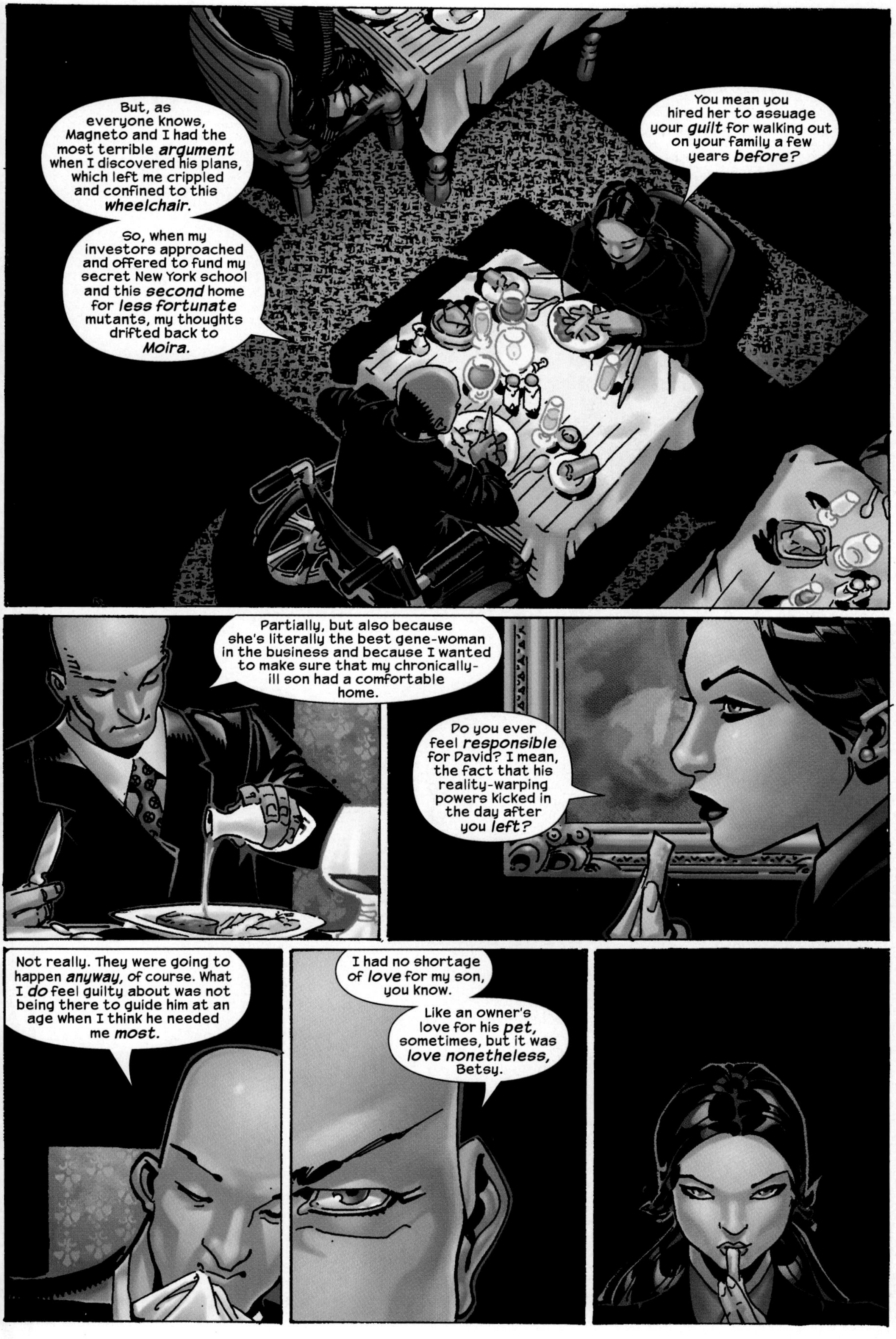

But, as everyone knows, Magneto and I had the most terrible *argument* when I discovered his plans, which left me crippled and confined to this *wheelchair*.
So, when my investors approached and offered to fund my secret New York school and this *second* home for *less fortunate* mutants, my thoughts drifted back to *Moira*.
You mean you hired her to assuage your *guilt* for walking out on your family a few years *before?*
Partially, but also because she's literally the best gene-woman in the business and because I wanted to make sure that my chronically-ill son had a comfortable home.
Do you ever feel *responsible* for David? I mean, the fact that his reality-warping powers kicked in the day after you *left?*
Not really. They were going to happen *anyway*, of course. What I *do* feel guilty about was not being there to guide him at an age when I think he needed me *most*.
I had no shortage of *love* for my son, you know.
Like an owner's love for his *pet*, sometimes, but it was *love nonetheless*, Betsy.

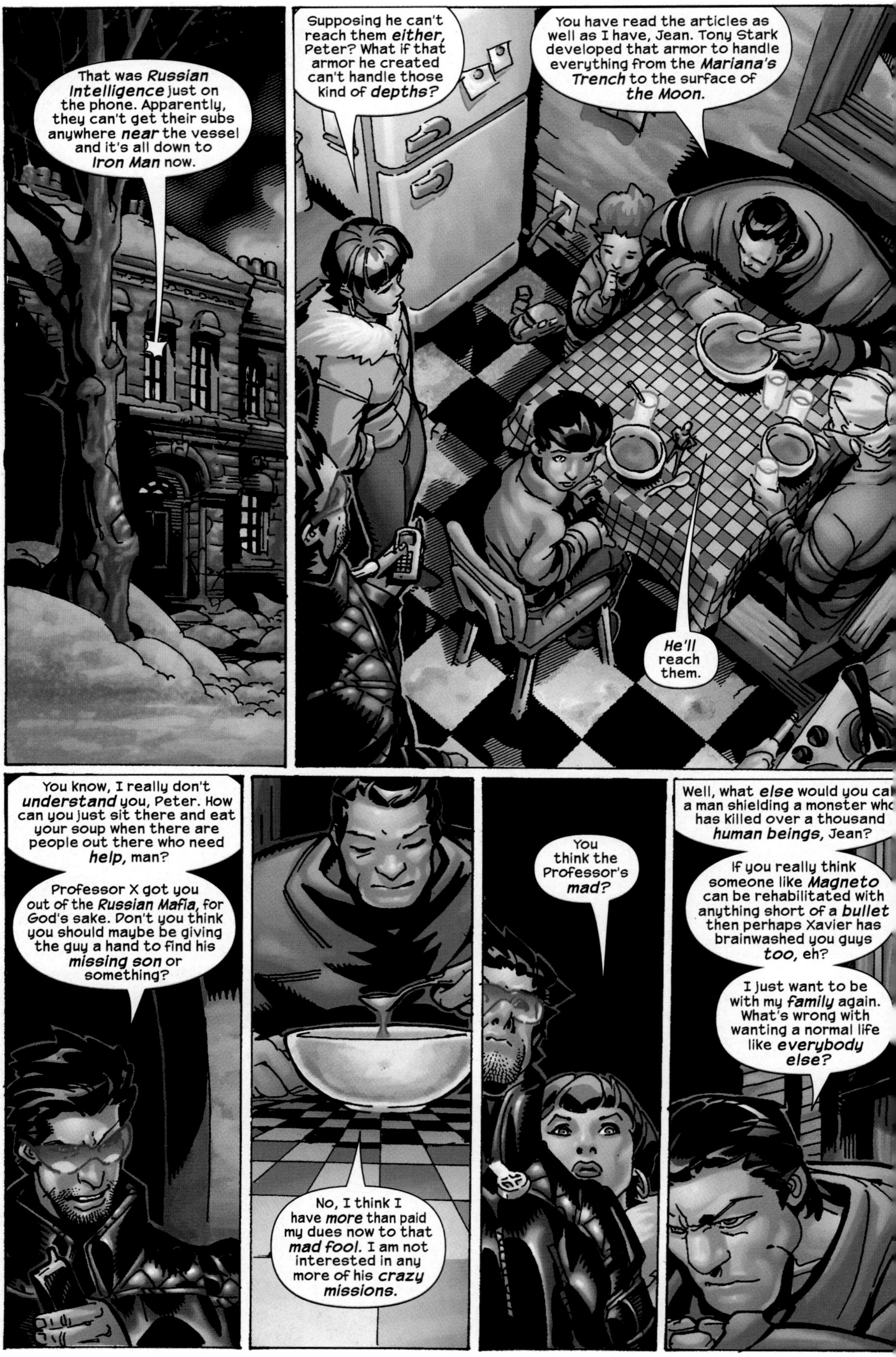
That was Russian Intelligence just on the phone. Apparently, they can't get their subs anywhere near the vessel and it's all down to Iron Man now.
Supposing he can't reach them either, Peter? What if that armor he created can't handle those kind of depths?
You have read the articles as well as I have, Jean. Tony Stark developed that armor to handle everything from the Mariana's Trench to the surface of the Moon.
He'll reach them.
You know, I really don't understand you, Peter. How can you just sit there and eat your soup when there are people out there who need help, man?
Professor X got you out of the Russian Mafia, for God's sake. Don't you think you should maybe be giving the guy a hand to find his missing son or something?
No, I think I have more than paid my dues now to that mad fool. I am not interested in any more of his crazy missions.
You think the Professor's mad?
Well, what else would you ca a man shielding a monster wh has killed over a thousand human beings, Jean?
If you really think someone like Magneto can be rehabilitated with anything short of a bullet then perhaps Xavier has brainwashed you guys too, eh?
I just want to be with my family again. What's wrong with wanting a normal life like everybody else?

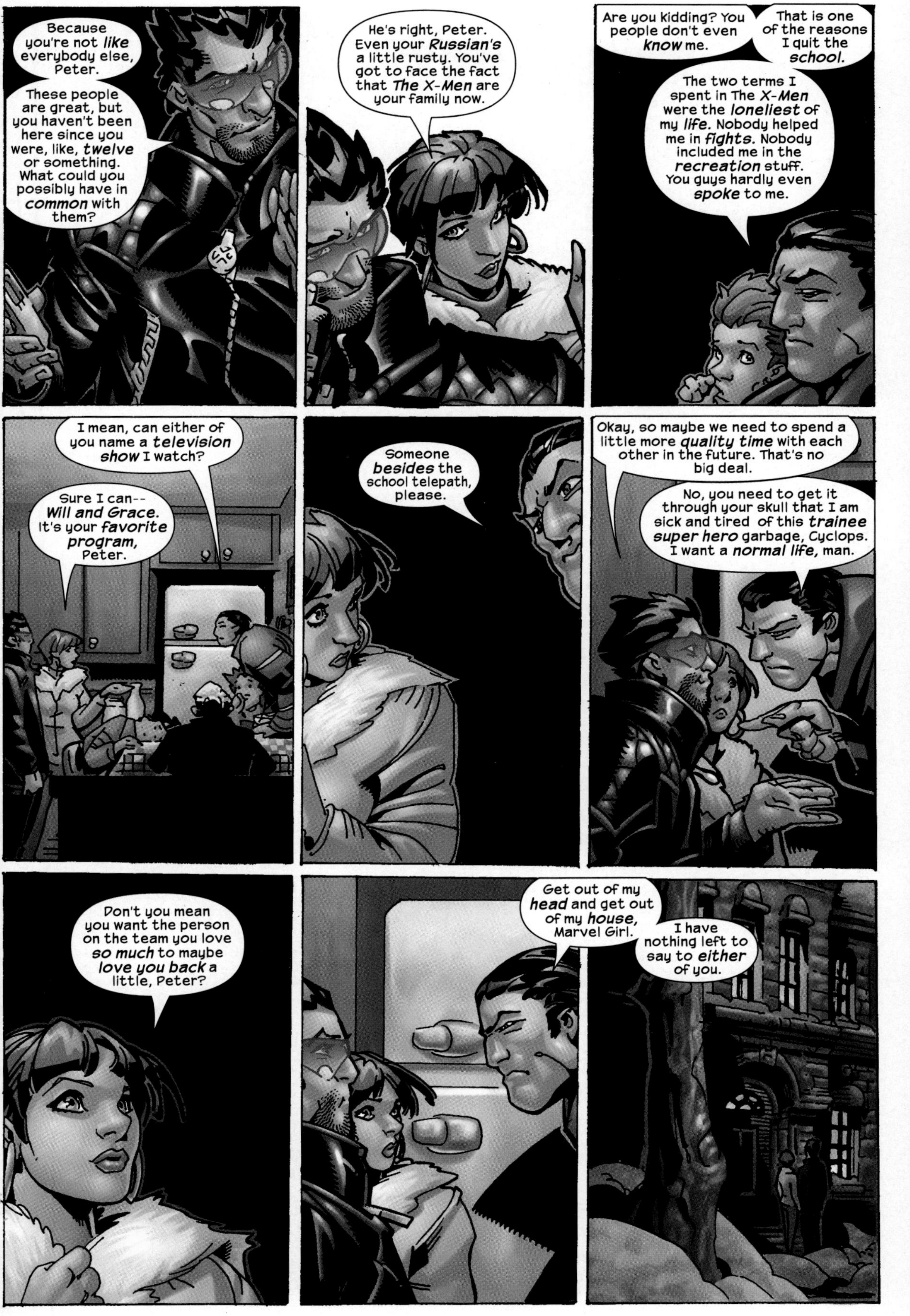
Because you're not like everybody else, Peter.
These people are great, but you haven't been here since you were, like, twelve or something. What could you possibly have in common with them?
He's right, Peter. Even your Russian's a little rusty. You've got to face the fact that The X-Men are your family now.
Are you kidding? You people don't even know me.
That is one of the reasons I quit the school.
The two terms I spent in The X-Men were the loneliest of my life. Nobody helped me in fights. Nobody included me in the recreation stuff. You guys hardly even spoke to me.
I mean, can either of you name a television show I watch?
Sure I can-- Will and Grace. It's your favorite program, Peter.
Someone besides the school telepath, please.
Okay, so maybe we need to spend a little more quality time with each other in the future. That's no big deal.
No, you need to get it through your skull that I am sick and tired of this trainee super hero garbage, Cyclops. I want a normal life, man.
Don't you mean you want the person on the team you love so much to maybe love you back a little, Peter?
Get out of my head and get out of my house, Marvel Girl.
I have nothing left to say to either of you.

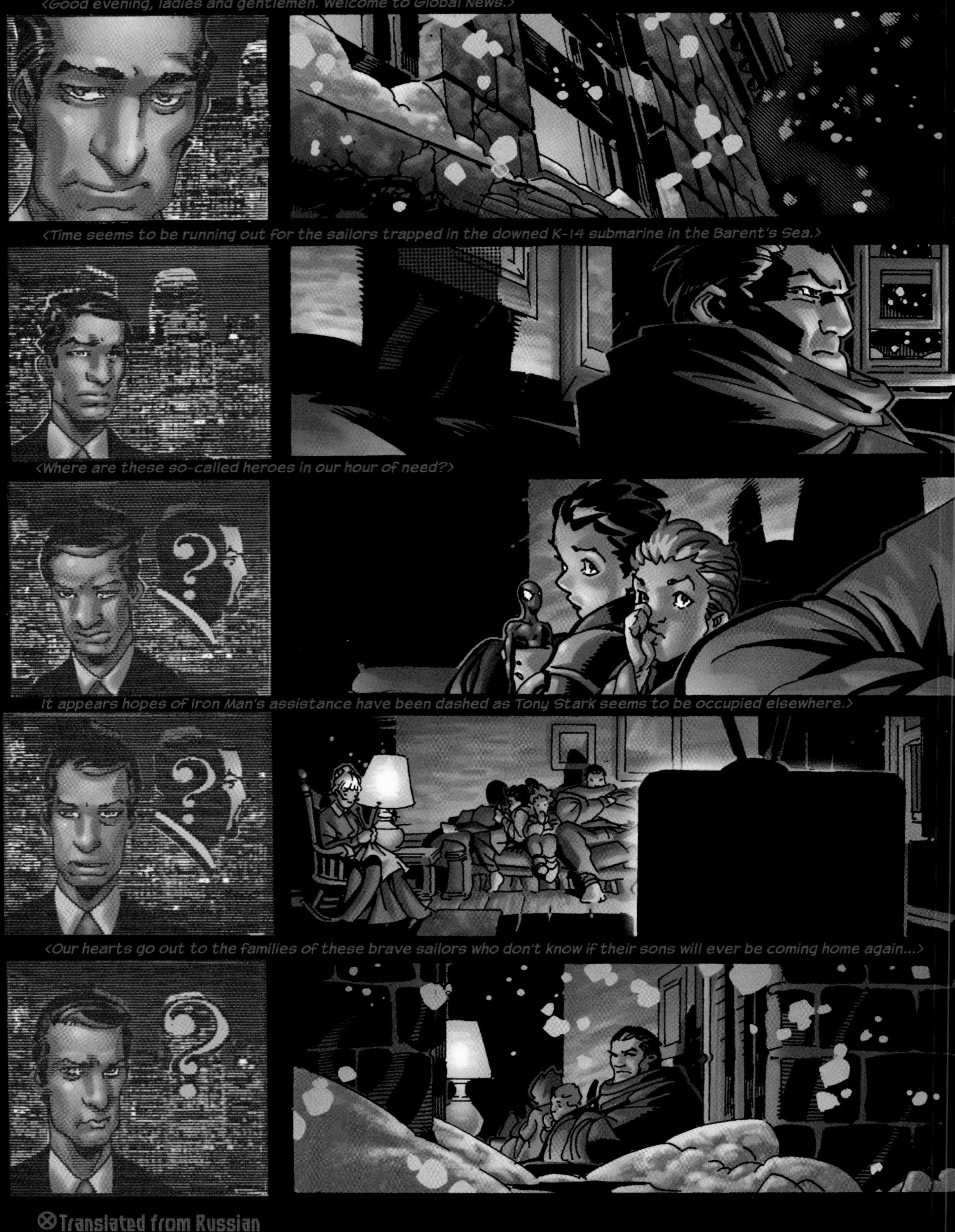
<Good evening, ladies and gentlemen. Welcome to Global News.>
<Time seems to be running out for the sailors trapped in the downed K-14 submarine in the Barent's Sea.>
<Where are these so-called heroes in our hour of need?>
It appears hopes of Iron Man's assistance have been dashed as Tony Stark seems to be occupied elsewhere.>
<Our hearts go out to the families of these brave sailors who don't know if their sons will ever be coming home again...>
Translated from Russian

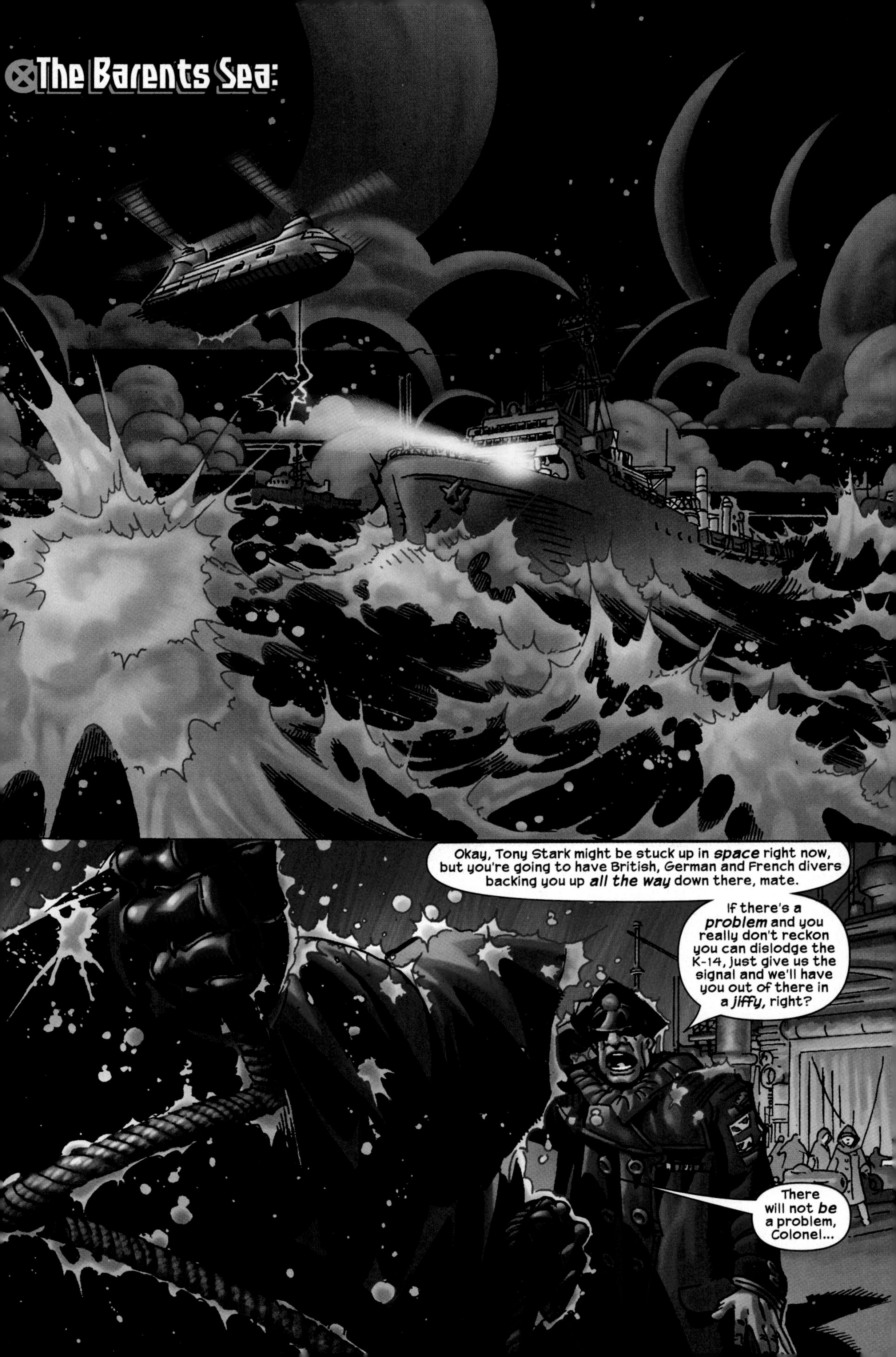
The Barents Sea:
Okay, Tony Stark might be stuck up in *space* right now, but you're going to have British, German and French divers backing you up *all the way* down there, mate.
If there's a *problem* and you really don't reckon you can dislodge the K-14, just give us the signal and we'll have you out of there in a *jiffy*, right?
There will not *be* a problem, Colonel...

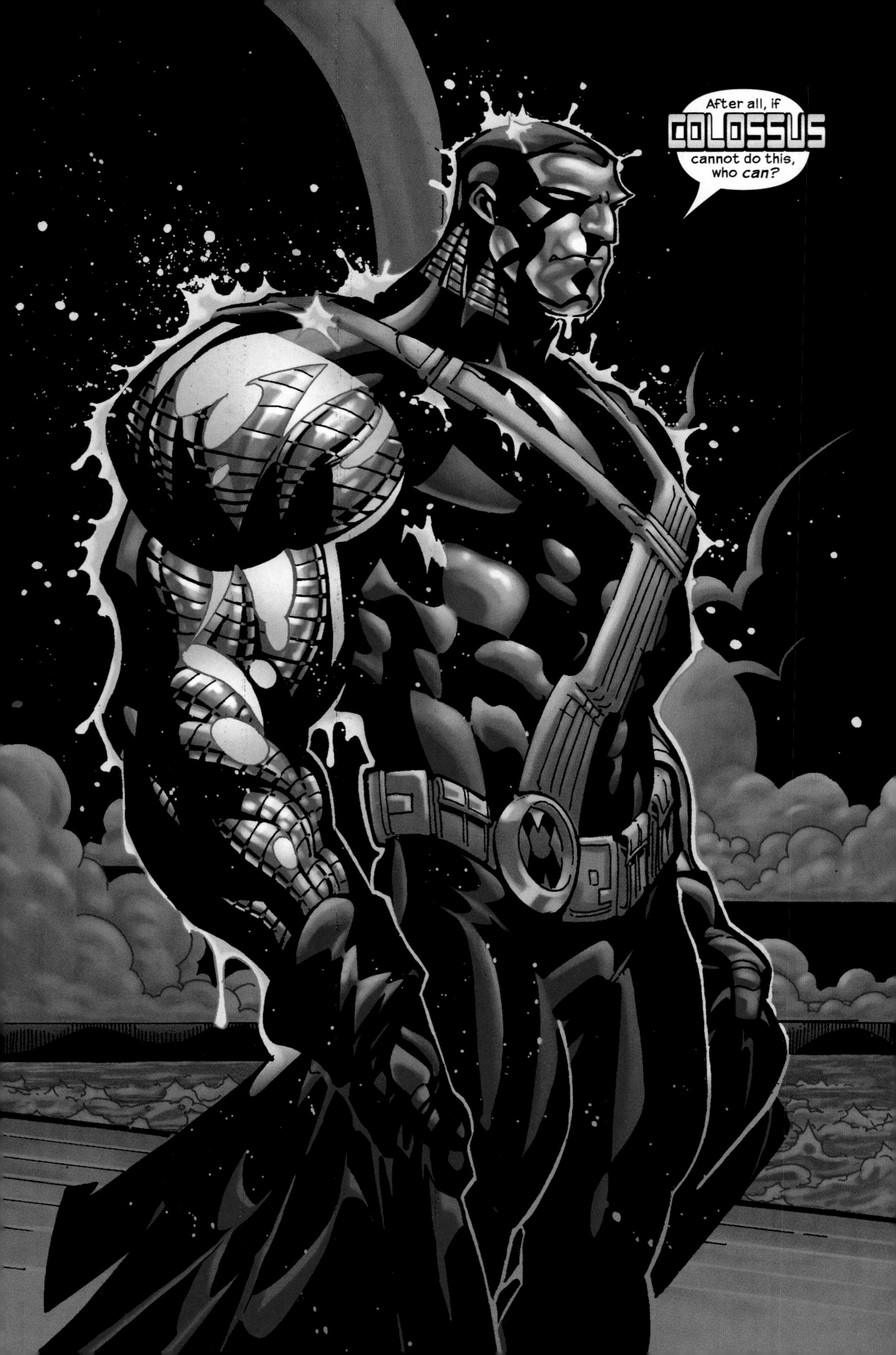
After all, if COLOSSUS cannot do this, who *can*?

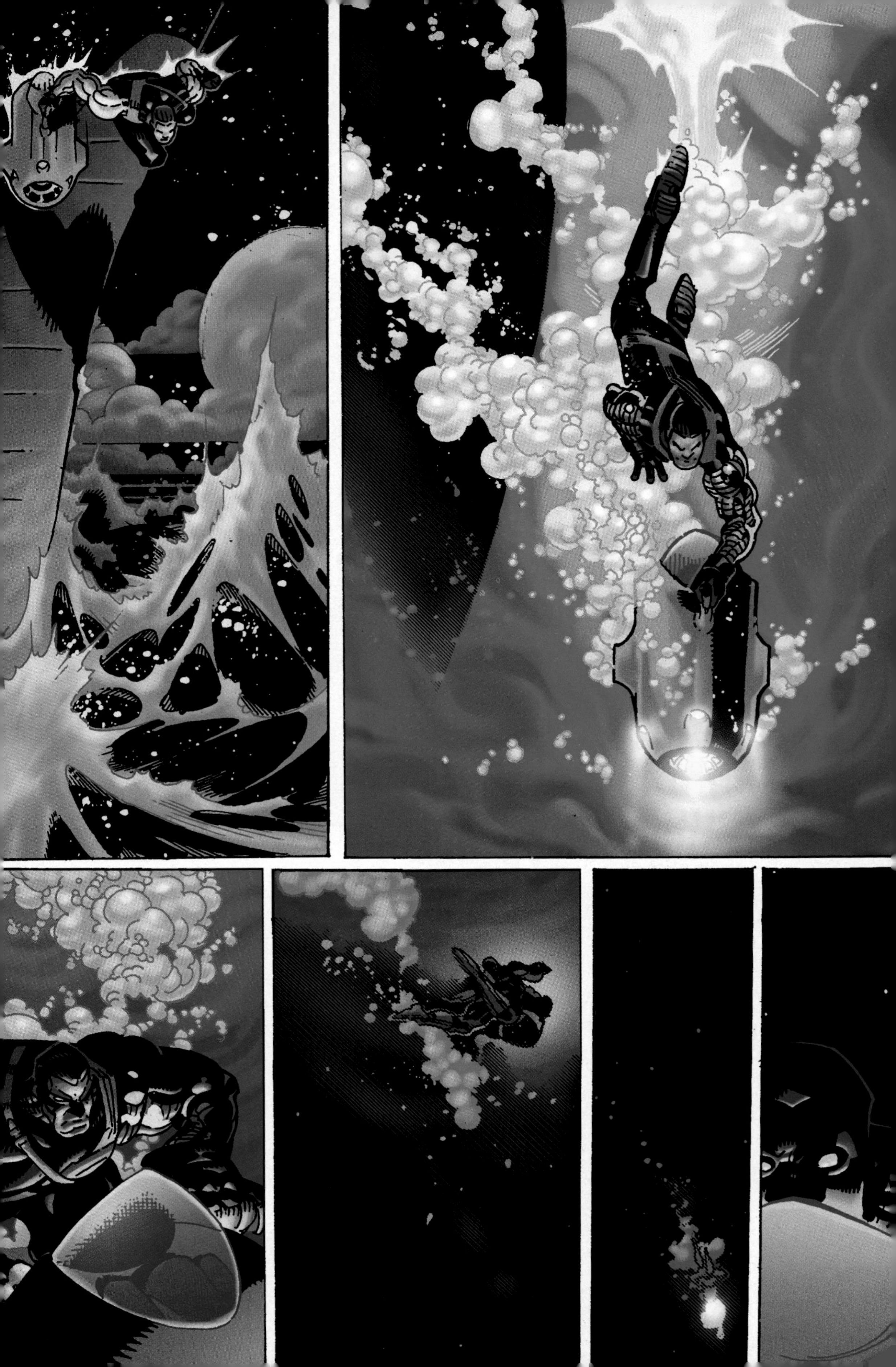

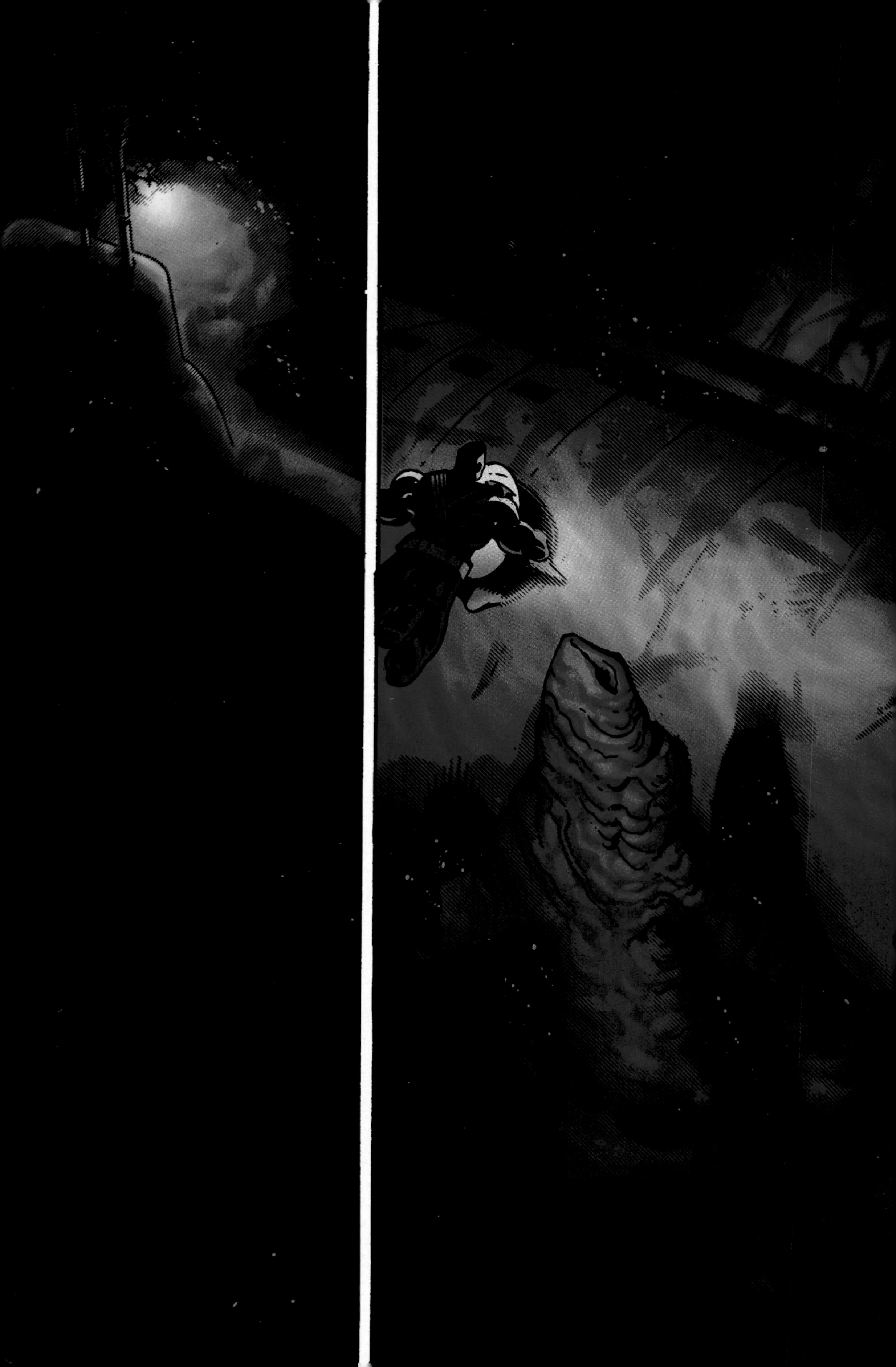

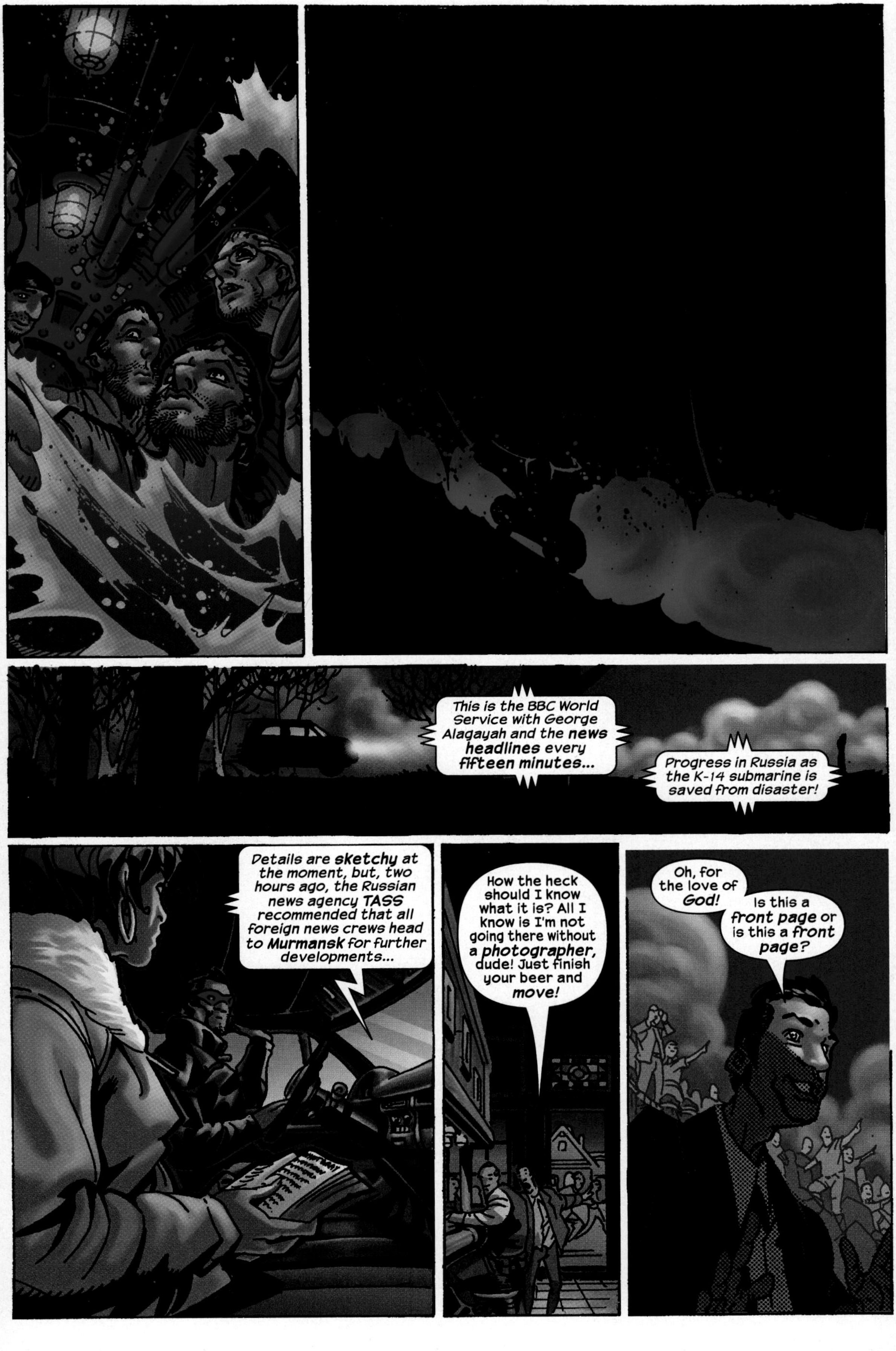
This is the BBC World Service with George Alagayah and the news headlines every fifteen minutes...
Progress in Russia as the K-14 submarine is saved from disaster!
Details are sketchy at the moment, but, two hours ago, the Russian news agency TASS recommended that all foreign news crews head to Murmansk for further developments...
How the heck should I know what it is? All I know is I'm not going there without a photographer, dude! Just finish your beer and move!
Oh, for the love of God!
Is this a front page or is this a front page?

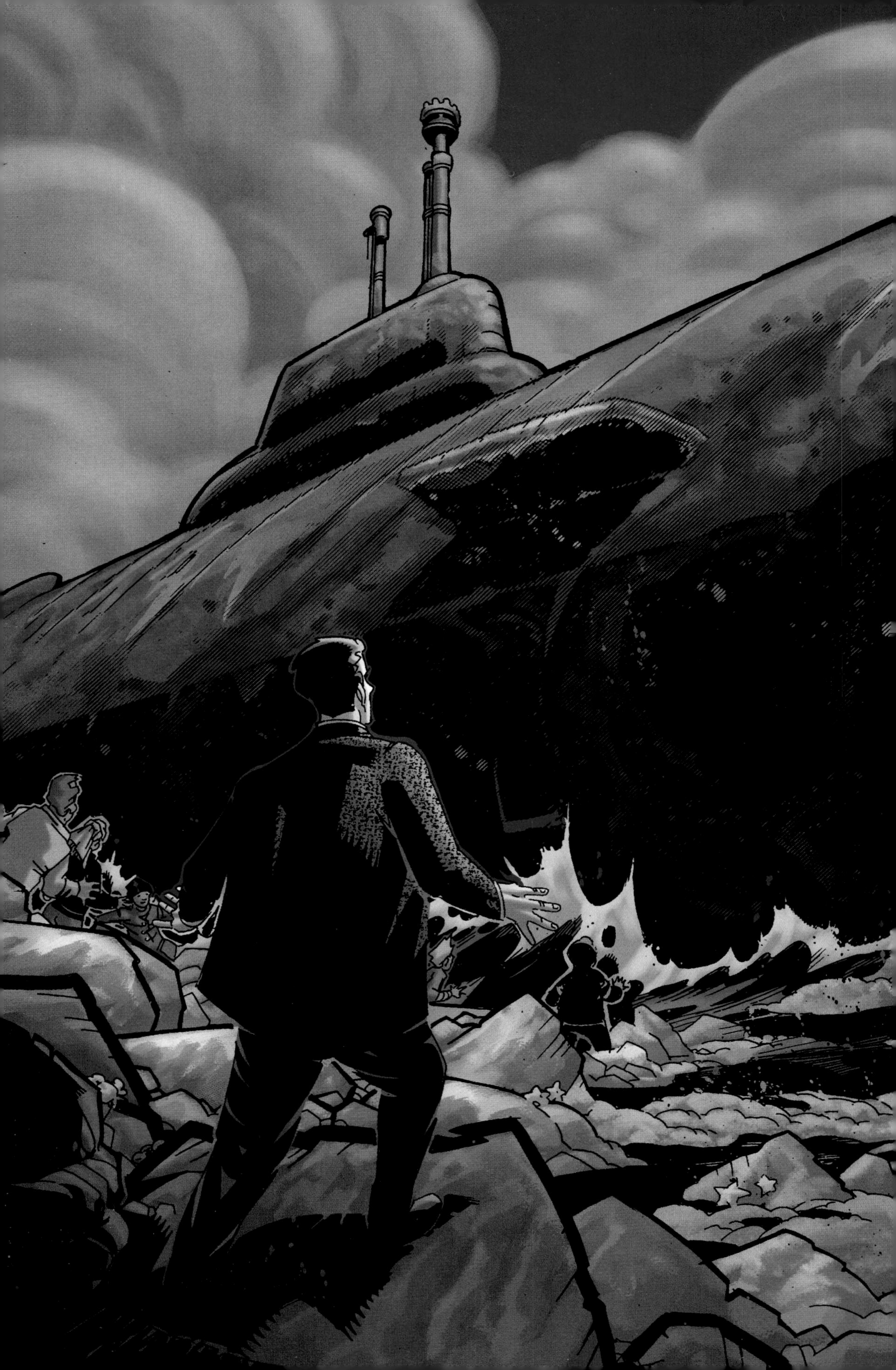

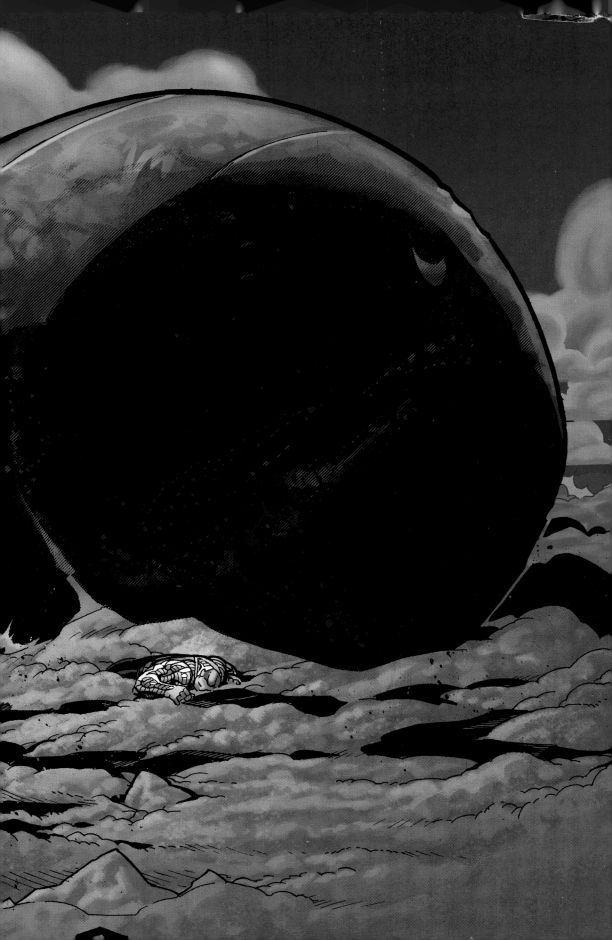

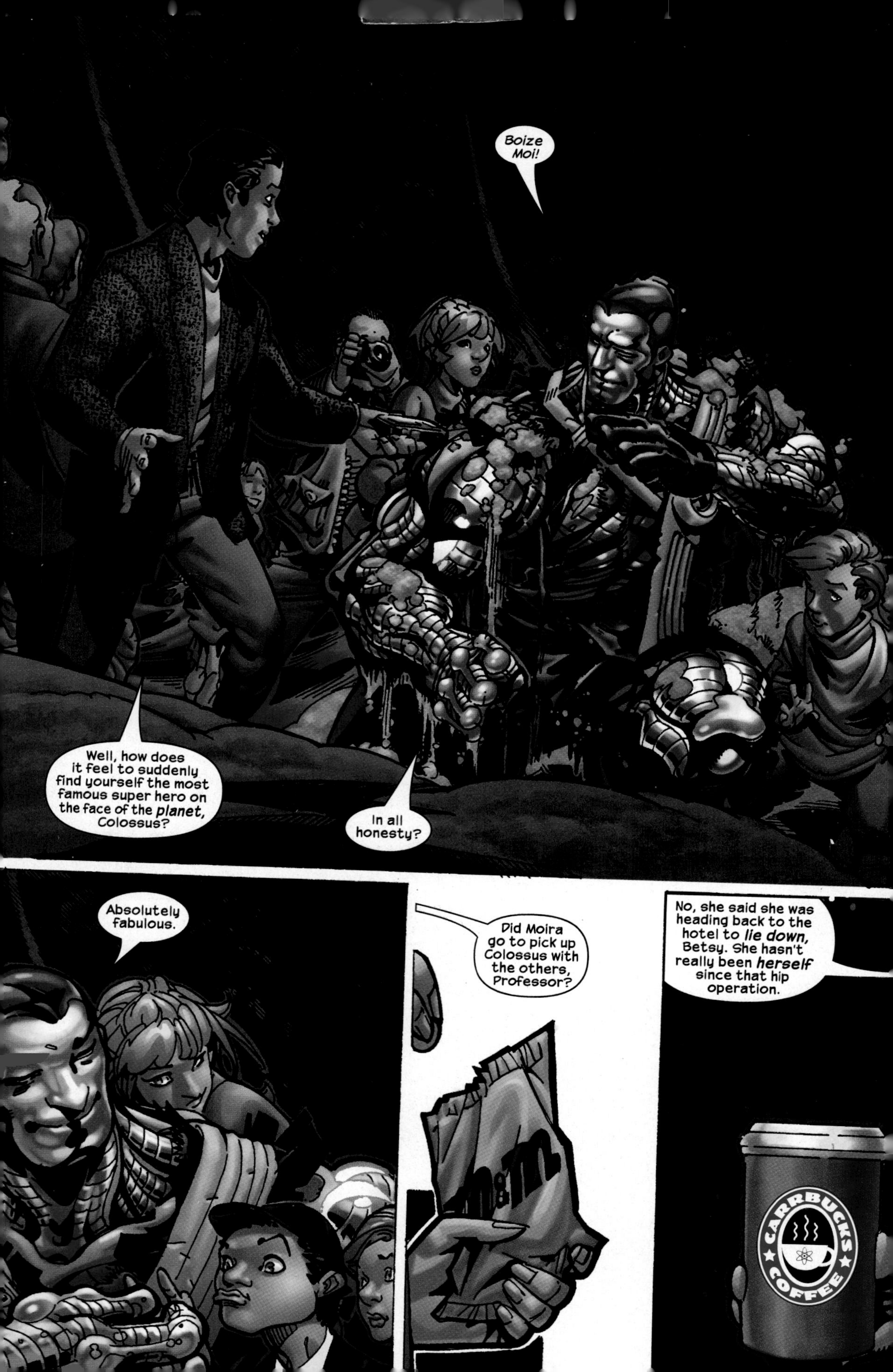
Boize Moi!
Well, how does it feel to suddenly find yourself the most famous super hero on the face of the *planet*, Colossus?
In all honesty?
Absolutely fabulous.
Did Moira go to pick up Colossus with the others, Professor?
No, she said she was heading back to the hotel to *lie down*, Betsy. She hasn't really been *herself* since that hip operation.
m&m
CARRBUCKS COFFEE

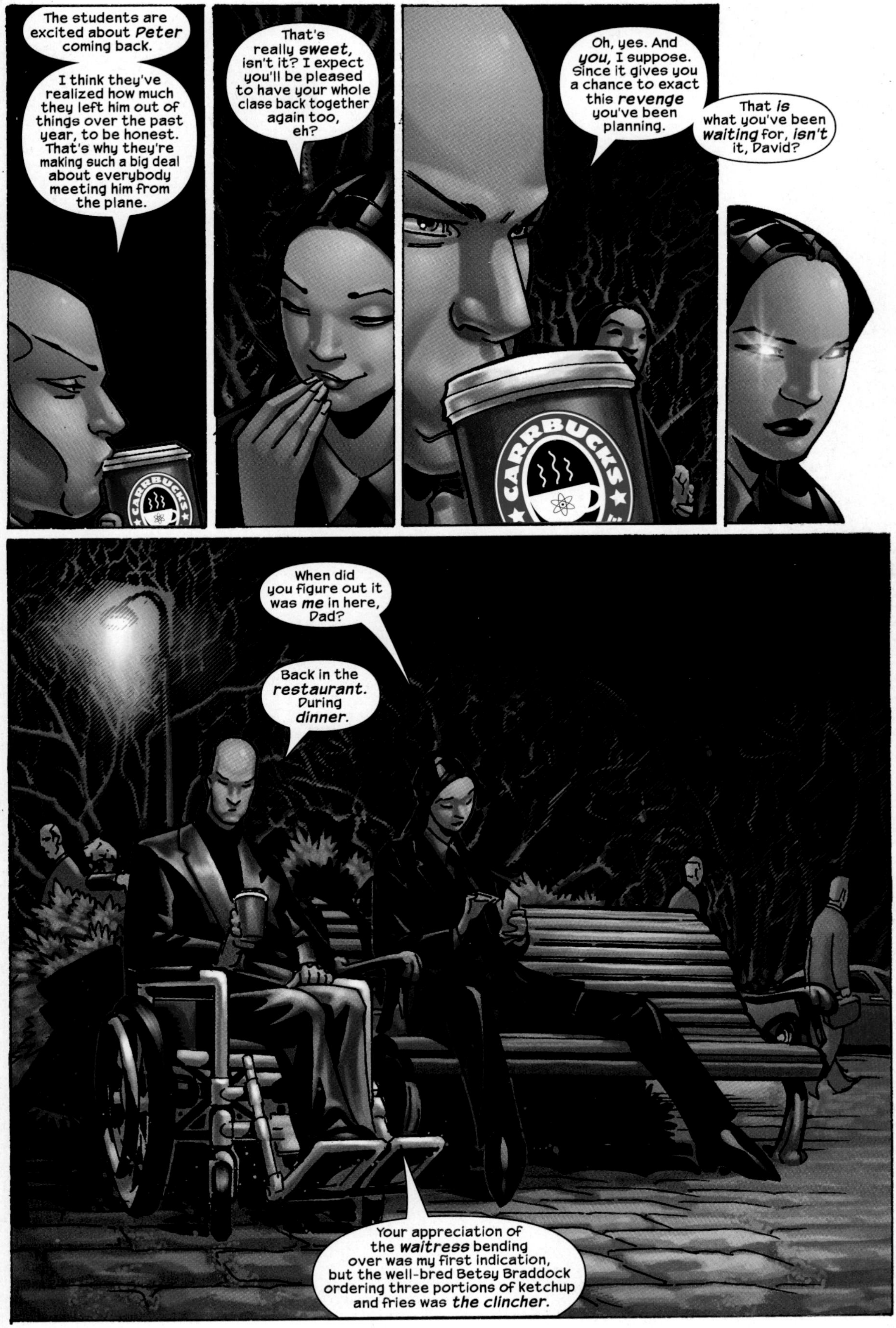
The students are excited about Peter coming back.
I think they've realized how much they left him out of things over the past year, to be honest. That's why they're making such a big deal about everybody meeting him from the plane.
That's really sweet, isn't it? I expect you'll be pleased to have your whole class back together again too, eh?
CARRBUCKS
Oh, yes. And you, I suppose. Since it gives you a chance to exact this revenge you've been planning.
That is what you've been waiting for, isn't it, David?
When did you figure out it was me in here, Dad?
Back in the restaurant. During dinner.
Your appreciation of the waitress bending over was my first indication, but the well-bred Betsy Braddock ordering three portions of ketchup and fries was the clincher.

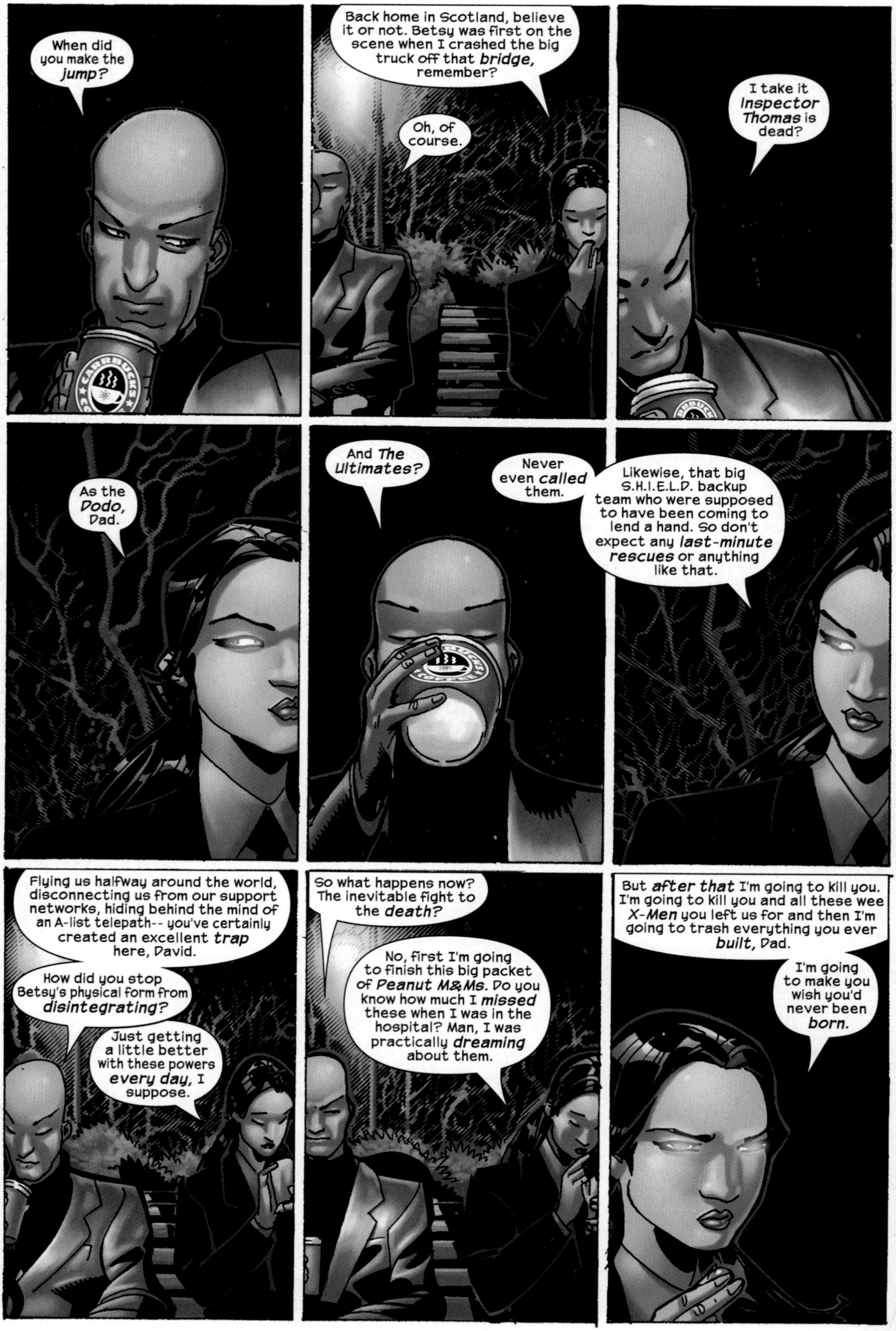

When did you make the *jump?*
Back home in Scotland, believe it or not. Betsy was first on the scene when I crashed the big truck off that *bridge,* remember?
Oh, of course.
I take it *Inspector Thomas* is dead?
As the *Dodo,* Dad.
And *The Ultimates?*
Never even *called* them.
Likewise, that big S.H.I.E.L.D. backup team who were supposed to have been coming to lend a hand. So don't expect any *last-minute rescues* or anything like that.
Flying us halfway around the world, disconnecting us from our support networks, hiding behind the mind of an A-list telepath-- you've certainly created an excellent *trap* here, David.
How did you stop Betsy's physical form from *disintegrating?*
Just getting a little better with these powers *every day,* I suppose.
So what happens now? The inevitable fight to the *death?*
No, first I'm going to finish this big packet of *Peanut M&Ms.* Do you know how much I *missed* these when I was in the hospital? Man, I was practically *dreaming* about them.
But *after that* I'm going to kill you. I'm going to kill you and all these wee *X-Men* you left us for and then I'm going to trash everything you ever *built,* Dad.
I'm going to make you wish you'd never been *born.*

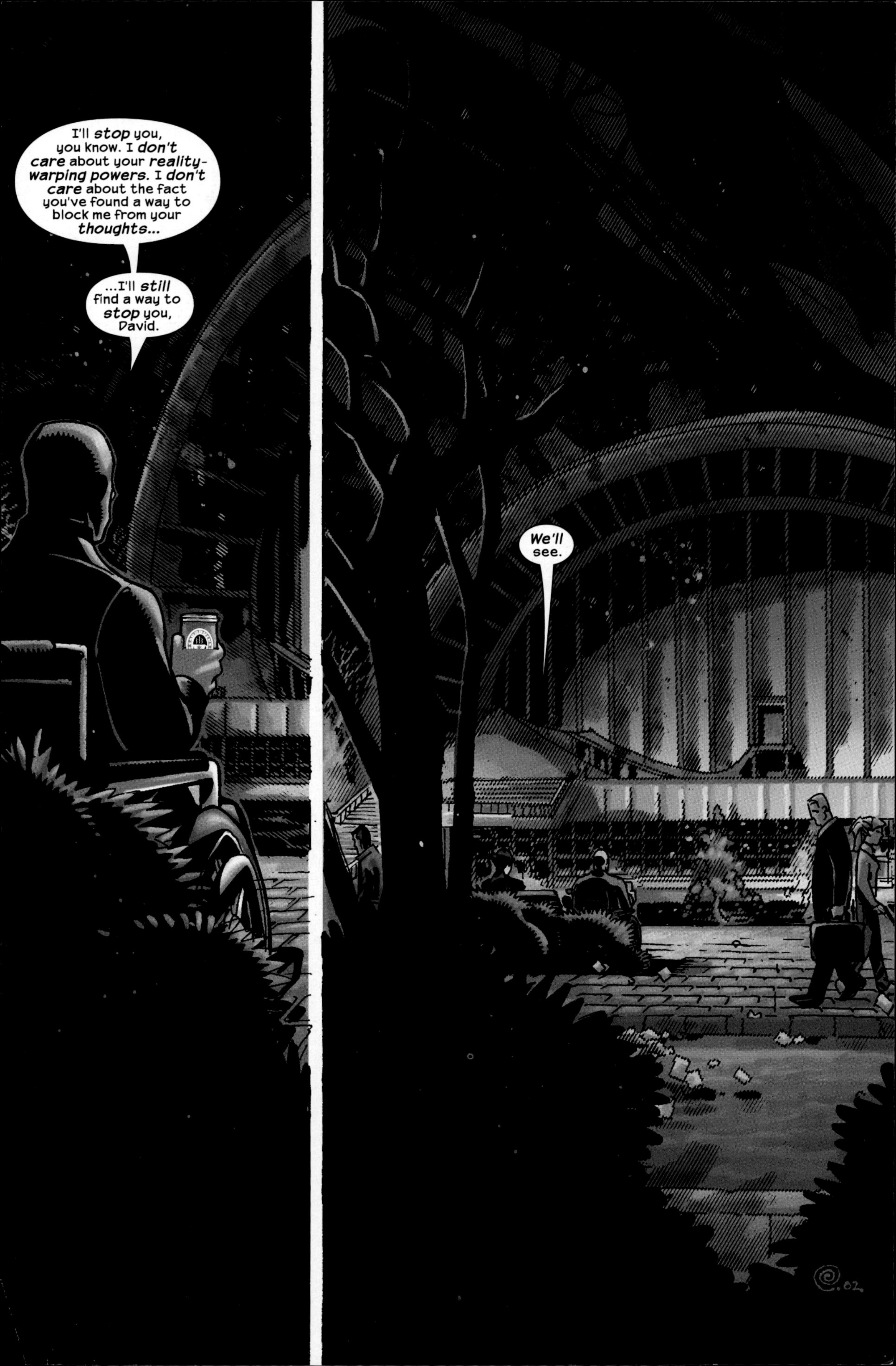
I'll stop you, you know. I don't care about your reality-warping powers. I don't care about the fact you've found a way to block me from your thoughts...
...I'll still find a way to stop you, David.
We'll see.

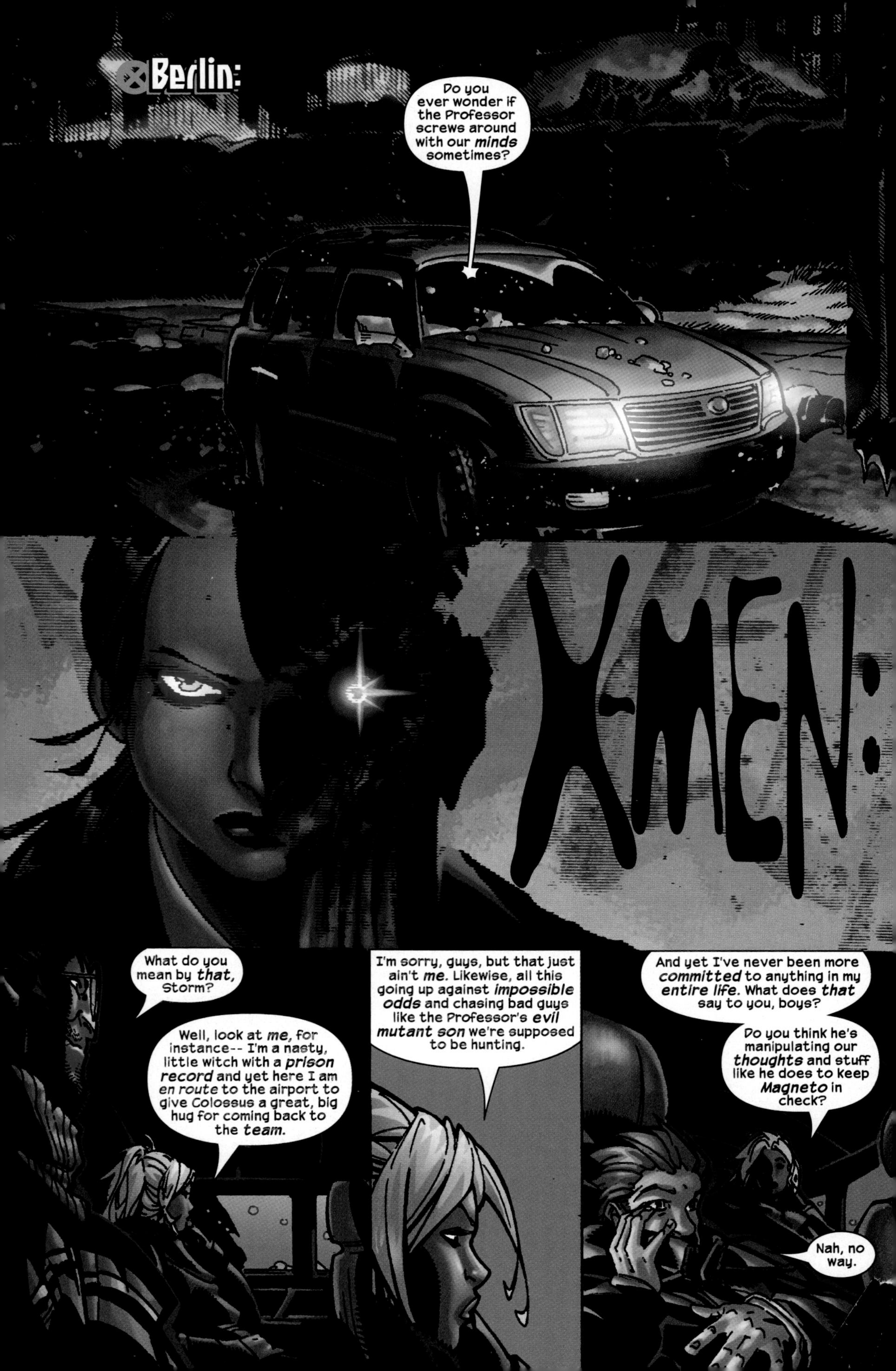
Berlin:
Do you ever wonder if the Professor screws around with our *minds* sometimes?
X-MEN:
What do you mean by *that*, Storm?
Well, look at *me*, for instance-- I'm a nasty, little witch with a *prison record* and yet here I am *en route* to the airport to give Colossus a great, big hug for coming back to the *team*.
I'm sorry, guys, but that just ain't *me*. Likewise, all this going up against *impossible odds* and chasing bad guys like the Professor's *evil mutant son* we're supposed to be hunting.
And yet I've never been more *committed* to anything in my *entire life*. What does *that* say to you, boys?
Do you think he's manipulating our *thoughts* and stuff like he does to keep *Magneto* in check?
Nah, no way.

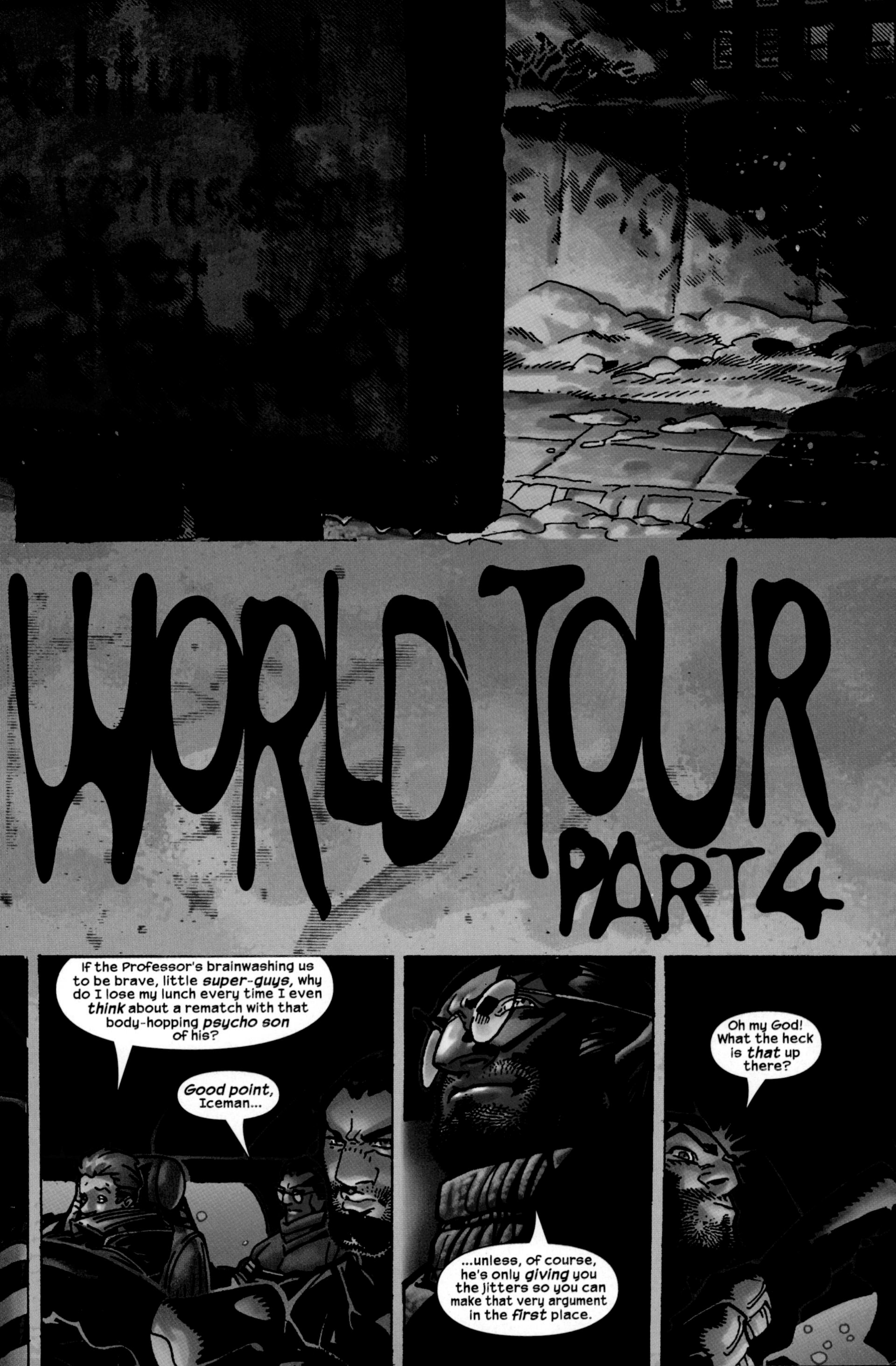
WORLD TOUR PART 4
If the Professor's brainwashing us to be brave, little super-guys, why do I lose my lunch every time I even think about a rematch with that body-hopping psycho son of his?
Good point, Iceman...
...unless, of course, he's only giving you the jitters so you can make that very argument in the first place.
Oh my God! What the heck is that up there?

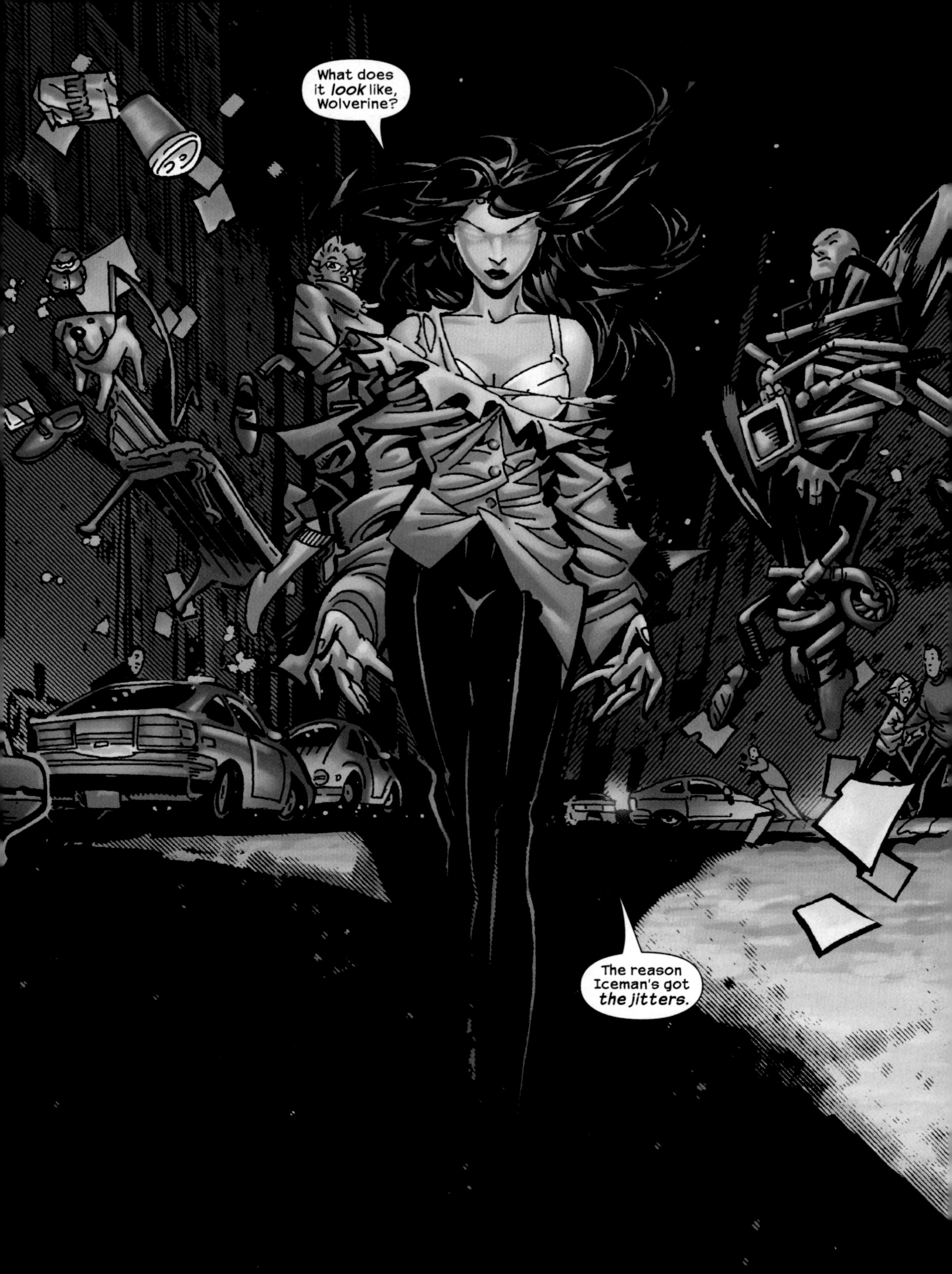
What does it *look* like, Wolverine?
The reason Iceman's got *the jitters.*

story **Mark Millar** **Chris Bachalo** artist

Dave Stewart colors
Chris Eliopoulos letters
C.B. Cebulski associate editor
Brian Smith associate editor
Ralph Macchio editor
Joe Quesada editor in chief
Bill Jemas president & inspiration

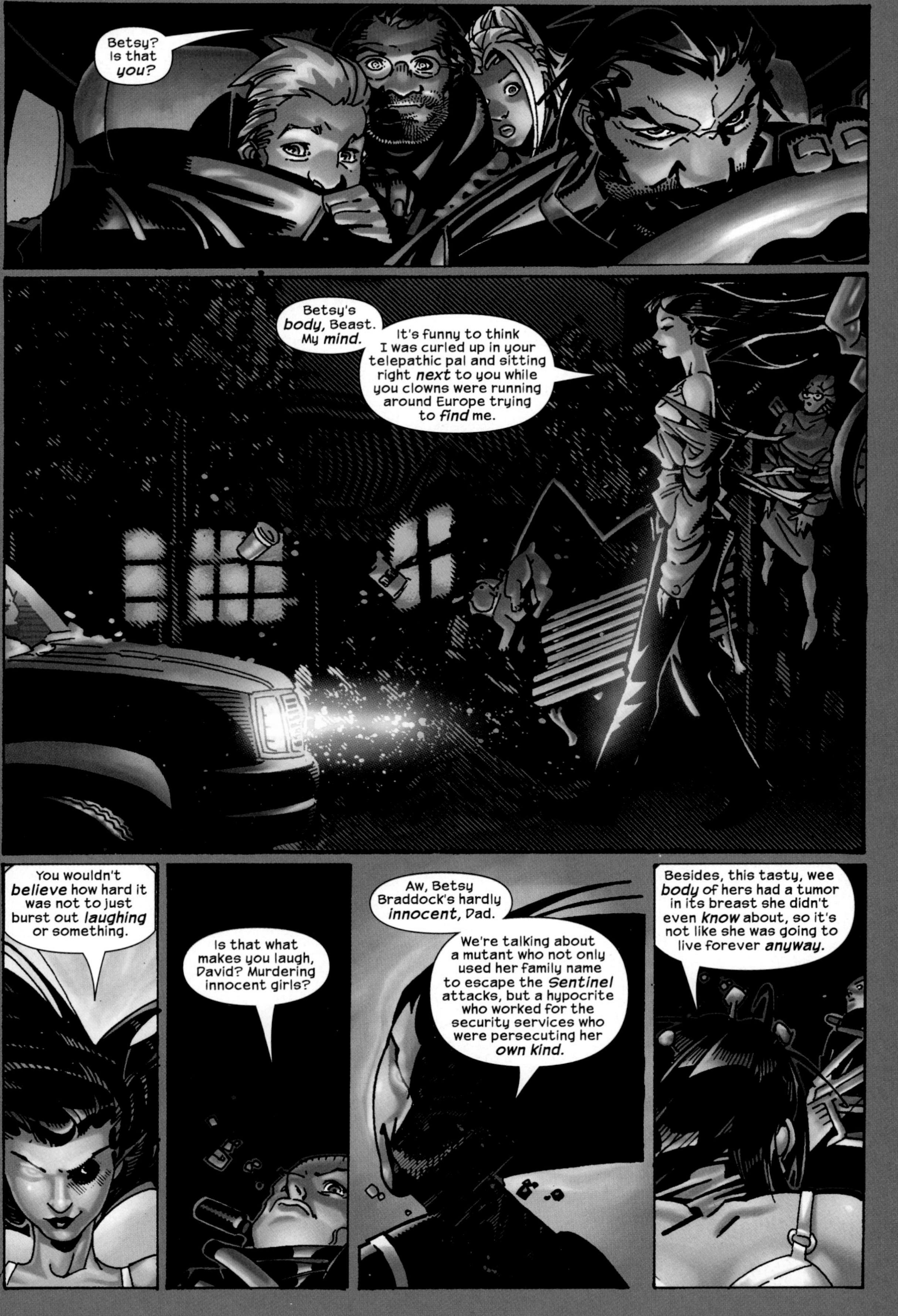
Betsy? Is that *you*?
Betsy's *body*, Beast. My *mind*.
It's funny to think I was curled up in your telepathic pal and sitting right *next* to you while you clowns were running around Europe trying to *find* me.
You wouldn't *believe* how hard it was not to just burst out *laughing* or something.
Is that what makes you laugh, David? Murdering innocent girls?
Aw, Betsy Braddock's hardly *innocent*, Dad.
We're talking about a mutant who not only used her family name to escape the *Sentinel* attacks, but a hypocrite who worked for the security services who were persecuting her *own kind*.
Besides, this tasty, wee *body* of hers had a tumor in its breast she didn't even *know* about, so it's not like she was going to live forever *anyway*.

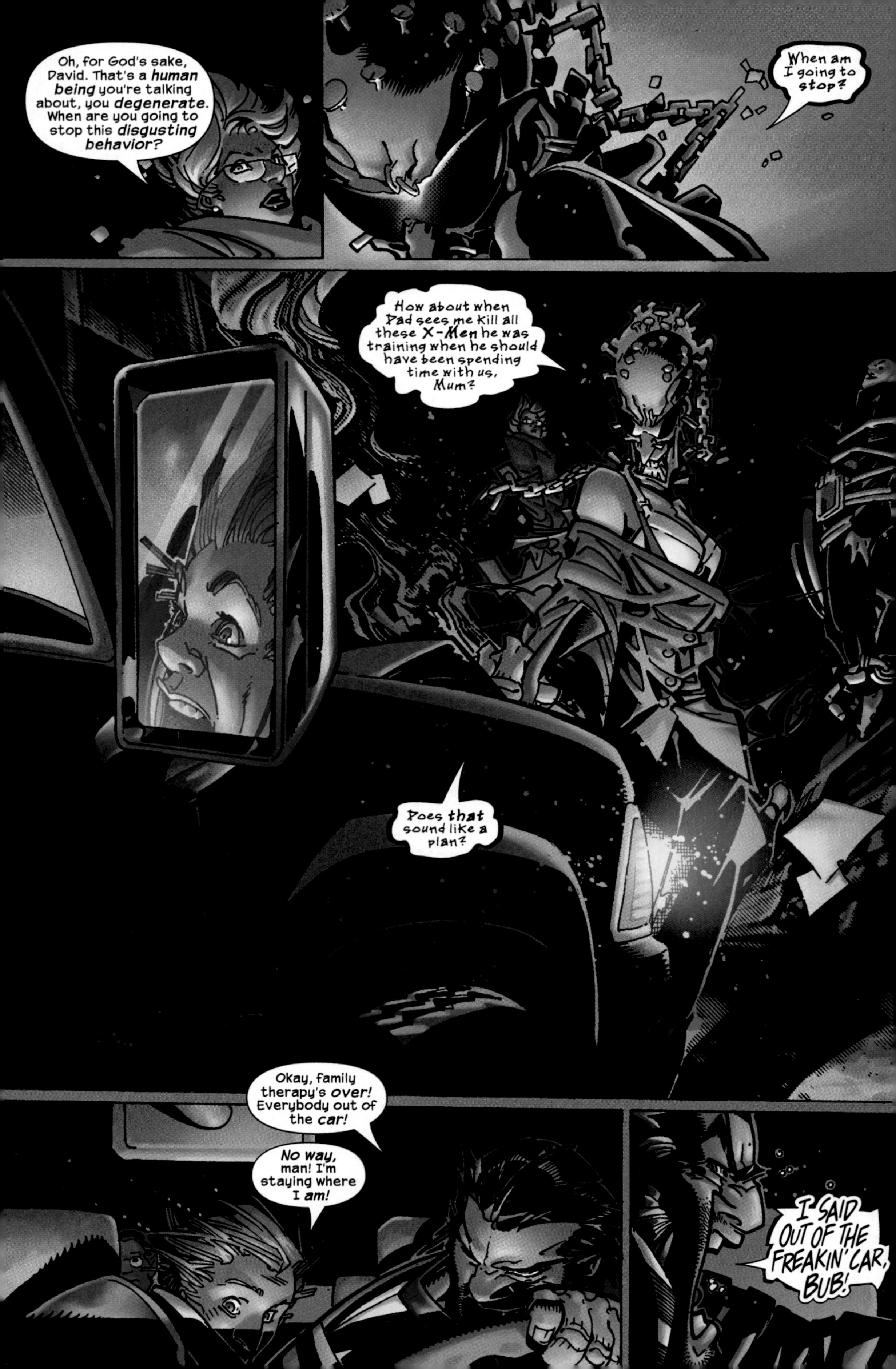
Oh, for God's sake, David. That's a human being you're talking about, you degenerate. When are you going to stop this disgusting behavior?
When am I going to stop?
How about when Dad sees me kill all these X-Men he was training when he should have been spending time with us, Mum?
Does that sound like a plan?
Okay, family therapy's over! Everybody out of the car!
No way, man! I'm staying where I am!
I SAID OUT OF THE FREAKIN' CAR, BUB!

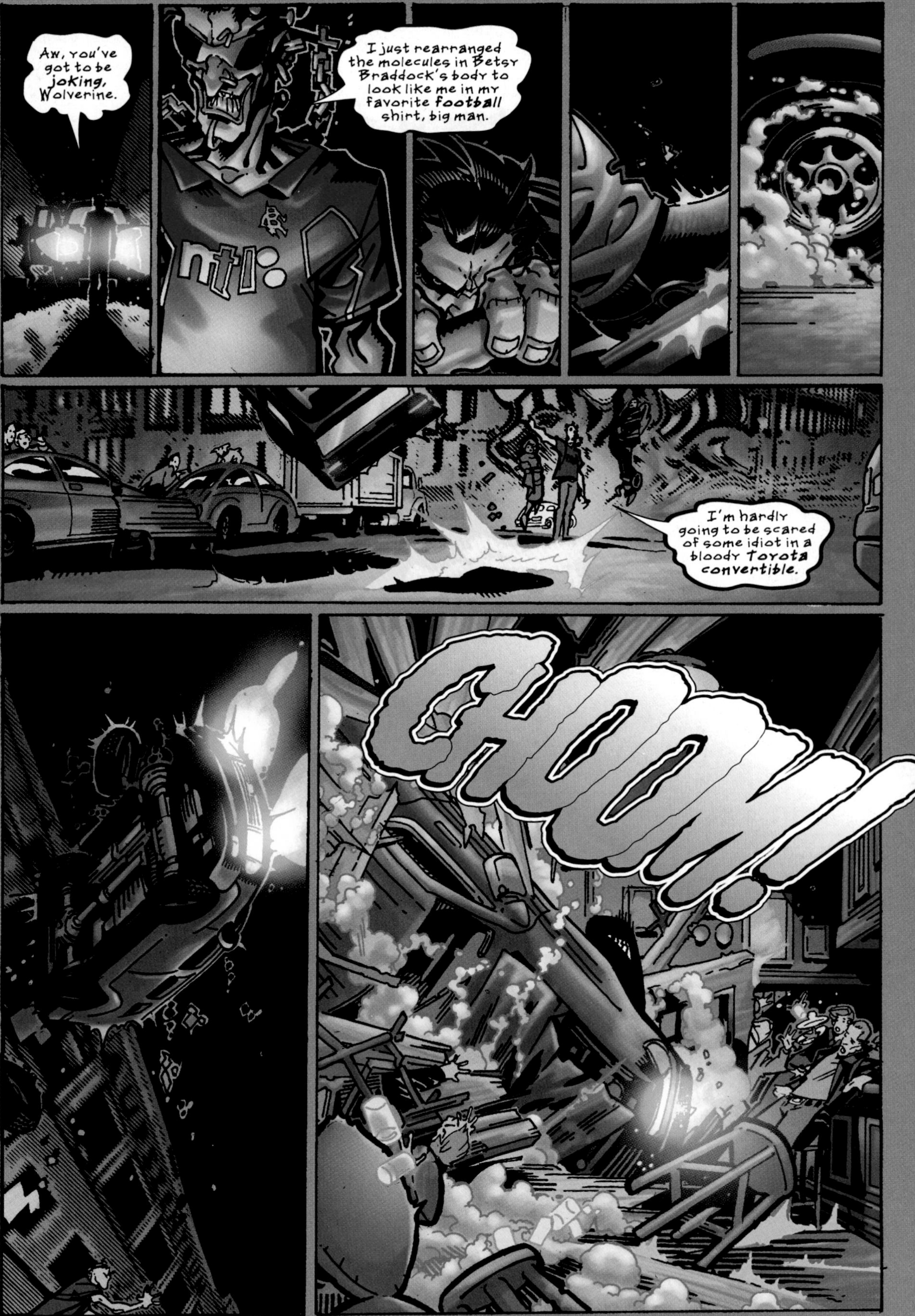
Aw, you've got to be joking, Wolverine.
I just rearranged the molecules in Betsy Braddock's body to look like me in my favorite football shirt, big man.
ntl:
I'm hardly going to be scared of some idiot in a bloody Toyota convertible.
CHOOM!!

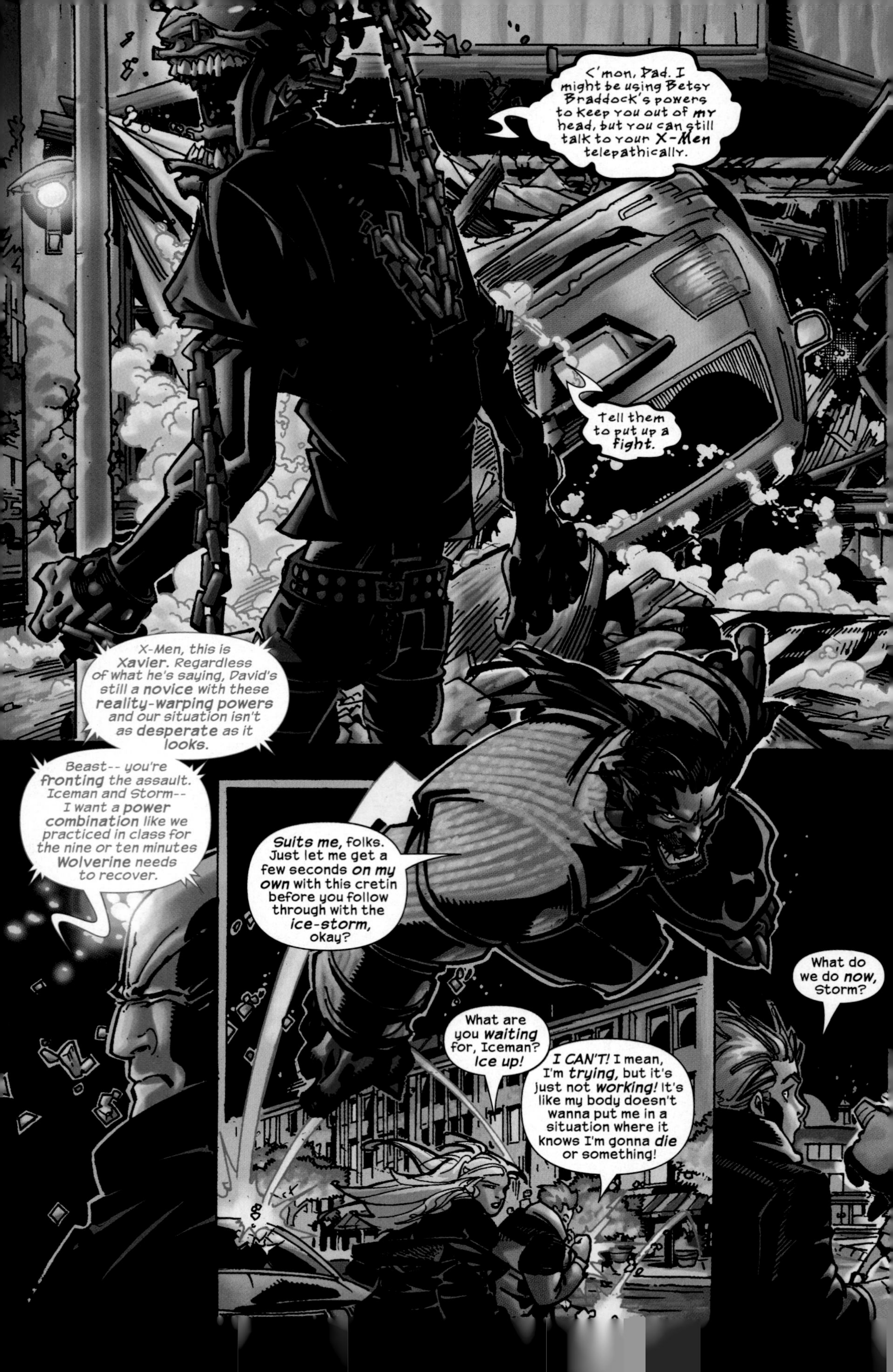
C'mon, Dad. I might be using Betsy Braddock's powers to keep you out of my head, but you can still talk to your X-Men telepathically.
Tell them to put up a fight.
X-Men, this is Xavier. Regardless of what he's saying, David's still a novice with these reality-warping powers and our situation isn't as desperate as it looks.
Beast-- you're fronting the assault. Iceman and Storm-- I want a power combination like we practiced in class for the nine or ten minutes Wolverine needs to recover.
Suits me, folks. Just let me get a few seconds on my own with this cretin before you follow through with the ice-storm, okay?
What do we do now, Storm?
What are you waiting for, Iceman? Ice up!
I CAN'T! I mean, I'm trying, but it's just not working! It's like my body doesn't wanna put me in a situation where it knows I'm gonna die or something!

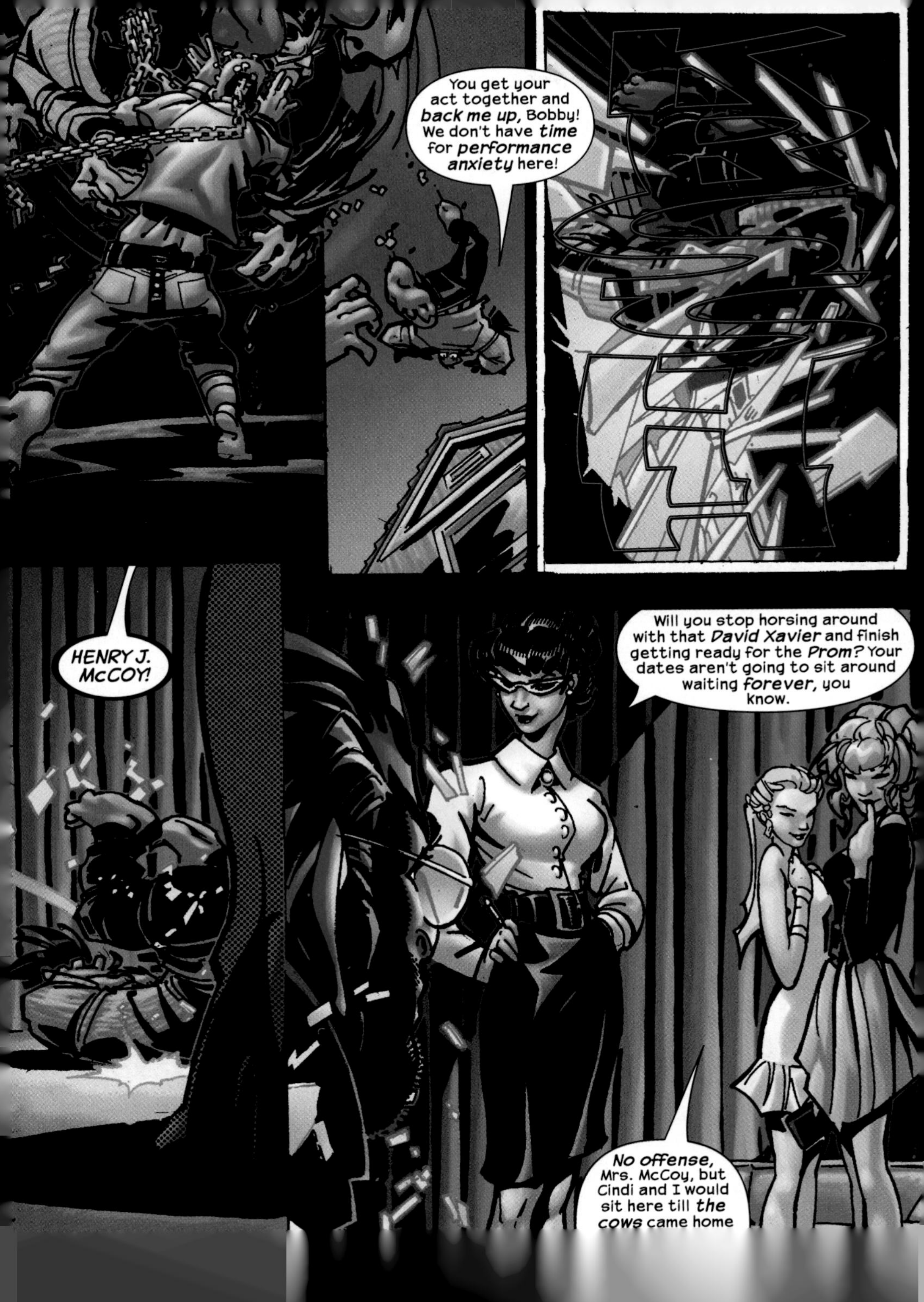
You get your act together and back me up, Bobby! We don't have time for performance anxiety here!
HENRY J. McCOY!
Will you stop horsing around with that David Xavier and finish getting ready for the Prom? Your dates aren't going to sit around waiting forever, you know.
No offense, Mrs. McCoy, but Cindi and I would sit here till the cows came home

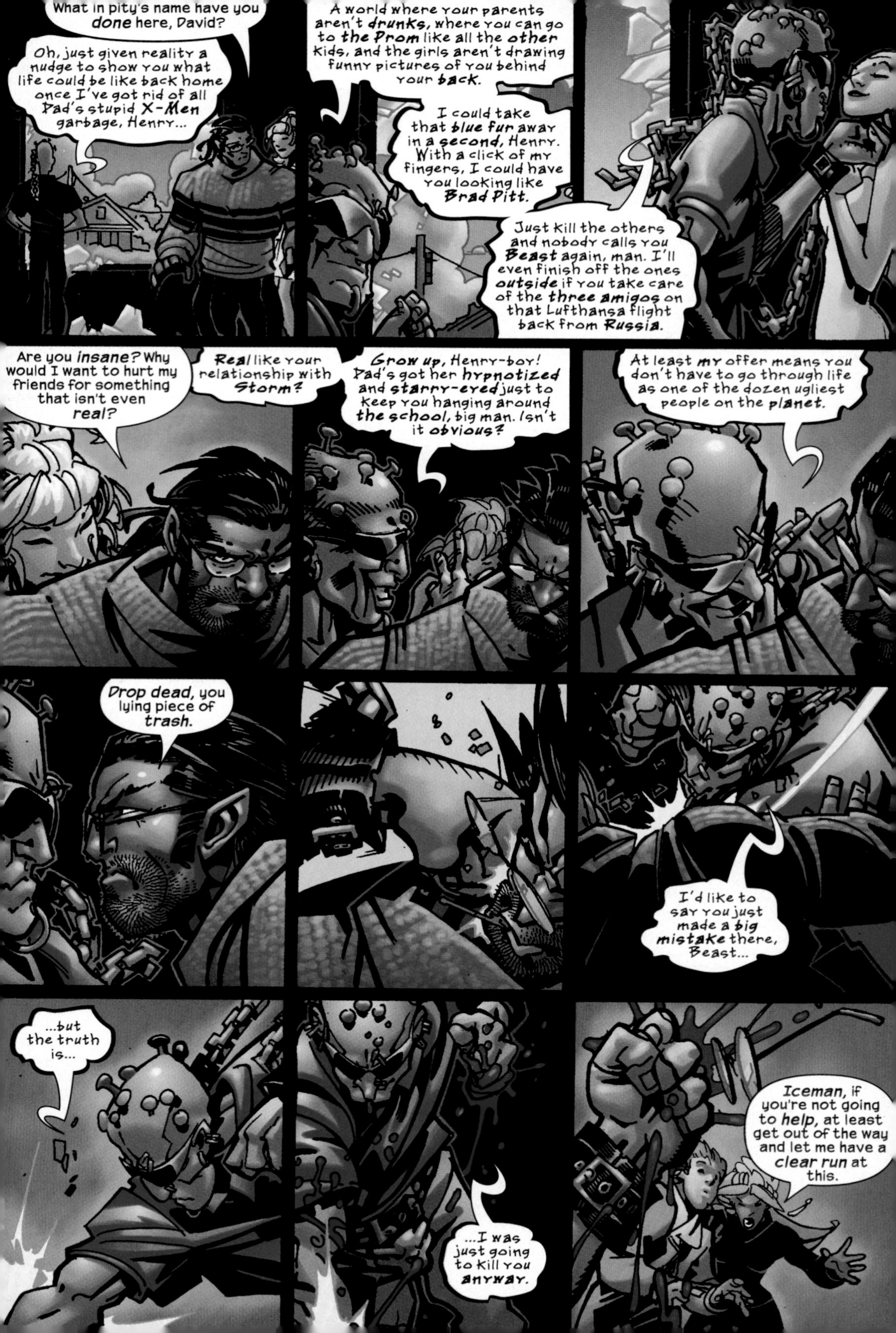
What in pity's name have you done here, David?
Oh, just given reality a nudge to show you what life could be like back home once I've got rid of all Dad's stupid X-Men garbage, Henry...
A world where your parents aren't drunks, where you can go to the Prom like all the other kids, and the girls aren't drawing funny pictures of you behind your back.
I could take that blue fur away in a second, Henry. With a click of my fingers, I could have you looking like Brad Pitt.
Just kill the others and nobody calls you Beast again, man. I'll even finish off the ones outside if you take care of the three amigos on that Lufthansa flight back from Russia.
Are you insane? Why would I want to hurt my friends for something that isn't even real?
Real like your relationship with Storm?
Grow up, Henry-boy! Dad's got her hypnotized and starry-eyed just to keep you hanging around the school, big man. Isn't it obvious?
At least my offer means you don't have to go through life as one of the dozen ugliest people on the planet.
Drop dead, you lying piece of trash.
I'd like to say you just made a big mistake there, Beast...
...but the truth is...
...I was just going to kill you anyway.
Iceman, if you're not going to help, at least get out of the way and let me have a clear run at this.

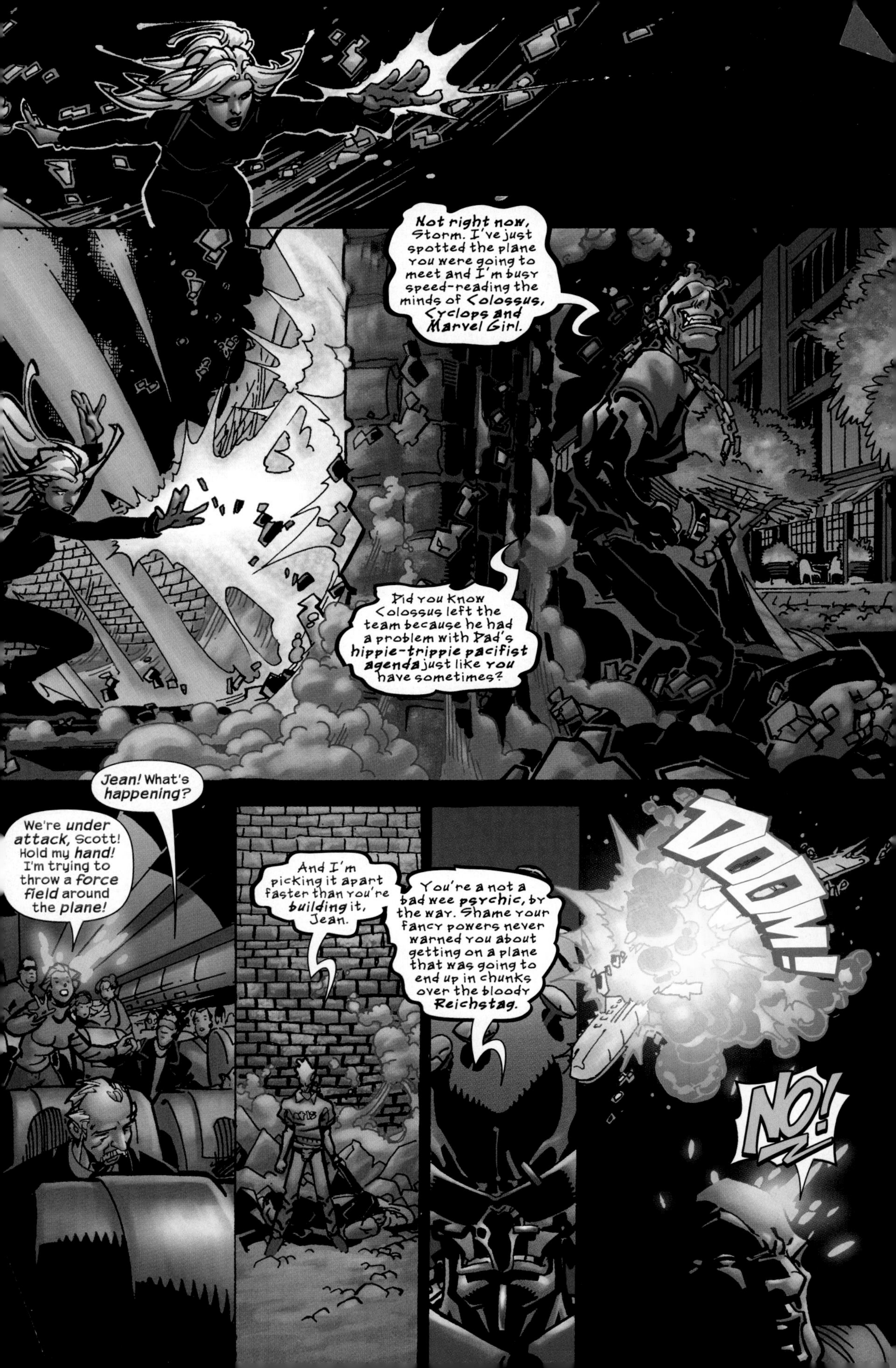
Not right now, Storm. I've just spotted the plane you were going to meet and I'm busy speed-reading the minds of Colossus, Cyclops and Marvel Girl.
Did you know Colossus left the team because he had a problem with Dad's hippie-trippie pacifist agenda just like you have sometimes?
Jean! What's happening?
We're under attack, Scott! Hold my hand! I'm trying to throw a force field around the plane!
And I'm picking it apart faster than you're building it, Jean.
You're a not a bad wee psychic, by the way. Shame your fancy powers never warned you about getting on a plane that was going to end up in chunks over the bloody Reichstag.
DOOM!
NO!

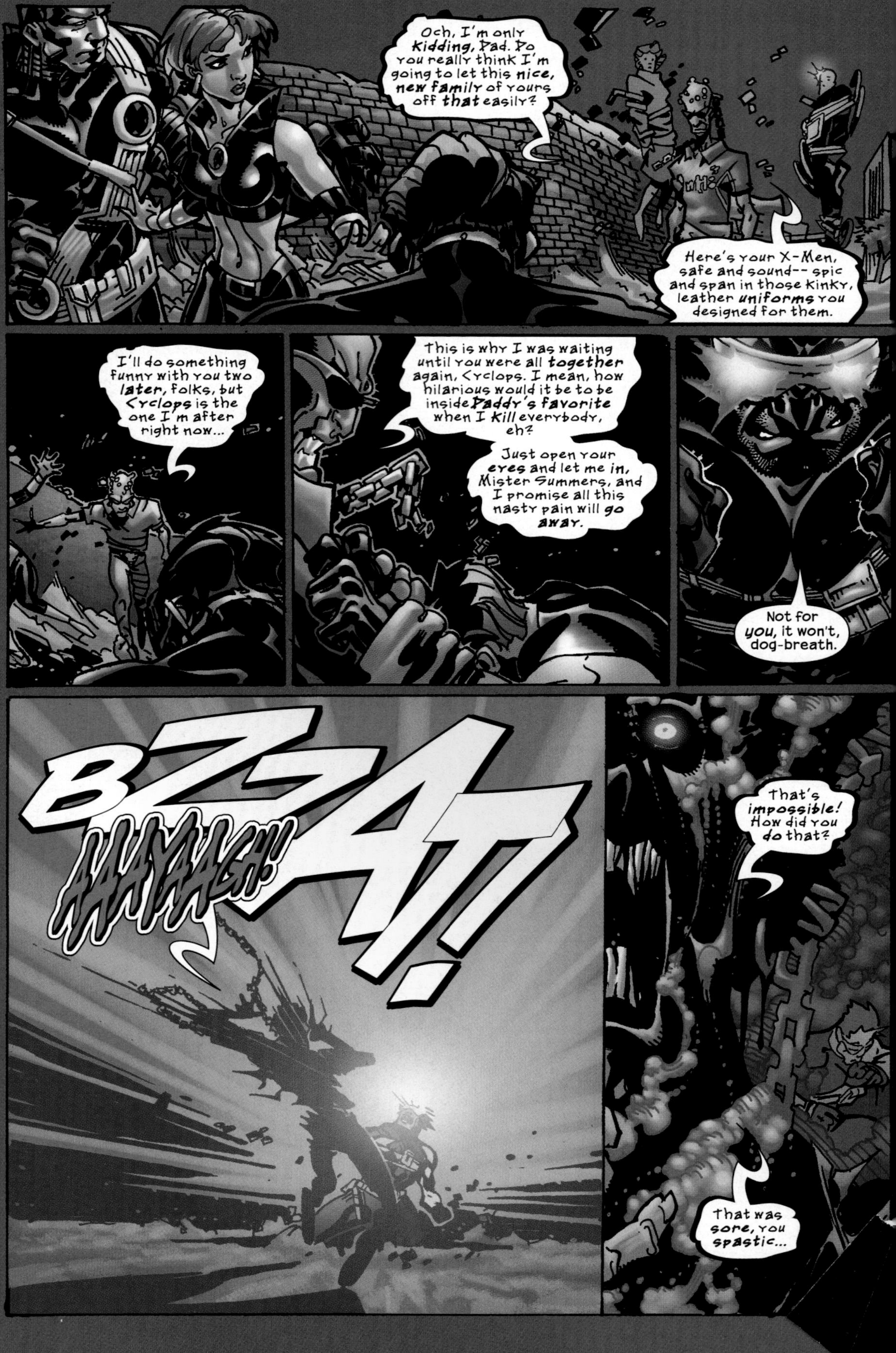
Och, I'm only kidding, Dad. Do you really think I'm going to let this nice, new family of yours off that easily?
Here's your X-Men, safe and sound-- spic and span in those kinky, leather uniforms you designed for them.
I'll do something funny with you two later, folks, but Cyclops is the one I'm after right now...
This is why I was waiting until you were all together again, Cyclops. I mean, how hilarious would it be to be inside Daddy's favorite when I kill everybody, eh?
Just open your eyes and let me in, Mister Summers, and I promise all this nasty pain will go away.
Not for you, it won't, dog-breath.
BZZAT!
AAAYAAGH!
That's impossible! How did you do that?
That was sore, you spastic...

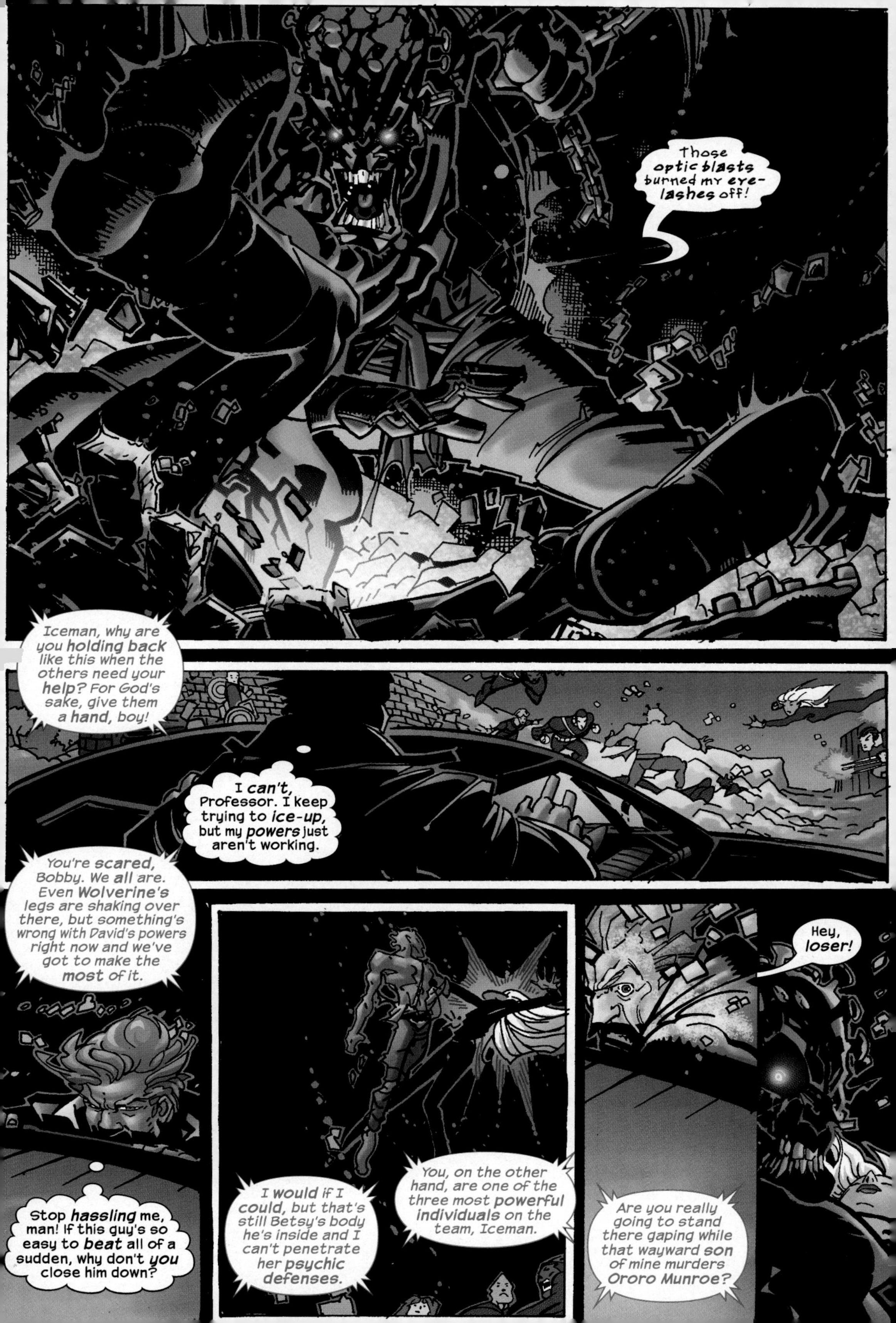
Those optic blasts burned my eye-lashes off!
Iceman, why are you holding back like this when the others need your help? For God's sake, give them a hand, boy!
I can't, Professor. I keep trying to ice-up, but my powers just aren't working.
You're scared, Bobby. We all are. Even Wolverine's legs are shaking over there, but something's wrong with David's powers right now and we've got to make the most of it.
Stop hassling me, man! If this guy's so easy to beat all of a sudden, why don't you close him down?
I would if I could, but that's still Betsy's body he's inside and I can't penetrate her psychic defenses.
You, on the other hand, are one of the three most powerful individuals on the team, Iceman.
Hey, loser!
Are you really going to stand there gaping while that wayward son of mine murders Ororo Munroe?

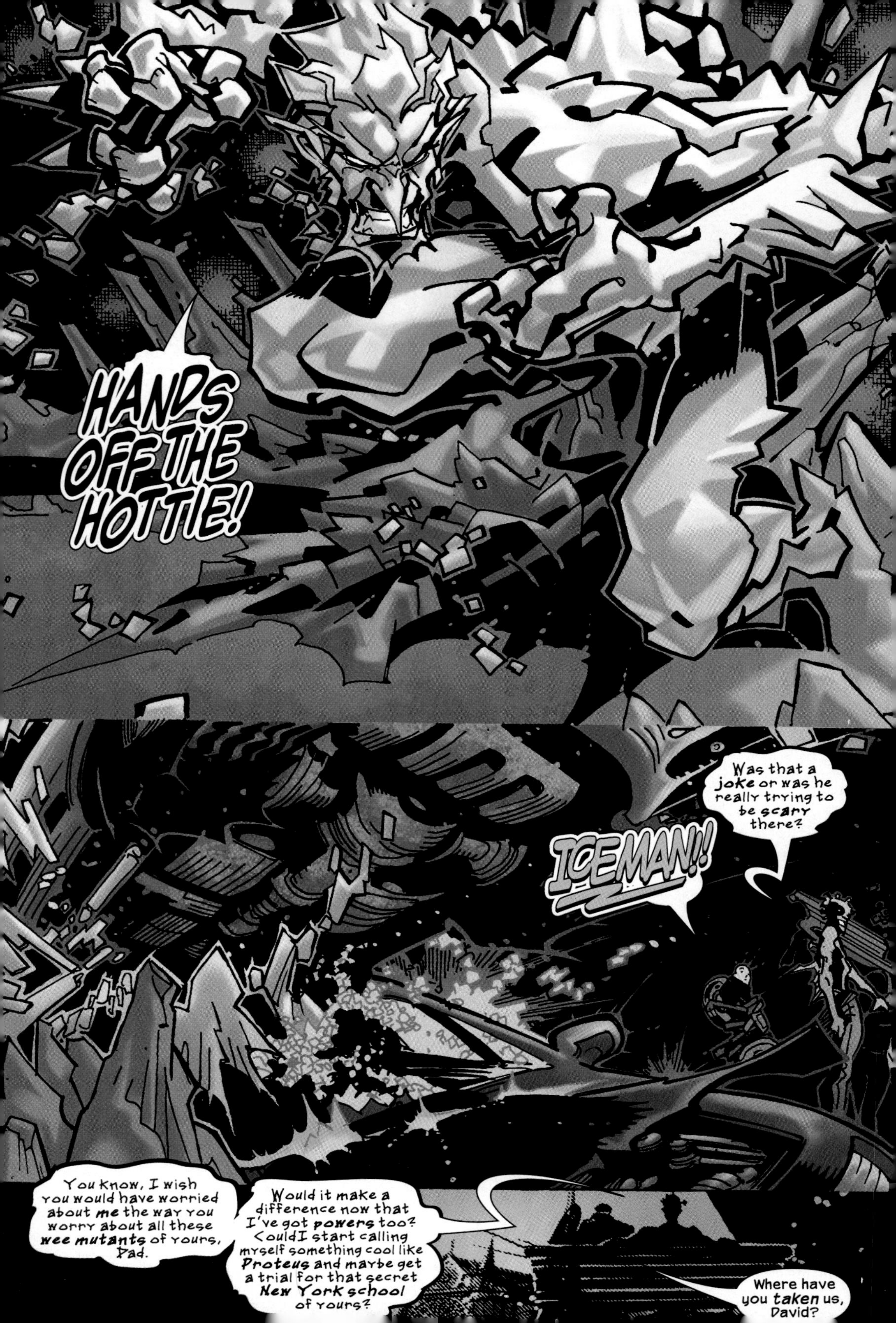

HANDS OFF THE HOTTIE!
ICEMAN!!
Was that a joke or was he really trying to be scary there?
You know, I wish you would have worried about me the way you worry about all these wee mutants of yours, Dad.
Would it make a difference now that I've got powers too? Could I start calling myself something cool like Proteus and maybe get a trial for that secret New York school of yours?
Where have you taken us, David?

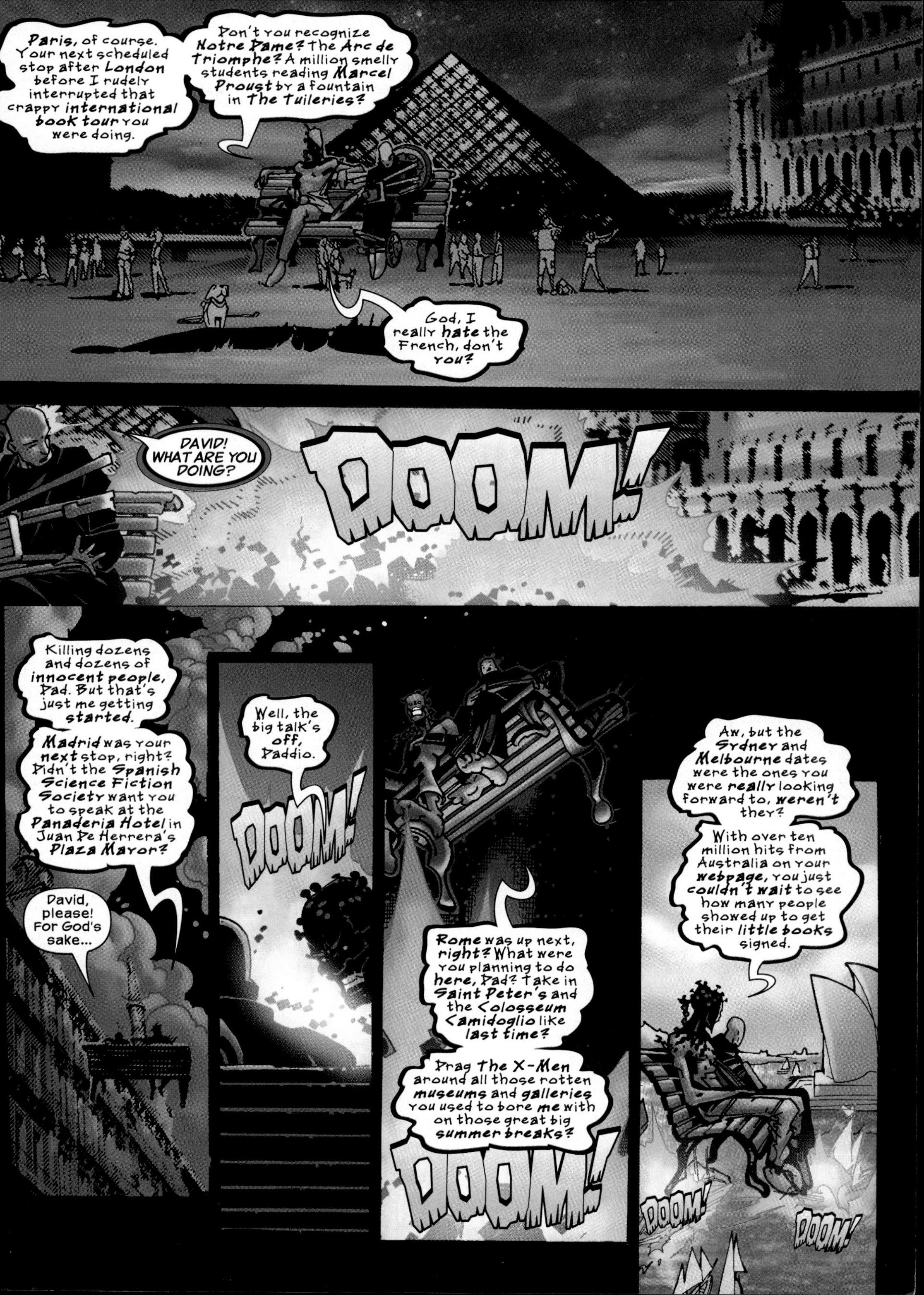

Paris, of course. Your next scheduled stop after London before I rudely interrupted that crappy international book tour you were doing.
Don't you recognize Notre Dame? The Arc de Triomphe? A million smelly students reading Marcel Proust by a fountain in The Tuileries?
God, I really hate the French, don't you?
DAVID! WHAT ARE YOU DOING?
DOOM!
Killing dozens and dozens of innocent people, Dad. But that's just me getting started.
Madrid was your next stop, right? Didn't the Spanish Science Fiction Society want you to speak at the Panaderia Hotel in Juan De Herrera's Plaza Mayor?
David, please! For God's sake...
Well, the big talk's off, Daddio.
DOOM!
Rome was up next, right? What were you planning to do here, Dad? Take in Saint Peter's and the Colosseum Camidoglio like last time?
Drag the X-Men around all those rotten museums and galleries you used to bore me with on those great big summer breaks?
DOOM!
Aw, but the Sydney and Melbourne dates were the ones you were really looking forward to, weren't they?
With over ten million hits from Australia on your webpage, you just couldn't wait to see how many people showed up to get their little books signed.
DOOM!
DOOM!

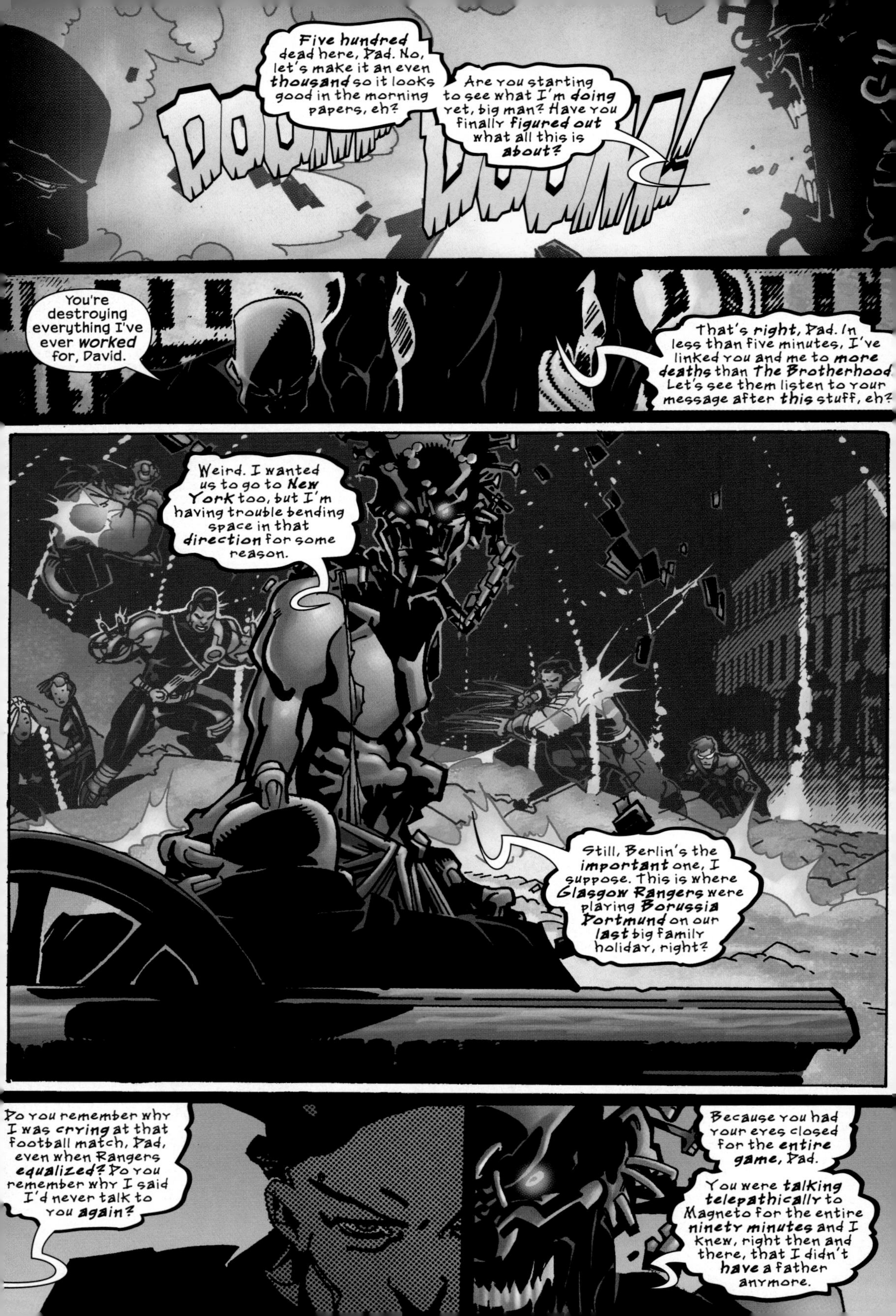
Five hundred dead here, Dad. No, let's make it an even thousand so it looks good in the morning papers, eh?
Are you starting to see what I'm doing yet, big man? Have you finally figured out what all this is about?
You're destroying everything I've ever worked for, David.
That's right, Dad. In less than five minutes, I've linked you and me to more deaths than the Brotherhood. Let's see them listen to your message after this stuff, eh?
Weird. I wanted us to go to New York too, but I'm having trouble bending space in that direction for some reason.
Still, Berlin's the important one, I suppose. This is where Glasgow Rangers were playing Borussia Dortmund on our last big family holiday, right?
Do you remember why I was crying at that football match, Dad, even when Rangers equalized? Do you remember why I said I'd never talk to you again?
Because you had your eyes closed for the entire game, Dad.
You were talking telepathically to Magneto for the entire ninety minutes and I knew, right then and there, that I didn't have a father anymore.

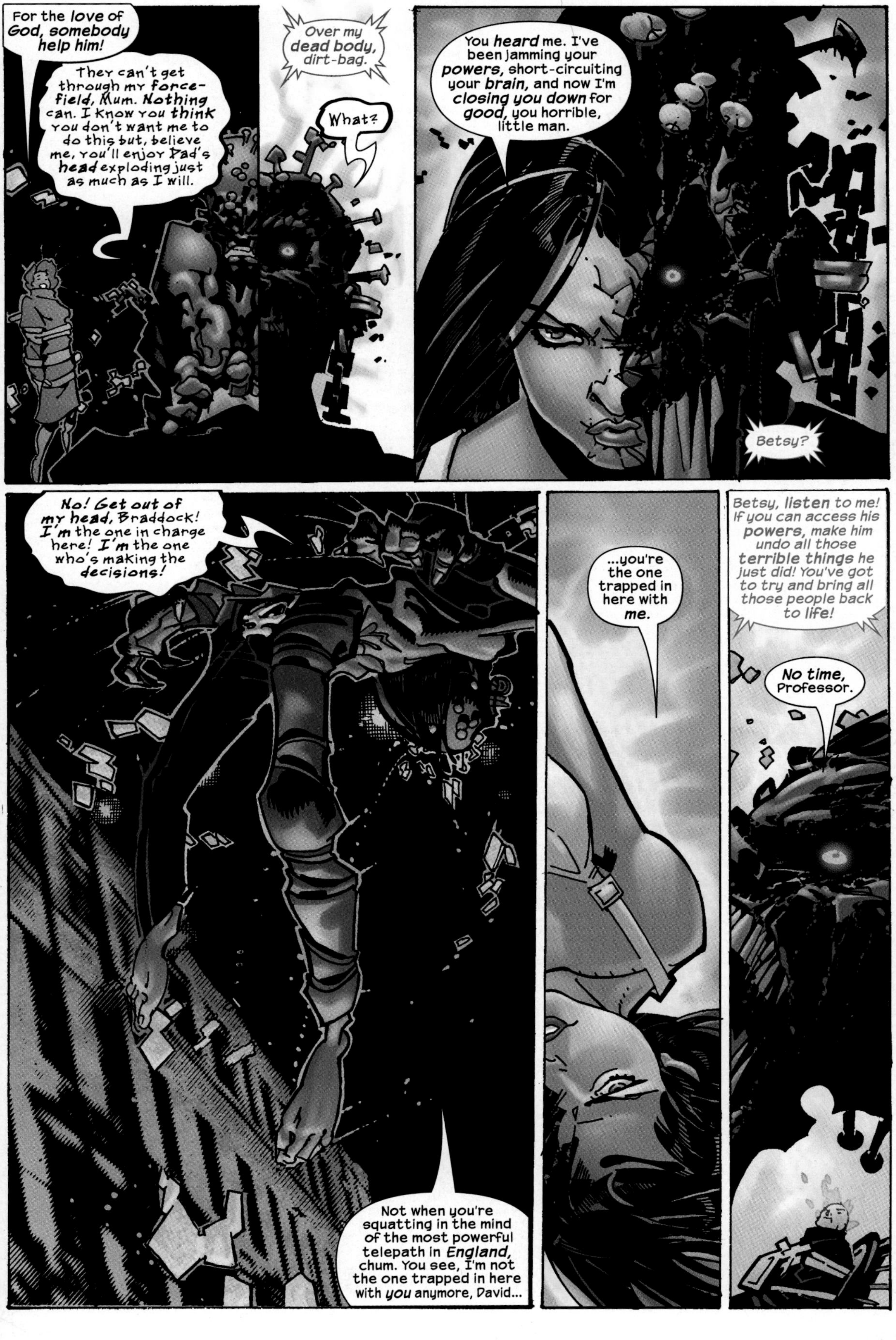
For the love of God, somebody help him!
They can't get through my force-field, Mum. Nothing can. I know you think you don't want me to do this but, believe me, you'll enjoy Dad's head exploding just as much as I will.
Over my dead body, dirt-bag.
What?
You heard me. I've been jamming your powers, short-circuiting your brain, and now I'm closing you down for good, you horrible, little man.
Betsy?
No! Get out of my head, Braddock! I'm the one in charge here! I'm the one who's making the decisions!
Not when you're squatting in the mind of the most powerful telepath in England, chum. You see, I'm not the one trapped in here with you anymore, David...
...you're the one trapped in here with me.
Betsy, listen to me! If you can access his powers, make him undo all those terrible things he just did! You've got to try and bring all those people back to life!
No time, Professor.

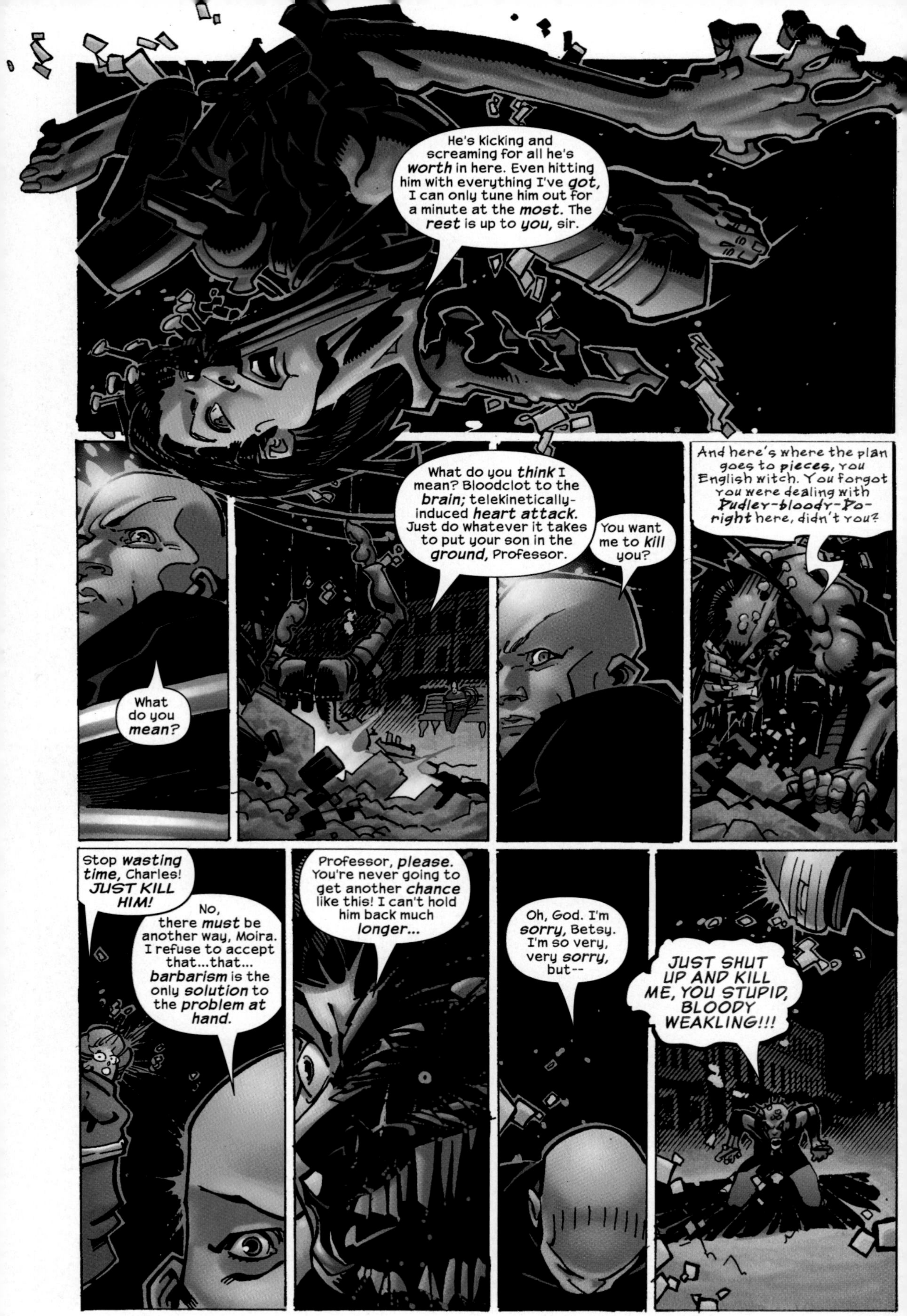
He's kicking and screaming for all he's worth in here. Even hitting him with everything I've got, I can only tune him out for a minute at the most. The rest is up to you, sir.
What do you mean?
What do you think I mean? Bloodclot to the brain; telekinetically-induced heart attack. Just do whatever it takes to put your son in the ground, Professor.
You want me to kill you?
And here's where the plan goes to pieces, you English witch. You forgot you were dealing with Dudley-bloody-Do-right here, didn't you?
Stop wasting time, Charles! JUST KILL HIM!
No, there must be another way, Moira. I refuse to accept that...that... barbarism is the only solution to the problem at hand.
Professor, please. You're never going to get another chance like this! I can't hold him back much longer...
Oh, God. I'm sorry, Betsy. I'm so very, very sorry, but--
JUST SHUT UP AND KILL ME, YOU STUPID, BLOODY WEAKLING!!!

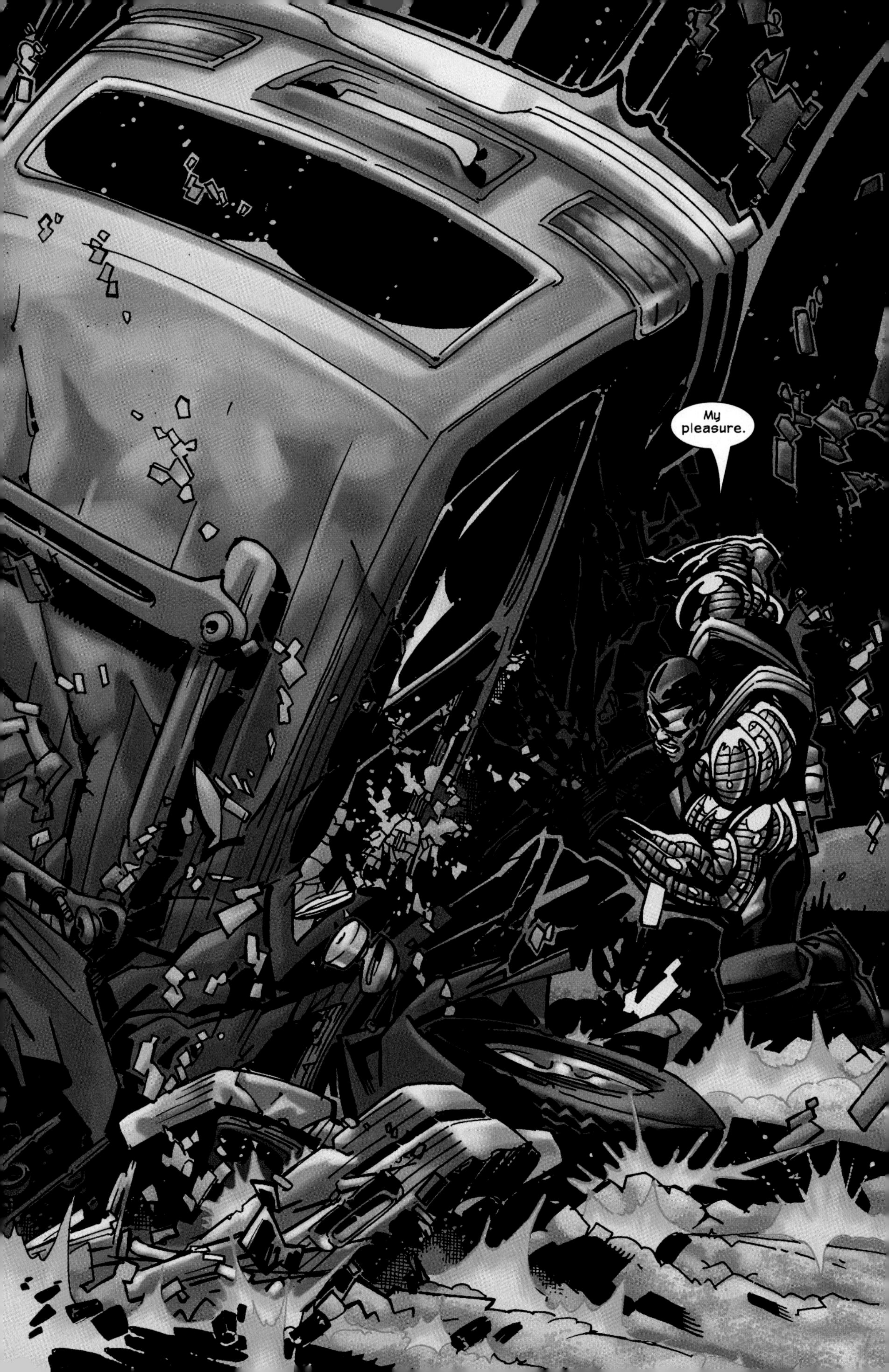
My pleasure.

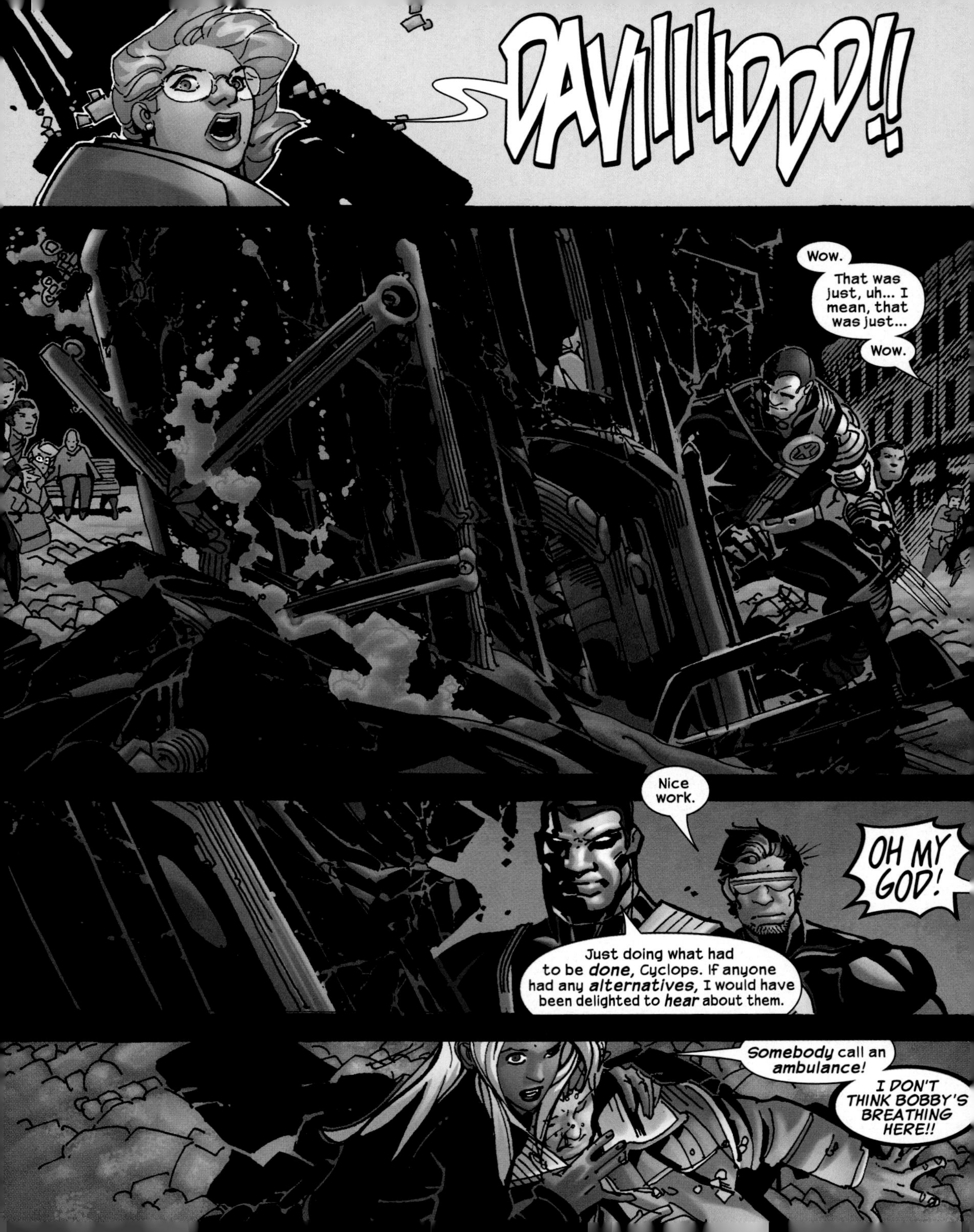
DAVIIIIDDD!!
Wow.
That was just, uh... I mean, that was just...
Wow.
Nice work.
OH MY GOD!
Just doing what had to be *done*, Cyclops. If anyone had any *alternatives*, I would have been delighted to *hear* about them.
Somebody call an *ambulance*!
I DON'T THINK BOBBY'S BREATHING HERE!!

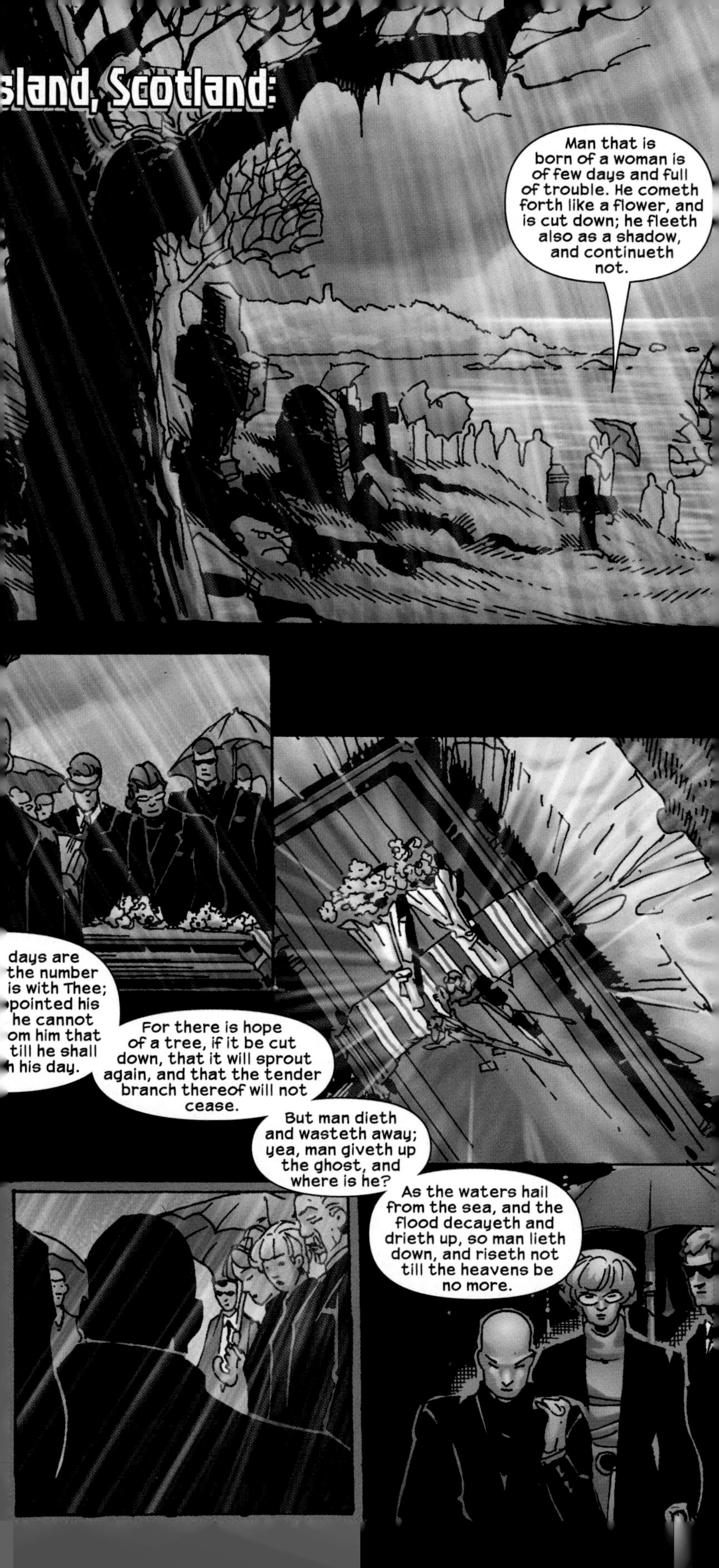
sland, Scotland:
Man that is born of a woman is of few days and full of trouble. He cometh forth like a flower, and is cut down; he fleeth also as a shadow, and continueth not.
days are the number is with Thee; pointed his he cannot om him that till he shall h his day.
For there is hope of a tree, if it be cut down, that it will sprout again, and that the tender branch thereof will not cease.
But man dieth and wasteth away; yea, man giveth up the ghost, and where is he?
As the waters hail from the sea, and the flood decayeth and drieth up, so man lieth down, and riseth not till the heavens be no more.

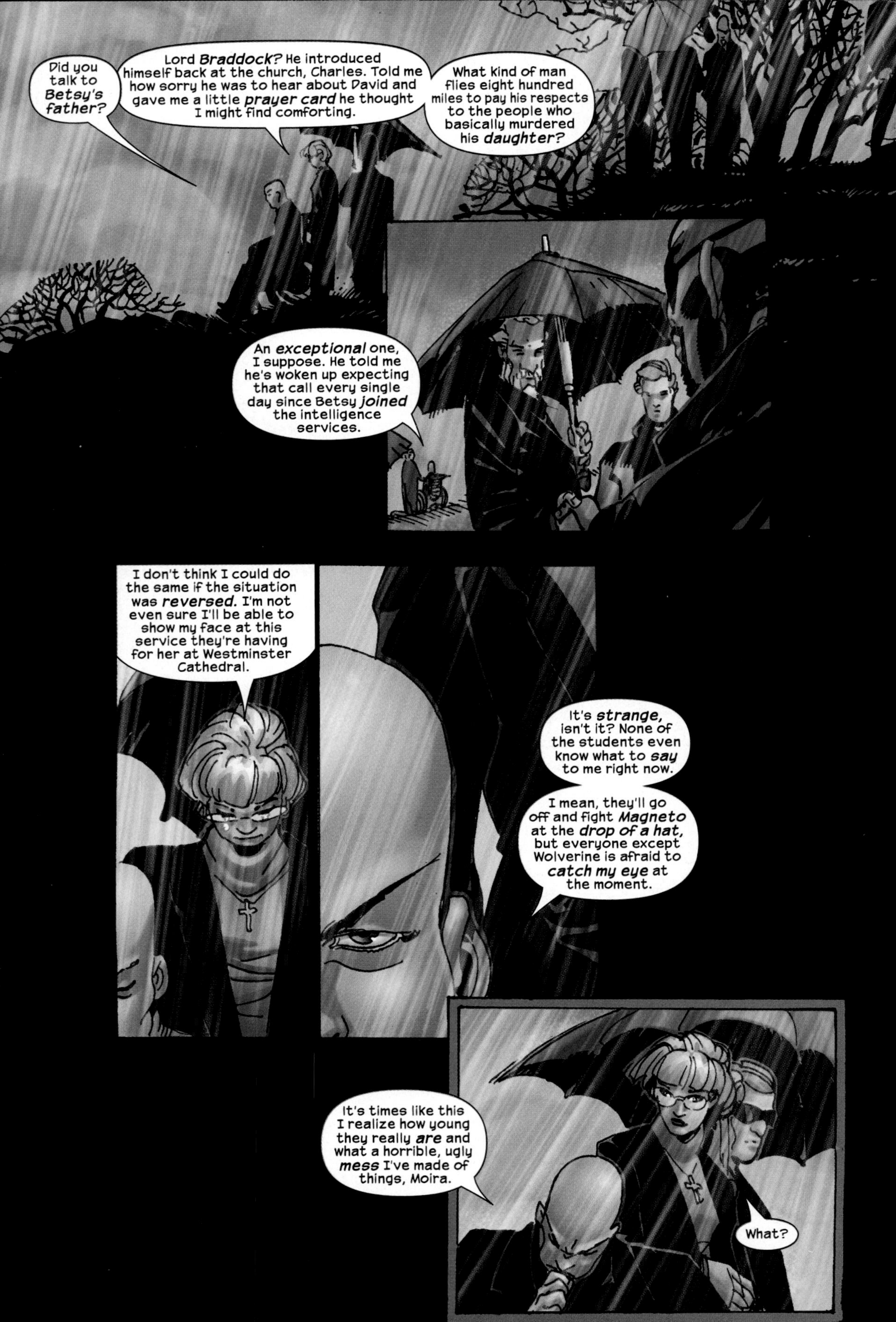
Did you talk to Betsy's father?
Lord Braddock? He introduced himself back at the church, Charles. Told me how sorry he was to hear about David and gave me a little prayer card he thought I might find comforting.
What kind of man flies eight hundred miles to pay his respects to the people who basically murdered his daughter?
An exceptional one, I suppose. He told me he's woken up expecting that call every single day since Betsy joined the intelligence services.
I don't think I could do the same if the situation was reversed. I'm not even sure I'll be able to show my face at this service they're having for her at Westminster Cathedral.
It's strange, isn't it? None of the students even know what to say to me right now.
I mean, they'll go off and fight Magneto at the drop of a hat, but everyone except Wolverine is afraid to catch my eye at the moment.
It's times like this I realize how young they really are and what a horrible, ugly mess I've made of things, Moira.
What?

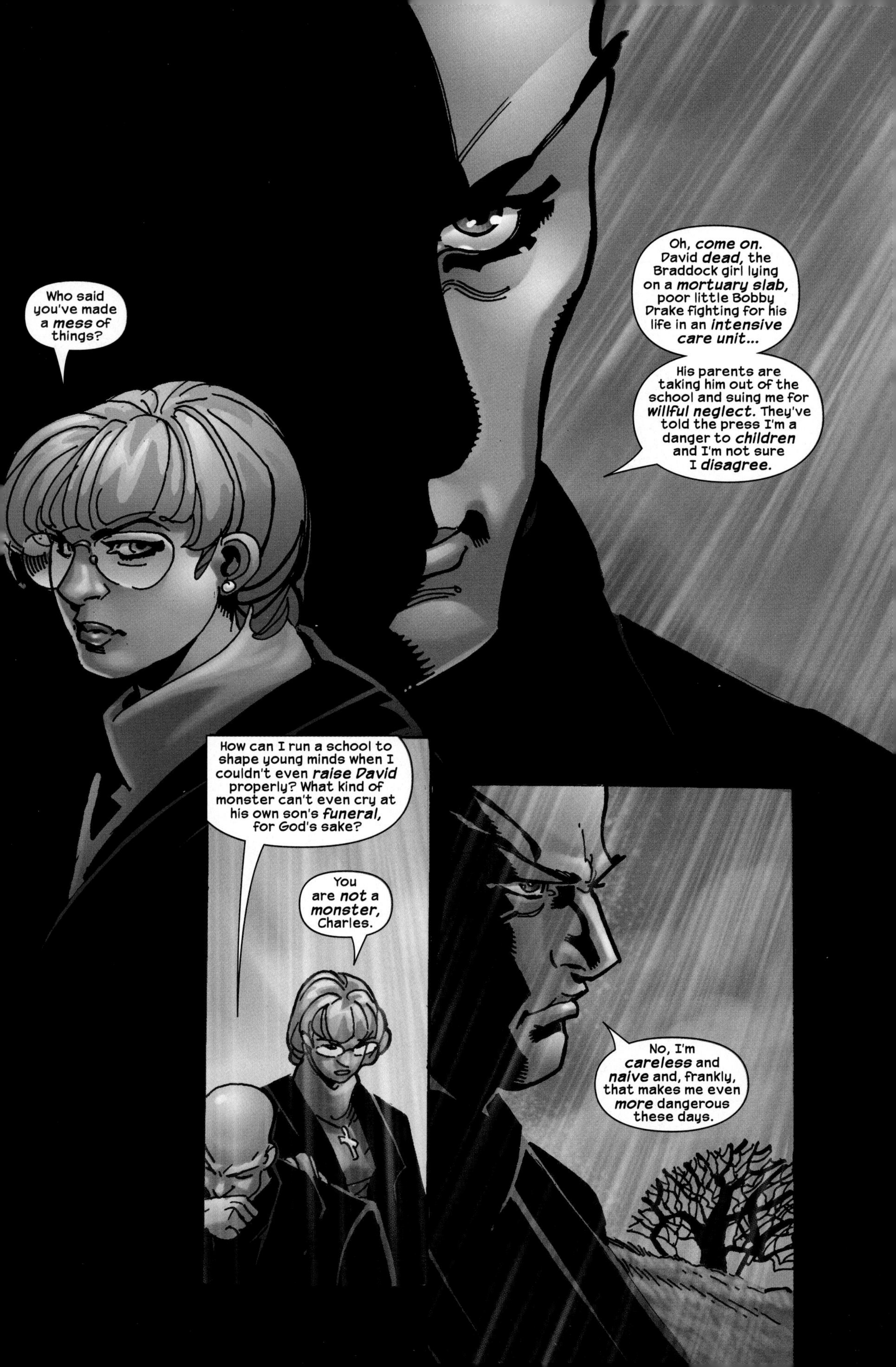
Who said you've made a mess of things?
Oh, come on. David dead, the Braddock girl lying on a mortuary slab, poor little Bobby Drake fighting for his life in an intensive care unit...
His parents are taking him out of the school and suing me for willful neglect. They've told the press I'm a danger to children and I'm not sure I disagree.
How can I run a school to shape young minds when I couldn't even raise David properly? What kind of monster can't even cry at his own son's funeral, for God's sake?
You are not a monster, Charles.
No, I'm careless and naive and, frankly, that makes me even more dangerous these days.

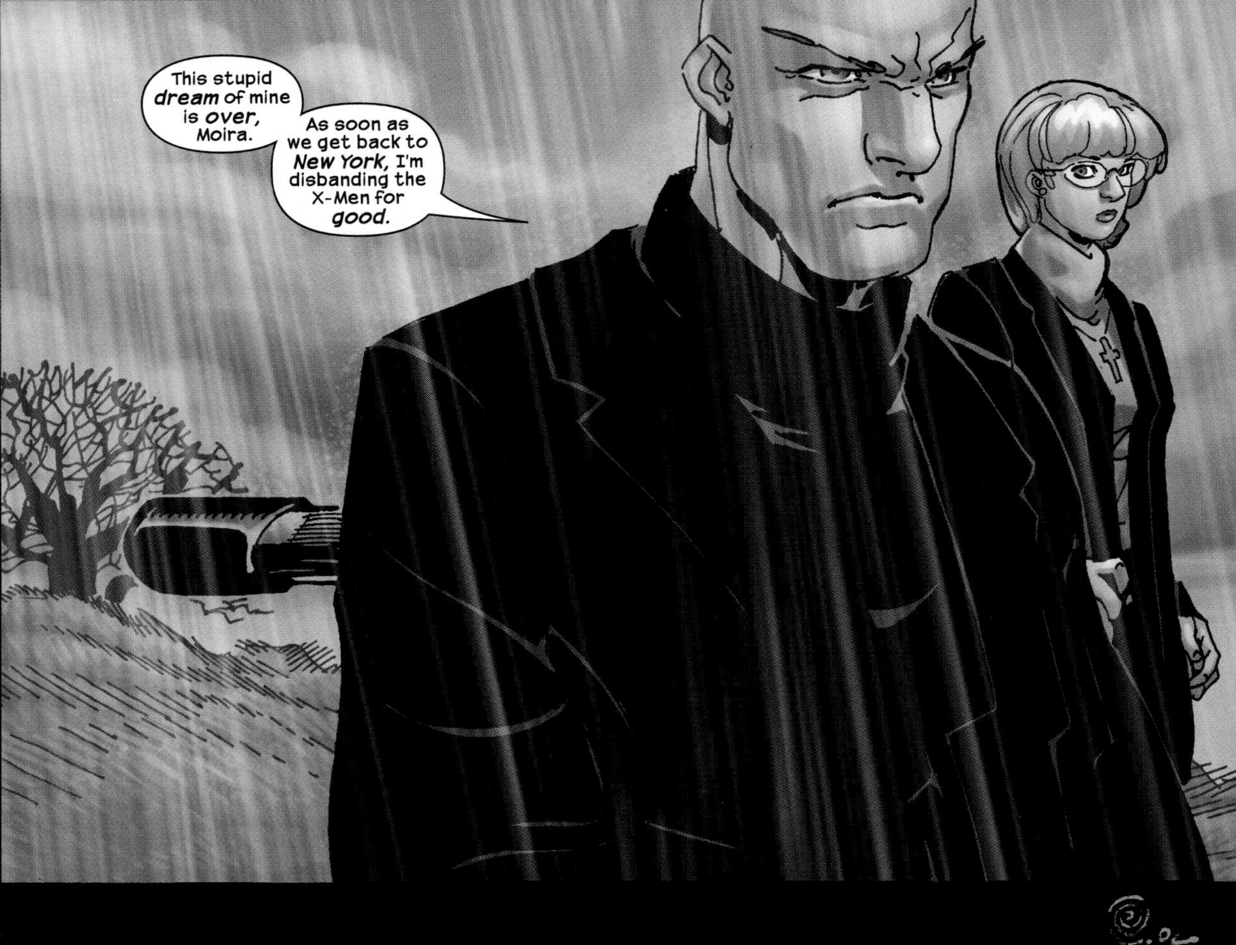
This stupid *dream* of mine is *over,* Moira.
As soon as we get back to *New York,* I'm disbanding the X-Men for *good.*

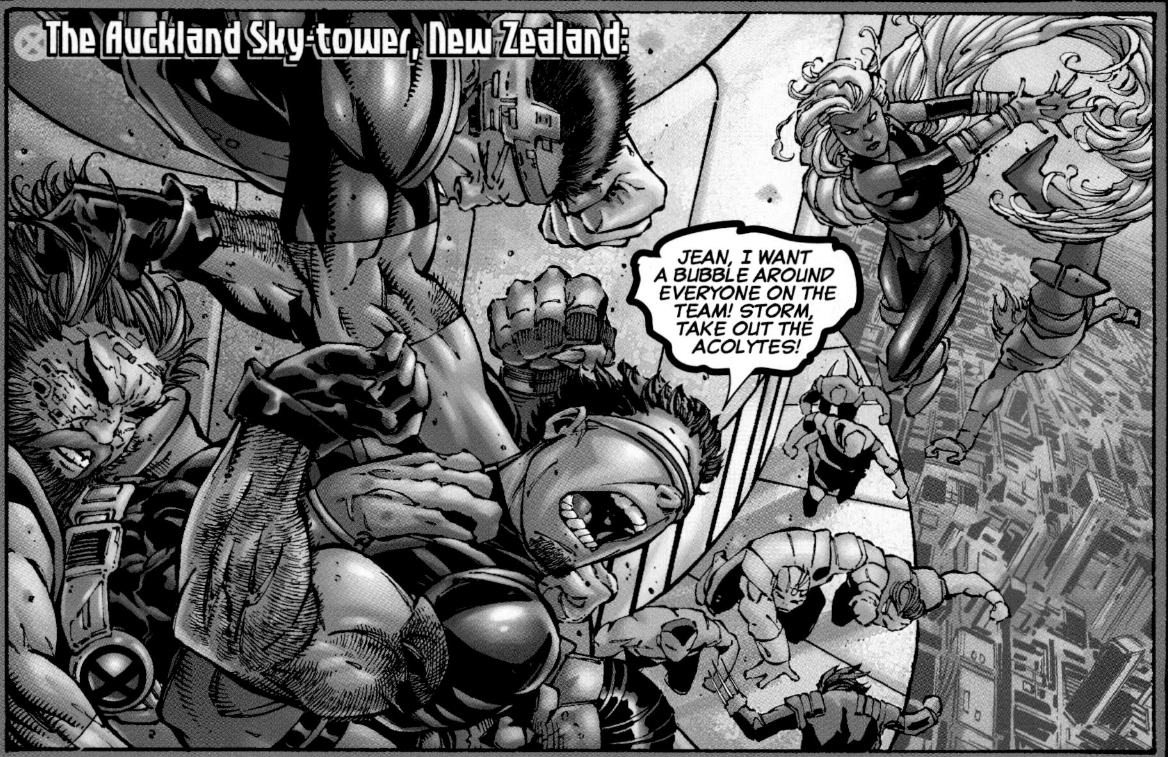
The Auckland Sky-tower, New Zealand:
JEAN, I WANT A BUBBLE AROUND EVERYONE ON THE TEAM! STORM, TAKE OUT THE ACOLYTES!

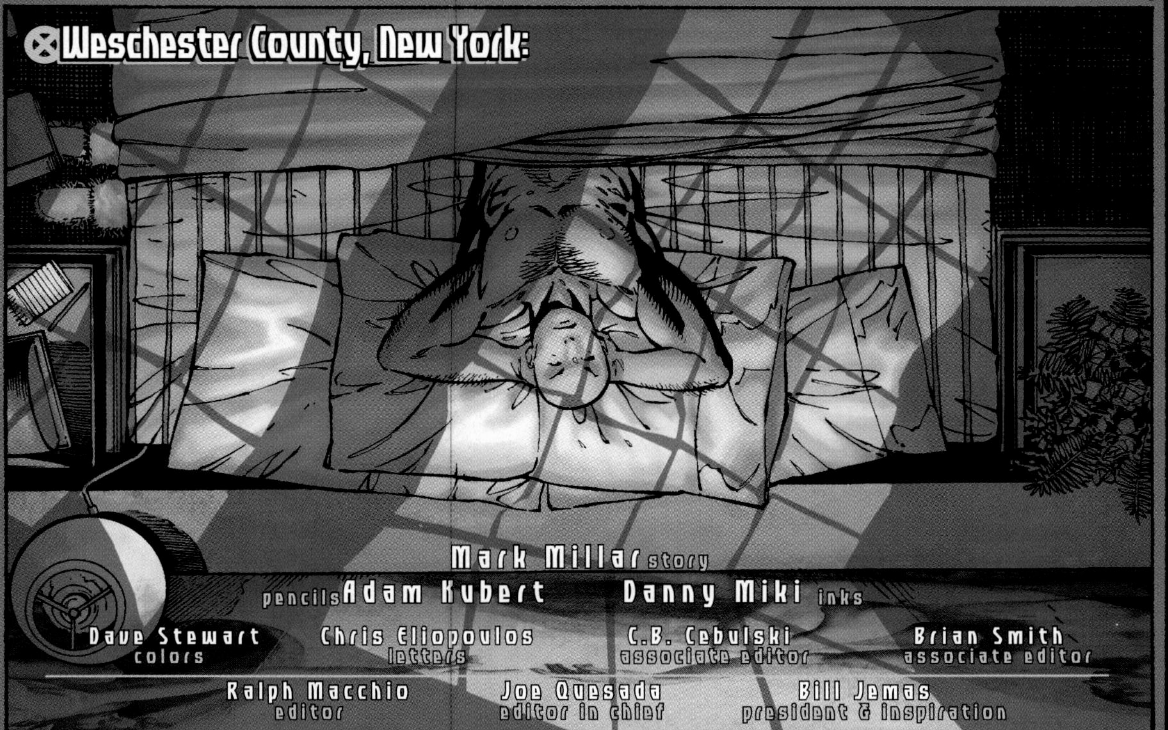
Weschester County, New York:
Mark Millar story
pencils Adam Kubert
Danny Miki inks
Dave Stewart colors
Chris Eliopoulos letters
C.B. Cebulski associate editor
Brian Smith associate editor
Ralph Macchio editor
Joe Quesada editor in chief
Bill Jemas president & inspiration

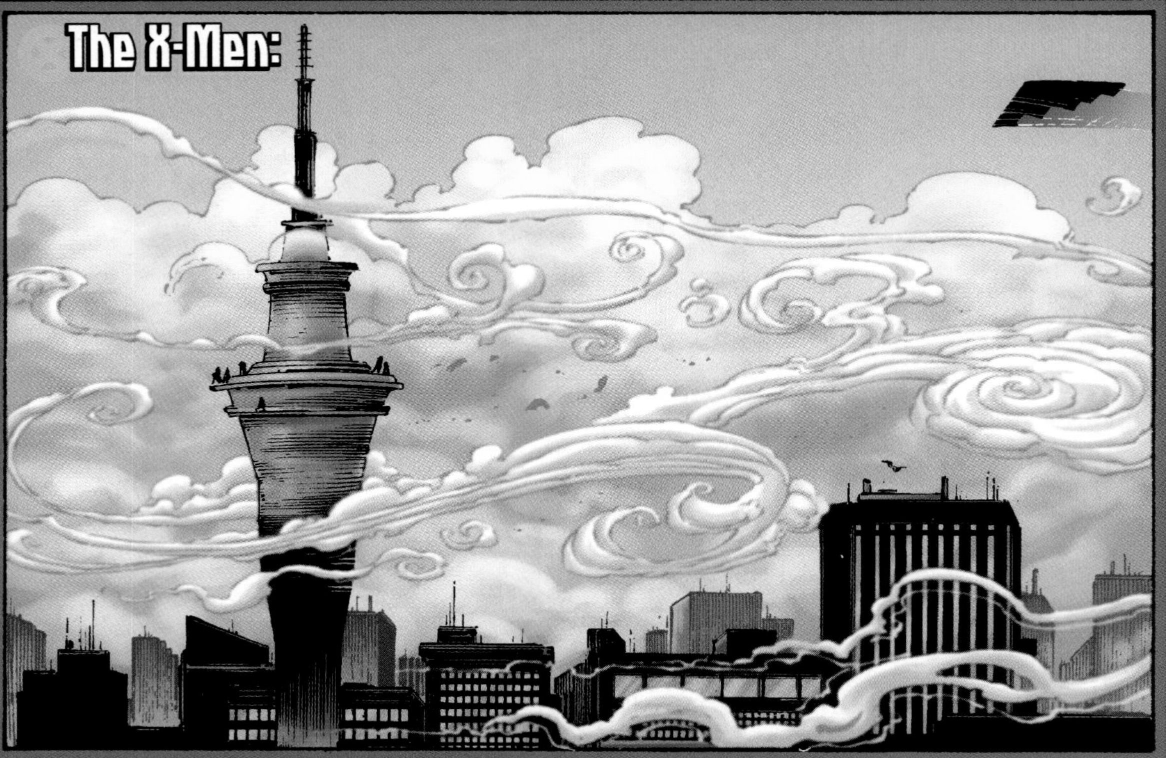
The X-Men:

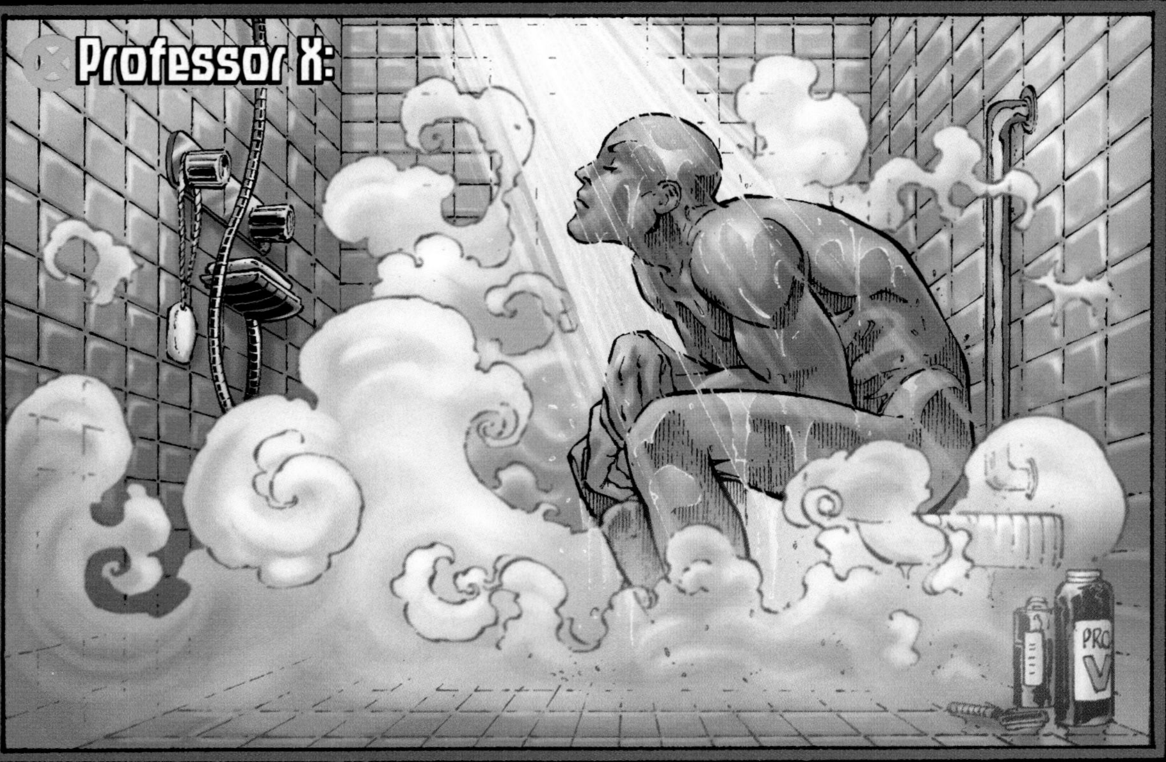
Professor X:

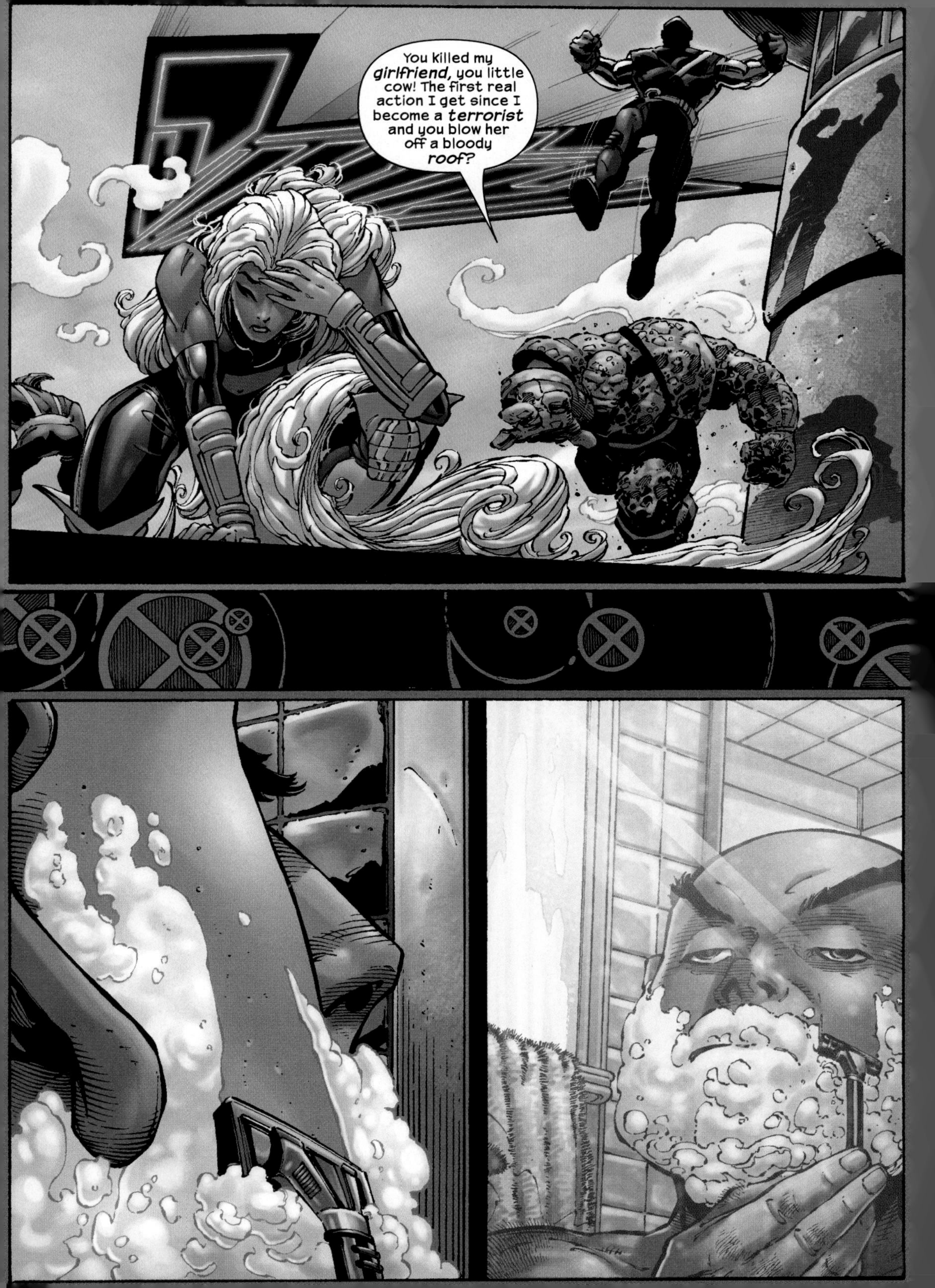
You killed my girlfriend, you little cow! The first real action I get since I become a terrorist and you blow her off a bloody roof?

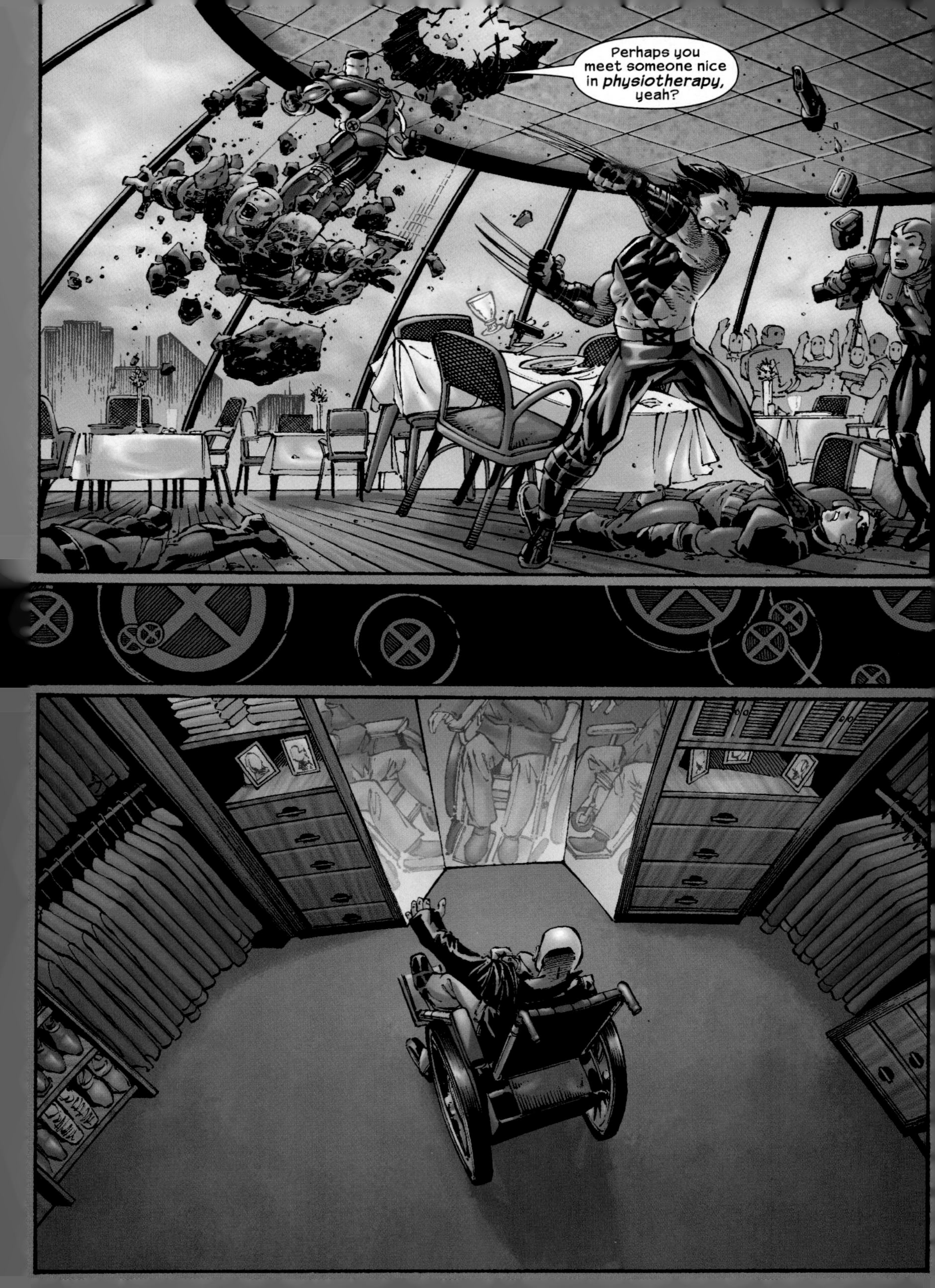
Perhaps you meet someone nice in *physiotherapy,* yeah?

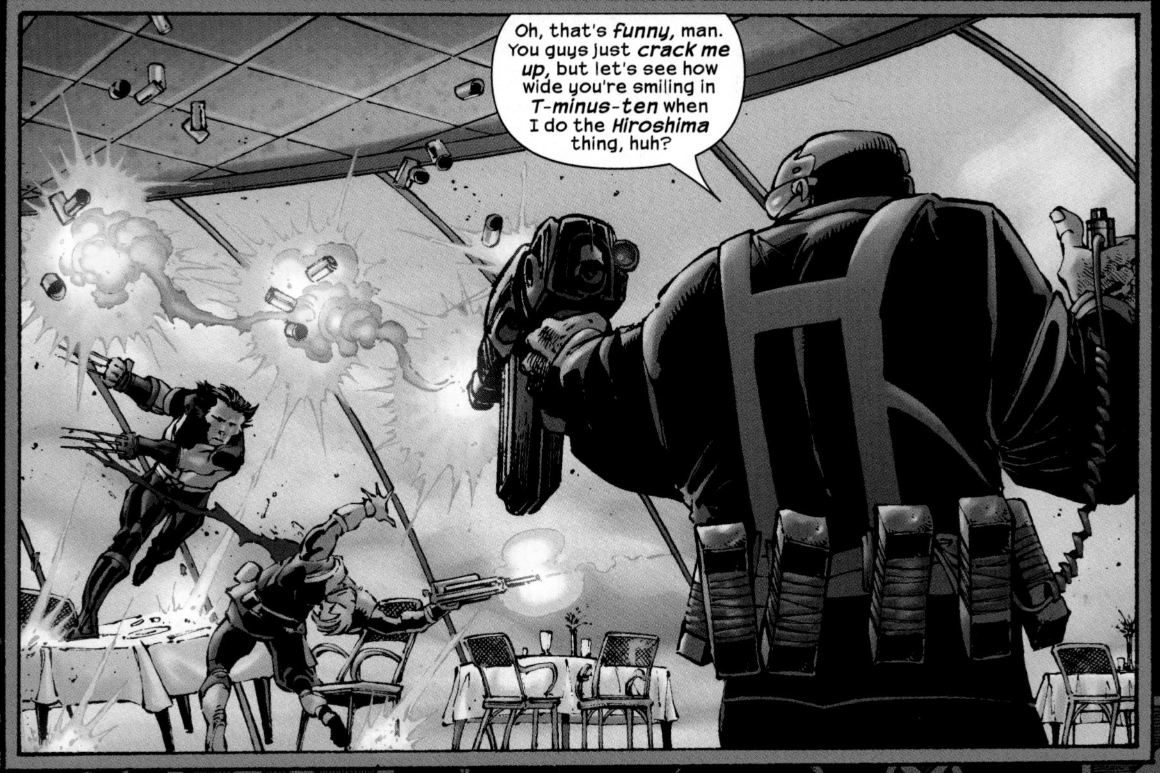
Oh, that's *funny,* man. You guys just *crack me up,* but let's see how wide you're smiling in *T-minus-ten* when I do the *Hiroshima* thing, huh?

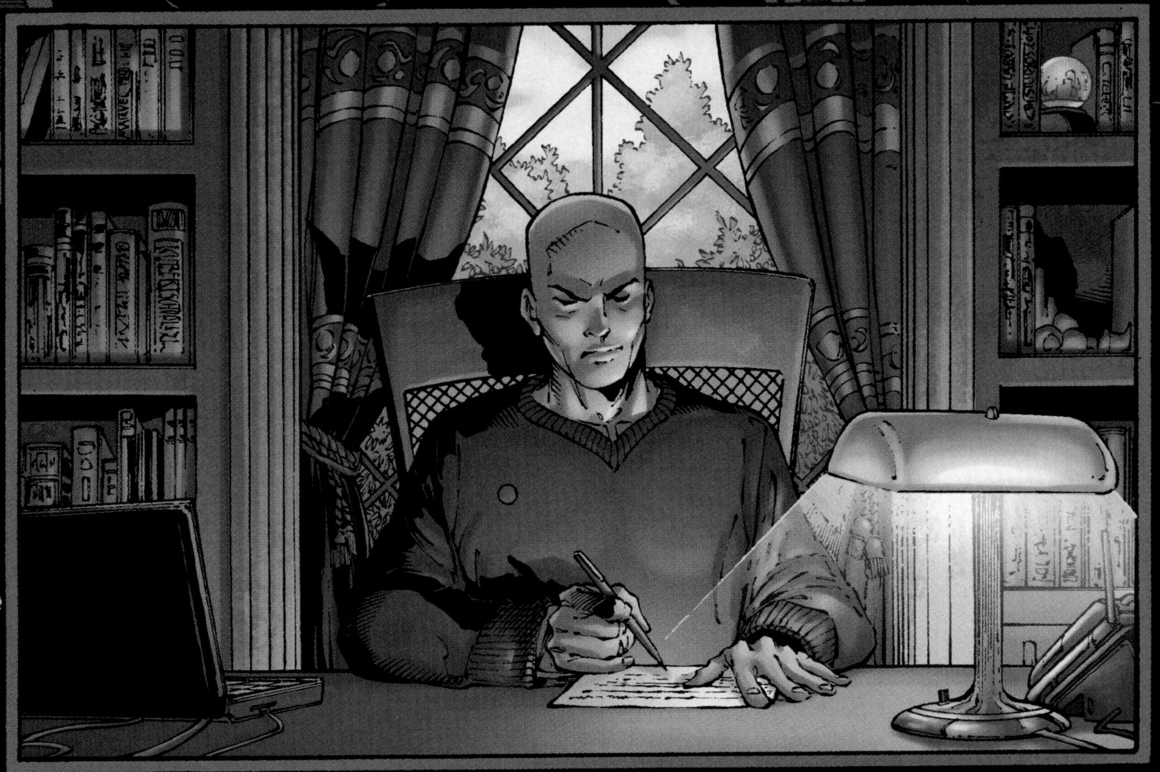

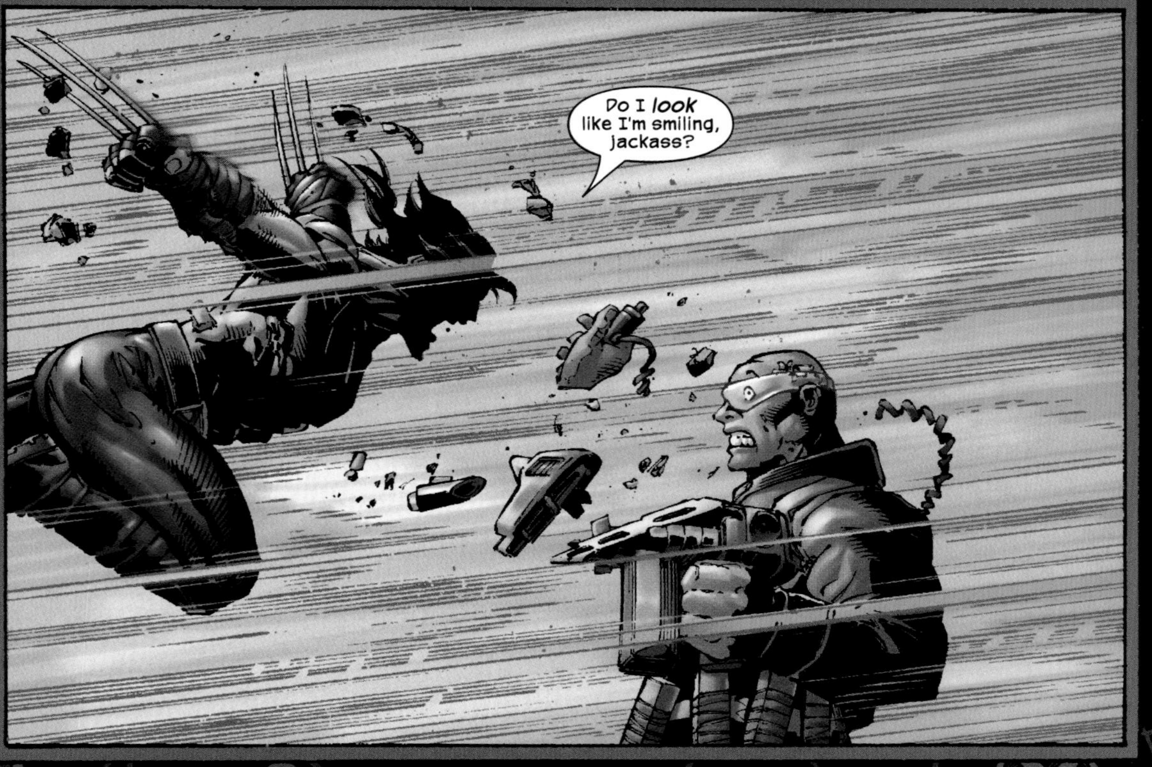
Do I *look* like I'm smiling, jackass?

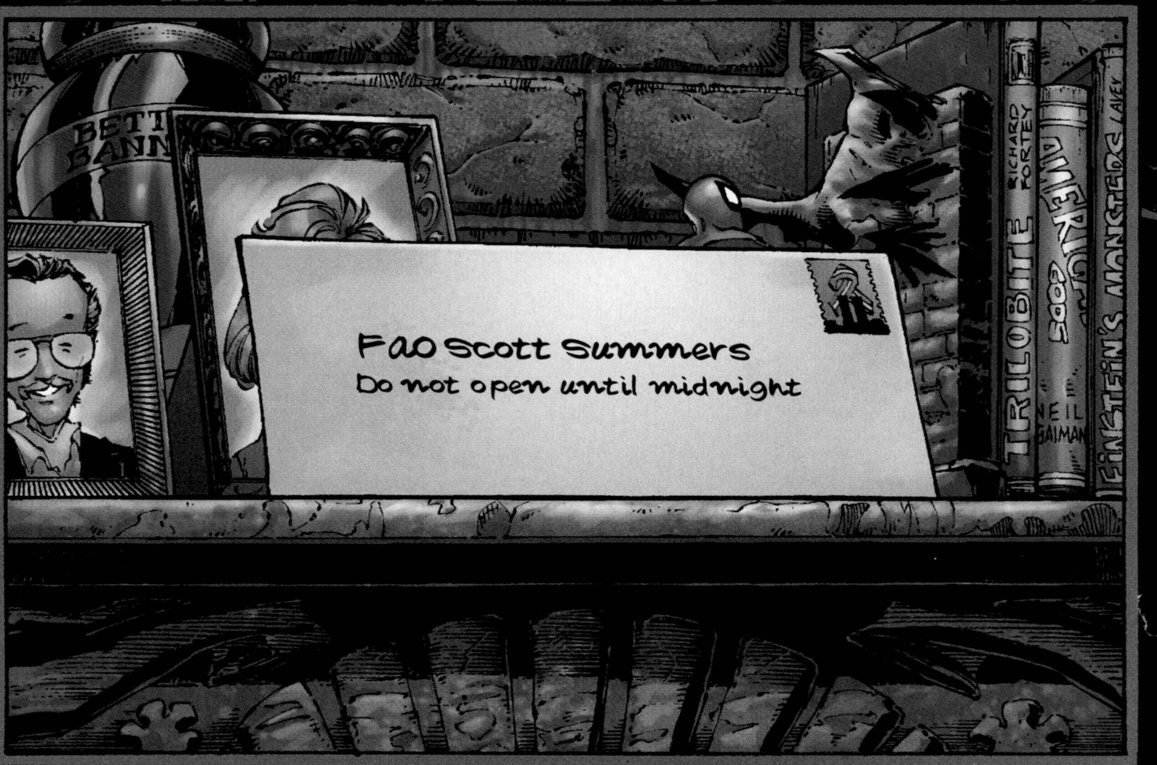
FAO Scott Summers
Do not open until midnight
TRILOBITE
RICHARD FORTEY
NEIL GAIMAN
EINSTEIN'S MONSTERS

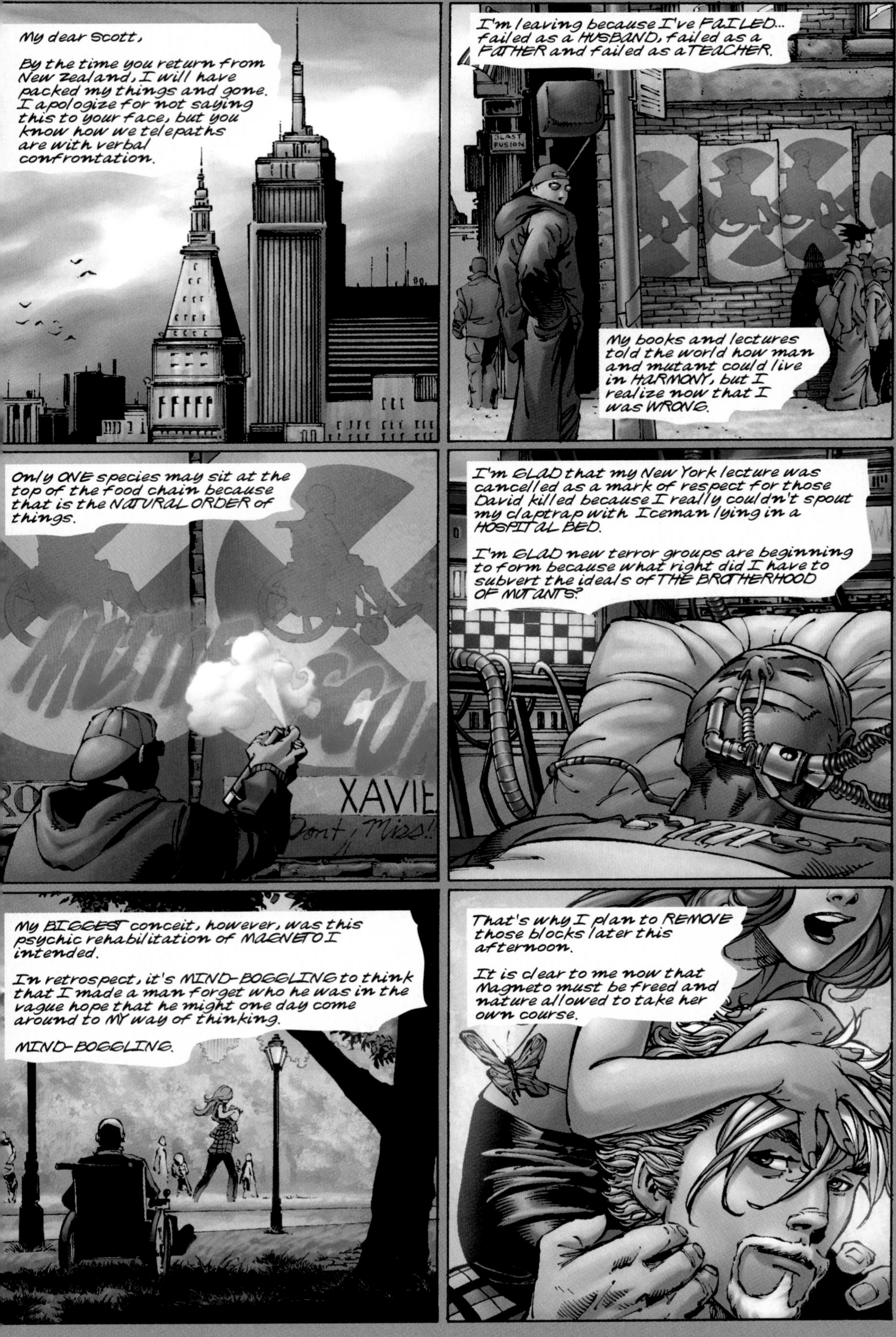
My dear Scott,
By the time you return from New Zealand, I will have packed my things and gone. I apologize for not saying this to your face, but you know how we telepaths are with verbal confrontation.
I'm leaving because I've FAILED... failed as a HUSBAND, failed as a FATHER and failed as a TEACHER.
BLAST FUSION
My books and lectures told the world how man and mutant could live in HARMONY, but I realize now that I was WRONG.
Only ONE species may sit at the top of the food chain because that is the NATURAL ORDER of things.
XAVIE
Dont Miss!
I'm GLAD that my New York lecture was cancelled as a mark of respect for those David killed because I really couldn't spout my claptrap with Iceman lying in a HOSPITAL BED.
I'm GLAD new terror groups are beginning to form because what right did I have to subvert the ideals of THE BROTHERHOOD OF MUTANTS?
My BIGGEST conceit, however, was this psychic rehabilitation of MAGNETO I intended.
In retrospect, it's MIND-BOGGLING to think that I made a man forget who he was in the vague hope that he might one day come around to MY way of thinking.
MIND-BOGGLING.
That's why I plan to REMOVE those blocks later this afternoon.
It is clear to me now that Magneto must be freed and nature allowed to take her own course.

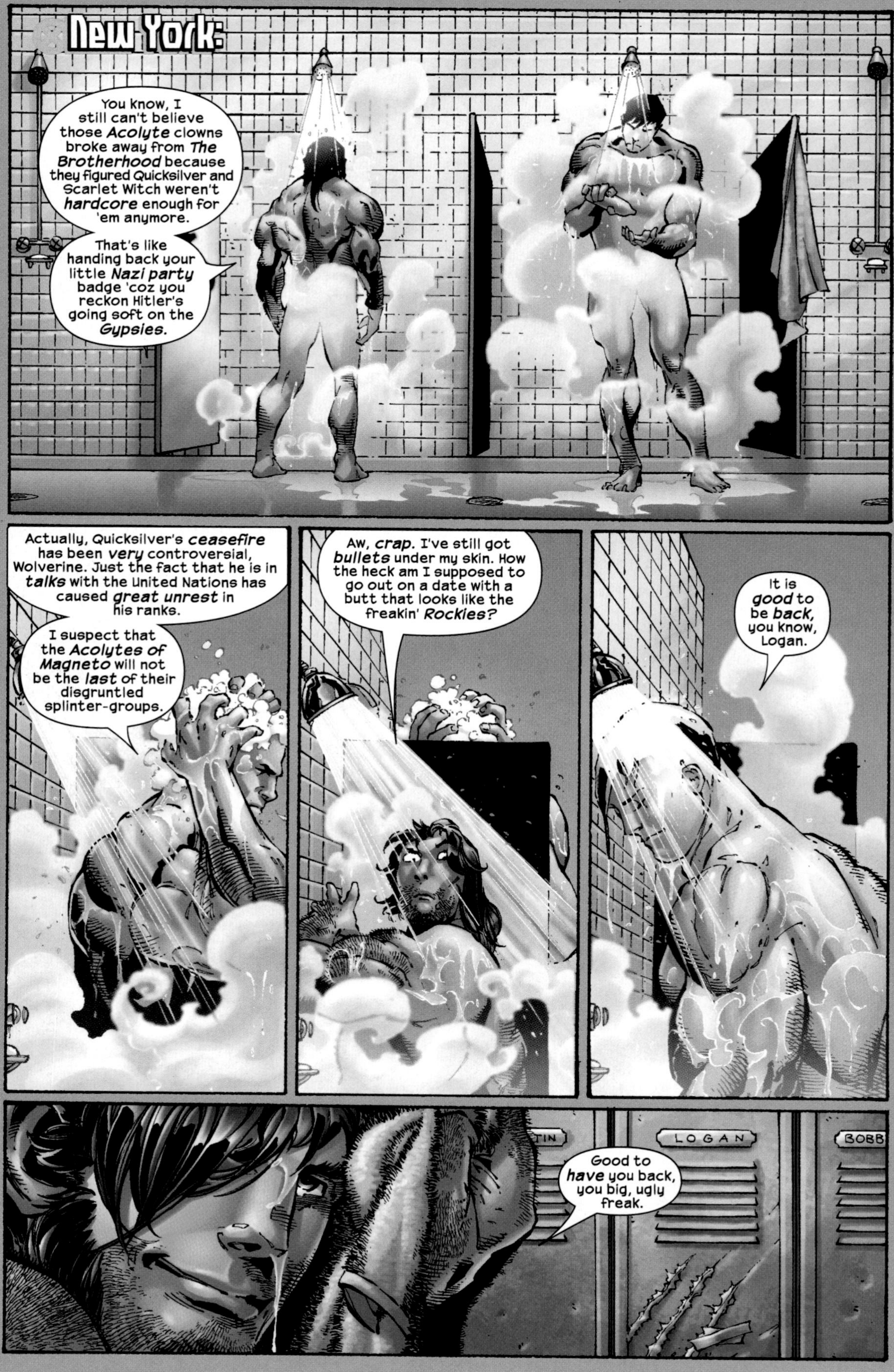
New York:
You know, I still can't believe those Acolyte clowns broke away from The Brotherhood because they figured Quicksilver and Scarlet Witch weren't hardcore enough for 'em anymore.
That's like handing back your little Nazi party badge 'coz you reckon Hitler's going soft on the Gypsies.
Actually, Quicksilver's ceasefire has been very controversial, Wolverine. Just the fact that he is in talks with the United Nations has caused great unrest in his ranks.
I suspect that the Acolytes of Magneto will not be the last of their disgruntled splinter-groups.
Aw, crap. I've still got bullets under my skin. How the heck am I supposed to go out on a date with a butt that looks like the freakin' Rockies?
It is good to be back, you know, Logan.
TIN
LOGAN
BOBB
Good to have you back, you big, ugly freak.

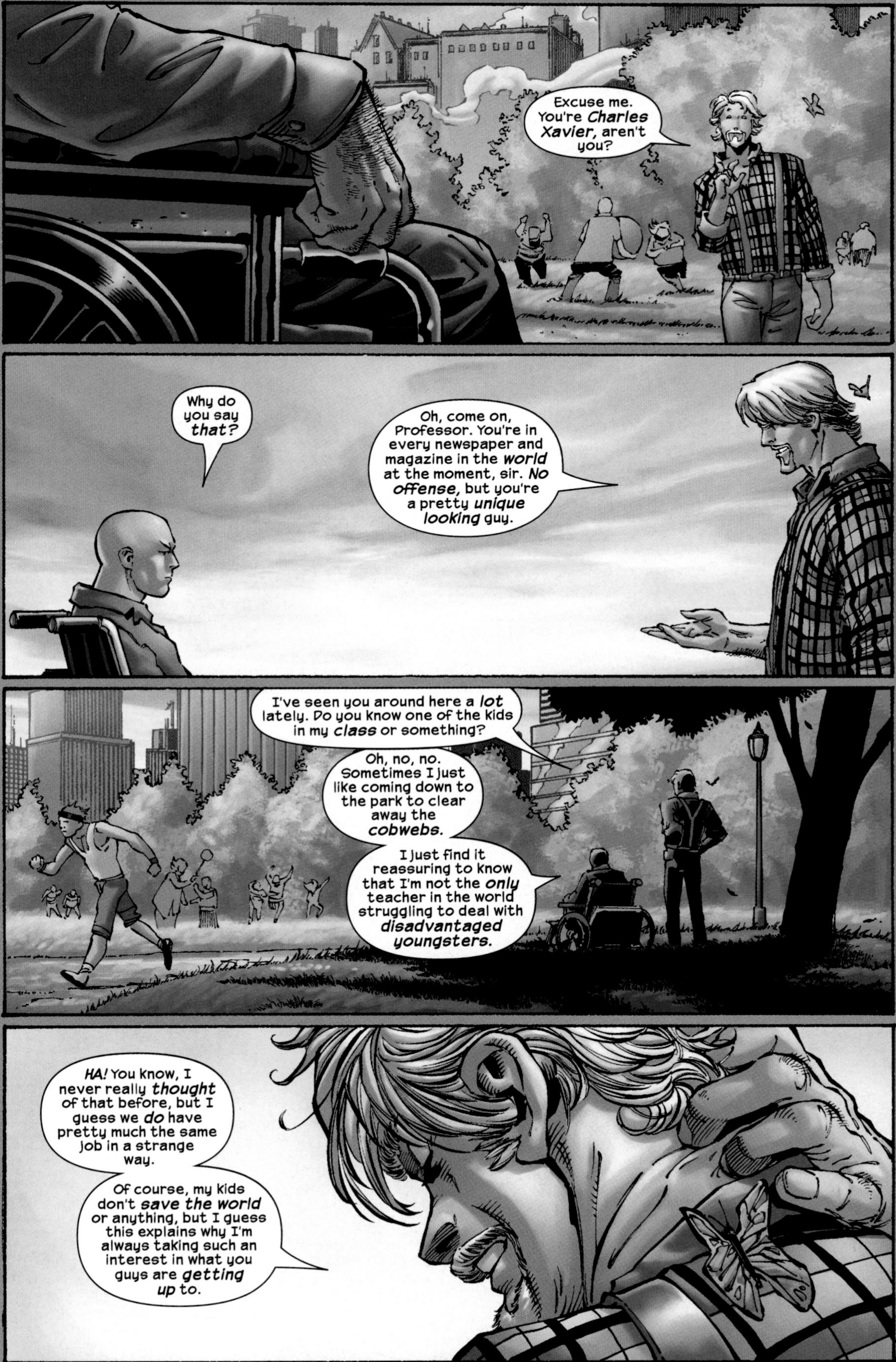

Excuse me. You're *Charles Xavier*, aren't you?
Why do you say *that?*
Oh, come on, Professor. You're in every newspaper and magazine in the *world* at the moment, sir. *No offense,* but you're a pretty *unique looking* guy.
I've seen you around here a *lot* lately. Do you know one of the kids in my *class* or something?
Oh, no, no. Sometimes I just like coming down to the park to clear away the *cobwebs.*
I just find it reassuring to know that I'm not the *only* teacher in the world struggling to deal with *disadvantaged youngsters.*
HA! You know, I never really *thought* of that before, but I guess we *do* have pretty much the same job in a strange way.
Of course, my kids don't *save the world* or anything, but I guess this explains why I'm always taking such an interest in what you guys are *getting up* to.

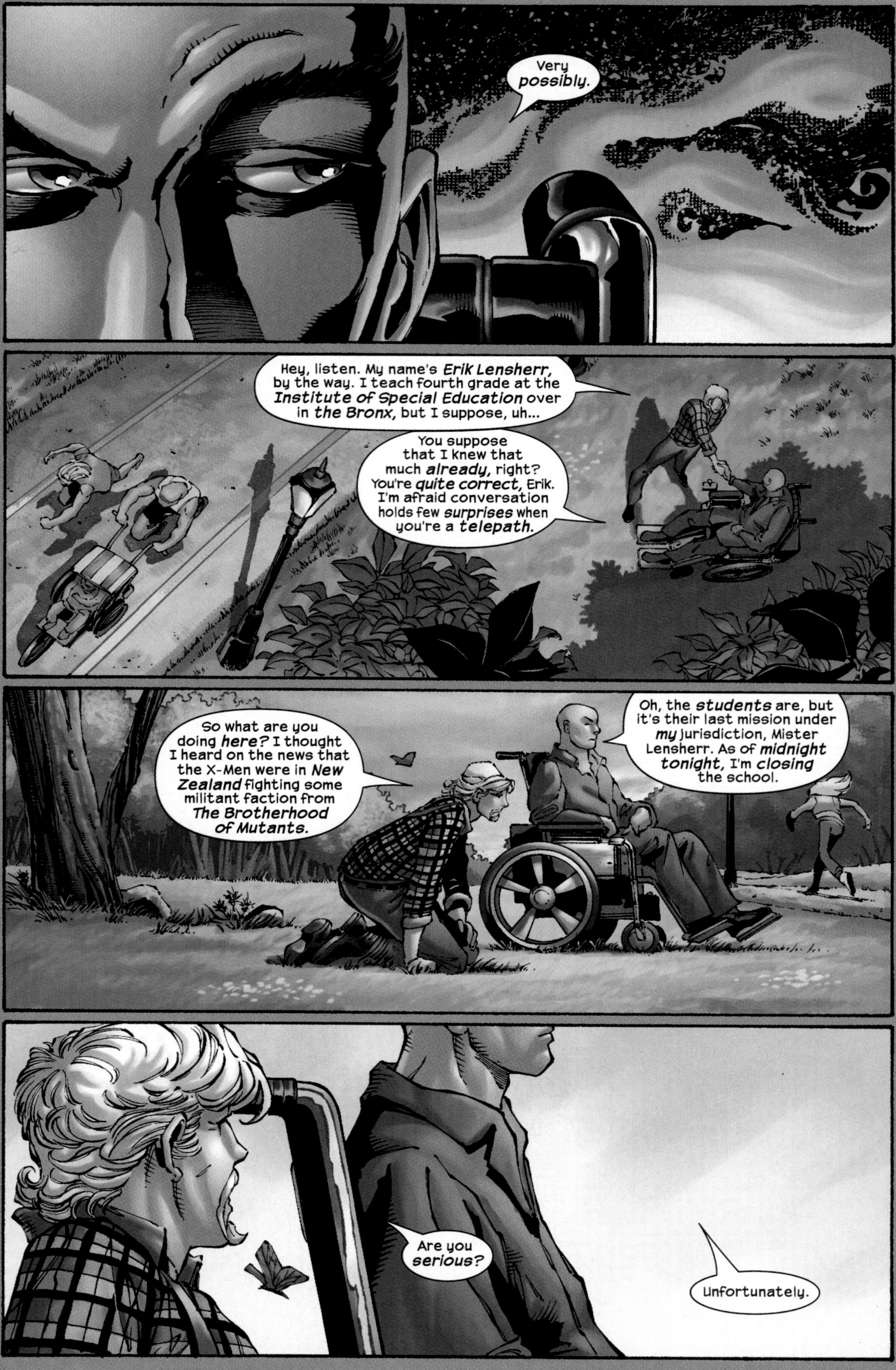

Very possibly.
Hey, listen. My name's Erik Lensherr, by the way. I teach fourth grade at the Institute of Special Education over in the Bronx, but I suppose, uh...
You suppose that I knew that much already, right? You're quite correct, Erik. I'm afraid conversation holds few surprises when you're a telepath.
So what are you doing here? I thought I heard on the news that the X-Men were in New Zealand fighting some militant faction from The Brotherhood of Mutants.
Oh, the students are, but it's their last mission under my jurisdiction, Mister Lensherr. As of midnight tonight, I'm closing the school.
Are you serious?
Unfortunately.

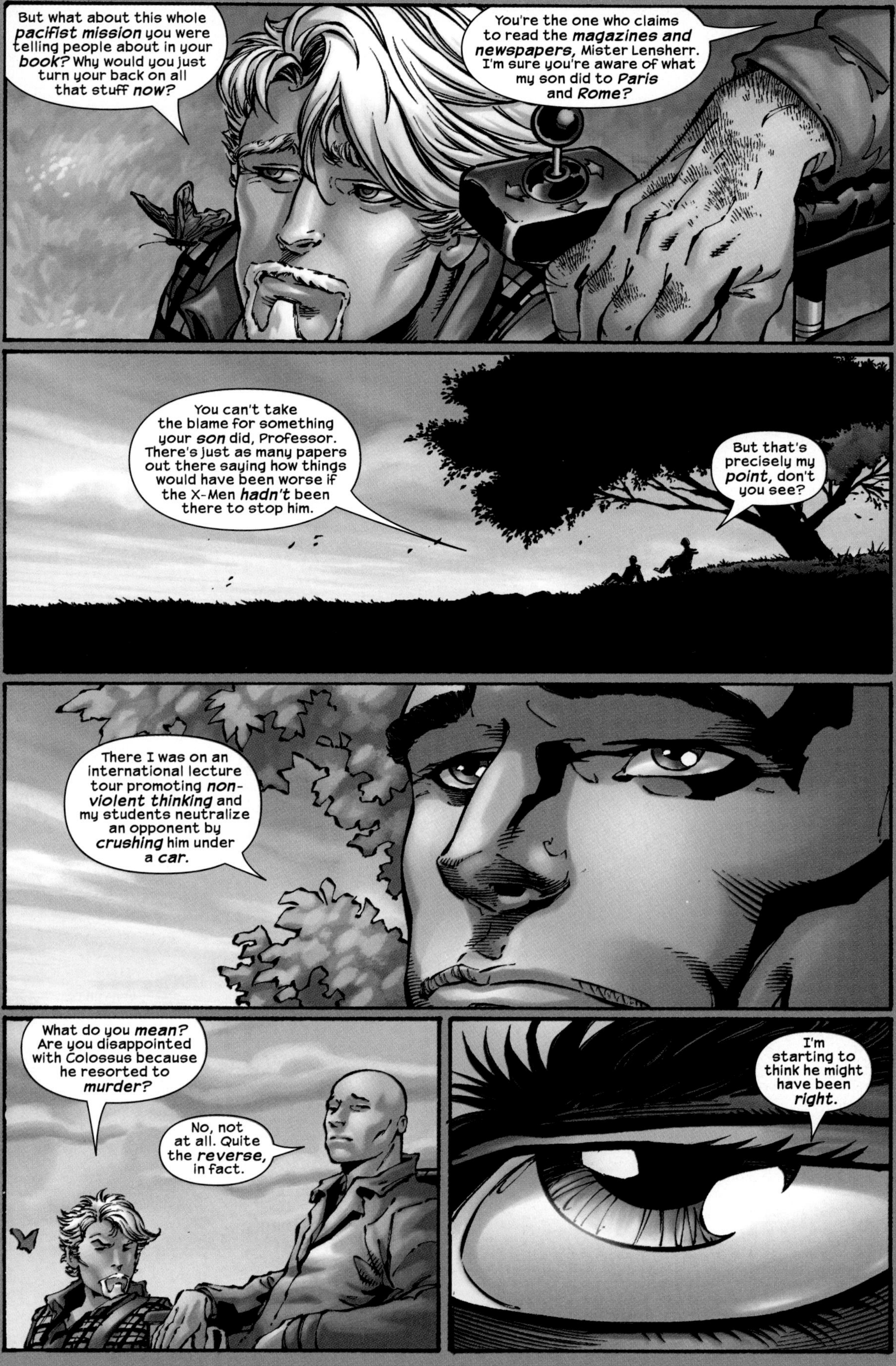

But what about this whole pacifist mission you were telling people about in your book? Why would you just turn your back on all that stuff now?
You're the one who claims to read the magazines and newspapers, Mister Lensherr. I'm sure you're aware of what my son did to Paris and Rome?
You can't take the blame for something your son did, Professor. There's just as many papers out there saying how things would have been worse if the X-Men hadn't been there to stop him.
But that's precisely my point, don't you see?
There I was on an international lecture tour promoting non-violent thinking and my students neutralize an opponent by crushing him under a car.
What do you mean? Are you disappointed with Colossus because he resorted to murder?
No, not at all. Quite the reverse, in fact.
I'm starting to think he might have been right.

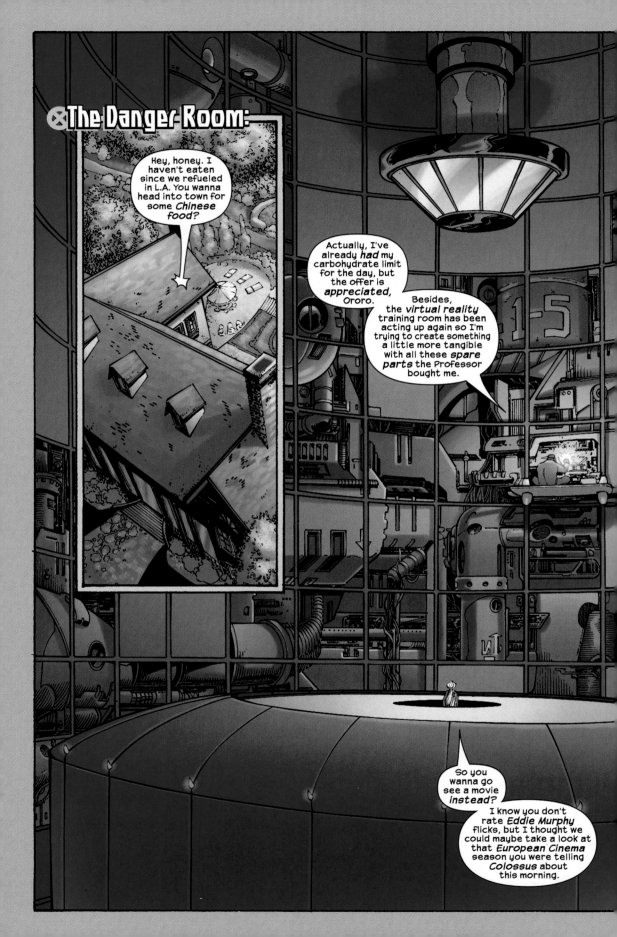

The Danger Room:

Hey, honey. I haven't eaten since we refueled in L.A. You wanna head into town for some *Chinese food?*

Actually, I've already *had* my carbohydrate limit for the day, but the offer is *appreciated*, Ororo.

Besides, the *virtual reality* training room has been acting up again so I'm trying to create something a little more tangible with all these *spare parts* the Professor bought me.

So you wanna go see a movie *instead?*

I know you don't rate *Eddie Murphy* flicks, but I thought we could maybe take a look at that *European Cinema* season you were telling *Colossus* about this morning.

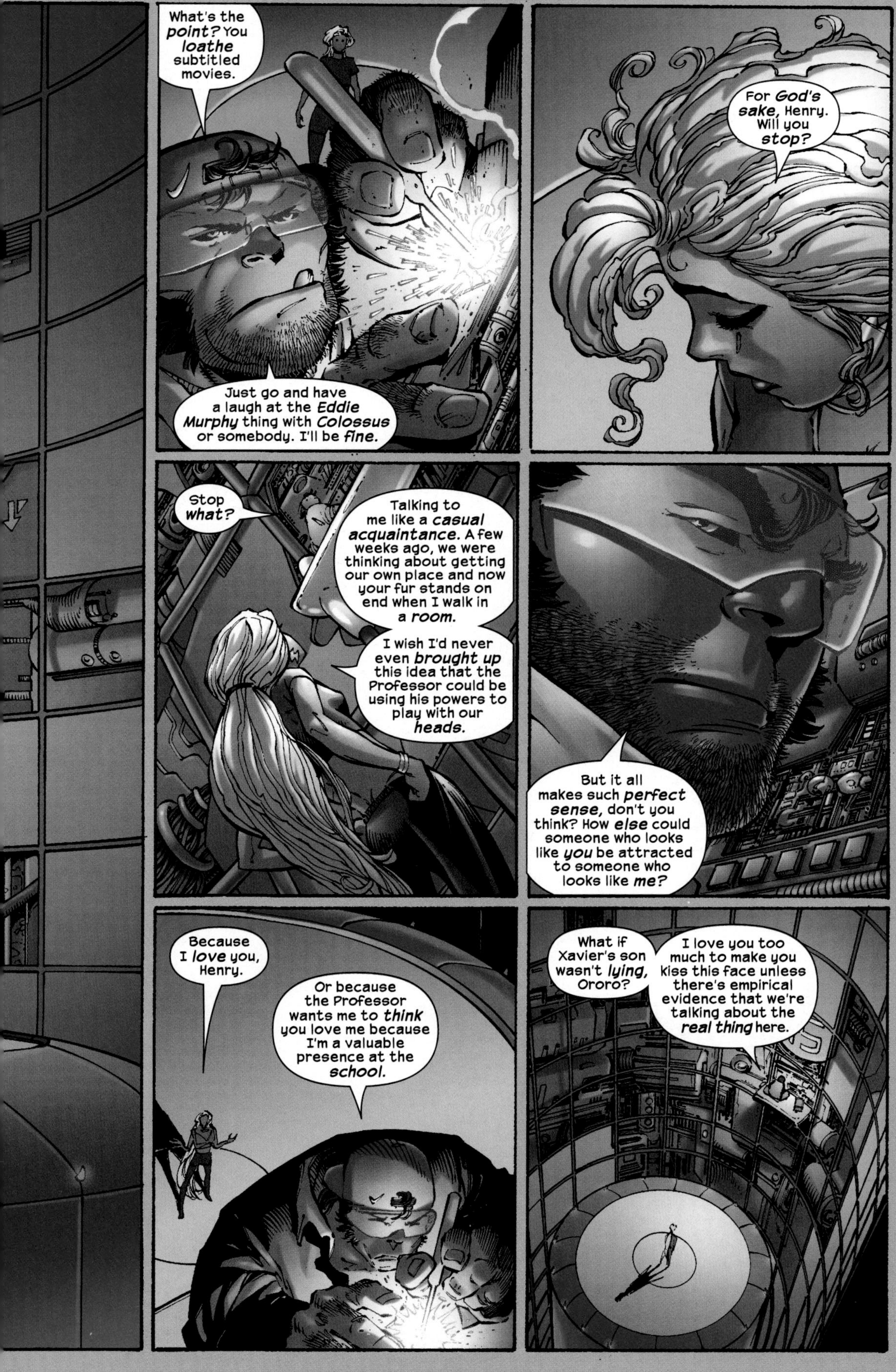

What's the point? You loathe subtitled movies.
Just go and have a laugh at the Eddie Murphy thing with Colossus or somebody. I'll be fine.
For God's sake, Henry. Will you stop?
Stop what?
Talking to me like a casual acquaintance. A few weeks ago, we were thinking about getting our own place and now your fur stands on end when I walk in a room.
I wish I'd never even brought up this idea that the Professor could be using his powers to play with our heads.
But it all makes such perfect sense, don't you think? How else could someone who looks like you be attracted to someone who looks like me?
Because I love you, Henry.
Or because the Professor wants me to think you love me because I'm a valuable presence at the school.
What if Xavier's son wasn't lying, Ororo?
I love you too much to make you kiss this face unless there's empirical evidence that we're talking about the real thing here.

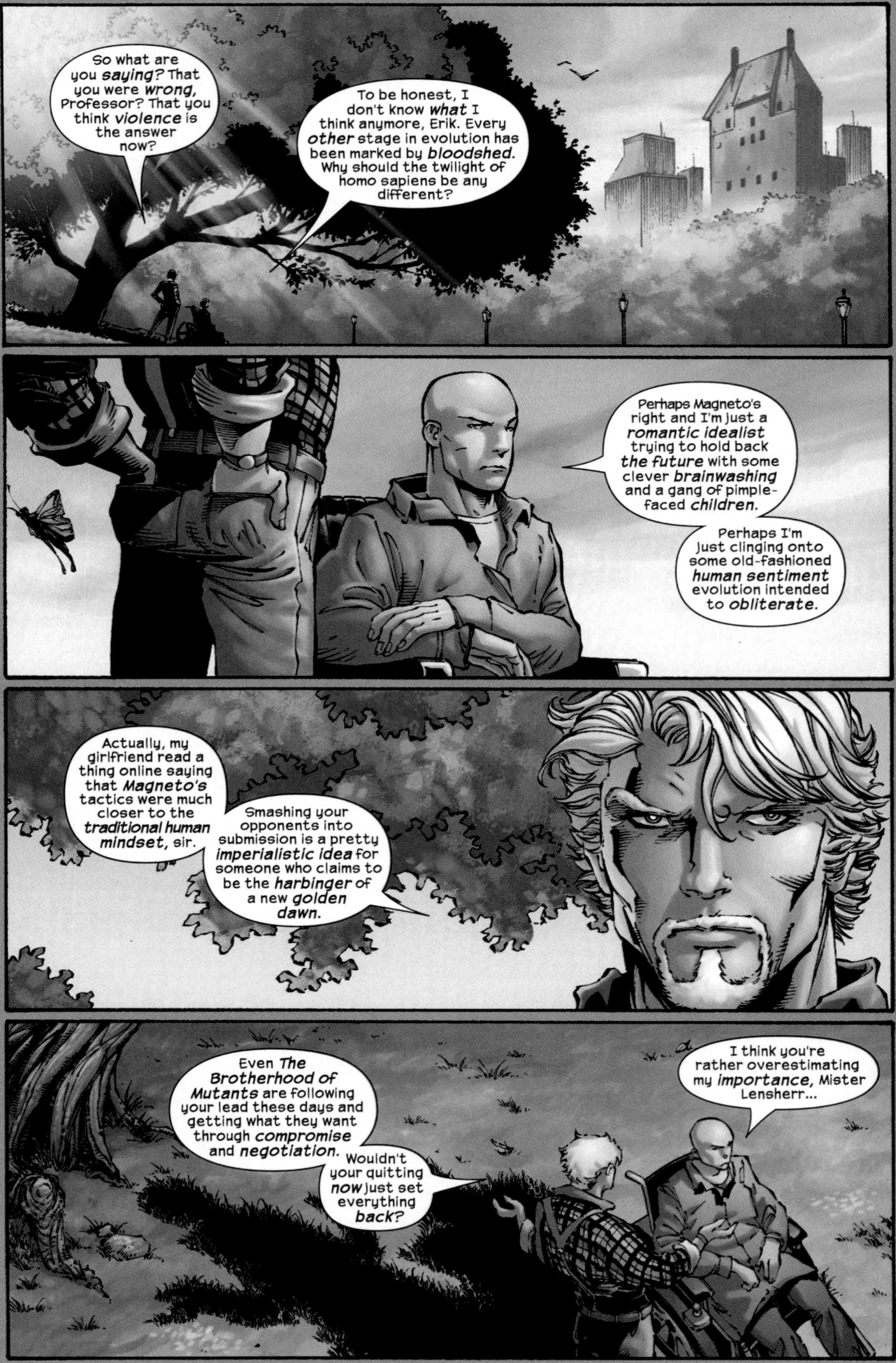

So what are you saying? That you were wrong, Professor? That you think violence is the answer now?
To be honest, I don't know what I think anymore, Erik. Every other stage in evolution has been marked by bloodshed. Why should the twilight of homo sapiens be any different?
Perhaps Magneto's right and I'm just a romantic idealist trying to hold back the future with some clever brainwashing and a gang of pimple-faced children.
Perhaps I'm just clinging onto some old-fashioned human sentiment evolution intended to obliterate.
Actually, my girlfriend read a thing online saying that Magneto's tactics were much closer to the traditional human mindset, sir.
Smashing your opponents into submission is a pretty imperialistic idea for someone who claims to be the harbinger of a new golden dawn.
Even The Brotherhood of Mutants are following your lead these days and getting what they want through compromise and negotiation.
Wouldn't your quitting now just set everything back?
I think you're rather overestimating my importance, Mister Lensherr...

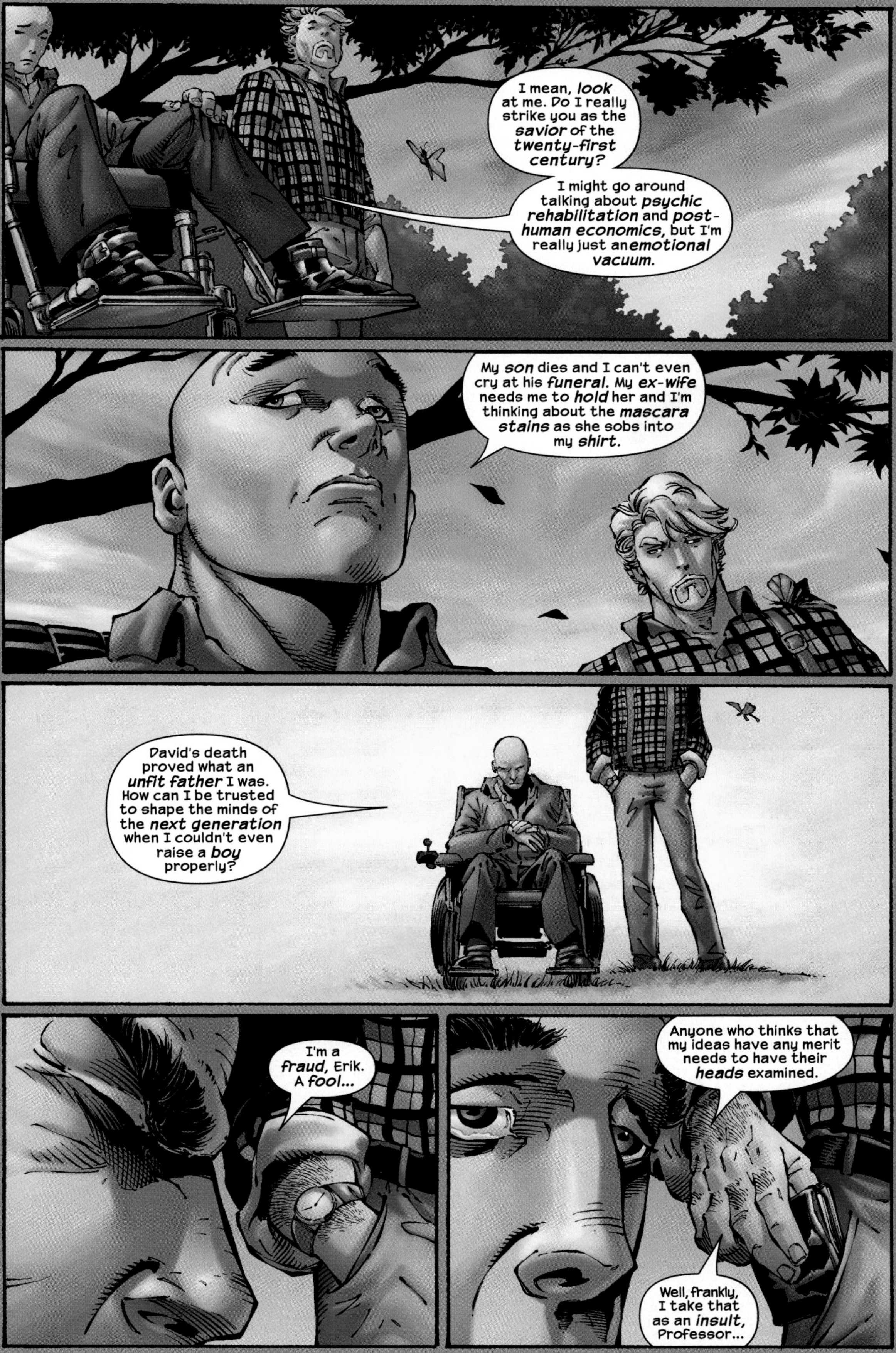
I mean, look at me. Do I really strike you as the savior of the twenty-first century?
I might go around talking about psychic rehabilitation and post-human economics, but I'm really just an emotional vacuum.
My son dies and I can't even cry at his funeral. My ex-wife needs me to hold her and I'm thinking about the mascara stains as she sobs into my shirt.
David's death proved what an unfit father I was. How can I be trusted to shape the minds of the next generation when I couldn't even raise a boy properly?
I'm a fraud, Erik. A fool...
Anyone who thinks that my ideas have any merit needs to have their heads examined.
Well, frankly, I take that as an insult, Professor...

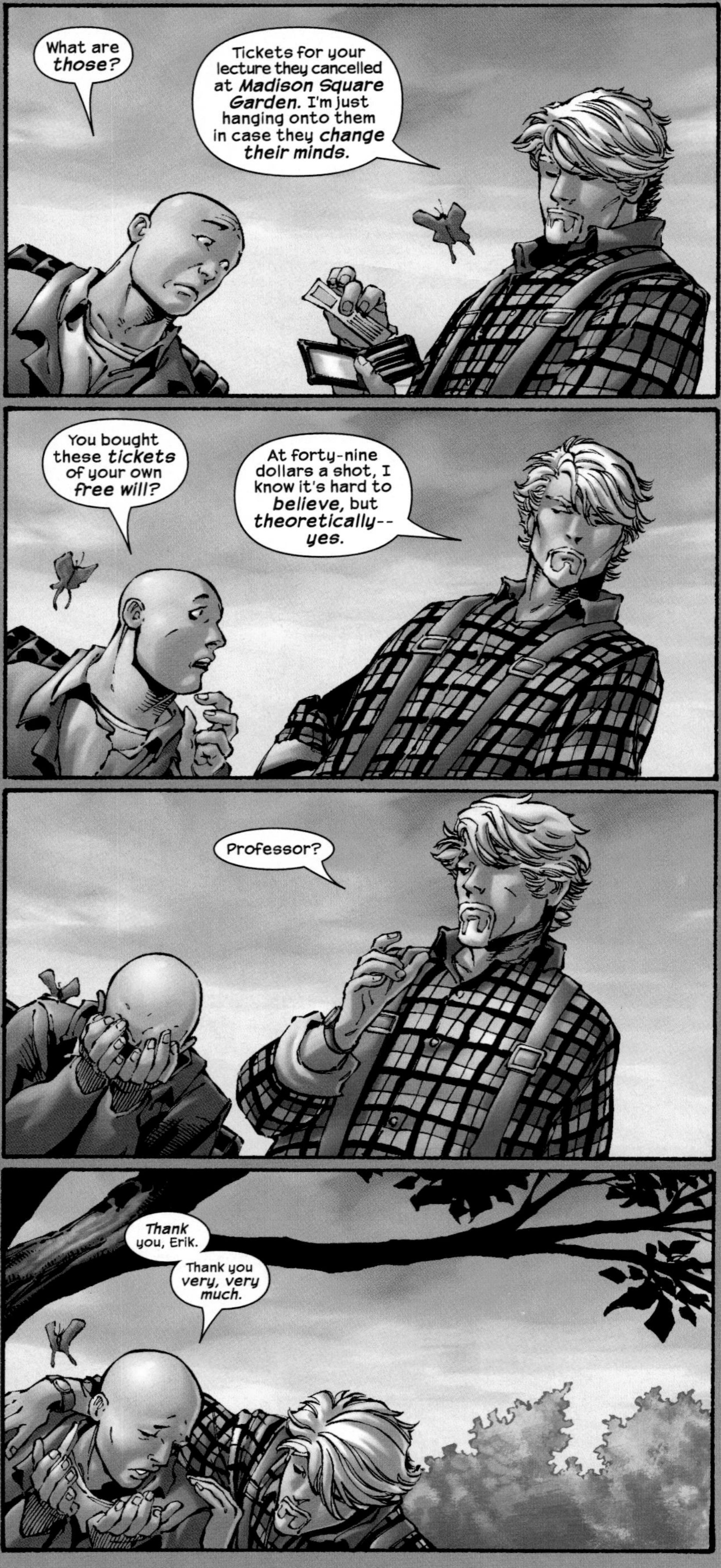
What are *those?*
Tickets for your lecture they cancelled at *Madison Square Garden.* I'm just hanging onto them in case they *change their minds.*
You bought these *tickets* of your own *free will?*
At forty-nine dollars a shot, I know it's hard to *believe,* but *theoretically--* *yes.*
Professor?
Thank you, Erik.
Thank you *very, very much.*

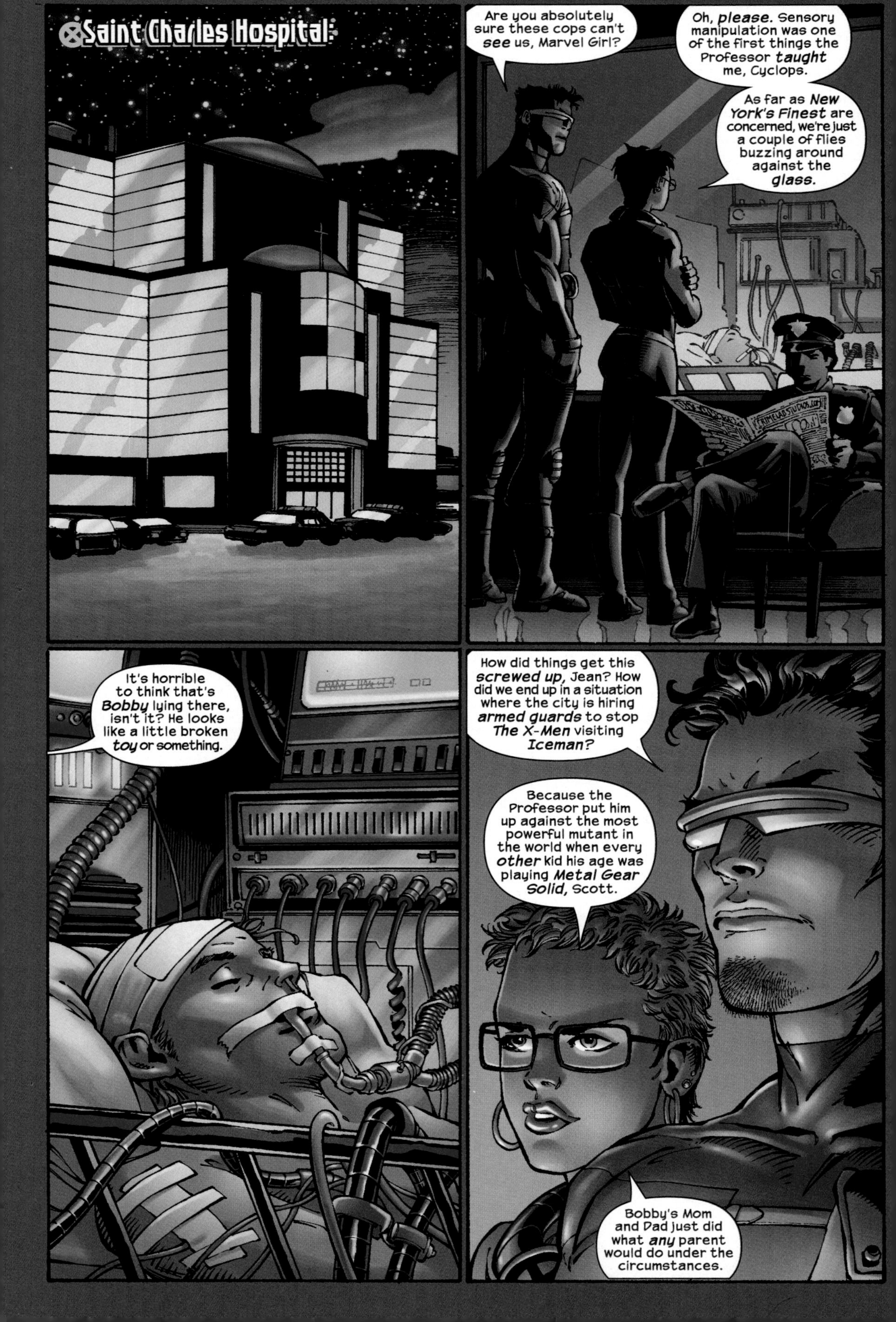
Saint Charles Hospital:
Are you absolutely sure these cops can't see us, Marvel Girl?
Oh, please. Sensory manipulation was one of the first things the Professor taught me, Cyclops.
As far as New York's Finest are concerned, we're just a couple of flies buzzing around against the glass.
It's horrible to think that's Bobby lying there, isn't it? He looks like a little broken toy or something.
How did things get this screwed up, Jean? How did we end up in a situation where the city is hiring armed guards to stop The X-Men visiting Iceman?
Because the Professor put him up against the most powerful mutant in the world when every other kid his age was playing Metal Gear Solid, Scott.
Bobby's Mom and Dad just did what any parent would do under the circumstances.

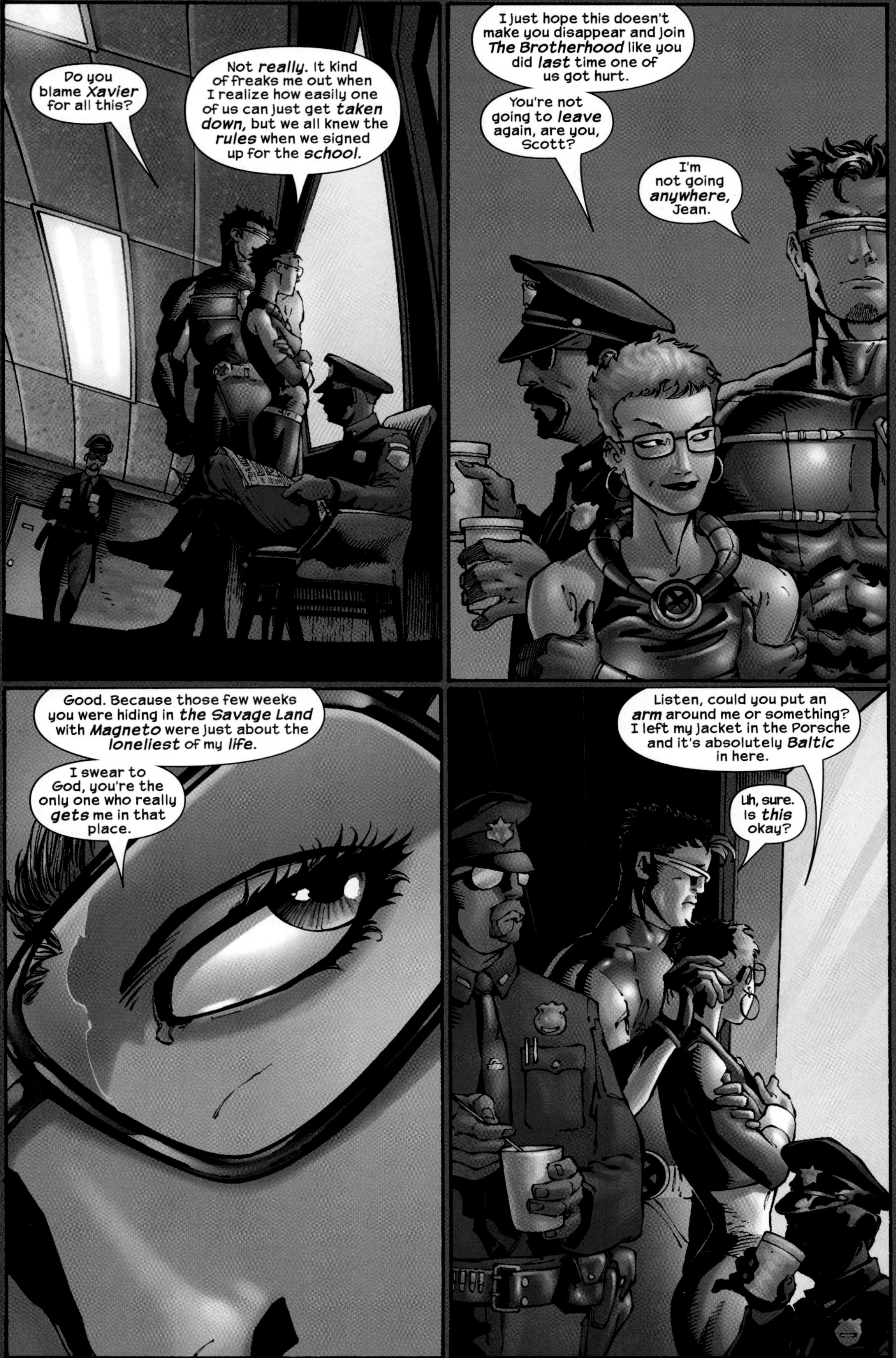
Do you blame Xavier for all this?
Not really. It kind of freaks me out when I realize how easily one of us can just get taken down, but we all knew the rules when we signed up for the school.
I just hope this doesn't make you disappear and join The Brotherhood like you did last time one of us got hurt.
You're not going to leave again, are you, Scott?
I'm not going anywhere, Jean.
Good. Because those few weeks you were hiding in the Savage Land with Magneto were just about the loneliest of my life.
I swear to God, you're the only one who really gets me in that place.
Listen, could you put an arm around me or something? I left my jacket in the Porsche and it's absolutely Baltic in here.
Uh, sure. Is this okay?

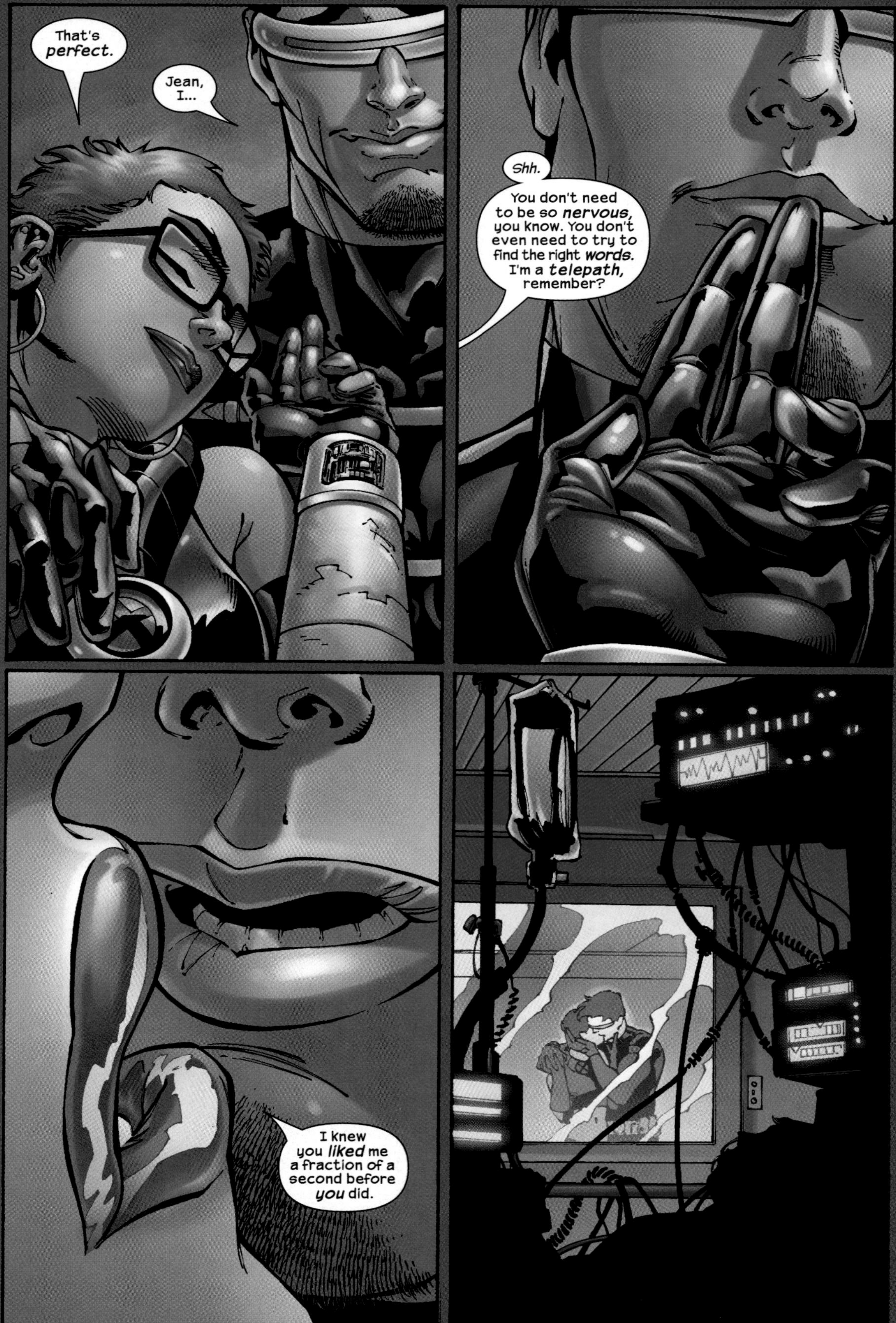
That's perfect.
Jean, I...
Shh.
You don't need to be so nervous, you know. You don't even need to try to find the right words. I'm a telepath, remember?
I knew you liked me a fraction of a second before you did.

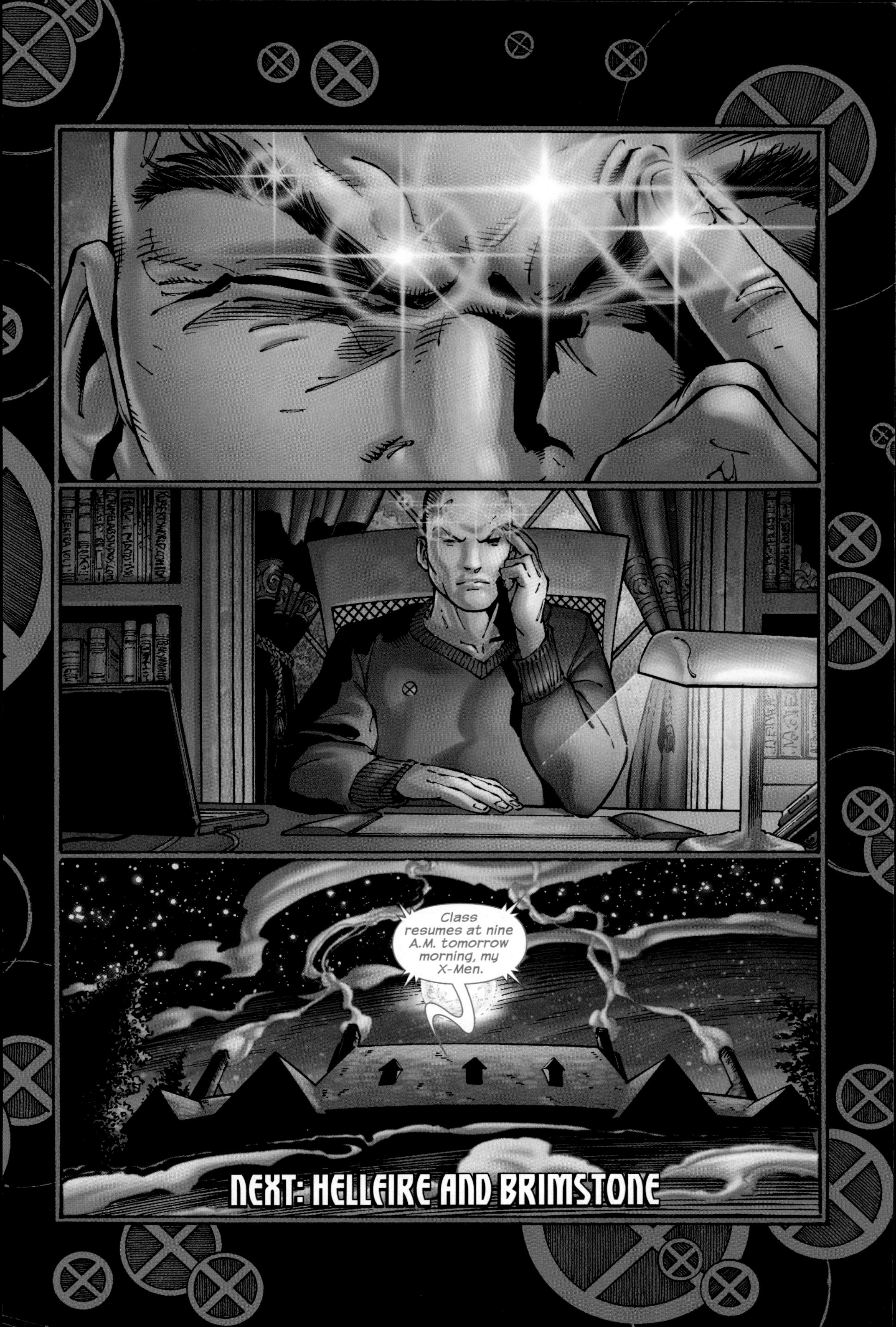
Class resumes at nine A.M. tomorrow morning, my X-Men.
NEXT: HELLFIRE AND BRIMSTONE

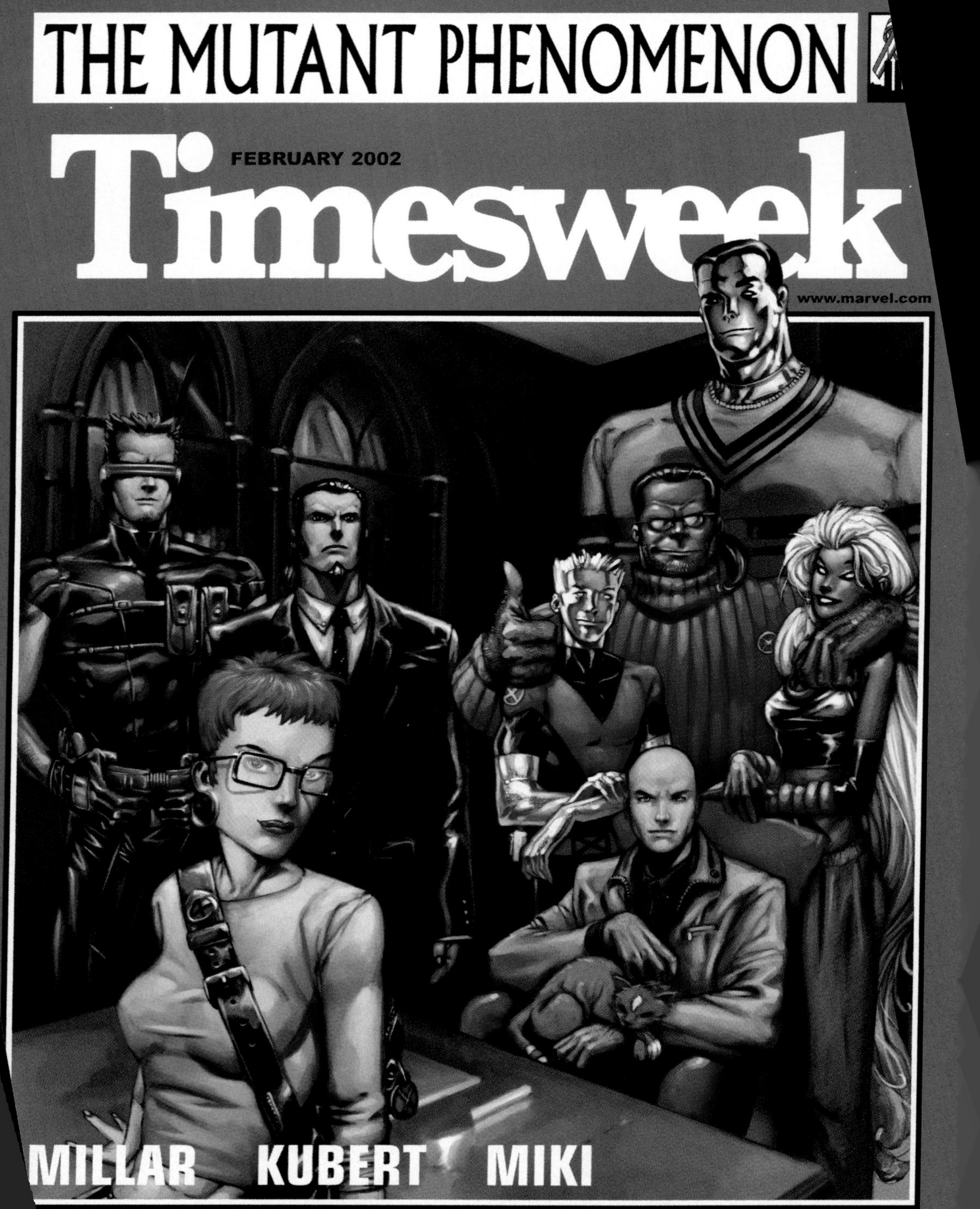
THE MUTANT PHENOMENON
FEBRUARY 2002
Timesweek
www.marvel.com
MILLAR KUBERT MIKI

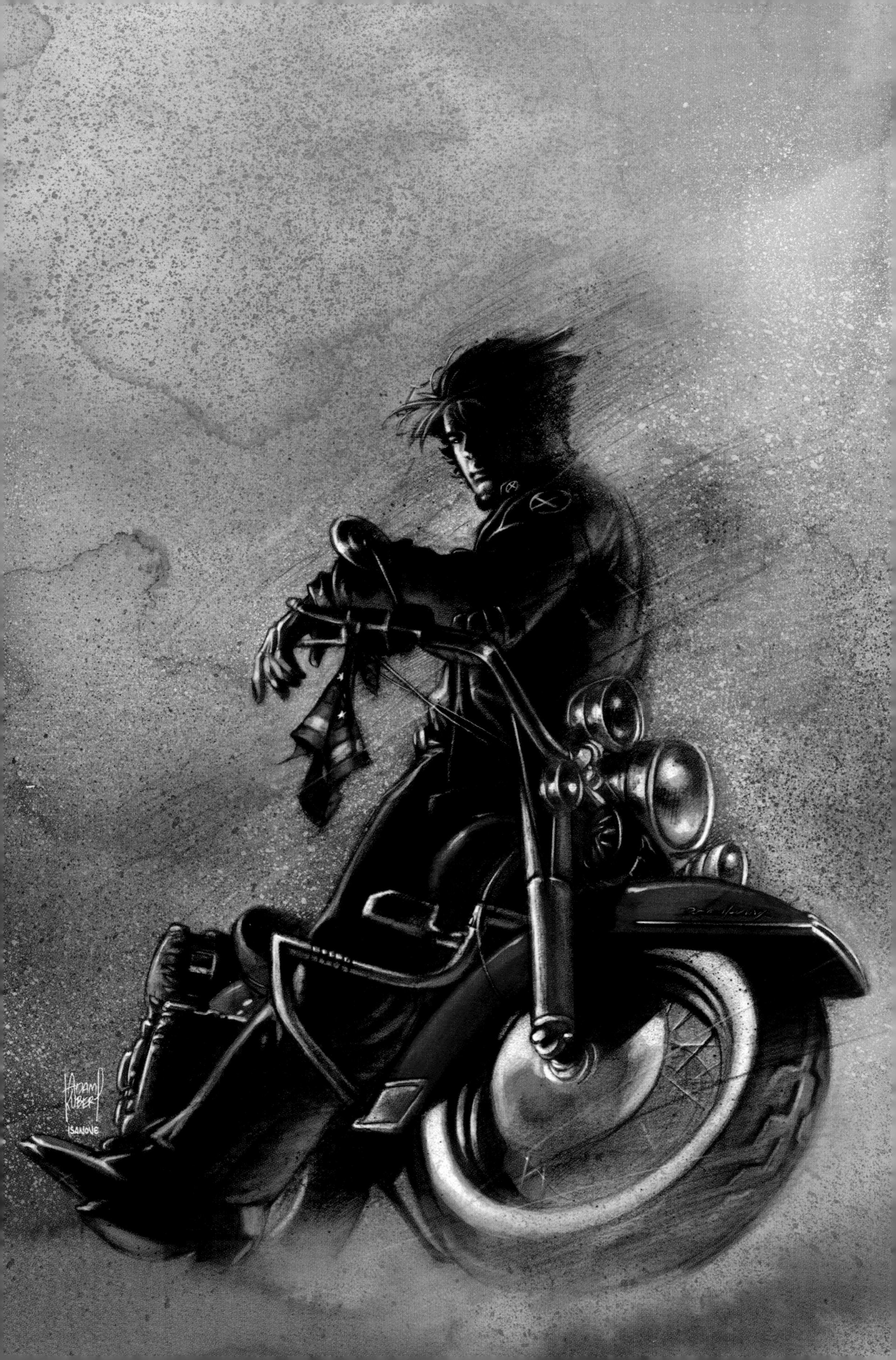
ADAM KUBERT
ISANOVE

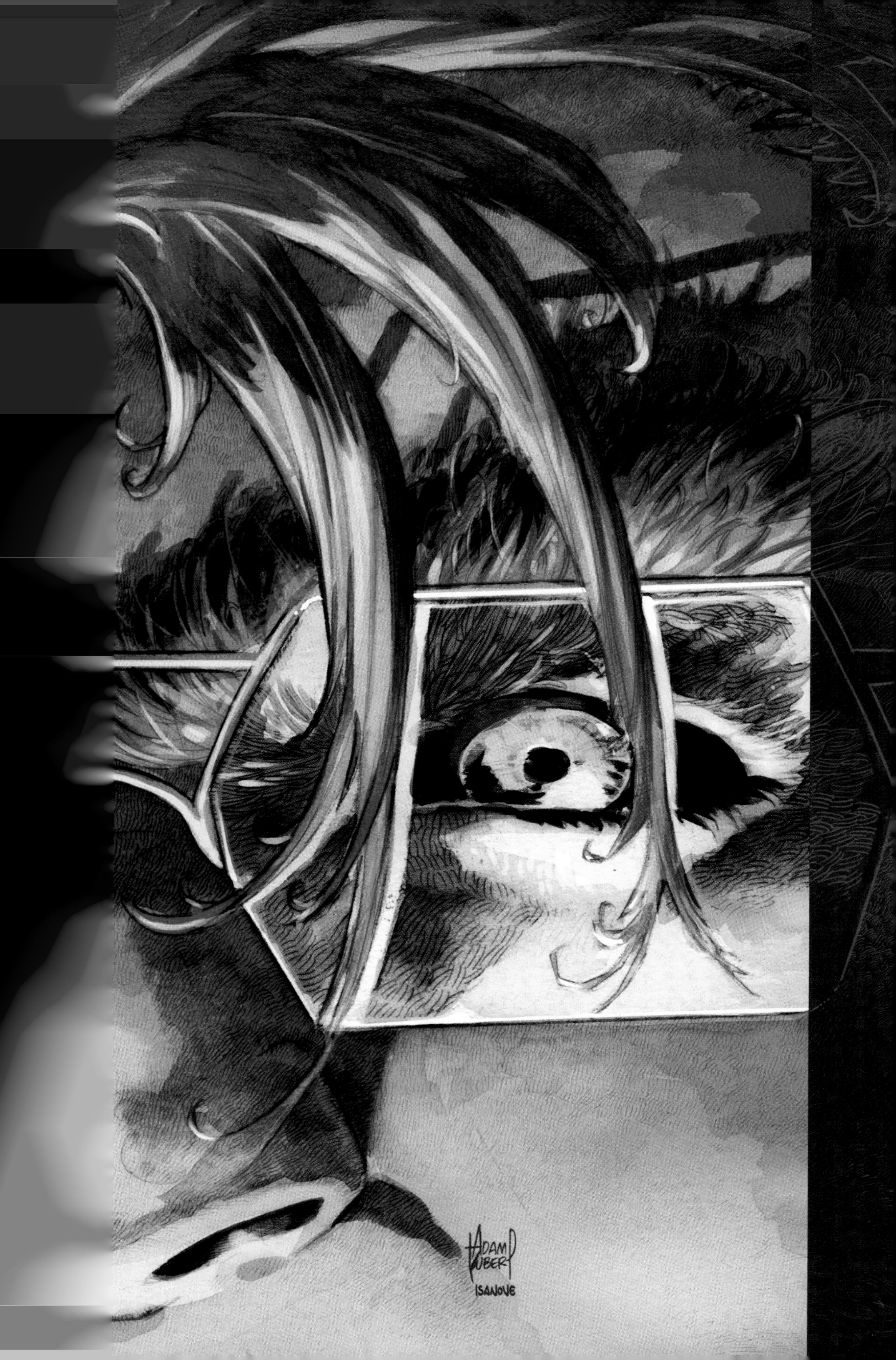
ADAM KUBERT
ISANOVE

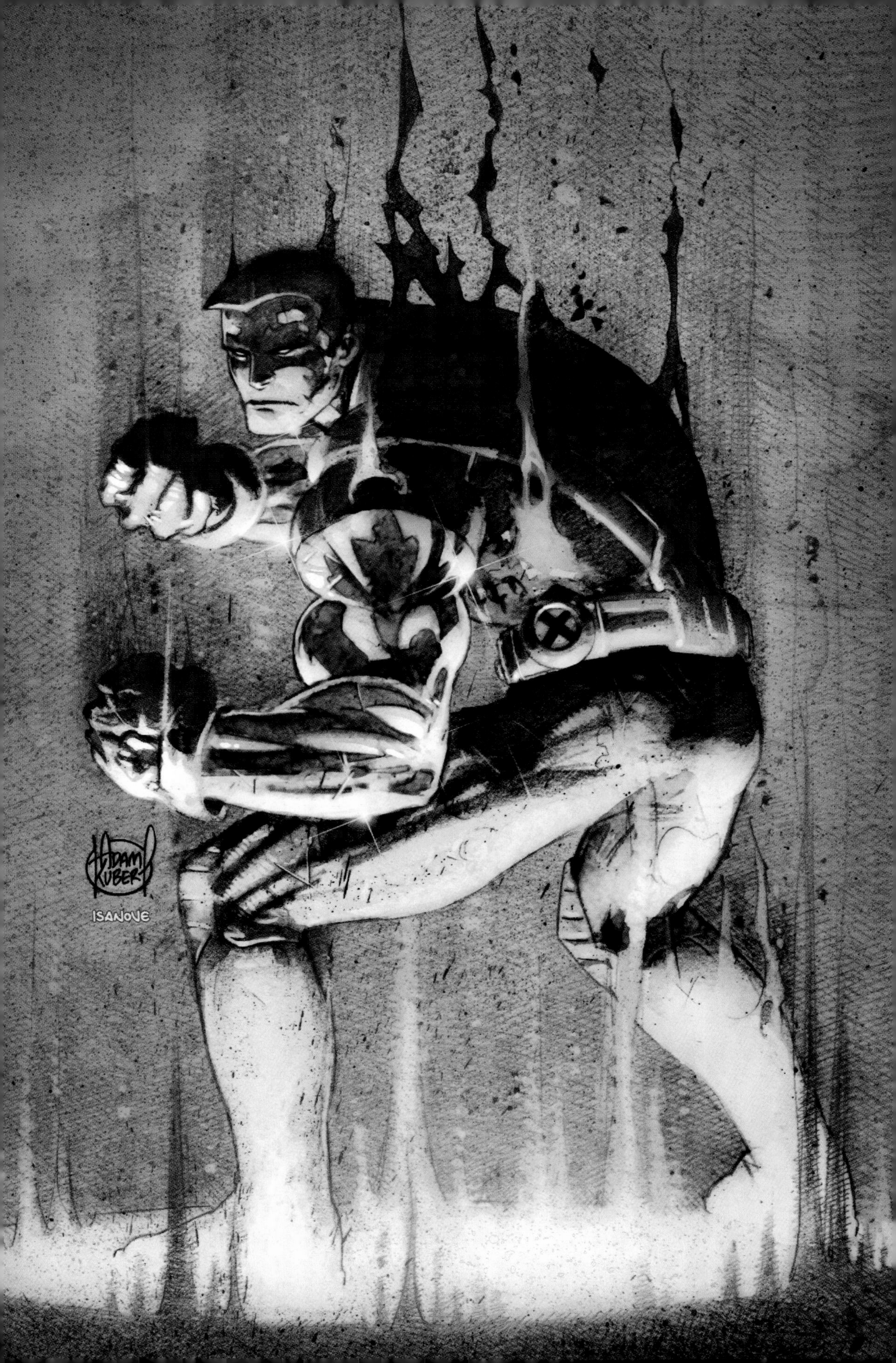
ADAM KUBERT
ISANOVE

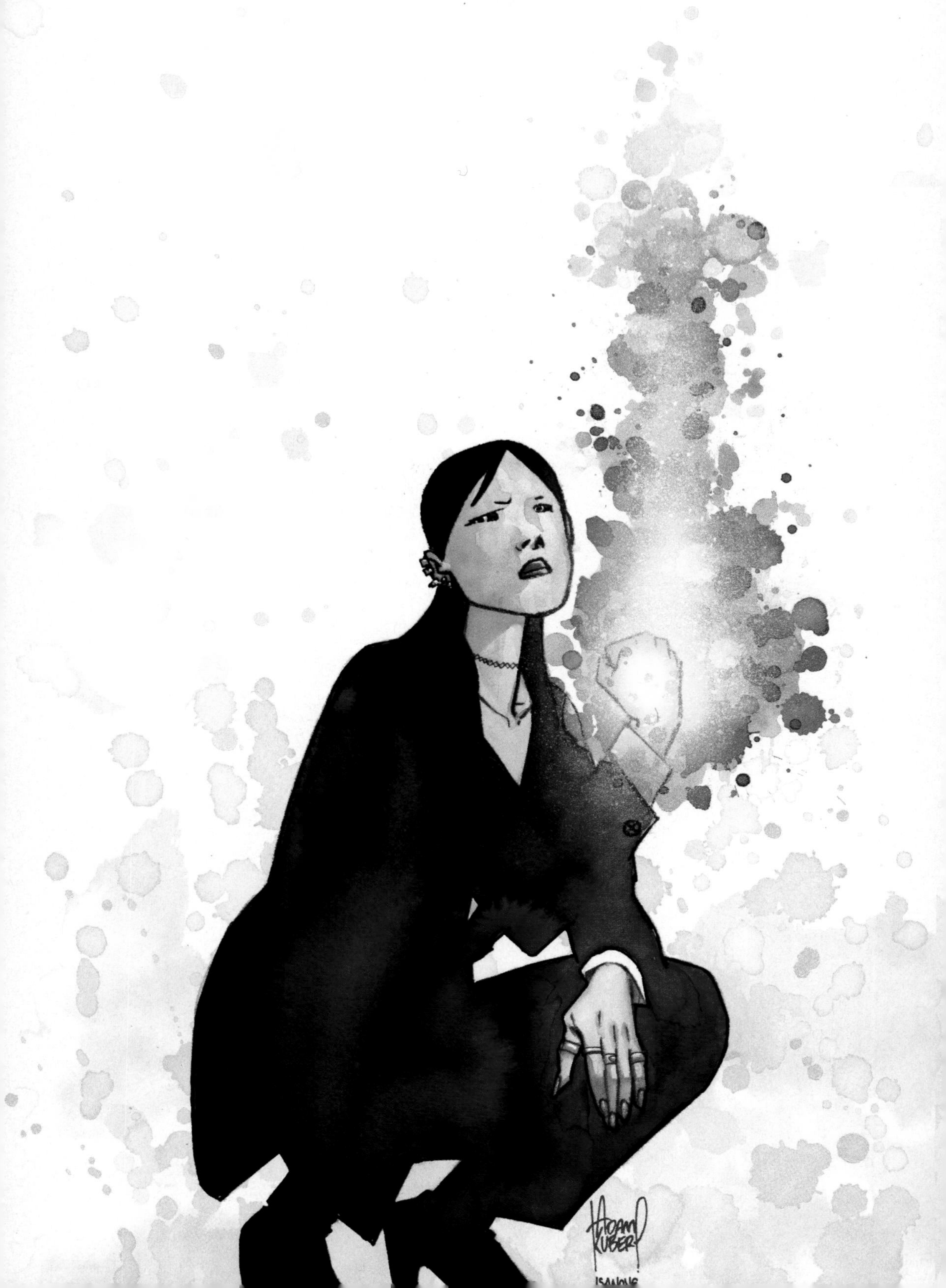

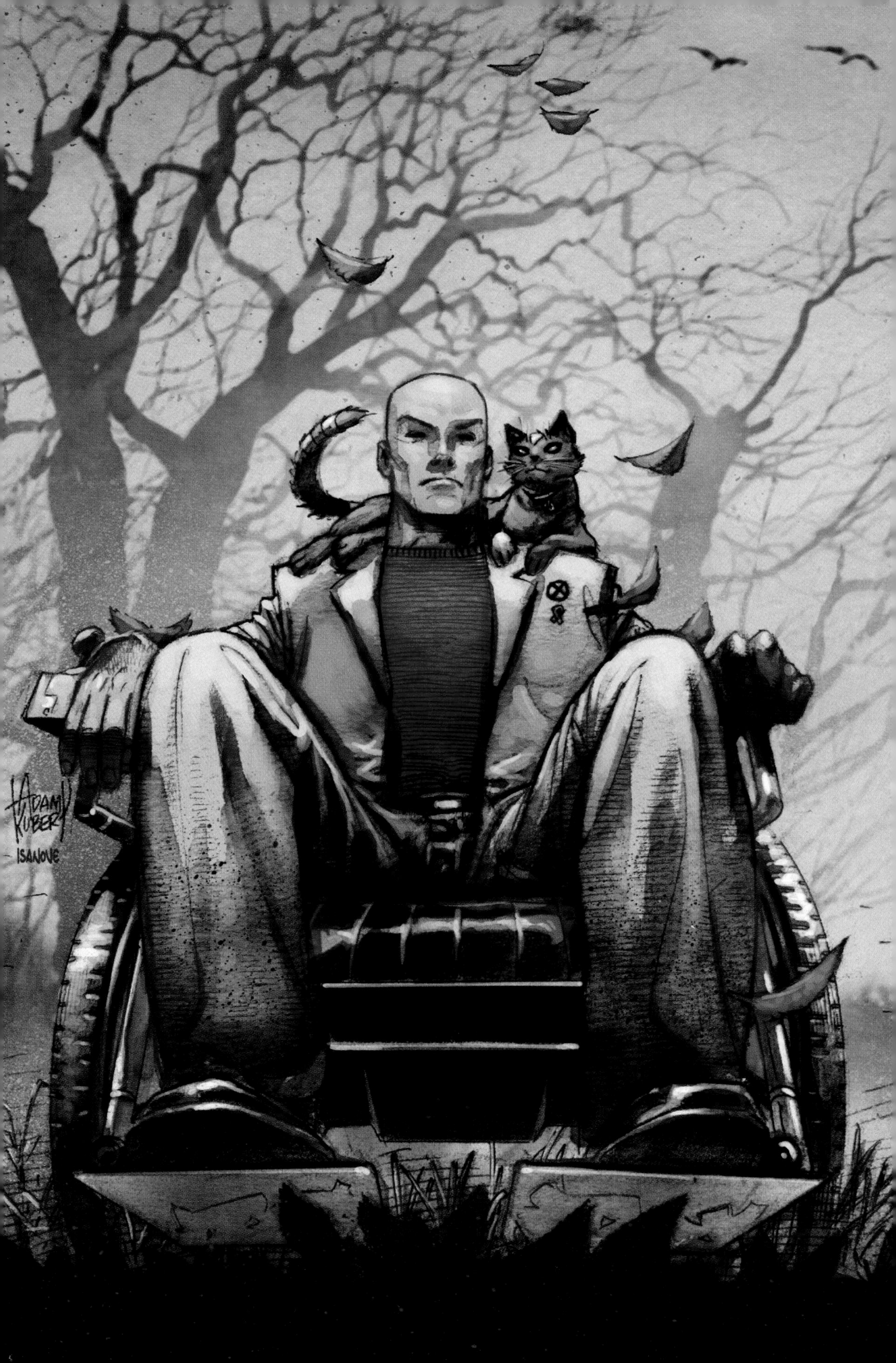
ADAM KUBERT
ISANOVE

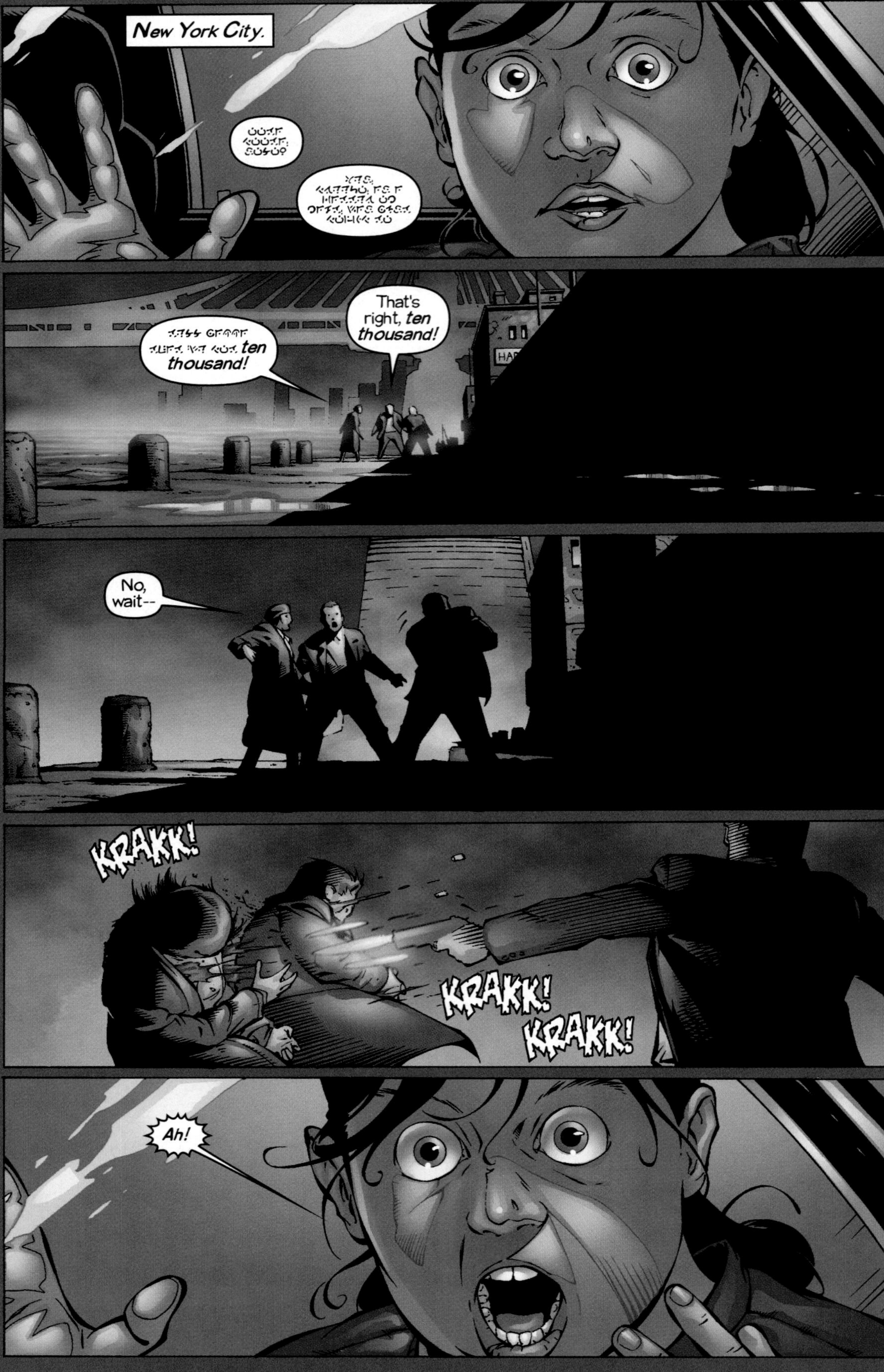
New York City.
ten thousand!
That's right, ten thousand!
No, wait--
KRAKK!
KRAKK!
KRAKK!
Ah!

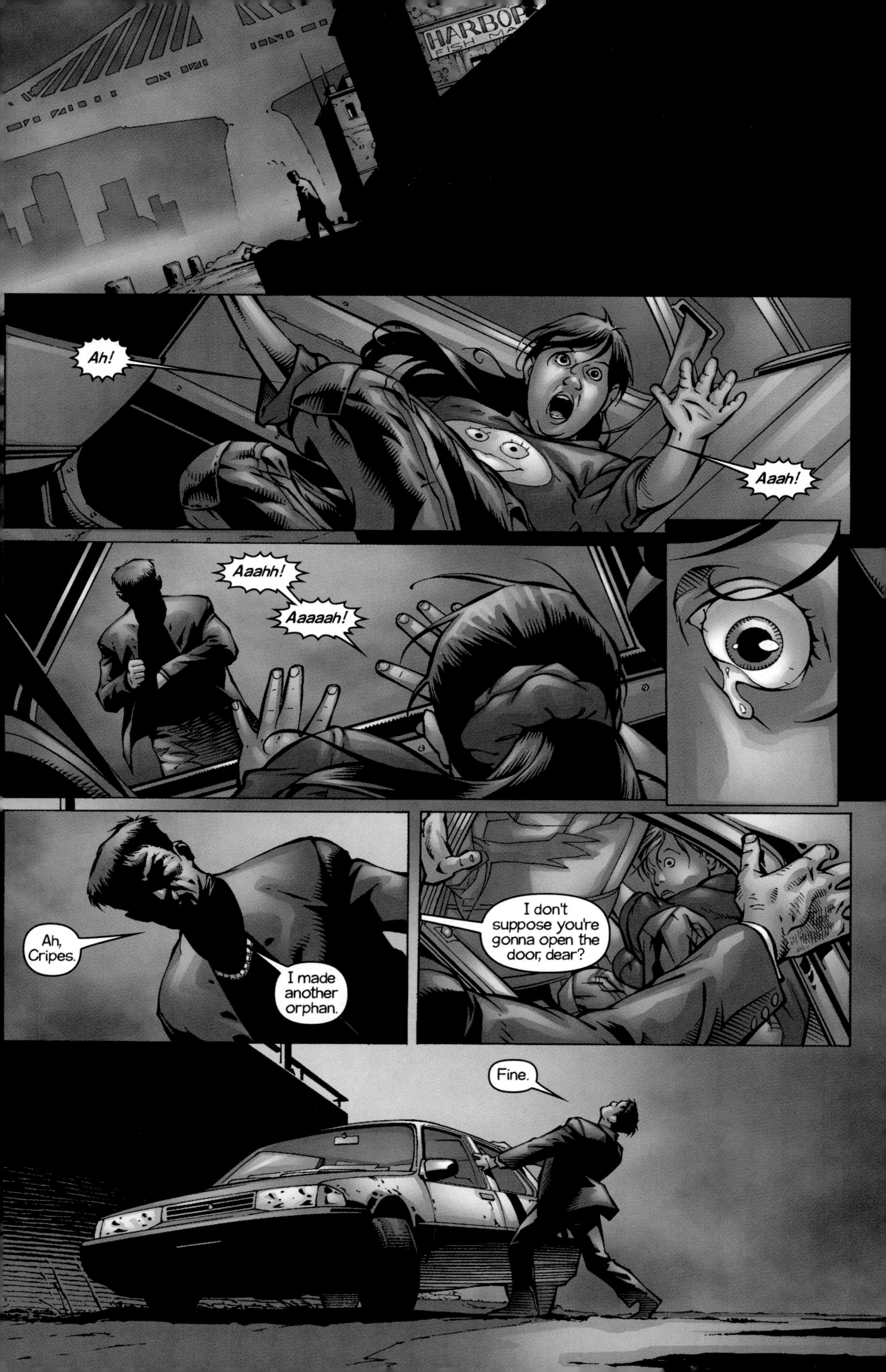
HARBOR
FISH MA
Ah!
Aaah!
Aaahh!
Aaaaah!
Ah, Cripes.
I made another orphan.
I don't suppose you're gonna open the door, dear?
Fine.

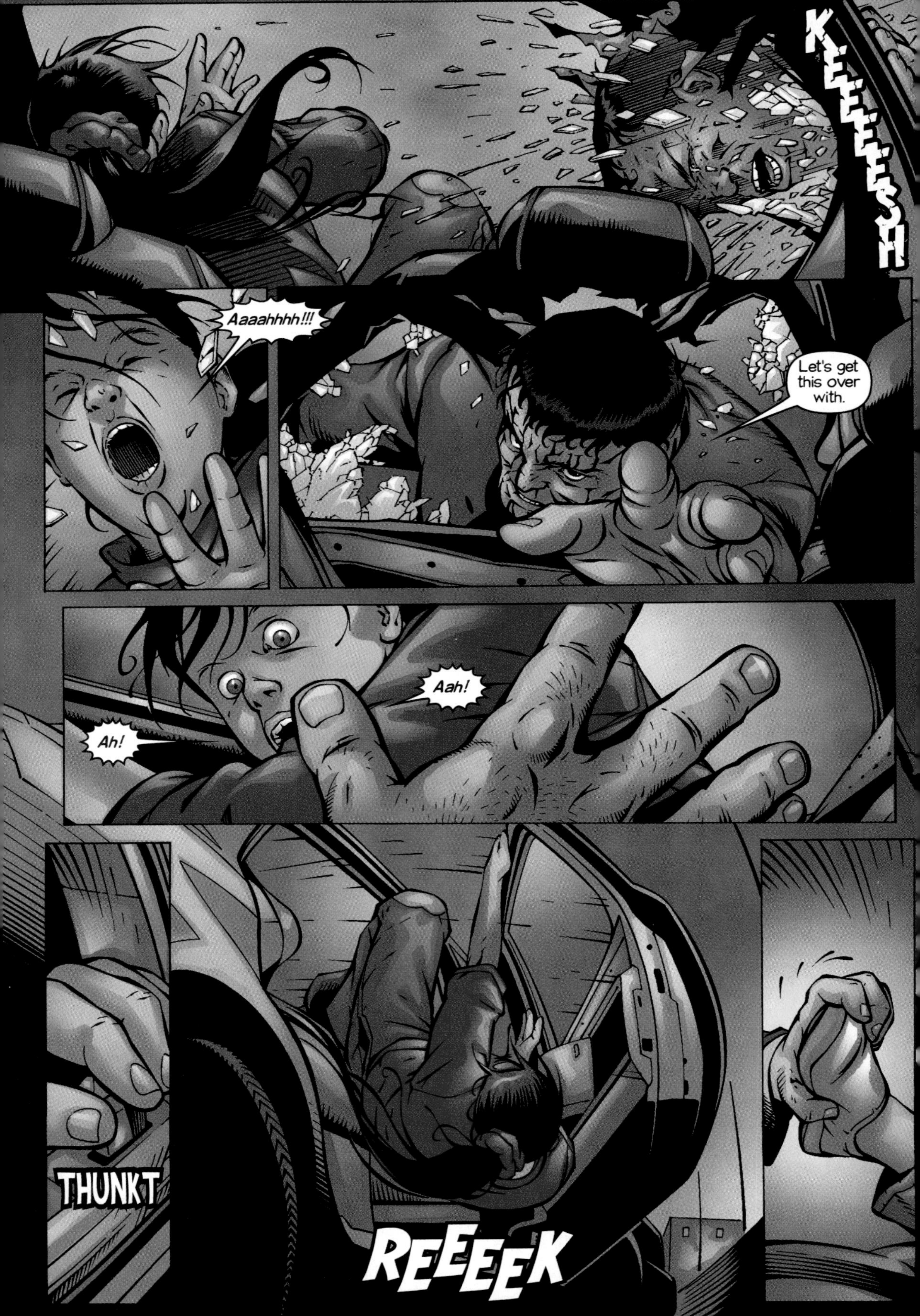
KEEEEESH
Aaaahhhh!!!
Let's get this over with.
Aah!
Ah!
THUNKT
REEEEK

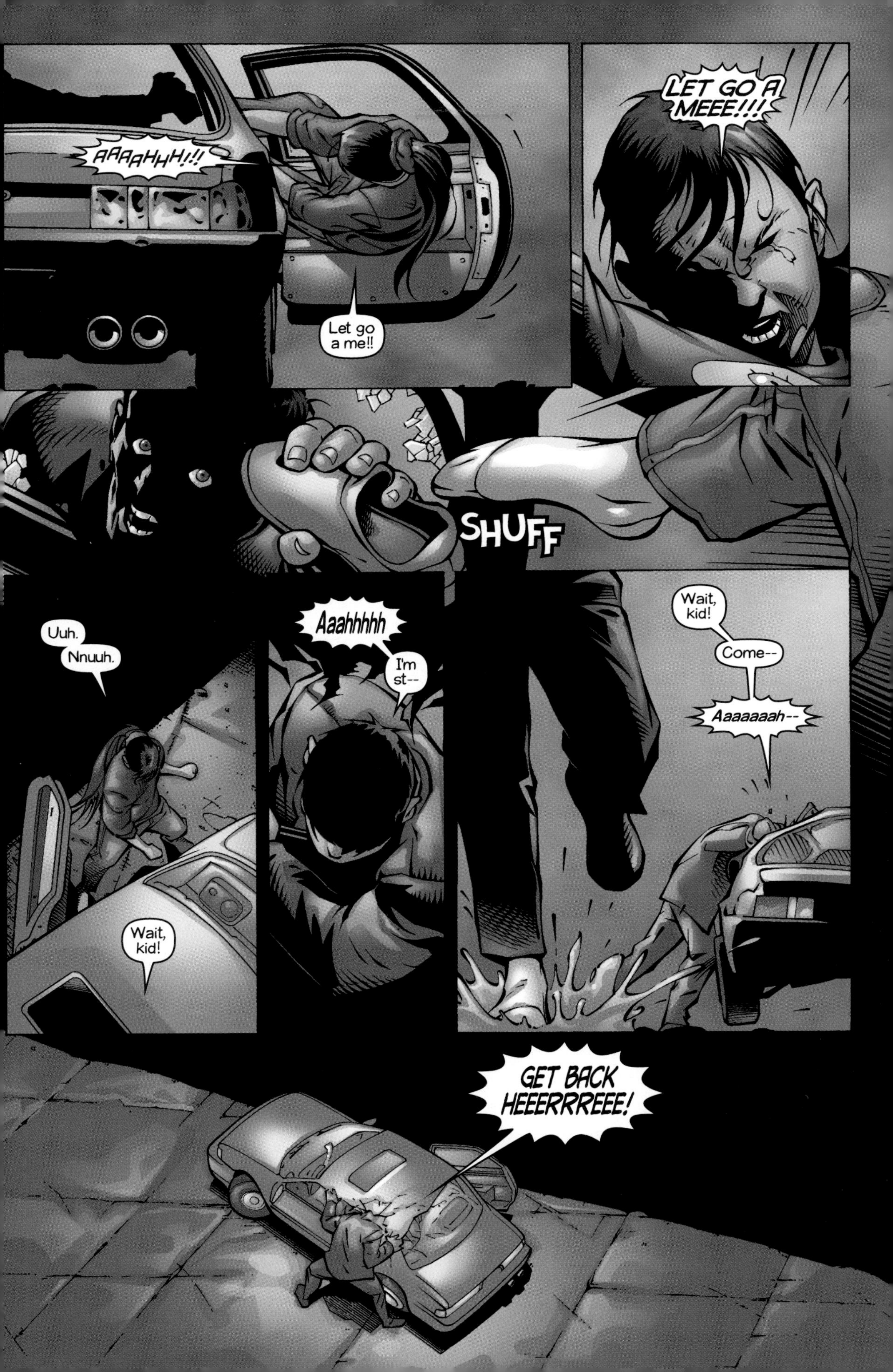
AAAAHHH!!!
Let go a me!!
LET GO A MEEE!!!
SHUFF
Uuh.
Nnuuh.
Wait, kid!
Aaahhhhh
I'm st--
Wait, kid!
Come--
Aaaaaaah--
GET BACK HEEERRREEE!

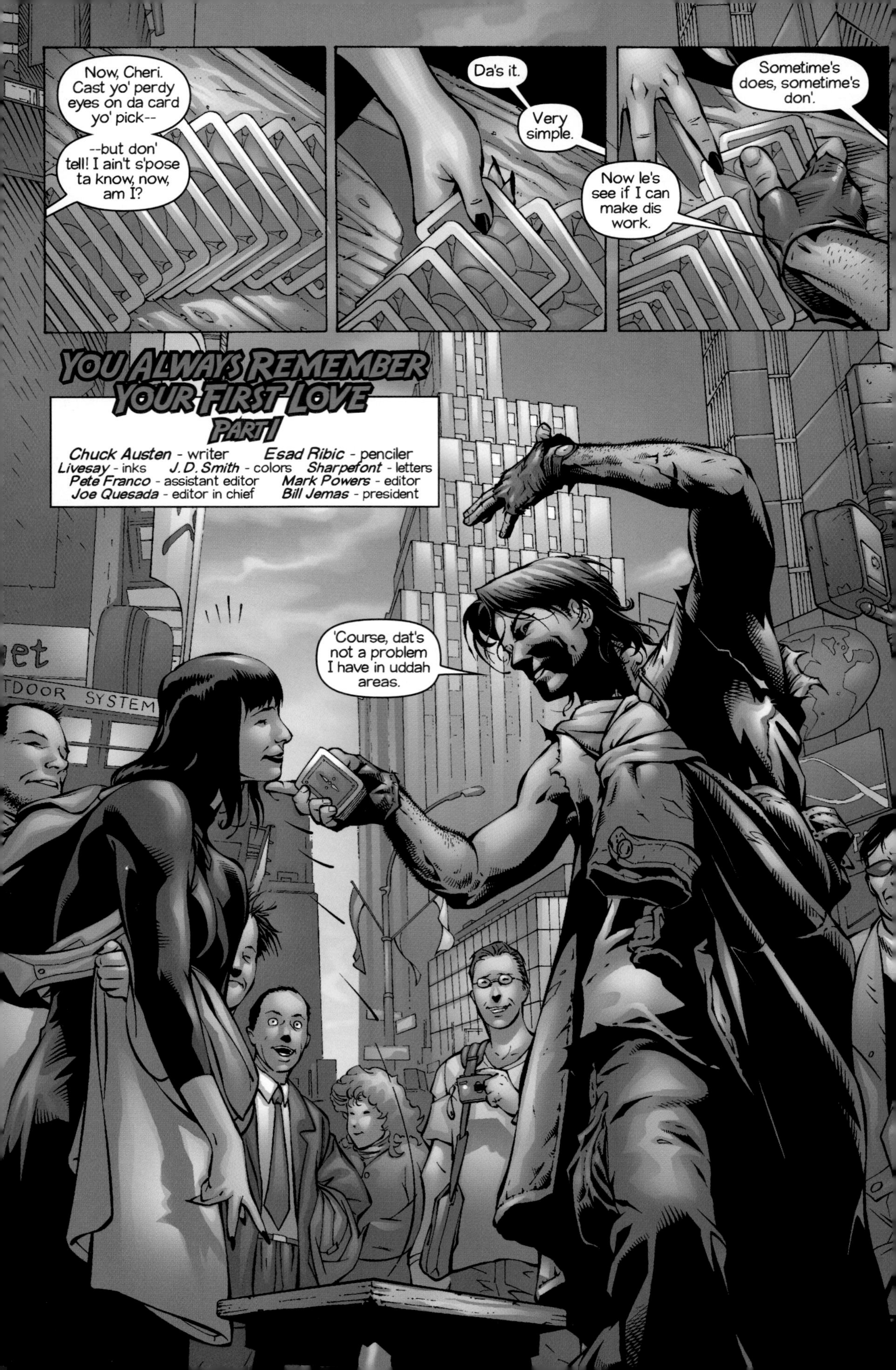

Now, Cheri. Cast yo' perdy eyes on da card yo' pick--
--but don' tell! I ain't s'pose ta know, now, am I?
Da's it.
Very simple.
Sometime's does, sometime's don'.
Now le's see if I can make dis work.
YOU ALWAYS REMEMBER YOUR FIRST LOVE
PART I
Chuck Austen - writer Esad Ribic - penciler
Livesay - inks J. D. Smith - colors Sharpefont - letters
Pete Franco - assistant editor Mark Powers - editor
Joe Quesada - editor in chief Bill Jemas - president
'Course, dat's not a problem I have in uddah areas.

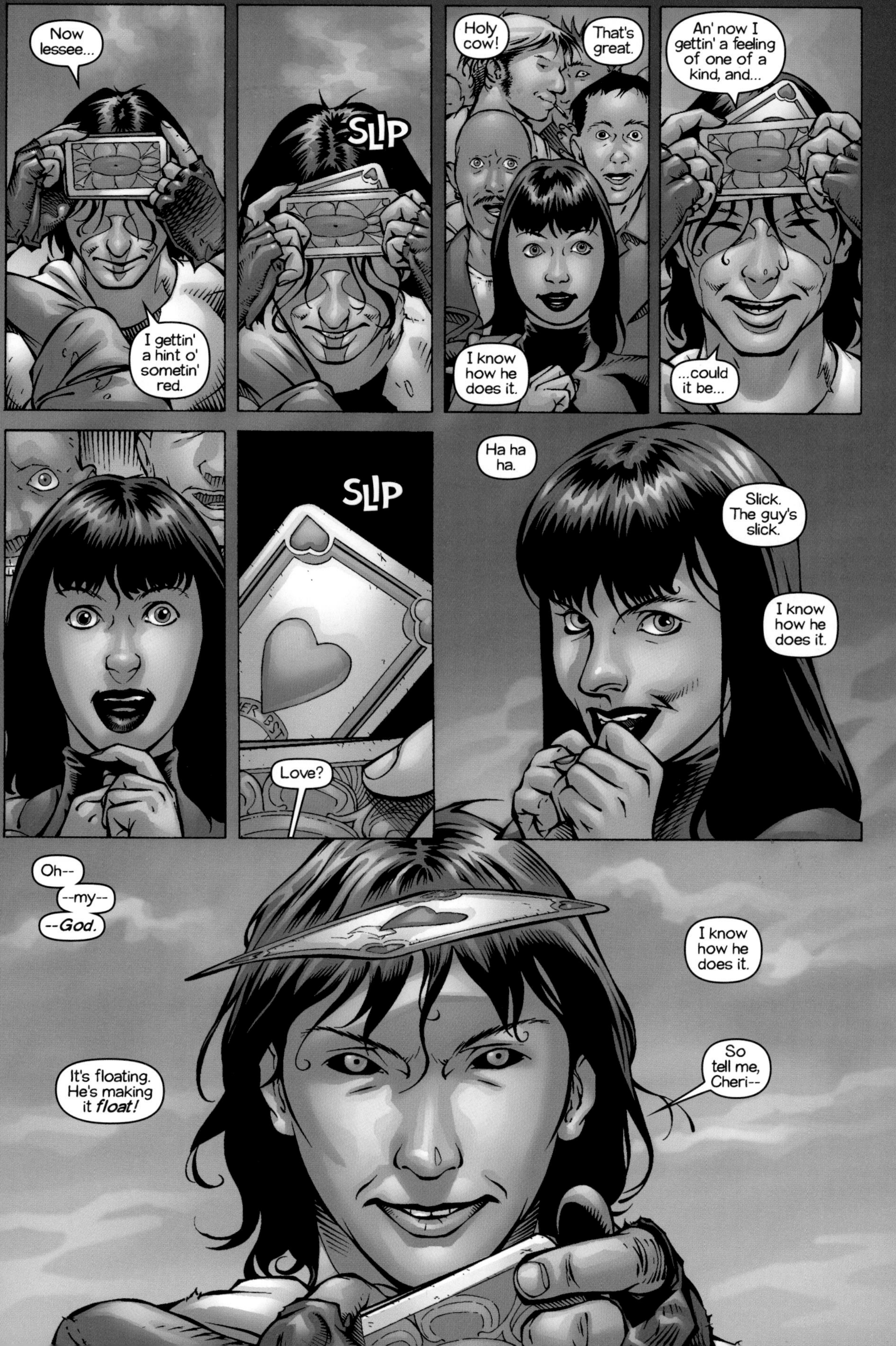
Now lessee...
I gettin' a hint o' sometin' red.
SLIP
Holy cow!
That's great.
I know how he does it.
An' now I gettin' a feeling of one of a kind, and...
...could it be...
SLIP
Love?
Ha ha ha.
Slick. The guy's slick.
I know how he does it.
Oh--
--my--
--*God.*
I know how he does it.
It's floating. He's making it *float!*
So tell me, Cheri--

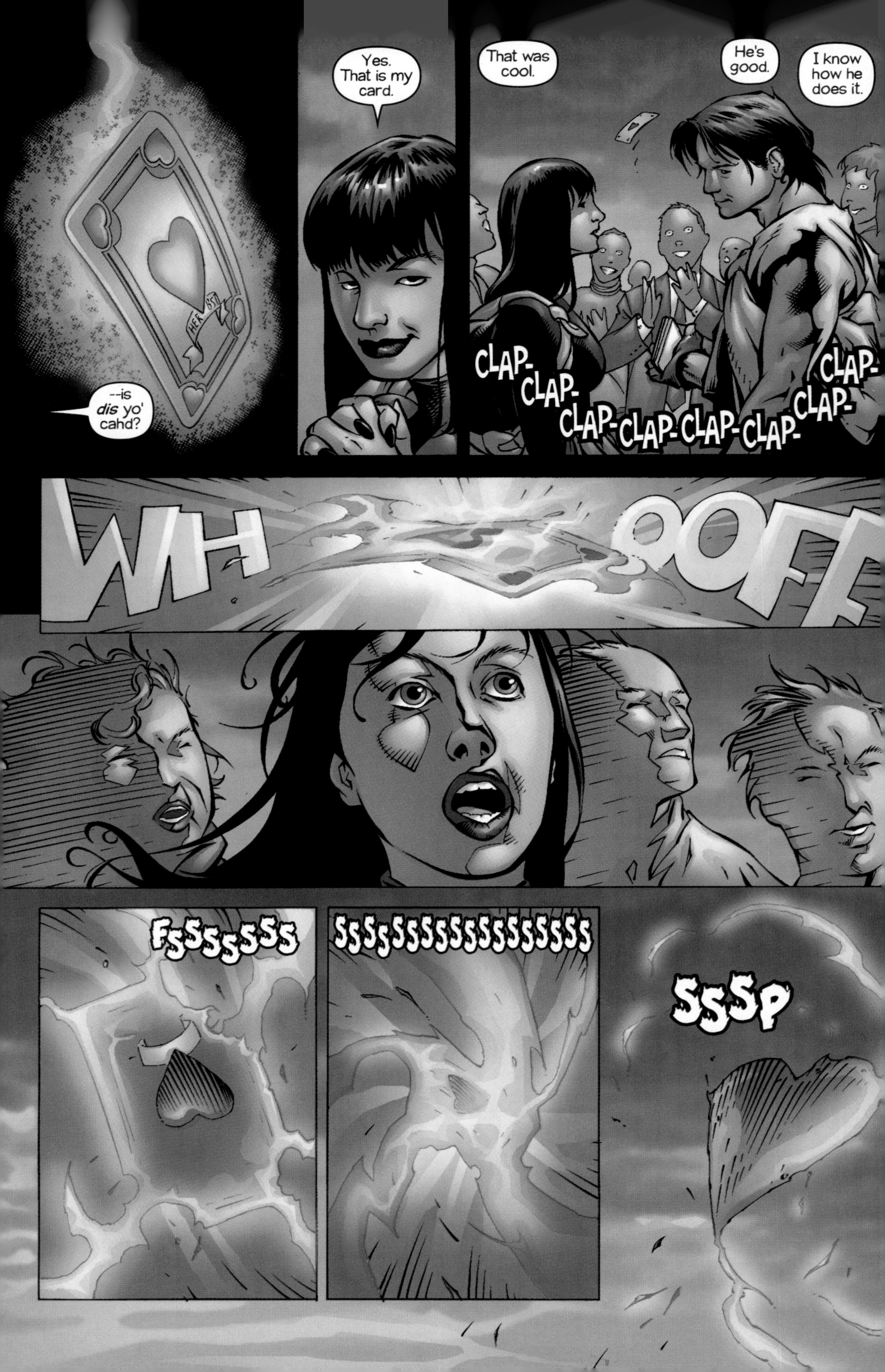

--is *dis* yo' cahd?
Yes. That is my card.
That was cool.
He's good.
I know how he does it.
CLAP-CLAP-CLAP-CLAP-CLAP-CLAP-CLAP-CLAP-
WHOOFF
FSSSSSSS
SSSSSSSSSSSSSSSSS
SSSP

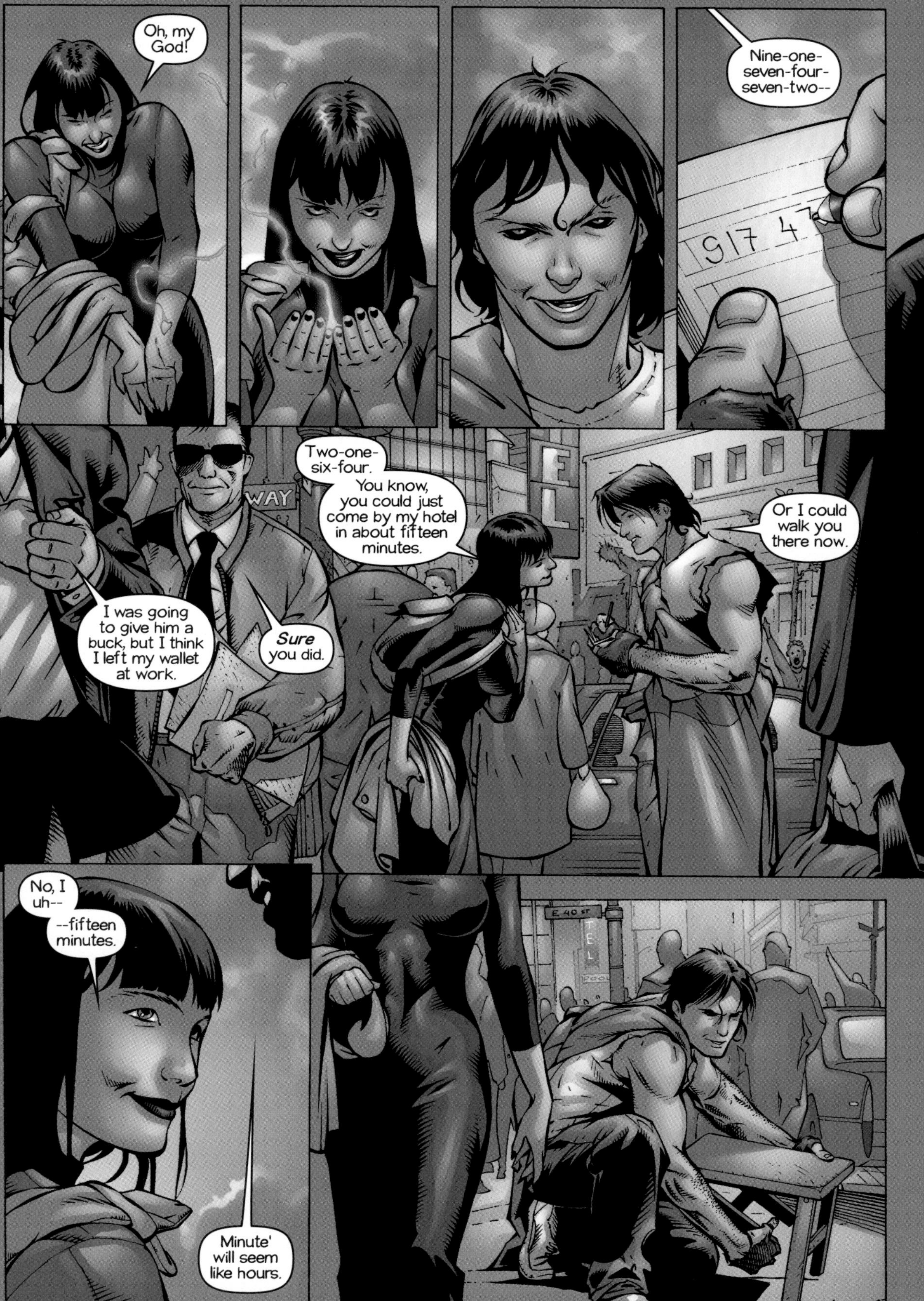
Oh, my God!
Nine-one-seven-four-seven-two--
917 47
Two-one-six-four. You know, you could just come by my hotel in about fifteen minutes.
Or I could walk you there now.
I was going to give him a buck, but I think I left my wallet at work.
Sure you did.
WAY
No, I uh--
--fifteen minutes.
Minute' will seem like hours.
E 40 ST
TEL
POOL

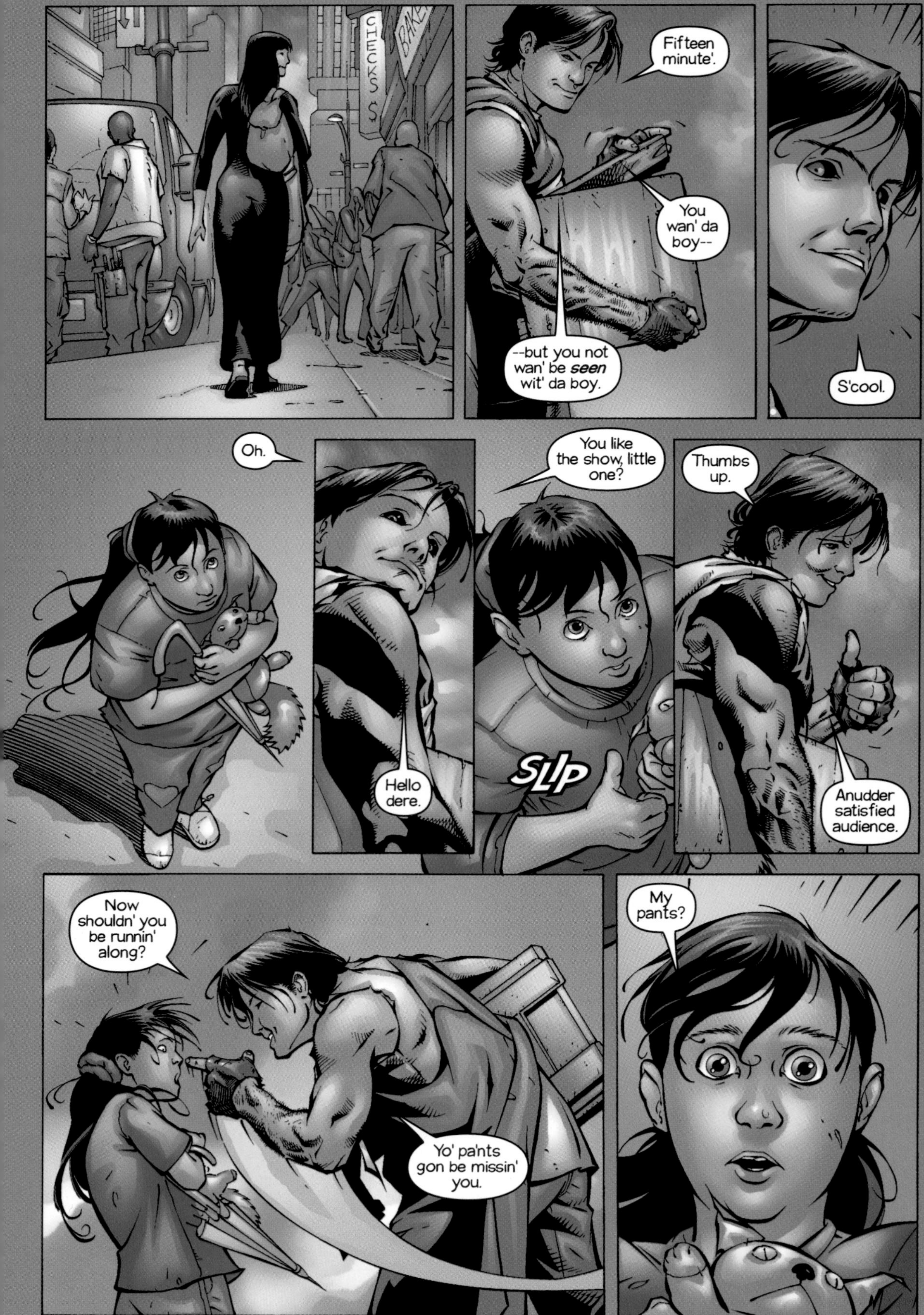

CHECKS $
Fifteen minute'.
You wan' da boy--
--but you not wan' be *seen* wit' da boy.
S'cool.
Oh.
Hello dere.
You like the show, little one?
SLIP
Thumbs up.
Anudder satisfied audience.
Now shouldn' you be runnin' along?
Yo' pa'nts gon be missin' you.
My pants?

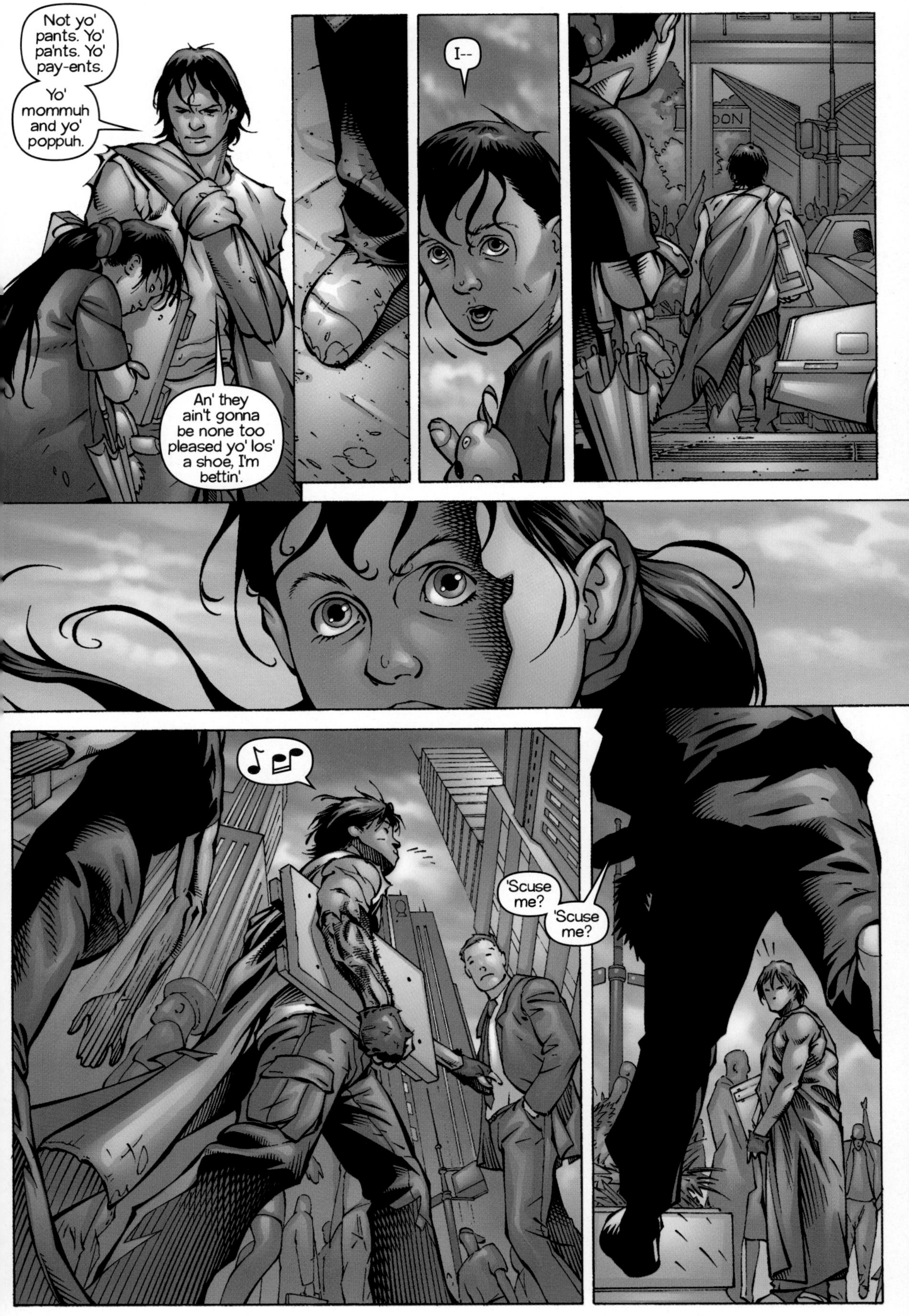
Not yo' pants. Yo' pa'nts. Yo' pay-ents.
Yo' mommuh and yo' poppuh.
An' they ain't gonna be none too pleased yo' los' a shoe, I'm bettin'.
I--
DON
'Scuse me?
'Scuse me?

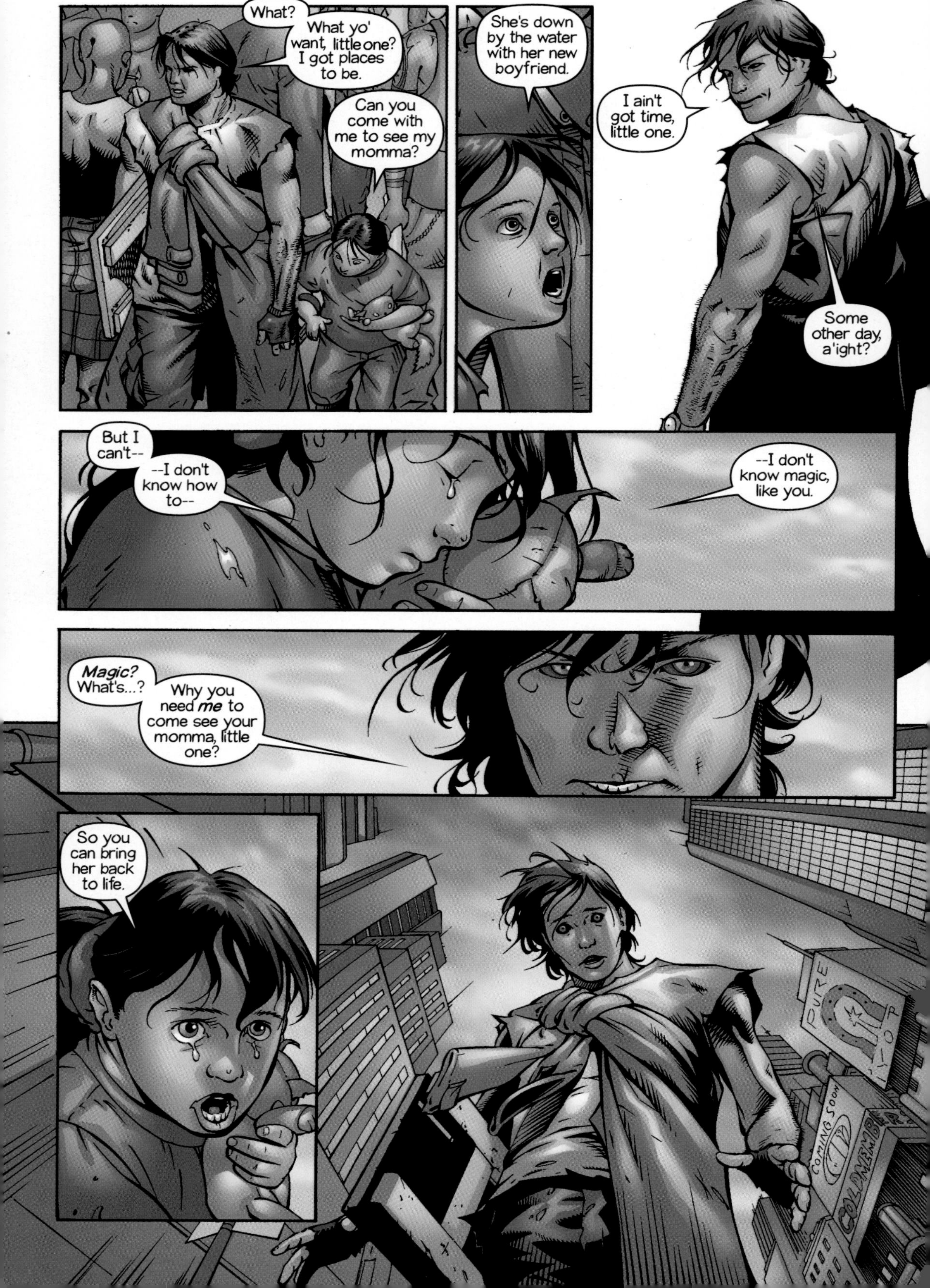
What?
What yo' want, little one? I got places to be.
Can you come with me to see my momma?
She's down by the water with her new boyfriend.
I ain't got time, little one.
Some other day, a'ight?
But I can't--
--I don't know how to--
--I don't know magic, like you.
Magic? What's...?
Why you need *me* to come see your momma, little one?
So you can bring her back to life.
PURE
COMING SOON
COLDVEMBER

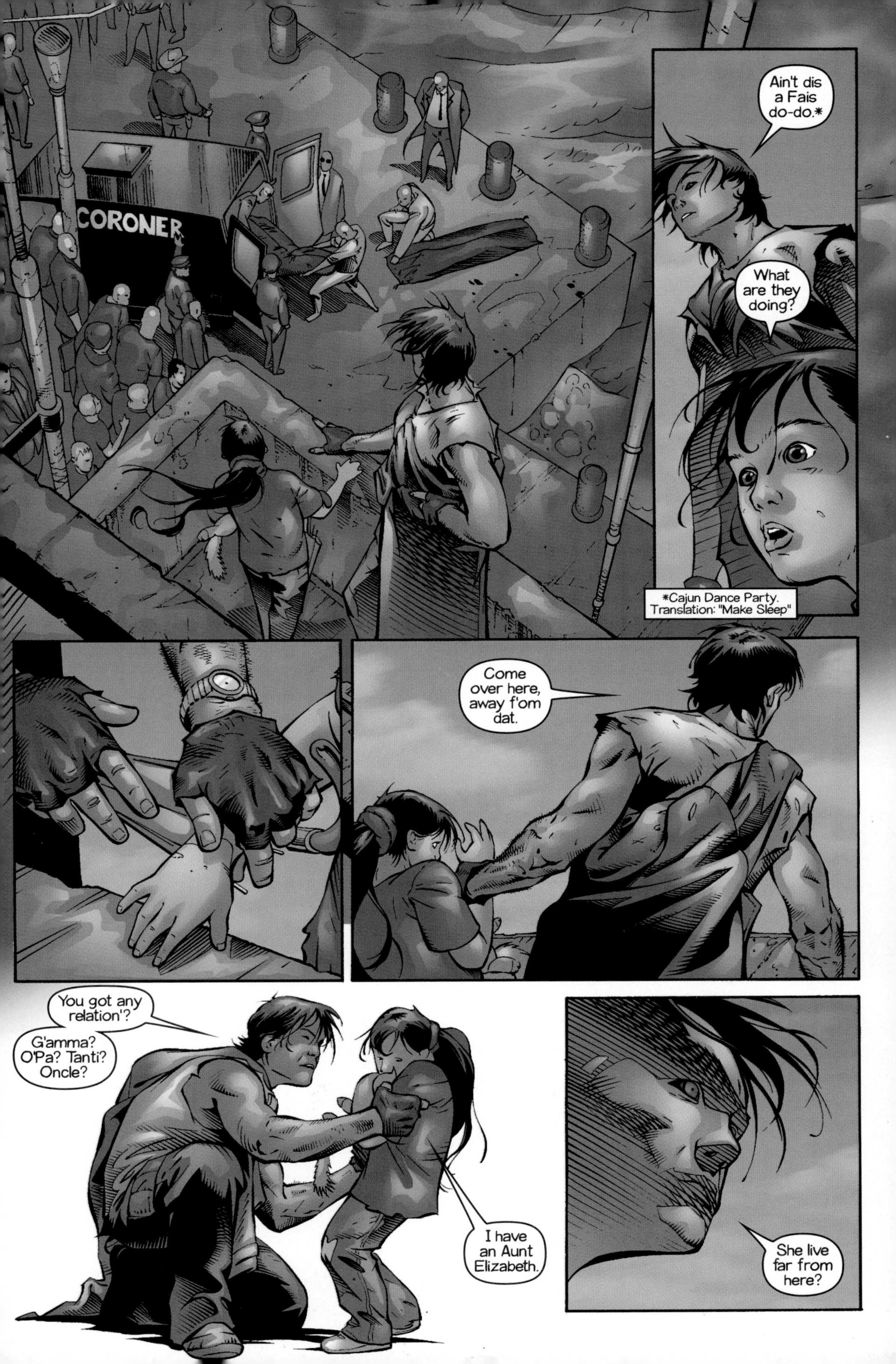
CORONER
Ain't dis a Fais do-do.*
What are they doing?
*Cajun Dance Party. Translation: "Make Sleep"
Come over here, away f'om dat.
You got any relation'?
G'amma? O'Pa? Tanti? Oncle?
I have an Aunt Elizabeth.
She live far from here?

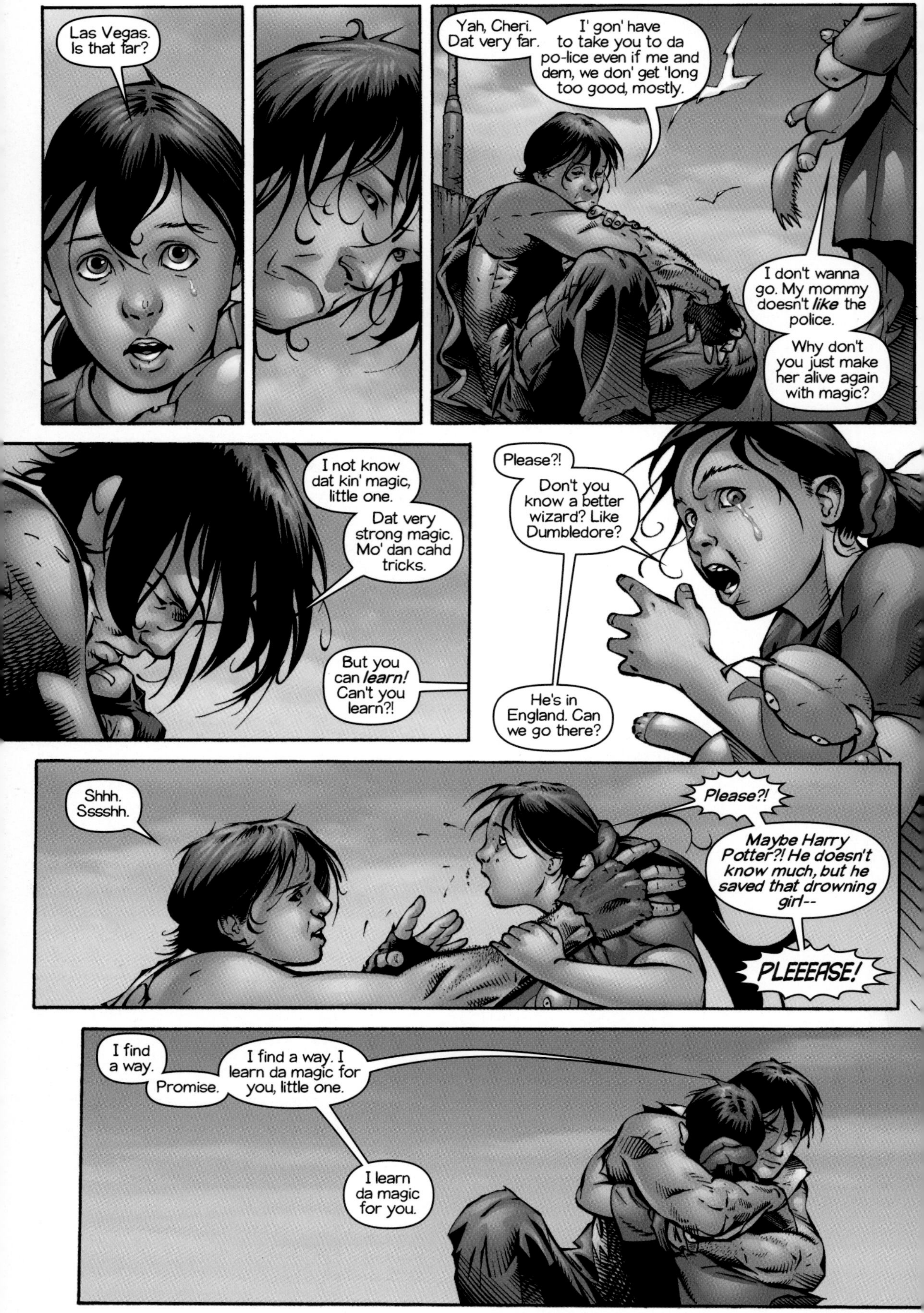

Las Vegas. Is that far?
Yah, Cheri. Dat very far.
I' gon' have to take you to da po-lice even if me and dem, we don' get 'long too good, mostly.
I don't wanna go. My mommy doesn't *like* the police.
Why don't you just make her alive again with magic?
I not know dat kin' magic, little one.
Dat very strong magic. Mo' dan cahd tricks.
But you can *learn!* Can't you learn?!
Please?!
Don't you know a better wizard? Like Dumbledore?
He's in England. Can we go there?
Shhh. Sssshh.
Please?!
Maybe Harry Potter?! He doesn't know much, but he saved that drowning girl--
PLEEEASE!
I find a way.
Promise.
I find a way. I learn da magic for you, little one.
I learn da magic for you.

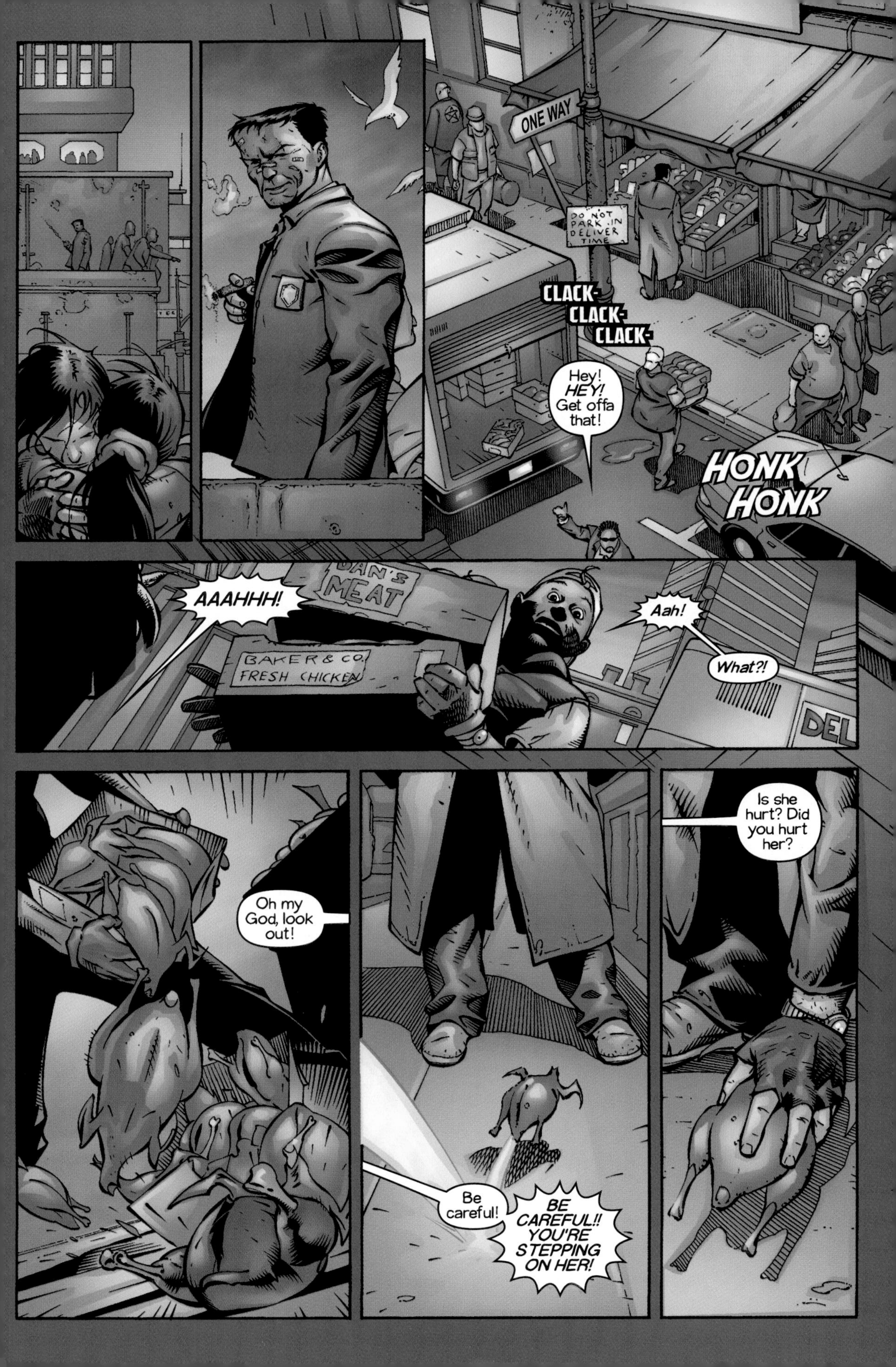
ONE WAY
DO NOT PARK IN DELIVER TIME
CLACK-
CLACK-
CLACK-
Hey! HEY! Get offa that!
HONK HONK
AAAHHH!
DAN'S MEAT
BAKER & CO. FRESH CHICKEN
Aah!
What?!
DEL
Oh my God, look out!
Be careful!
BE CAREFUL!! YOU'RE STEPPING ON HER!
Is she hurt? Did you hurt her?

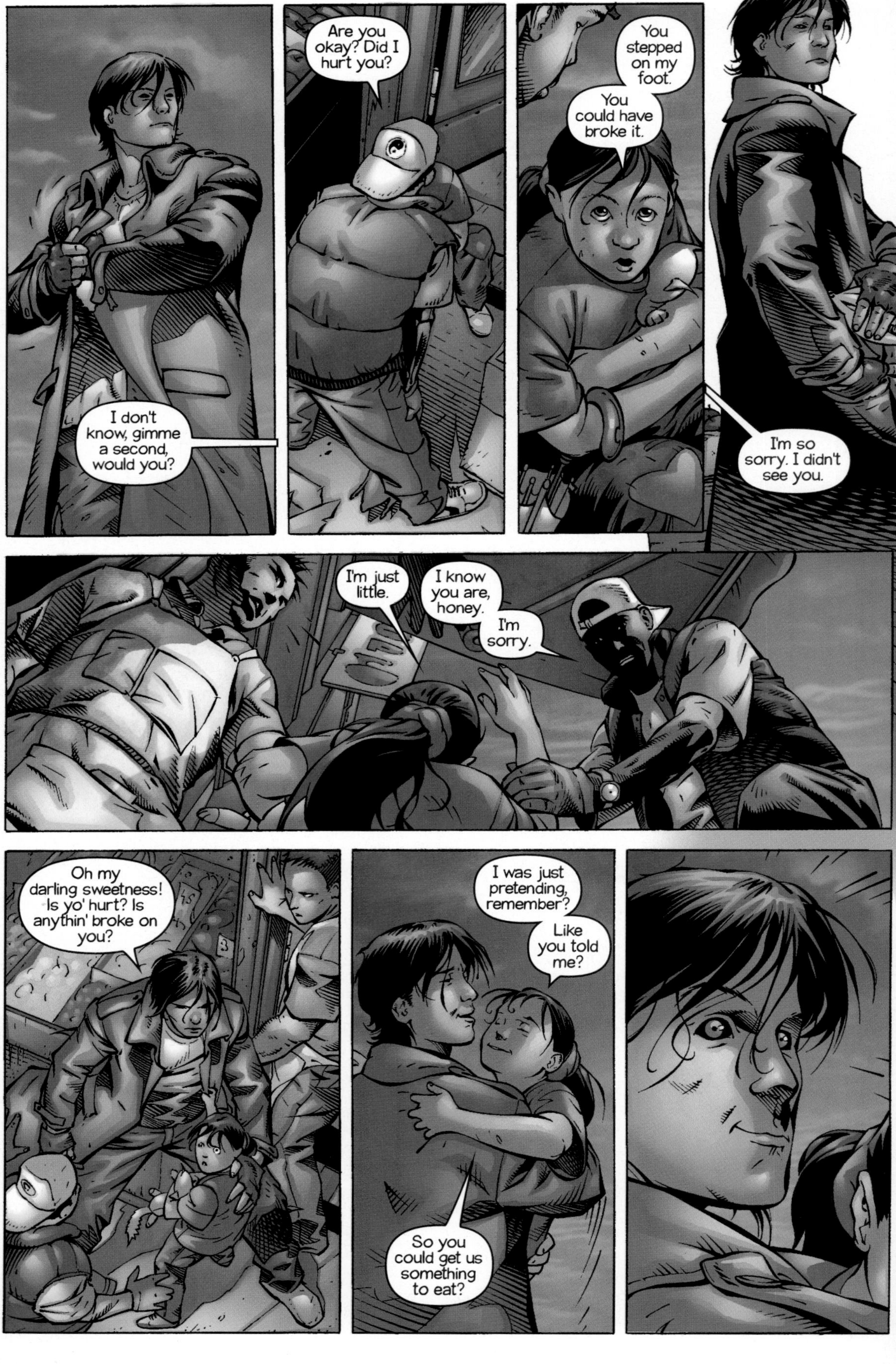
I don't know, gimme a second, would you?
Are you okay? Did I hurt you?
You stepped on my foot.
You could have broke it.
I'm so sorry. I didn't see you.
I'm just little.
I know you are, honey.
I'm sorry.
Oh my darling sweetness! Is yo' hurt? Is anythin' broke on you?
I was just pretending, remember?
Like you told me?
So you could get us something to eat?

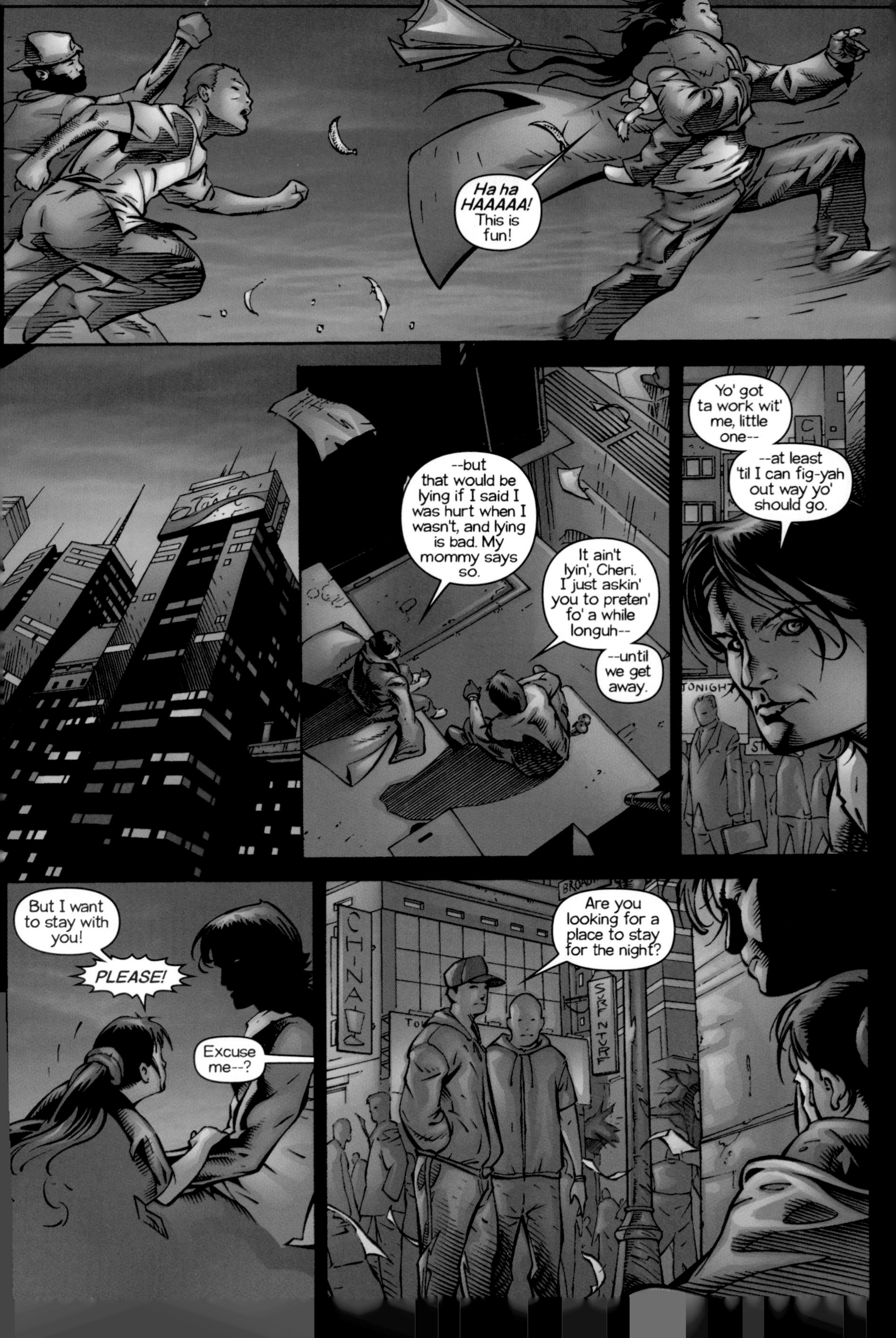

Ha ha HAAAAA! This is fun!
--but that would be lying if I said I was hurt when I wasn't, and lying is bad. My mommy says so.
It ain't lyin', Cheri. I just askin' you to preten' fo' a while longuh--
--until we get away.
Yo' got ta work wit' me, little one--
--at least 'til I can fig-yah out way yo' should go.
TONIGHT
But I want to stay with you!
PLEASE!
Excuse me--?
Are you looking for a place to stay for the night?
CHINA

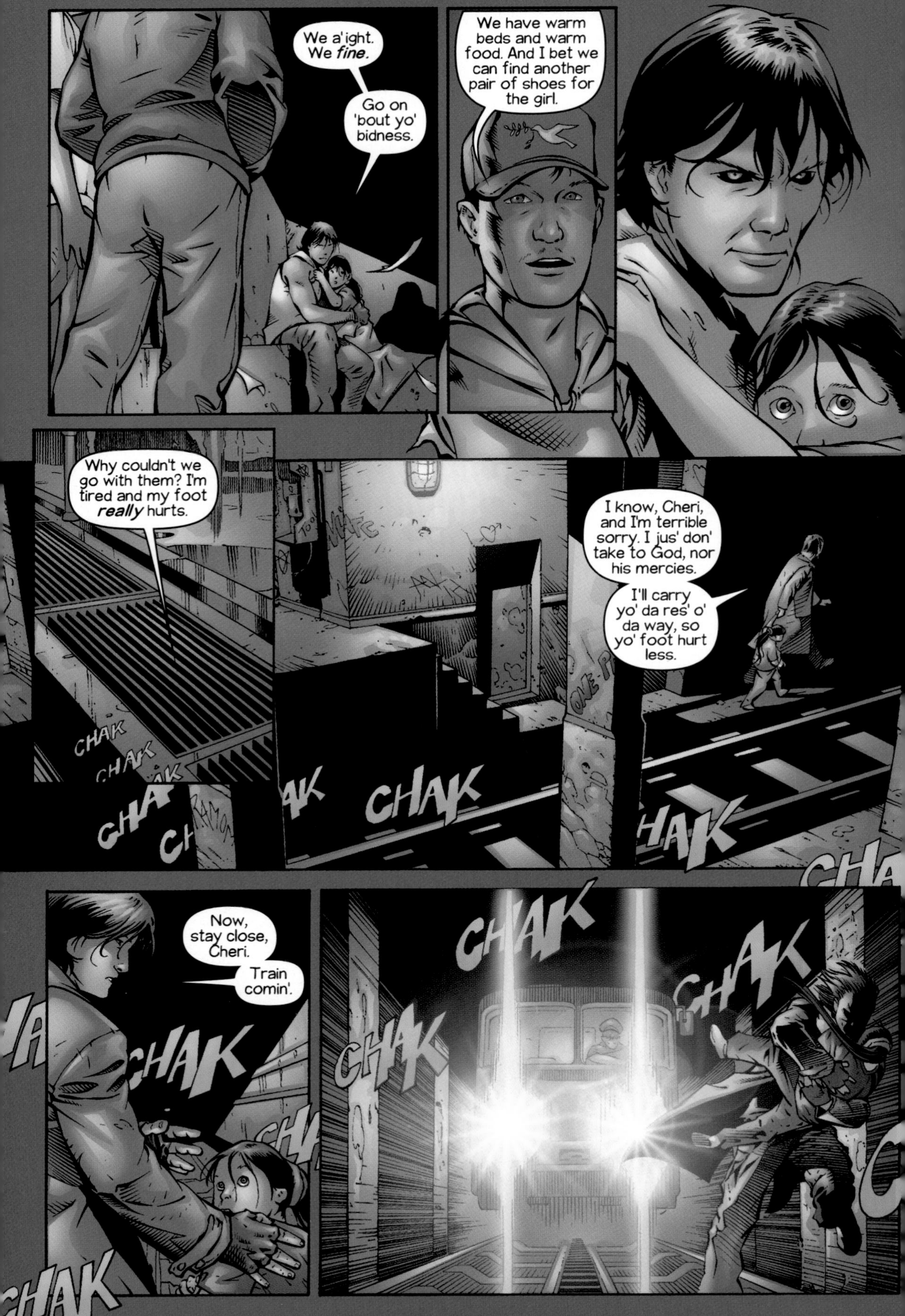
We a'ight. We *fine.*
Go on 'bout yo' bidness.
We have warm beds and warm food. And I bet we can find another pair of shoes for the girl.
Why couldn't we go with them? I'm tired and my foot ***really*** hurts.
I know, Cheri, and I'm terrible sorry. I jus' don' take to God, nor his mercies.
I'll carry yo' da res' o' da way, so yo' foot hurt less.
CHAK
CHAK
CHAK
CHAK
Now, stay close, Cheri.
Train comin'.
CHAK
CHAK
CHAK
CHAK
CHAK

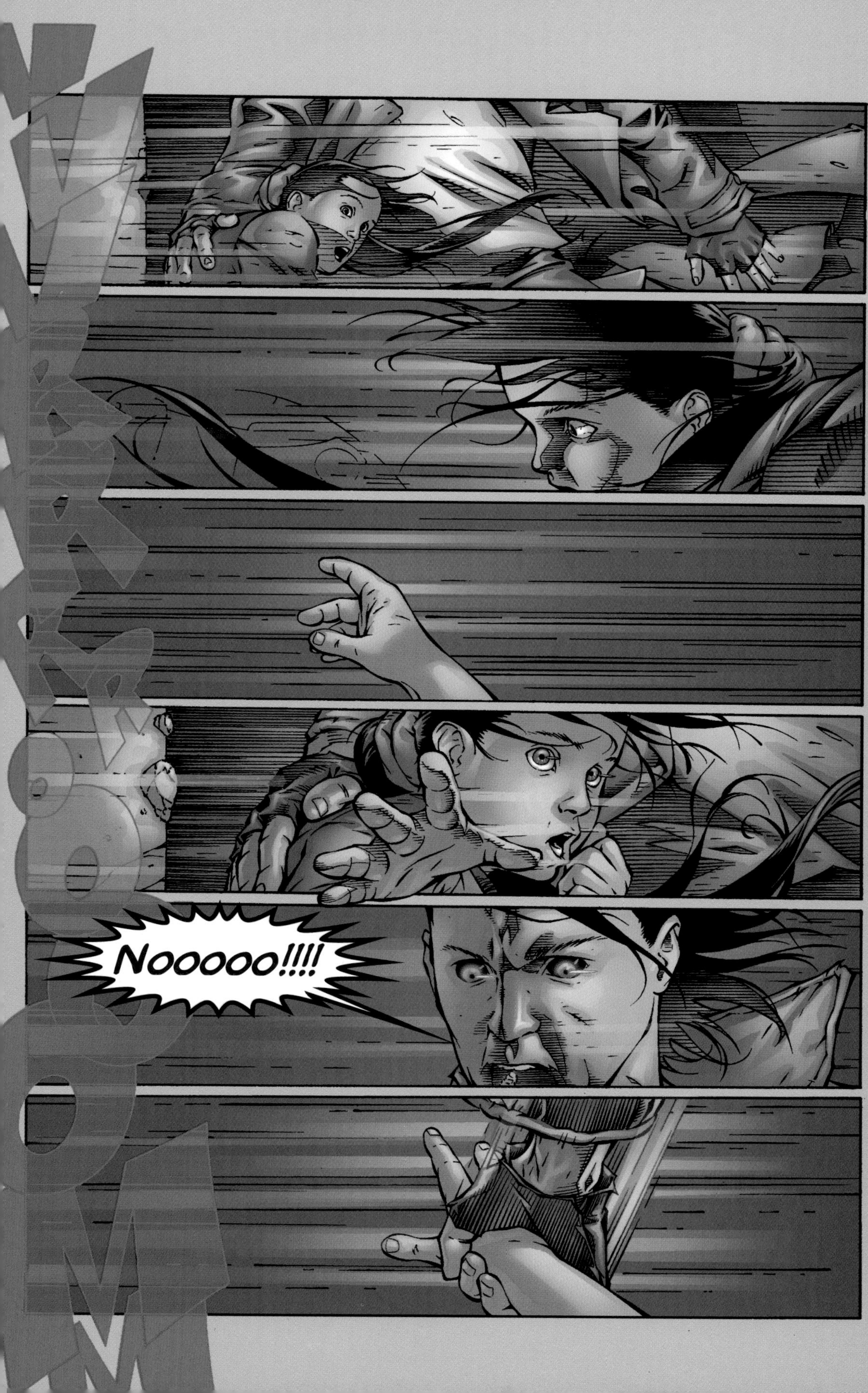
Nooooo!!!!

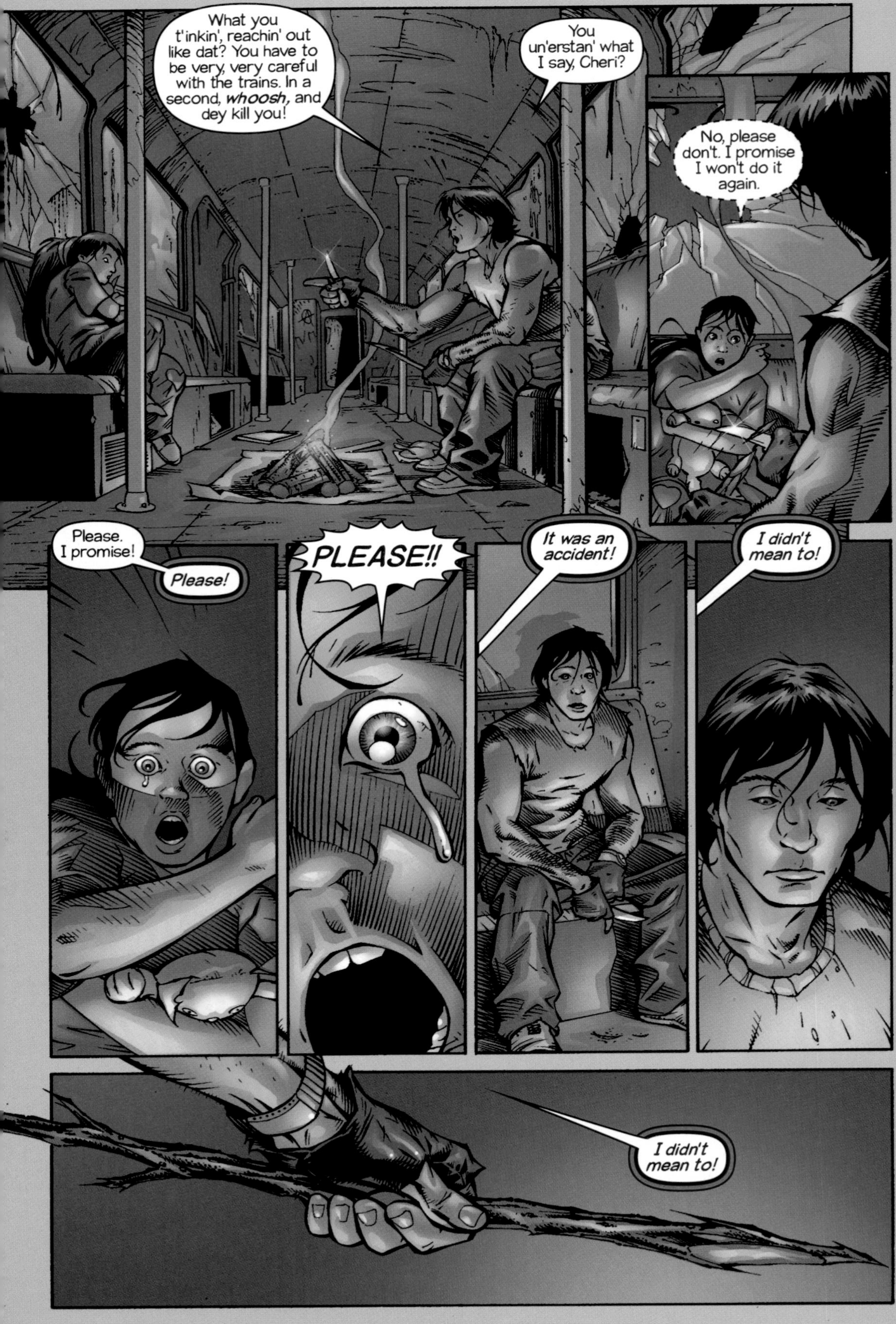

What you t'inkin', reachin' out like dat? You have to be very, very careful with the trains. In a second, **whoosh,** and dey kill you!
You un'erstan' what I say, Cheri?
No, please don't. I promise I won't do it again.
Please. I promise!
Please!
PLEASE!!
It was an accident!
I didn't mean to!
I didn't mean to!

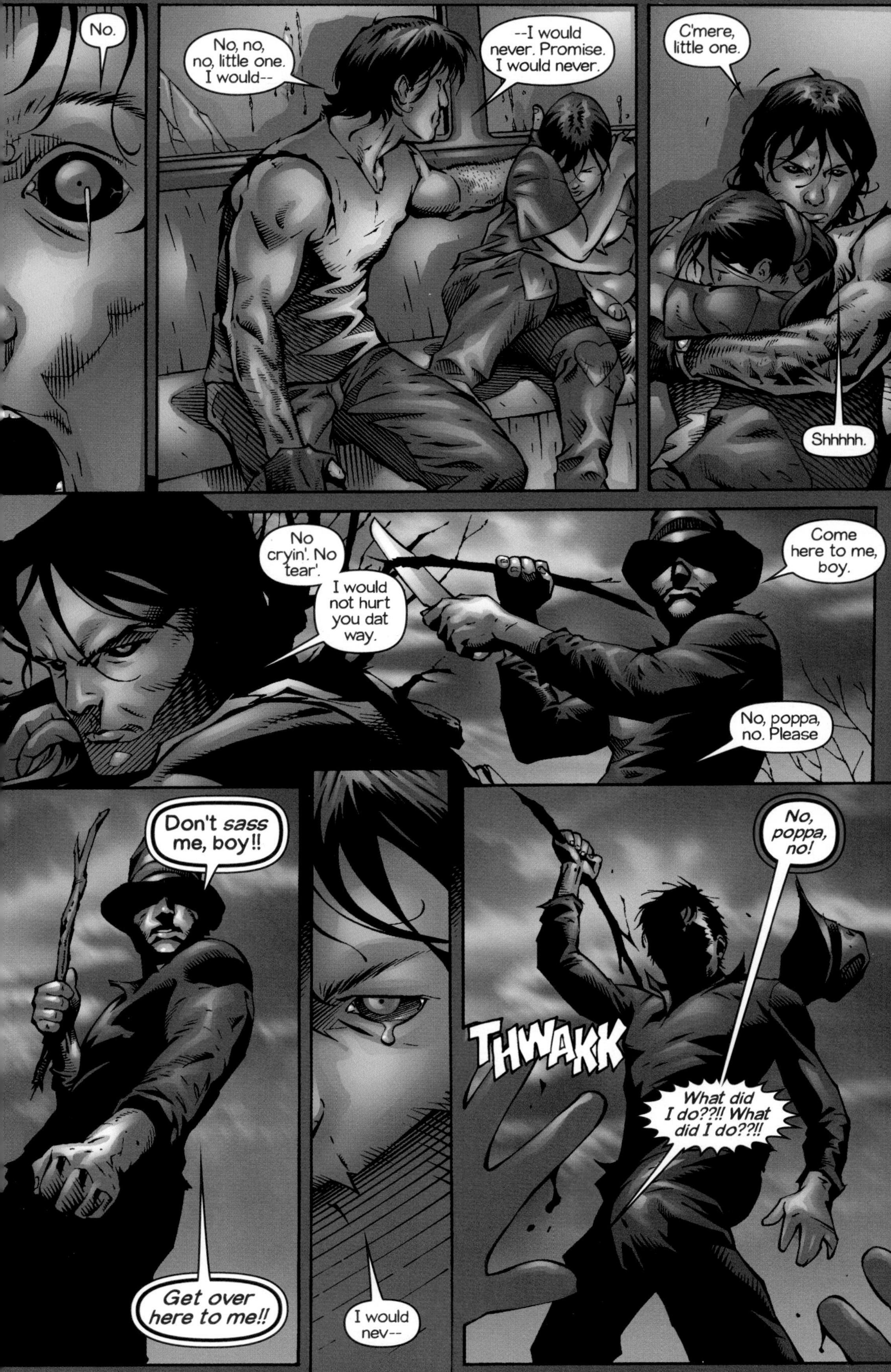
No.
No, no, no, little one. I would--
--I would never. Promise. I would never.
C'mere, little one.
Shhhhh.
No cryin'. No tear'.
I would not hurt you dat way.
Come here to me, boy.
No, poppa, no. Please
Don't *sass* me, boy!!
Get over here to me!!
I would nev--
THWAKK
No, poppa, no!
What did I do??!! What did I do??!!

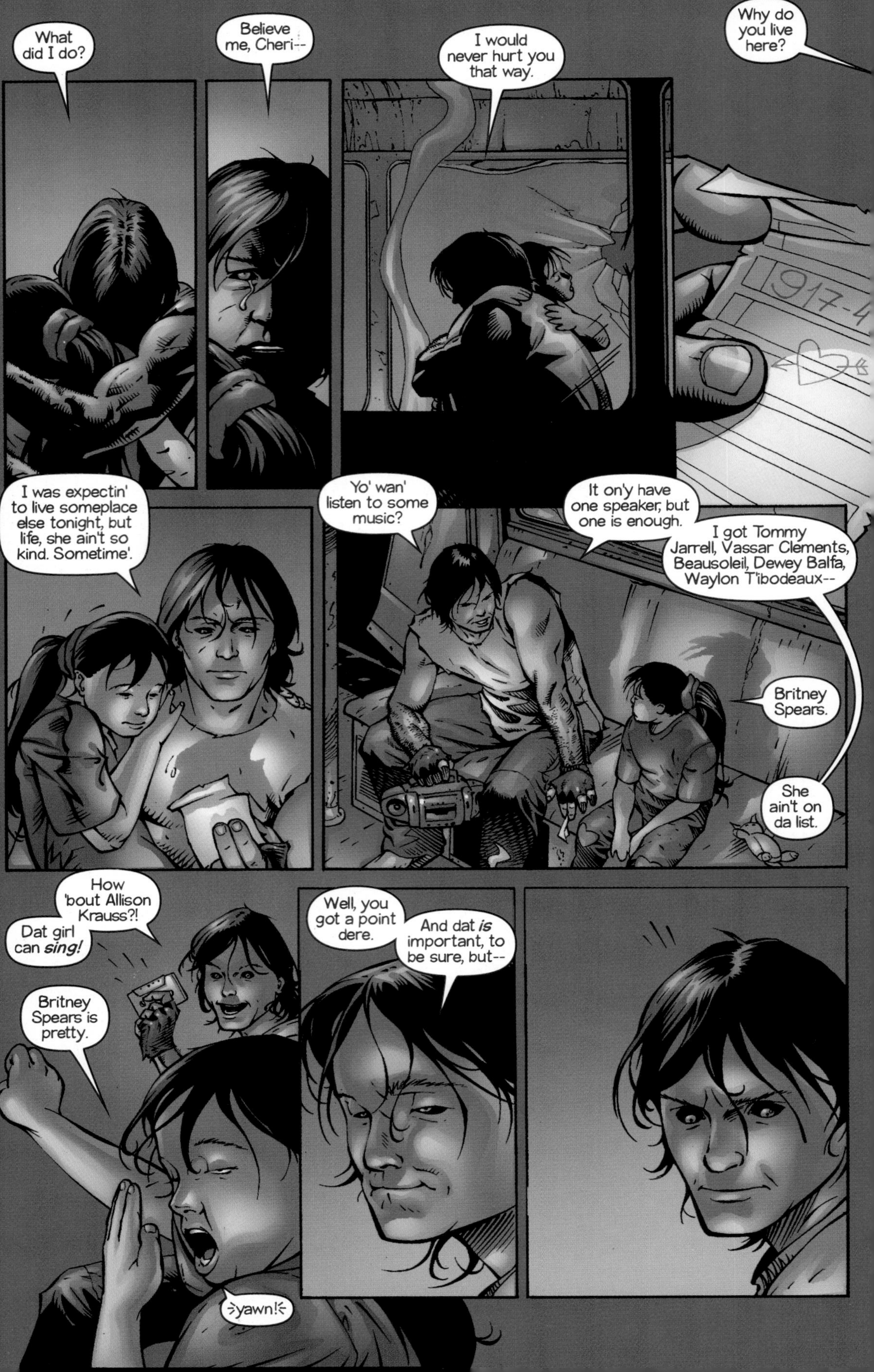
What did I do?
Believe me, Cheri--
I would never hurt you that way.
Why do you live here?
1917-4
I was expectin' to live someplace else tonight, but life, she ain't so kind. Sometime'.
Yo' wan' listen to some music?
It on'y have one speaker, but one is enough.
I got Tommy Jarrell, Vassar Clements, Beausoleil, Dewey Balfa, Waylon T'ibodeaux--
Britney Spears.
She ain't on da list.
How 'bout Allison Krauss?!
Dat girl can *sing!*
Britney Spears is pretty.
Well, you got a point dere.
And dat *is* important, to be sure, but--
yawn!

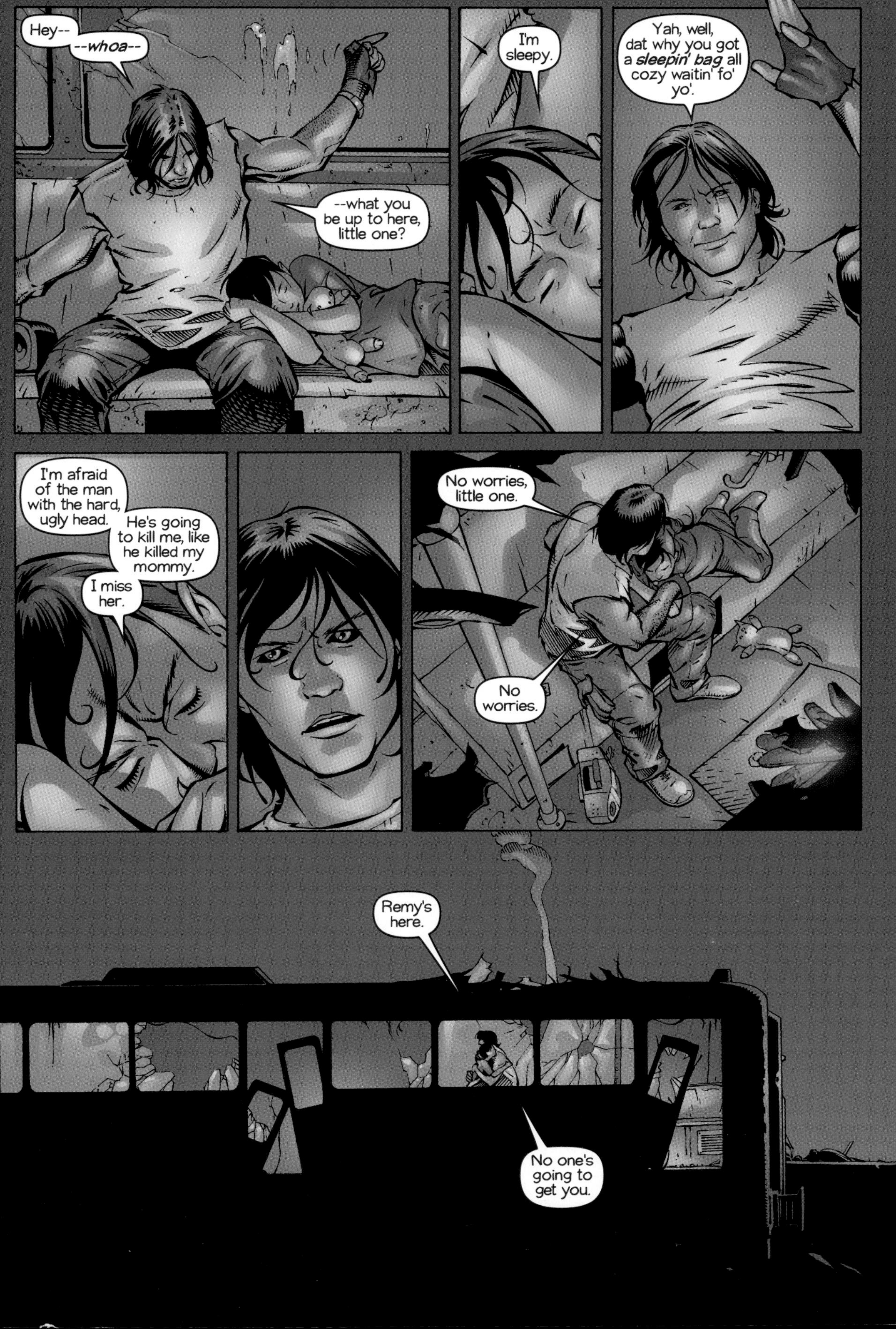

Hey--
--whoa--
--what you be up to here, little one?
I'm sleepy.
Yah, well, dat why you got a sleepin' bag all cozy waitin' fo' yo'.
I'm afraid of the man with the hard, ugly head.
He's going to kill me, like he killed my mommy.
I miss her.
No worries, little one.
No worries.
Remy's here.
No one's going to get you.

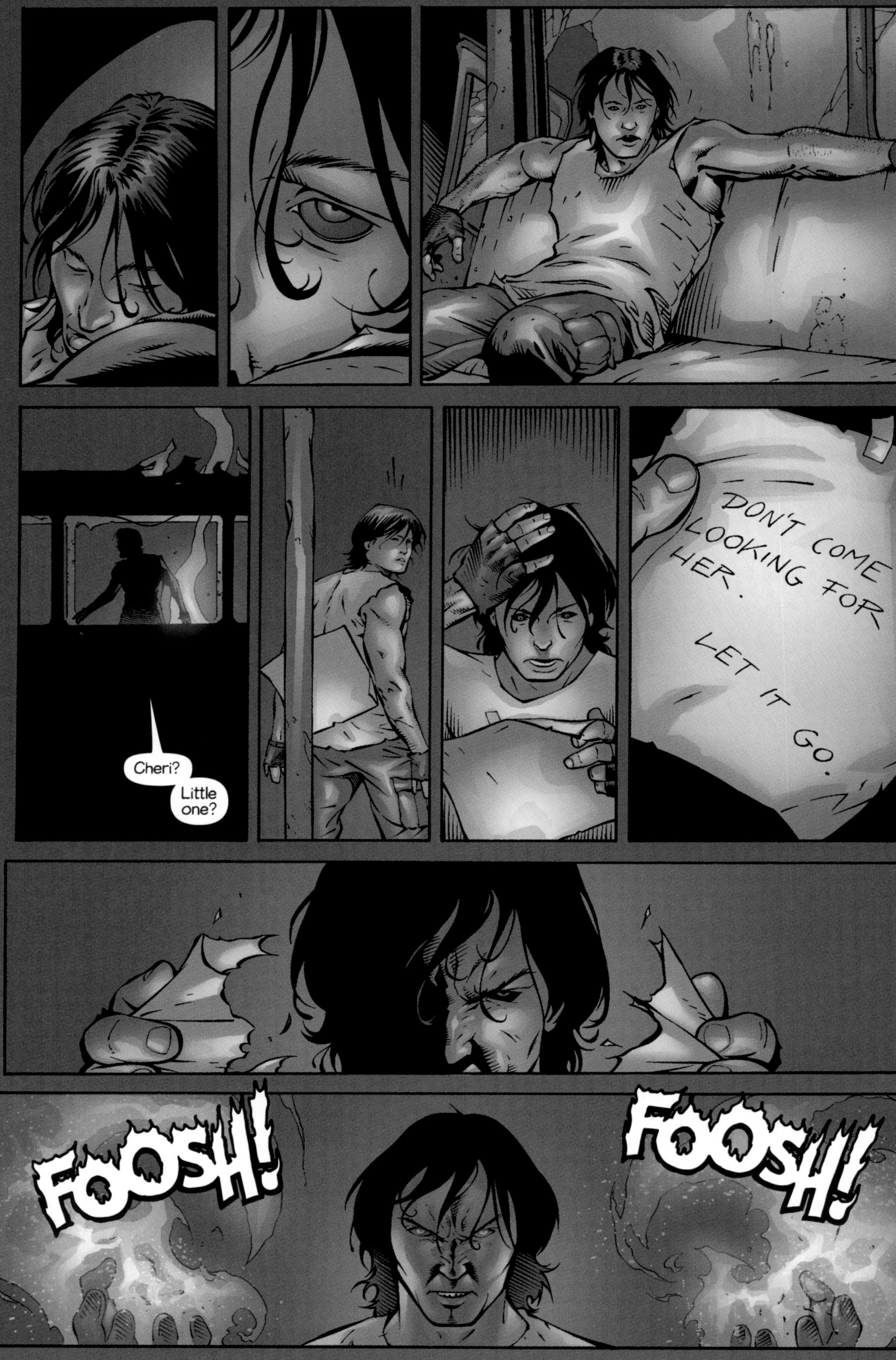
Cheri?
Little one?
DON'T COME LOOKING FOR HER.
LET IT GO.
FOOSH!
FOOSH!

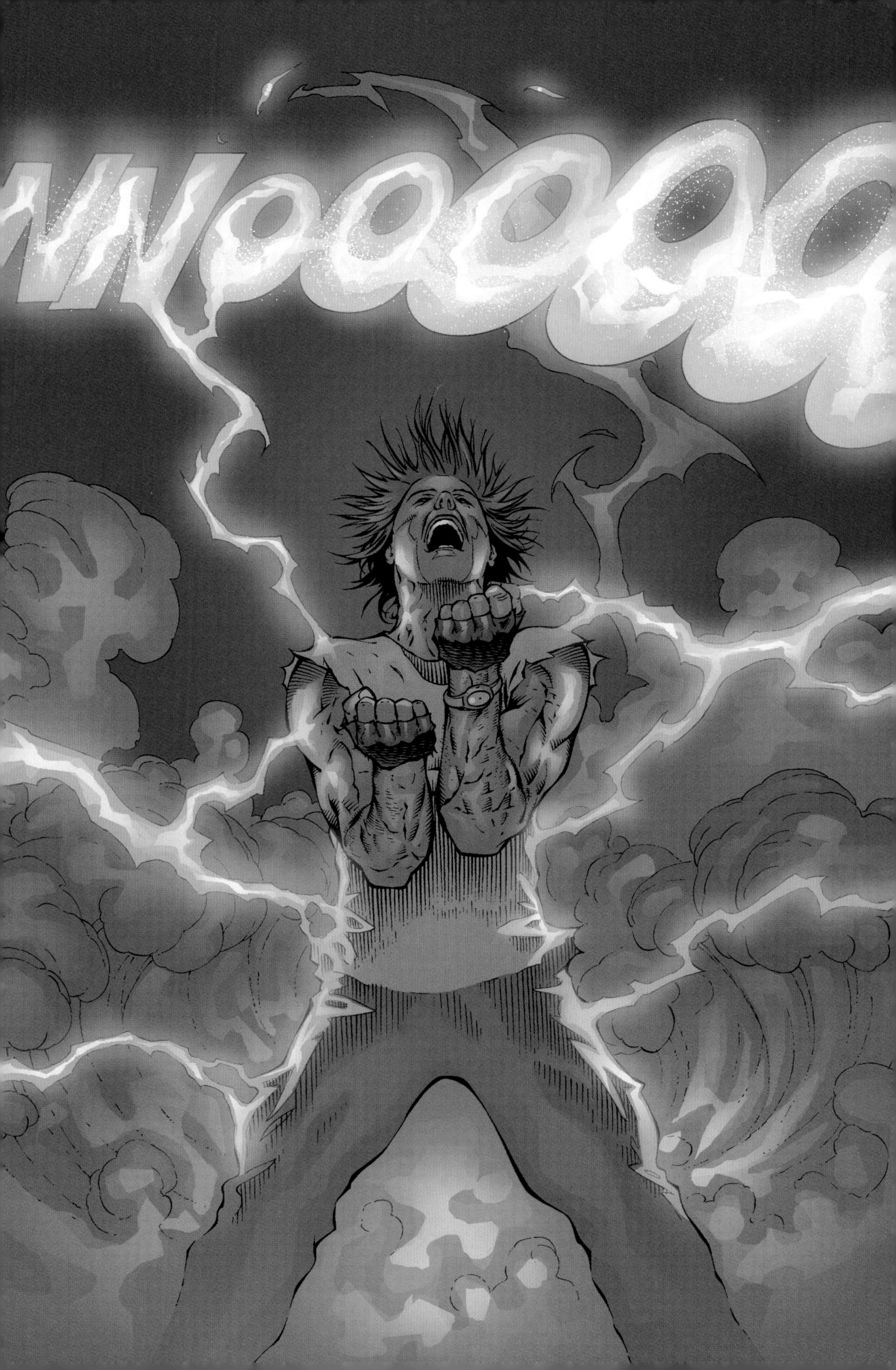
NOOOOOO

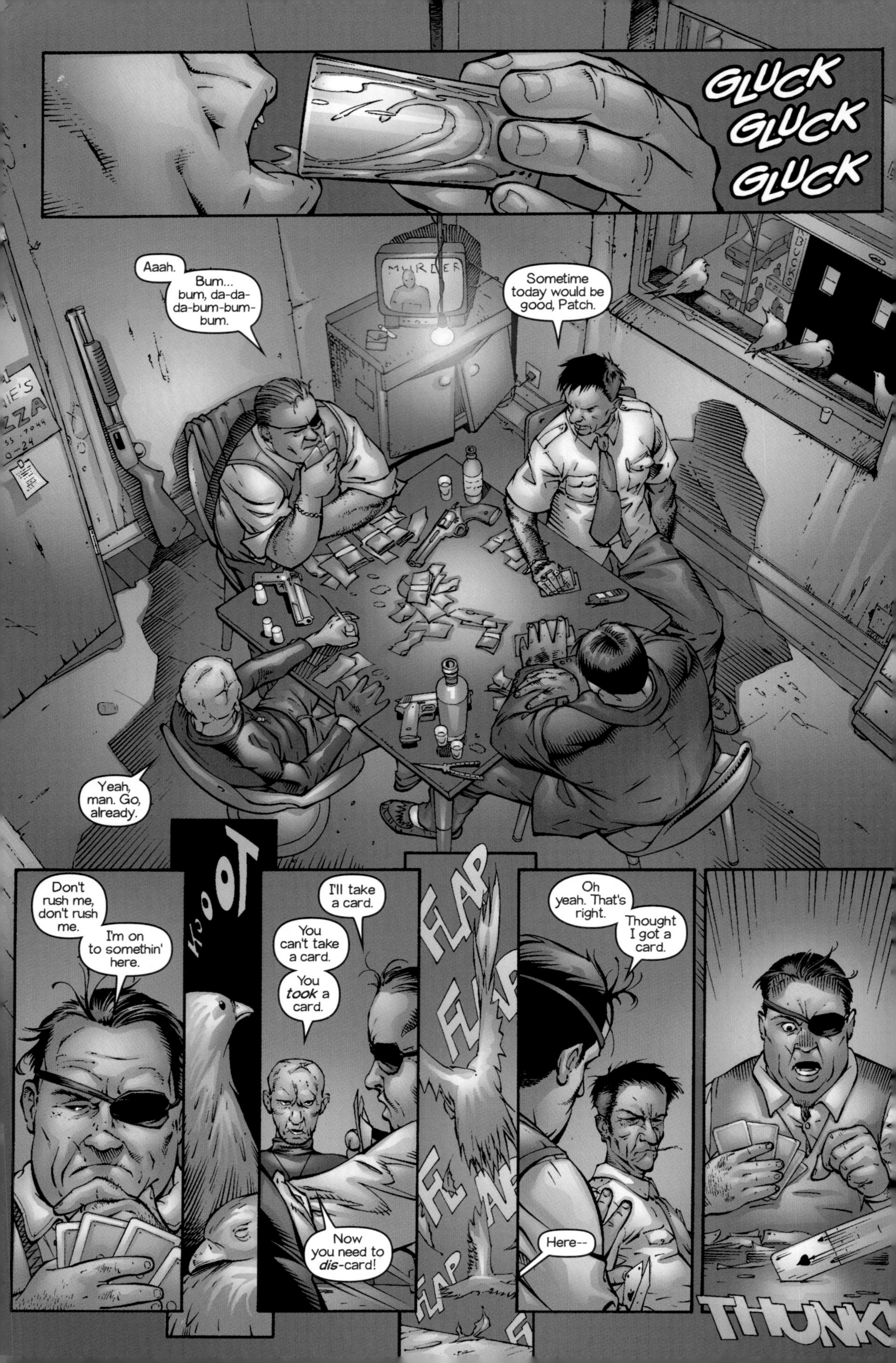
GLUCK
GLUCK
GLUCK
Aaah.
Bum... bum, da-da-da-bum-bum-bum.
MURDER
Sometime today would be good, Patch.
BUCKS
Yeah, man. Go, already.
Don't rush me, don't rush me.
I'm on to somethin' here.
HOOOT
I'll take a card.
You can't take a card.
You *took* a card.
Now you need to *dis*-card!
FLAP
FLAP
FLAP
FLAP
FLAP
Oh yeah. That's right.
Thought I got a card.
Here--
THUNK

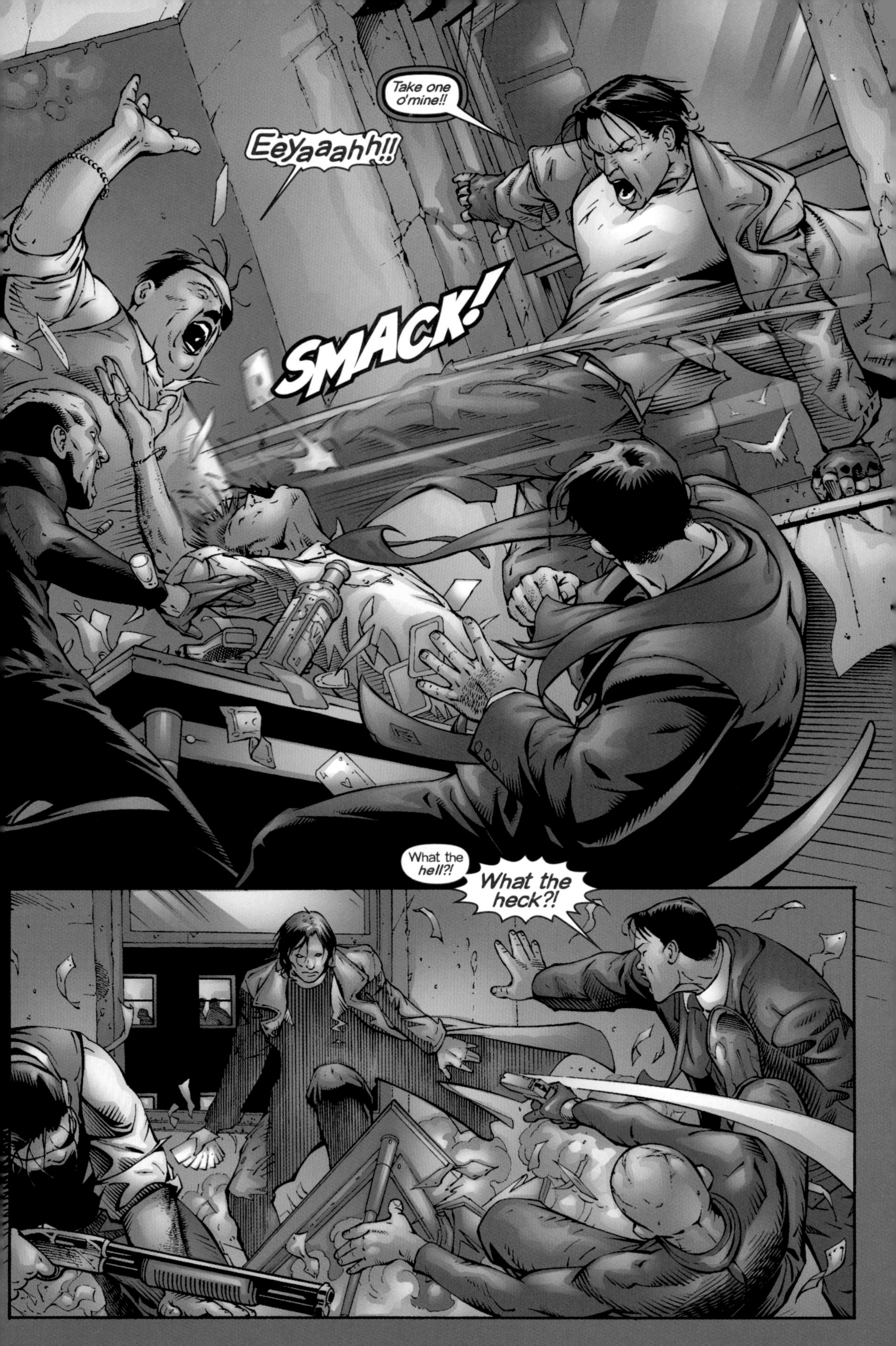
Take one o'mine!!
Eeyaaahh!!
SMACK!
What the hell?!
What the heck?!

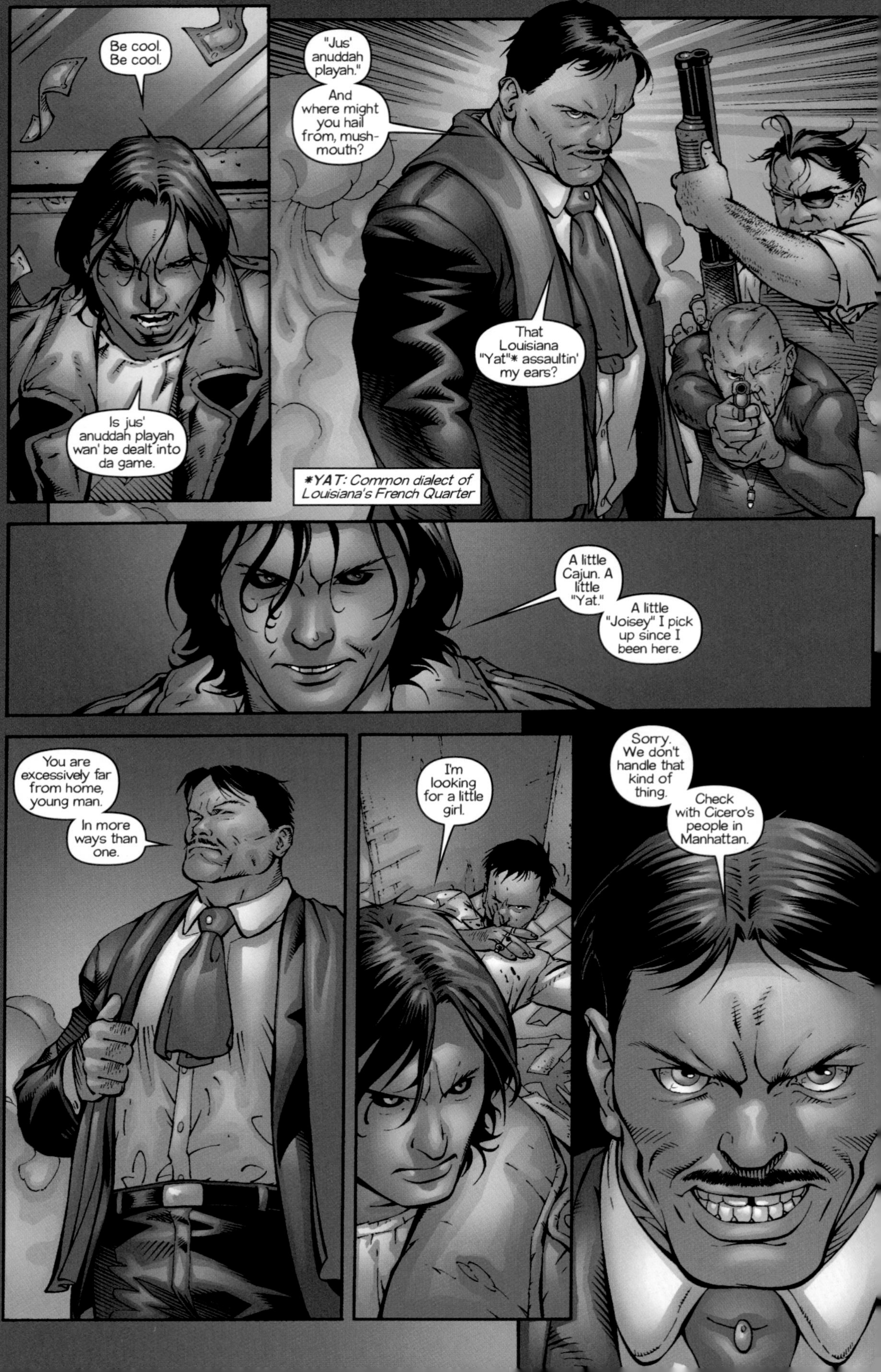
Be cool. Be cool.
Is jus' anuddah playah wan' be dealt into da game.
"Jus' anuddah playah."
And where might you hail from, mush-mouth?
That Louisiana "Yat"* assaultin' my ears?
*YAT: Common dialect of Louisiana's French Quarter
A little Cajun. A little "Yat."
A little "Joisey" I pick up since I been here.
You are excessively far from home, young man.
In more ways than one.
I'm looking for a little girl.
Sorry. We don't handle that kind of thing.
Check with Cicero's people in Manhattan.

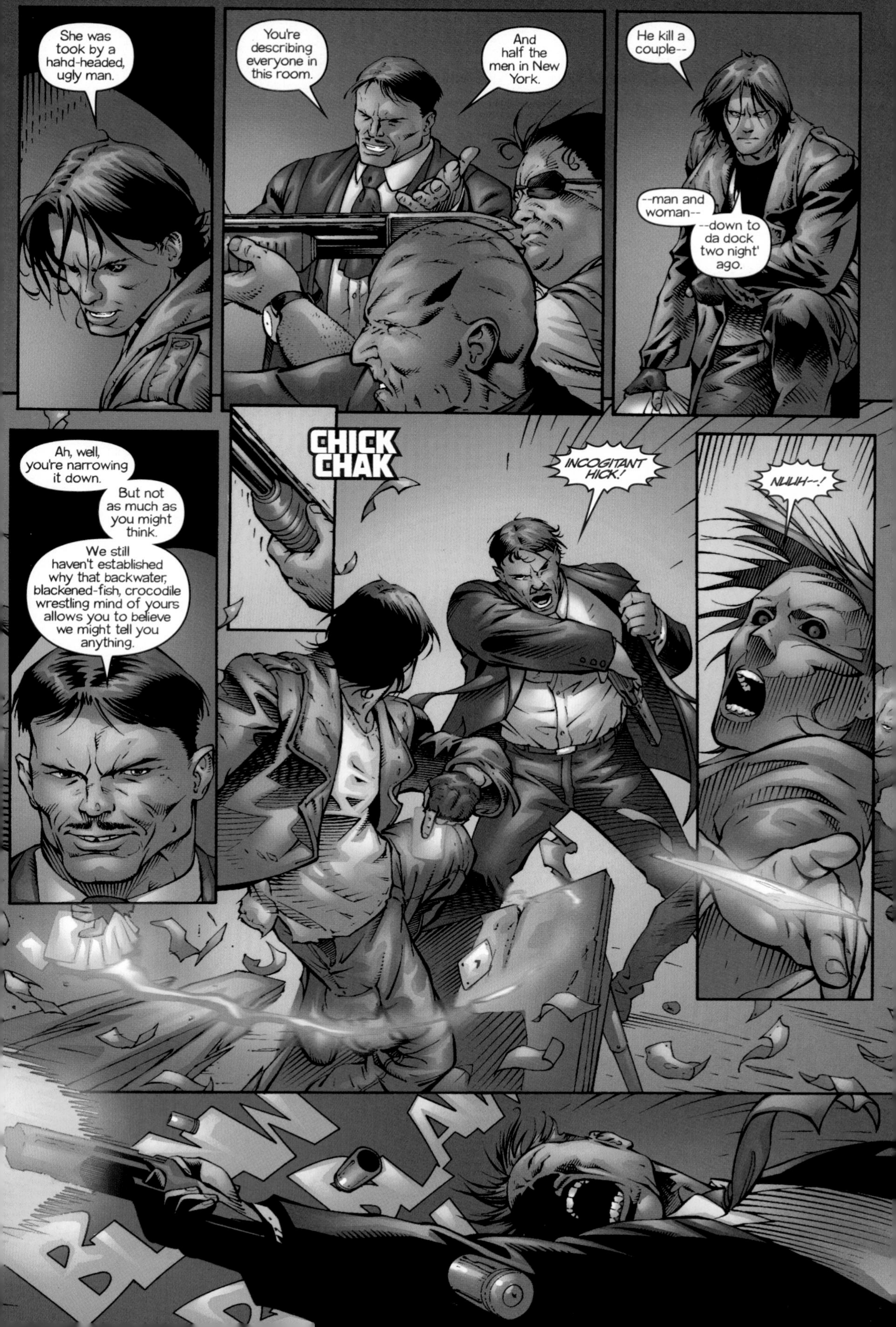
She was took by a hahd-headed, ugly man.
You're describing everyone in this room.
And half the men in New York.
He kill a couple--
--man and woman--
--down to da dock two night' ago.
Ah, well, you're narrowing it down.
But not as much as you might think.
We still haven't established why that backwater, blackened-fish, crocodile wrestling mind of yours allows you to believe we might tell you anything.
CHICK CHAK
INCOGITANT HICK!
NUUH--!

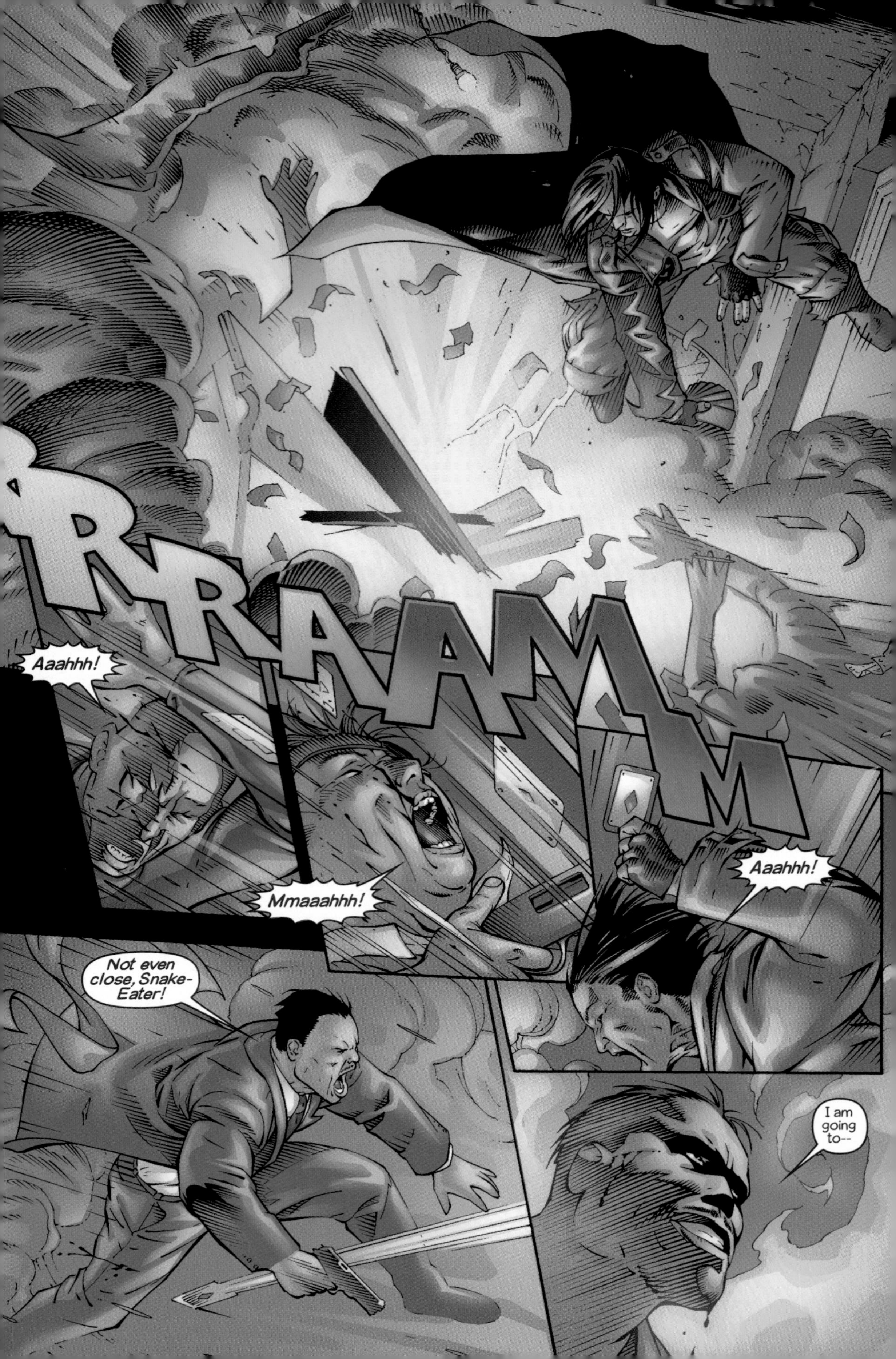
RRAAMM
Aaahhh!
Mmaaahhh!
Aaahhh!
Not even close, Snake-Eater!
I am going to--

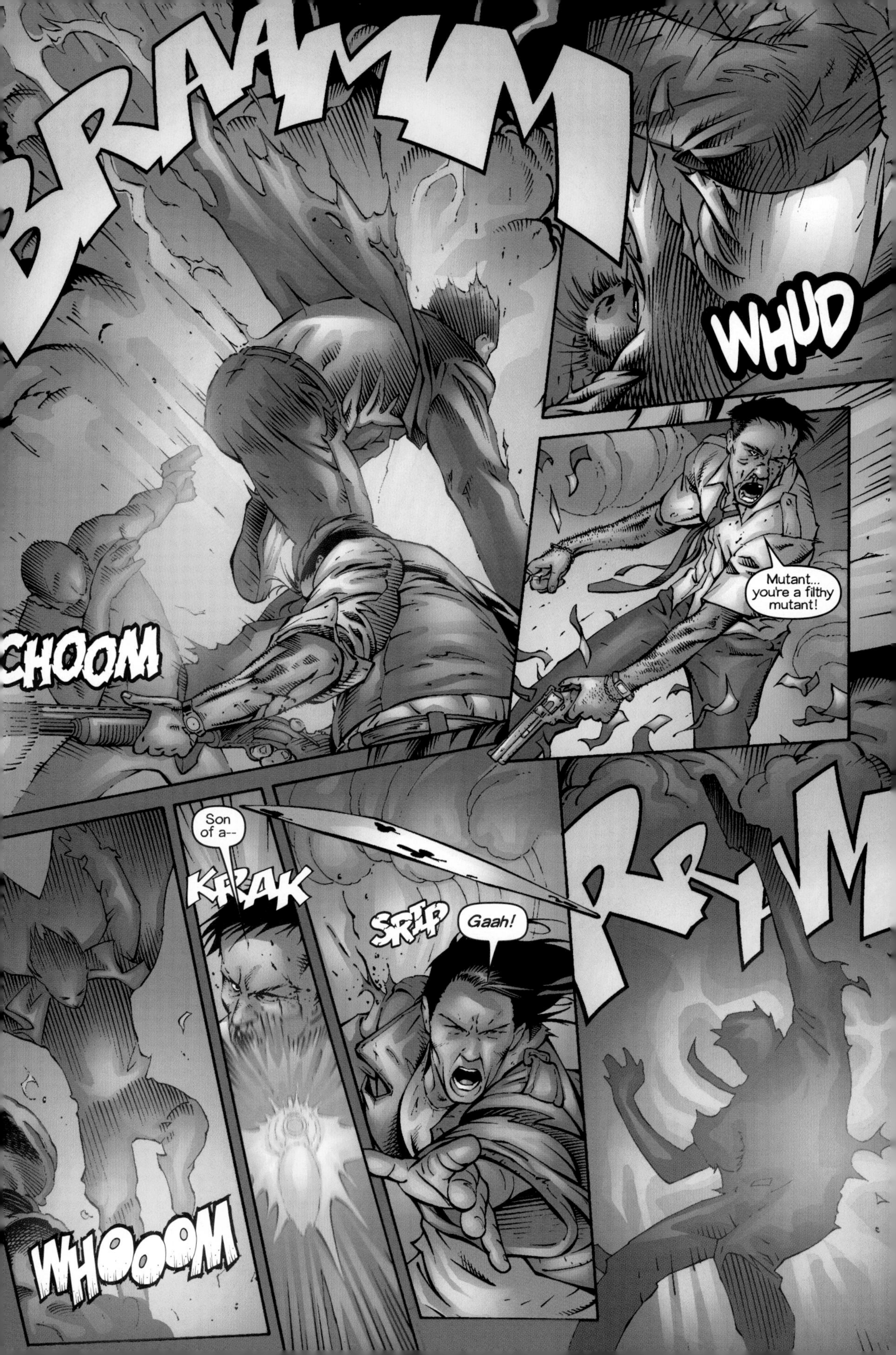
BRAAMM
WHUD
CHOOM
Mutant... you're a filthy mutant!
Son of a--
KRAK
SRIP
Gaah!
RAYM
WHOOOM

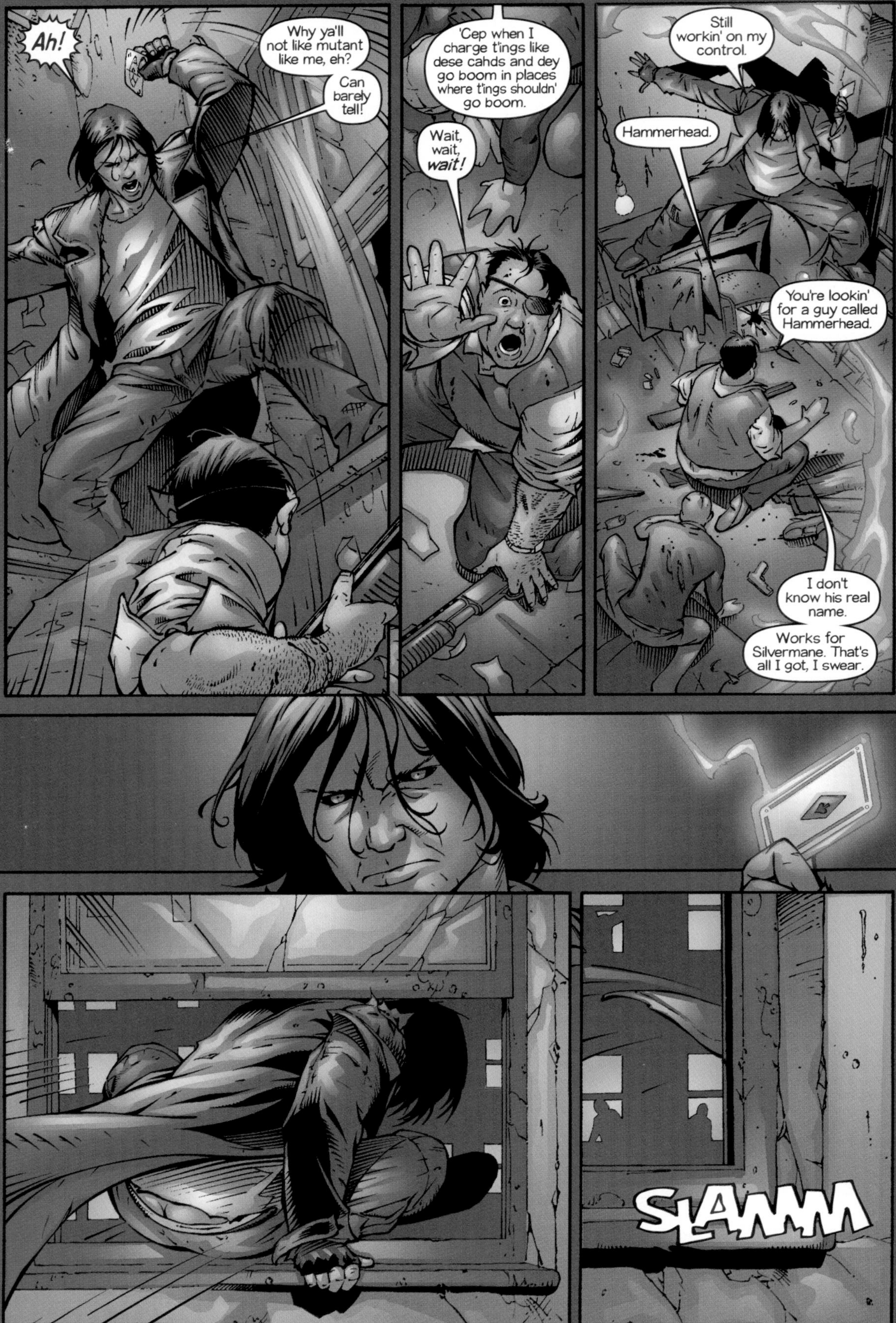
Ah!
Why ya'll not like mutant like me, eh?
Can barely tell!
'Cep when I charge t'ings like dese cahds and dey go boom in places where t'ings shouldn' go boom.
Wait, wait, *wait!*
Still workin' on my control.
Hammerhead.
You're lookin' for a guy called Hammerhead.
I don't know his real name.
Works for Silvermane. That's all I got, I swear.
SLAMM

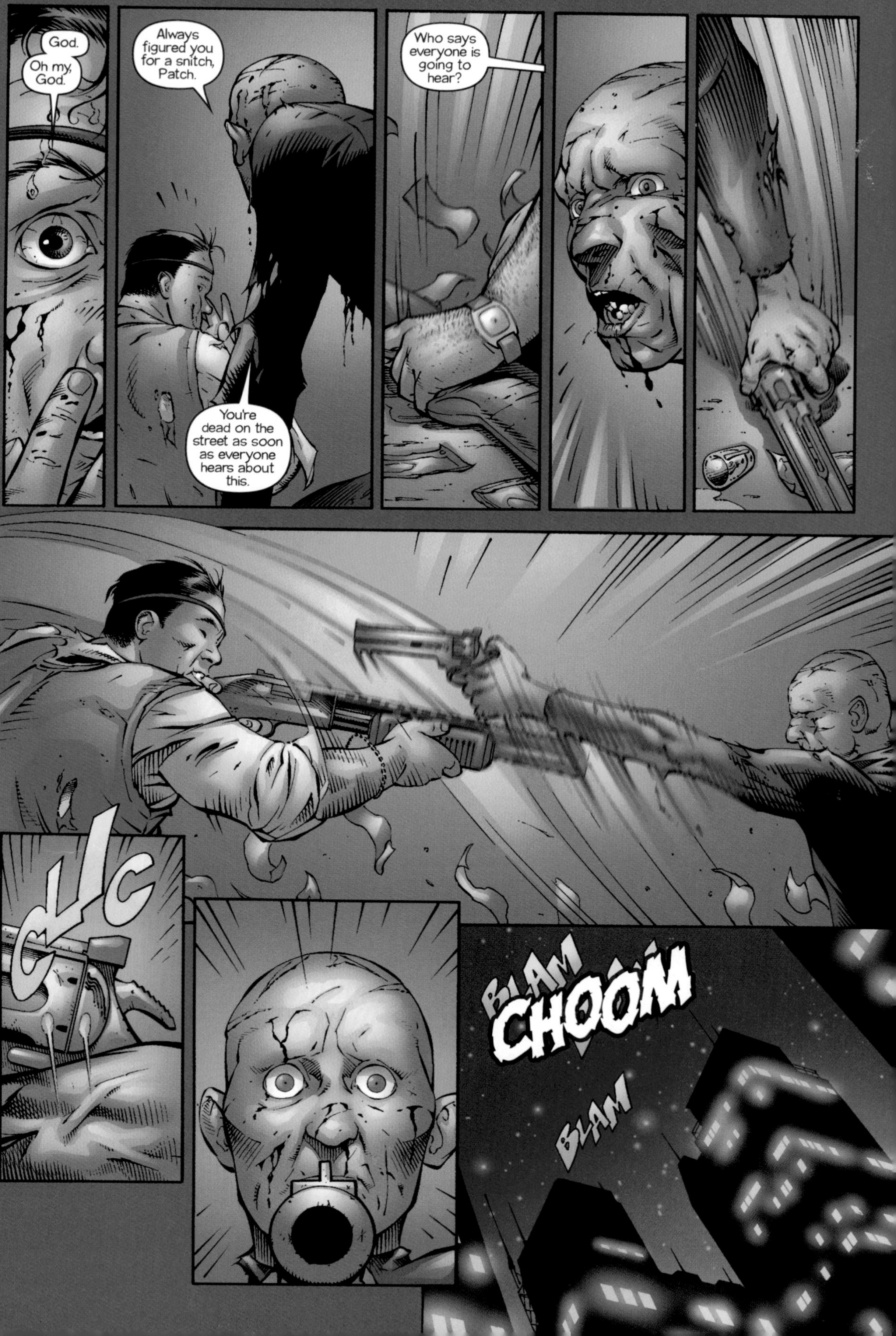
God.
Oh my, God.
Always figured you for a snitch, Patch.
You're dead on the street as soon as everyone hears about this.
Who says everyone is going to hear?
CLIC
BLAM
CHOOM
BLAM

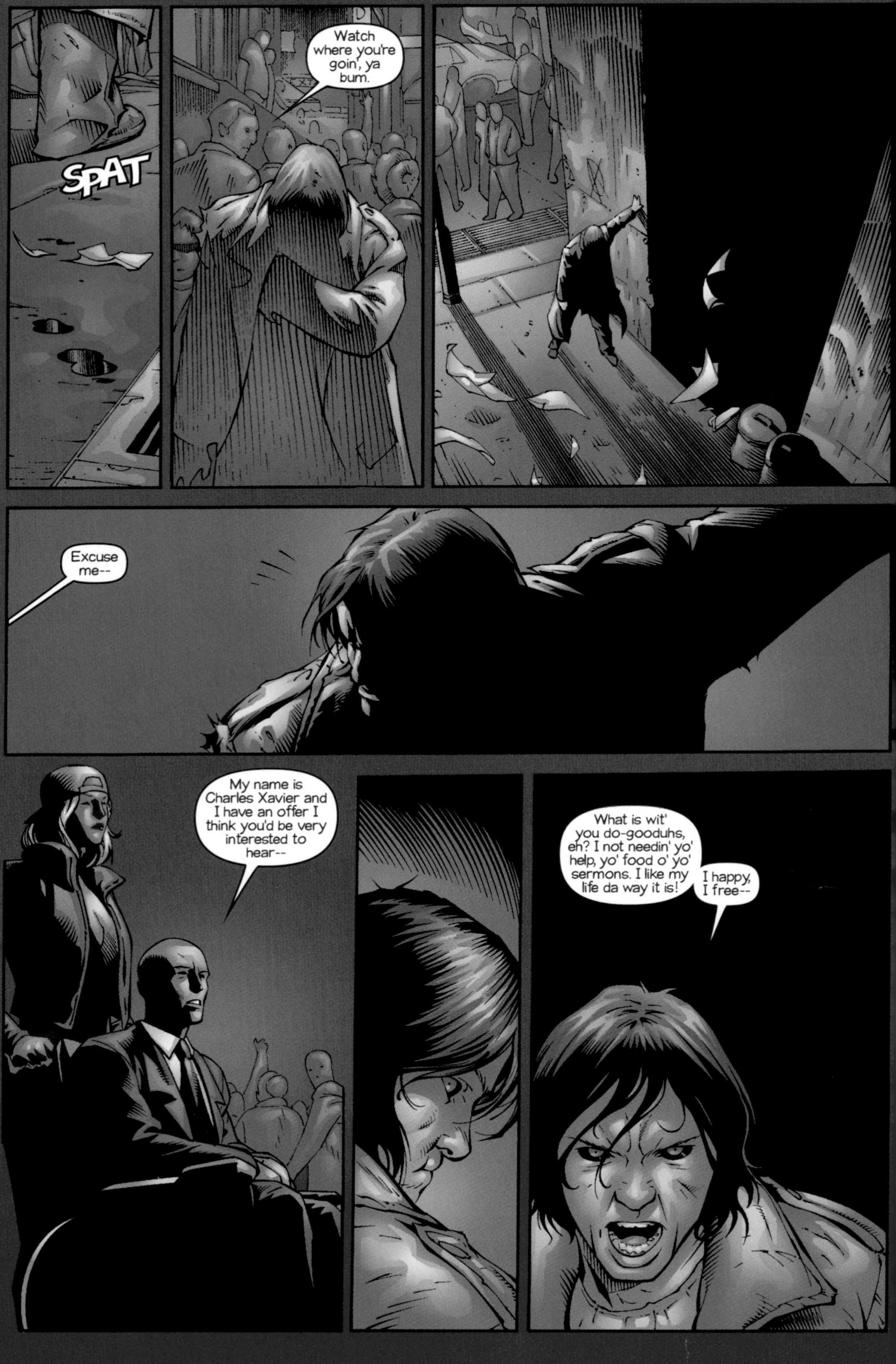
SPAT
Watch where you're goin', ya bum.
Excuse me--
My name is Charles Xavier and I have an offer I think you'd be very interested to hear--
What is wit' you do-gooduhs, eh? I not needin' yo' help, yo' food o' yo' sermons. I like my life da way it is!
I happy, I free--

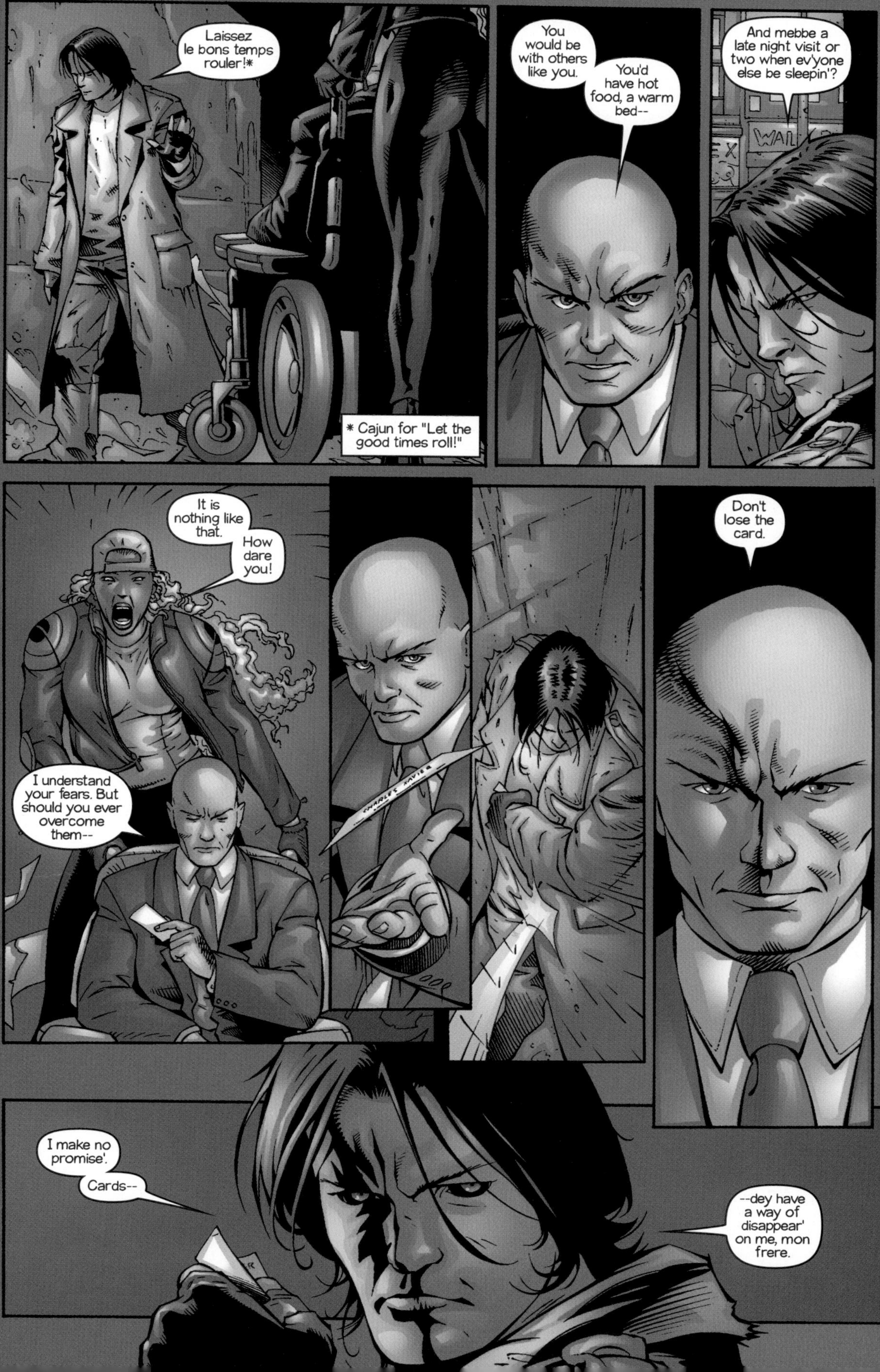
Laissez le bons temps rouler!*
* Cajun for "Let the good times roll!"
You would be with others like you.
You'd have hot food, a warm bed--
And mebbe a late night visit or two when ev'yone else be sleepin'?
It is nothing like that.
How dare you!
I understand your fears. But should you ever overcome them--
CHARLES XAVIER
Don't lose the card.
I make no promise'.
Cards--
--dey have a way of disappear' on me, mon frere.

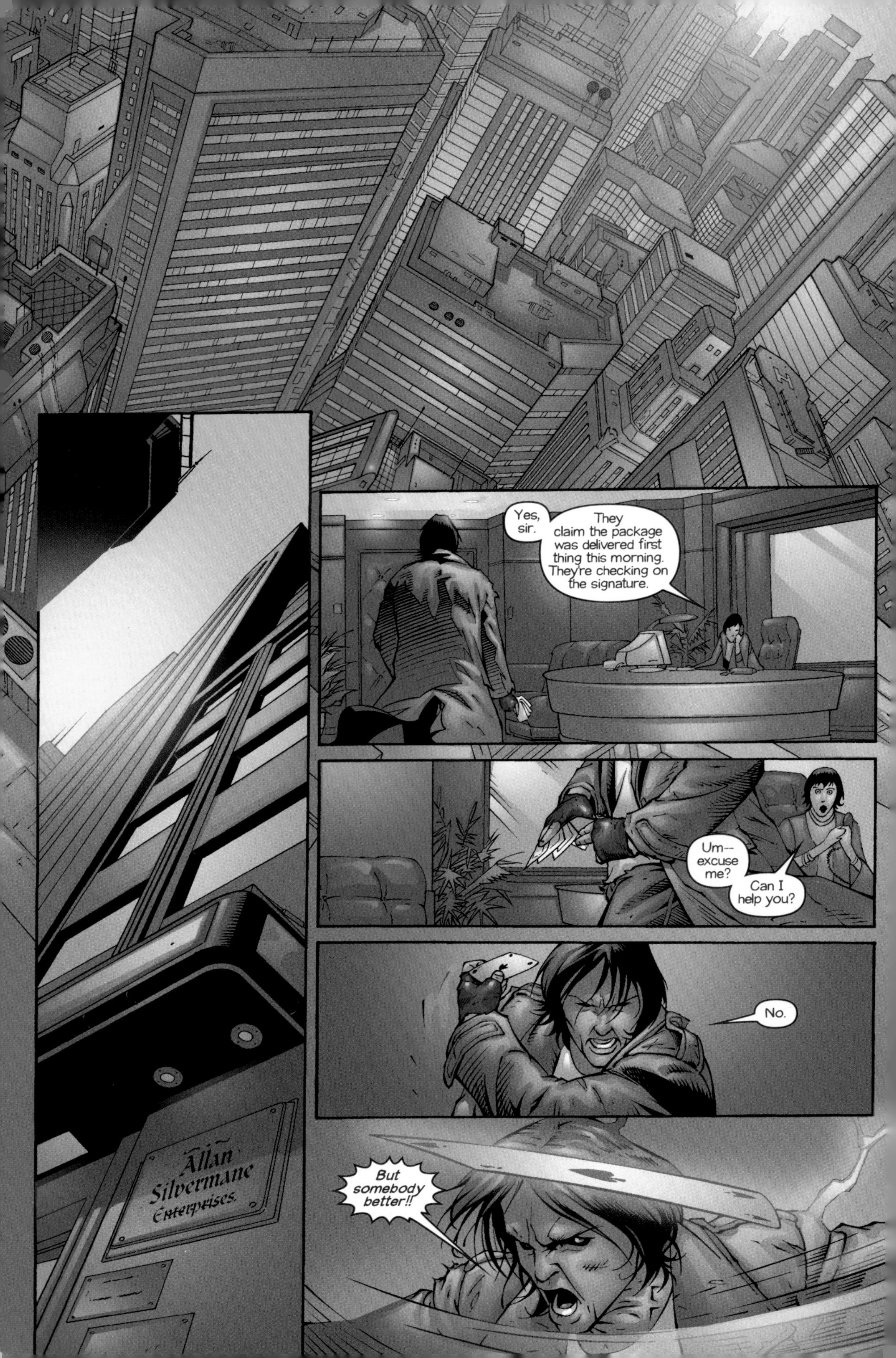

Allan Silvermane Enterprises.
Yes, sir.
They claim the package was delivered first thing this morning. They're checking on the signature.
Um-- excuse me?
Can I help you?
No.
But somebody better!!

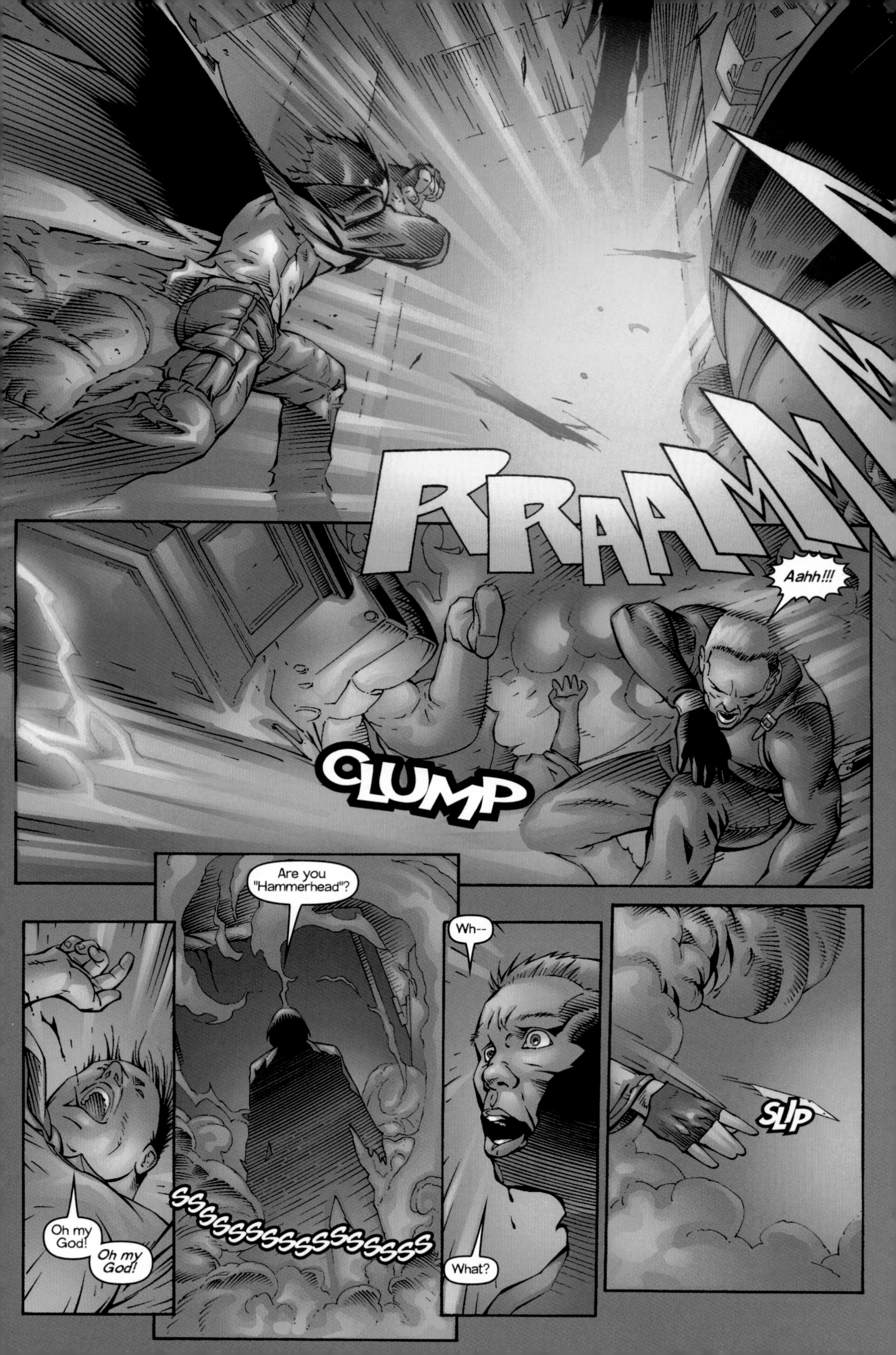
RRAAM
Aahh!!!
CLUMP
Oh my God!
Oh my God!
Are you "Hammerhead"?
SSSSSSSSSSSSSSSSSS
Wh--
What?
SLIP

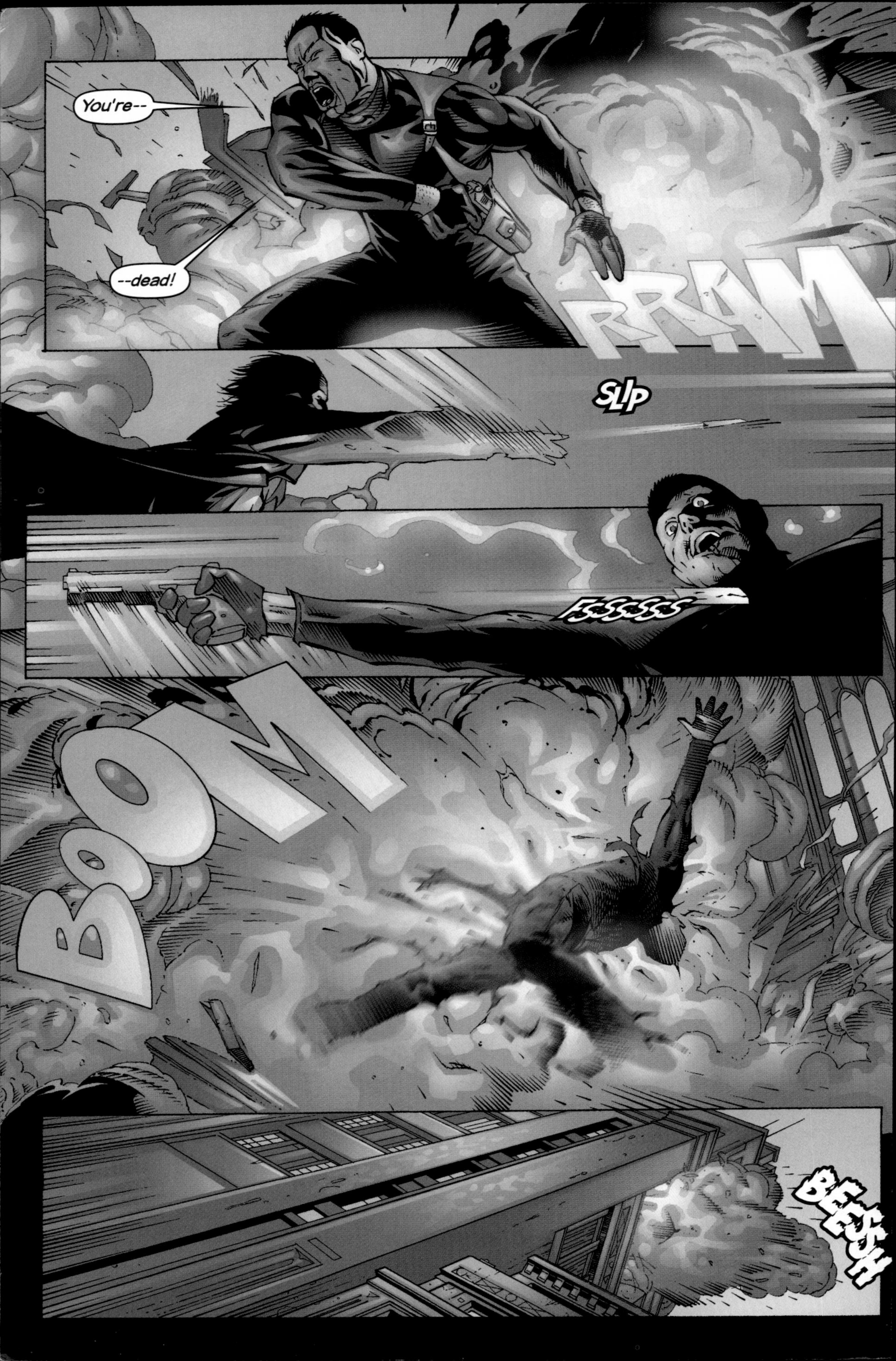
You're--
--dead!
RRAM
SLIP
FSSSSSS
BOOM
BLEESH

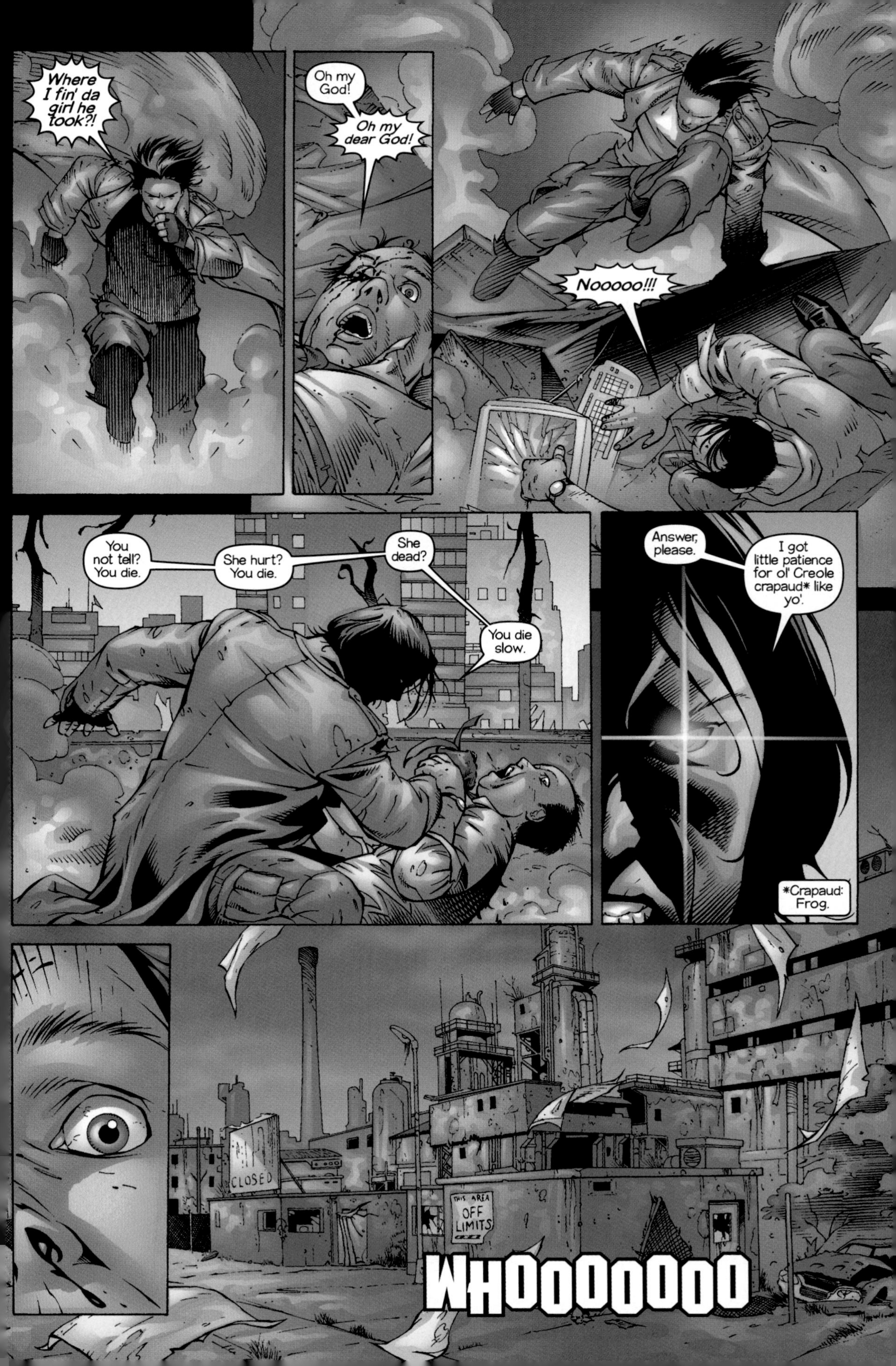

Where I fin' da girl he took?!
Oh my God!
Oh my dear God!
Nooooo!!!
You not tell? You die.
She hurt? You die.
She dead?
You die slow.
Answer, please.
I got little patience for ol' Creole crapaud* like yo'.
*Crapaud: Frog.
CLOSED
THIS AREA OFF LIMITS
WHOOOOOOOO

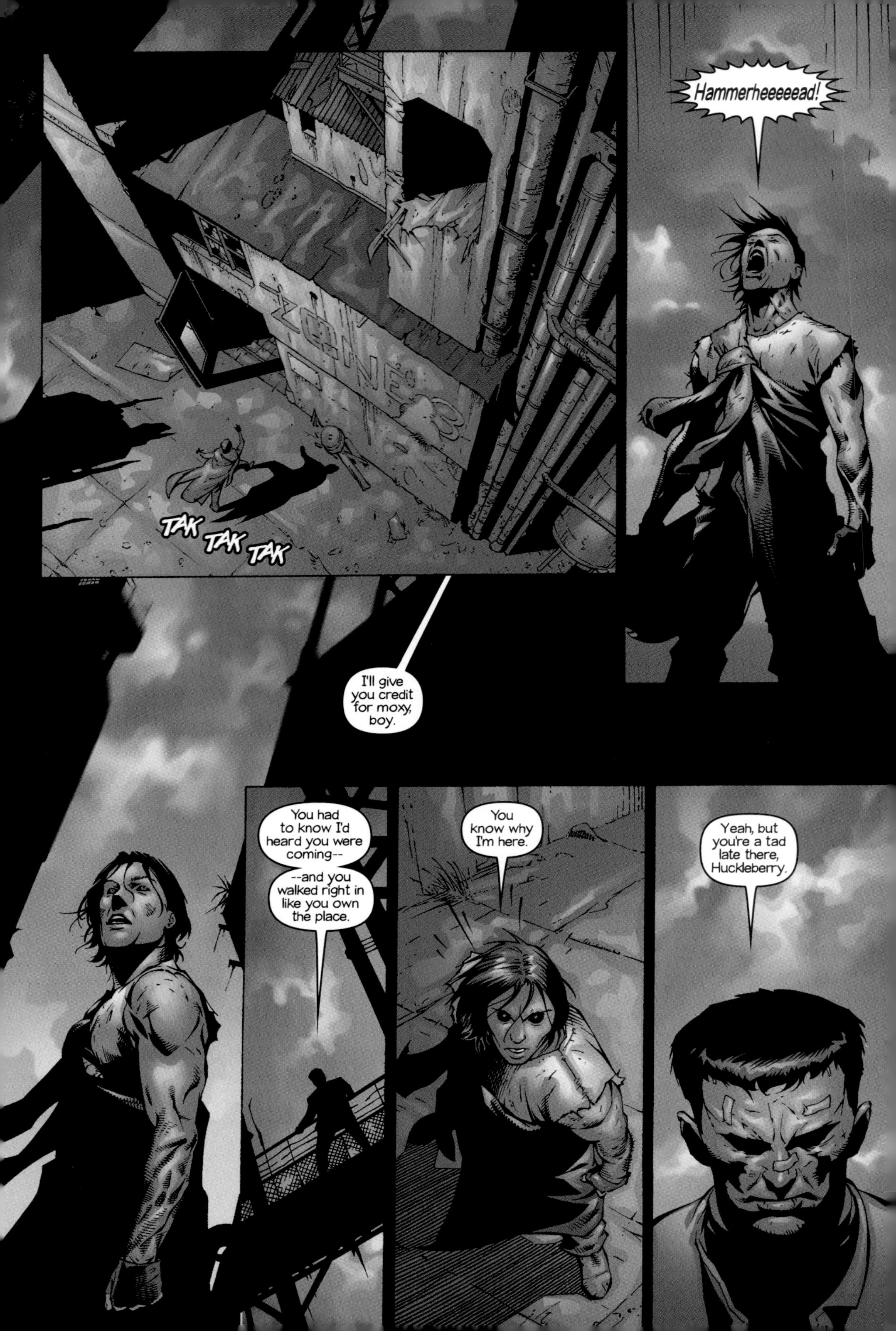
TAK TAK TAK
Hammerheeeeead!
I'll give you credit for moxy, boy.
You had to know I'd heard you were coming--
--and you walked right in like you own the place.
You know why I'm here.
Yeah, but you're a tad late there, Huckleberry.

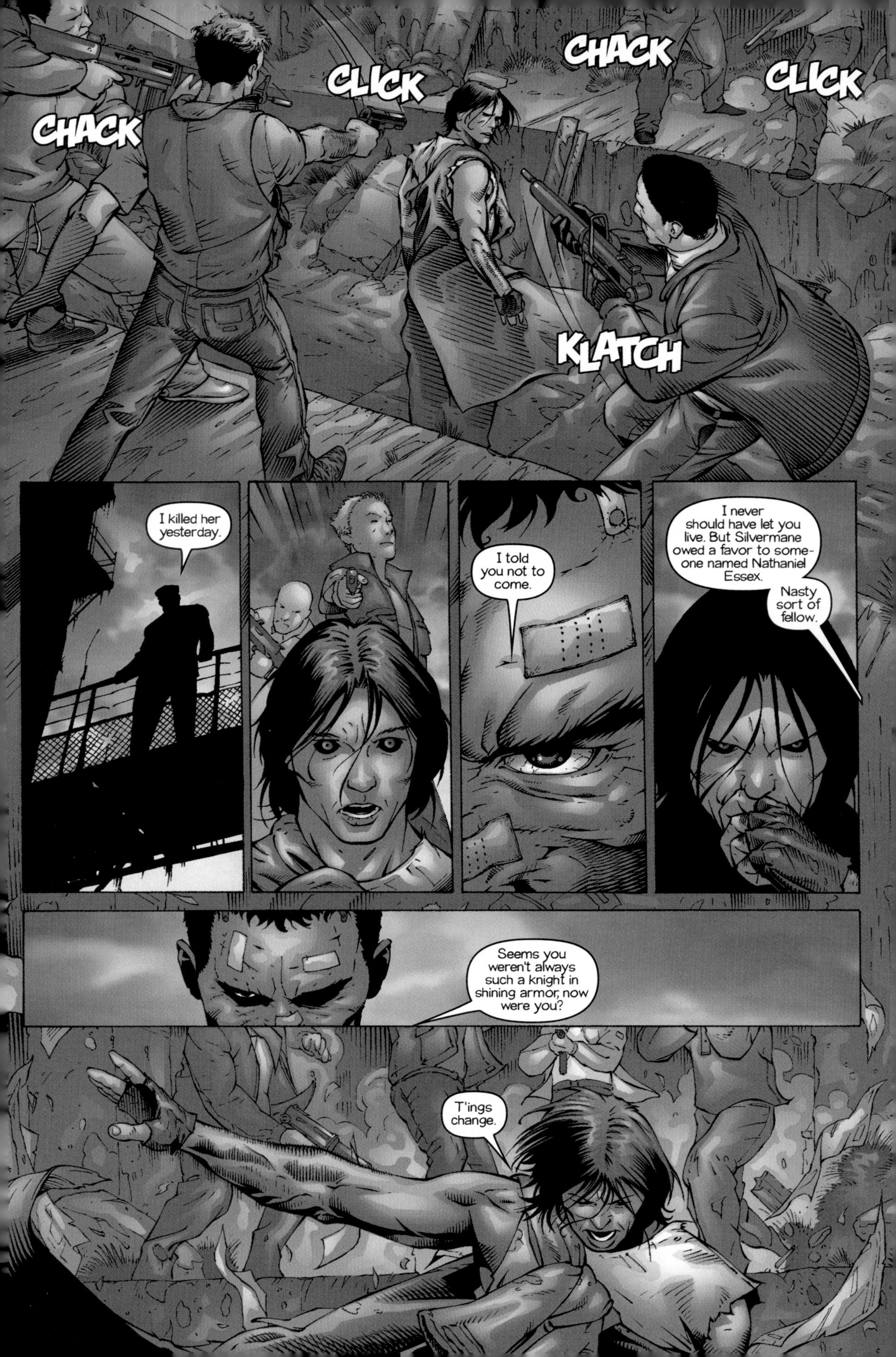
CHACK
CLICK
CHACK
CLICK
KLATCH
I killed her yesterday.
I told you not to come.
I never should have let you live. But Silvermane owed a favor to someone named Nathaniel Essex.
Nasty sort of fellow.
Seems you weren't always such a knight in shining armor, now were you?
T'ings change.

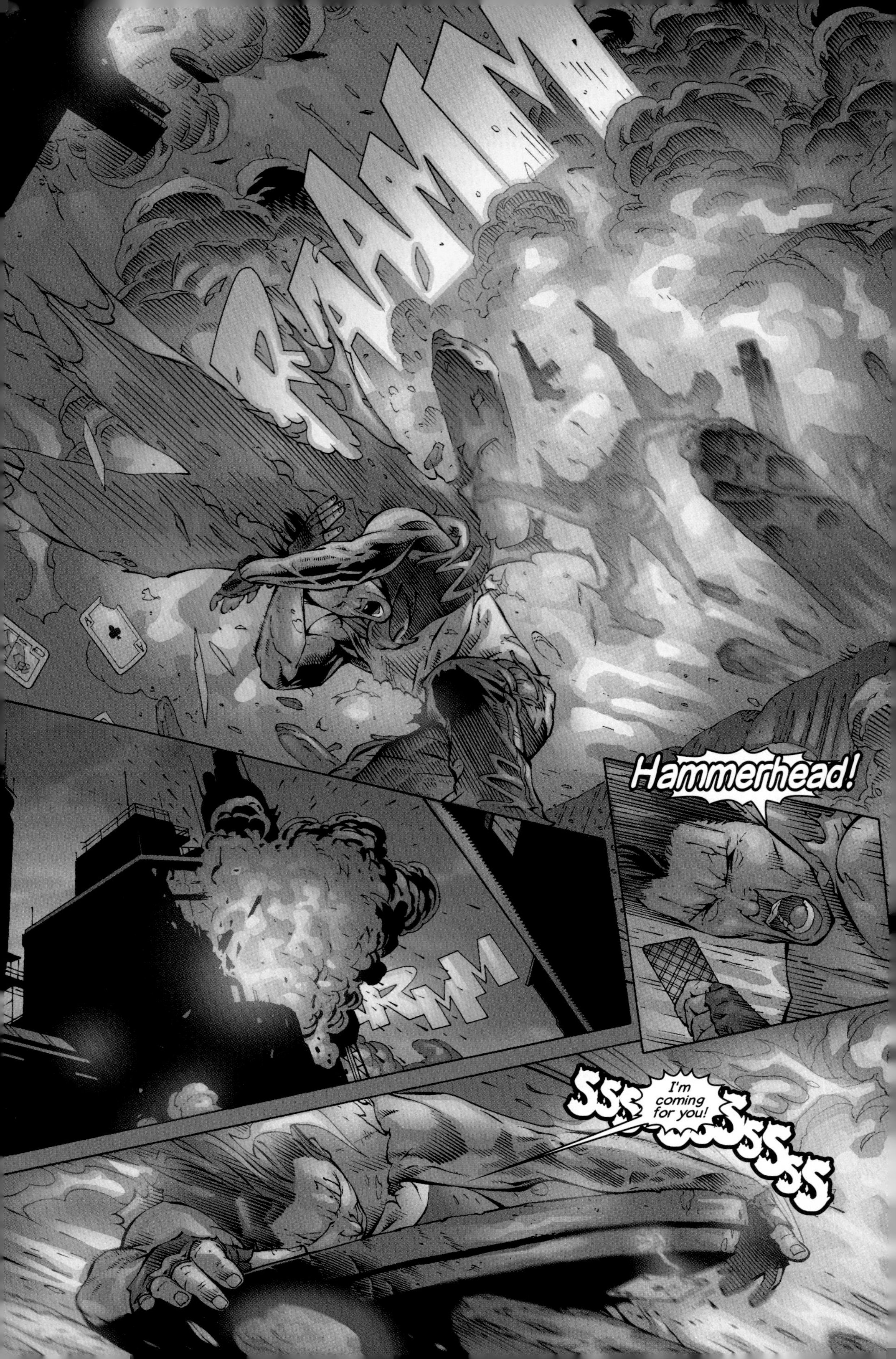
BRAAMM
BRAMM
Hammerhead!
SSSS
I'm coming for you!
SSSSS

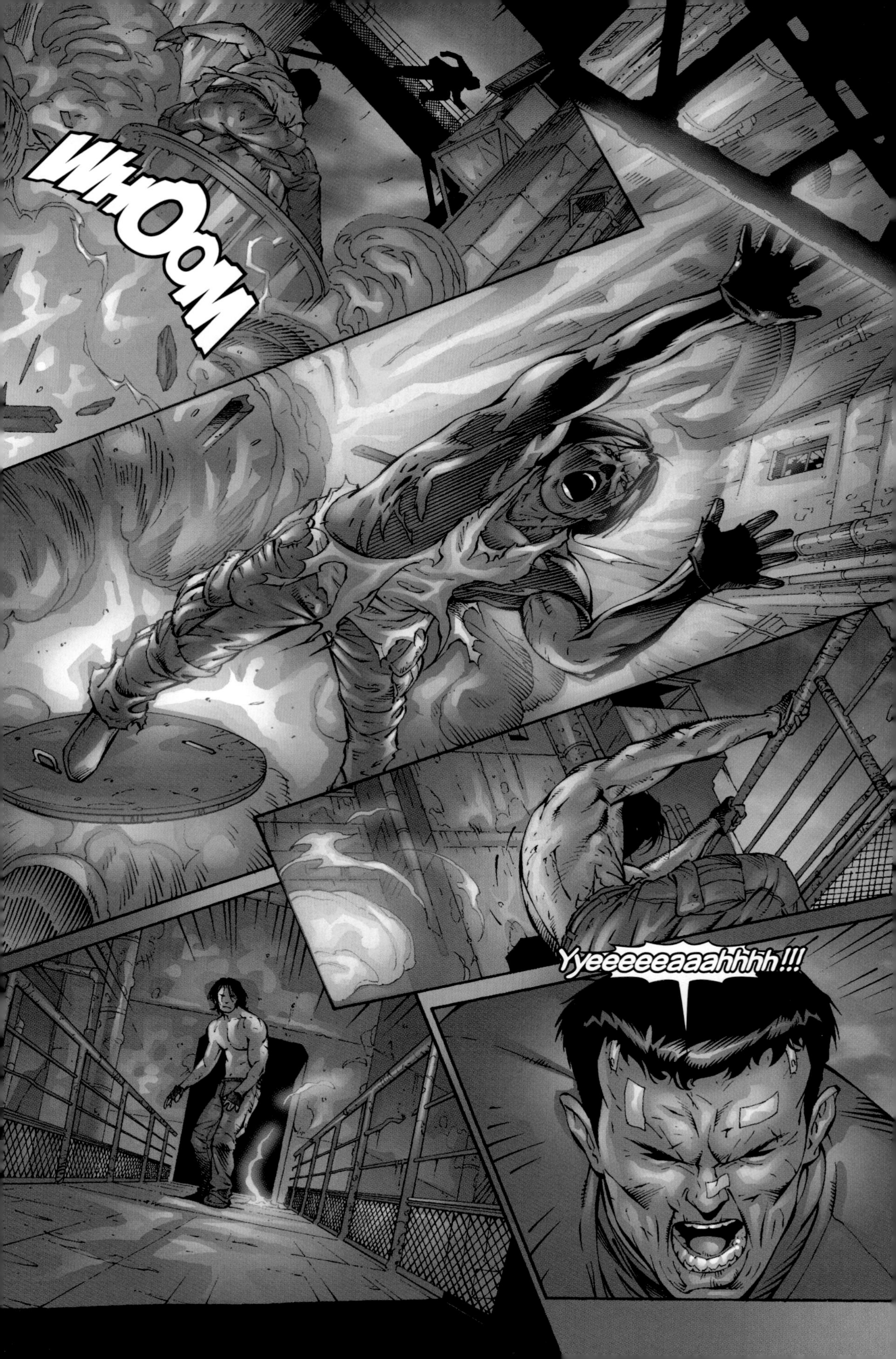
WHOOOM
Yyeeeeeeaaahhhh!!!

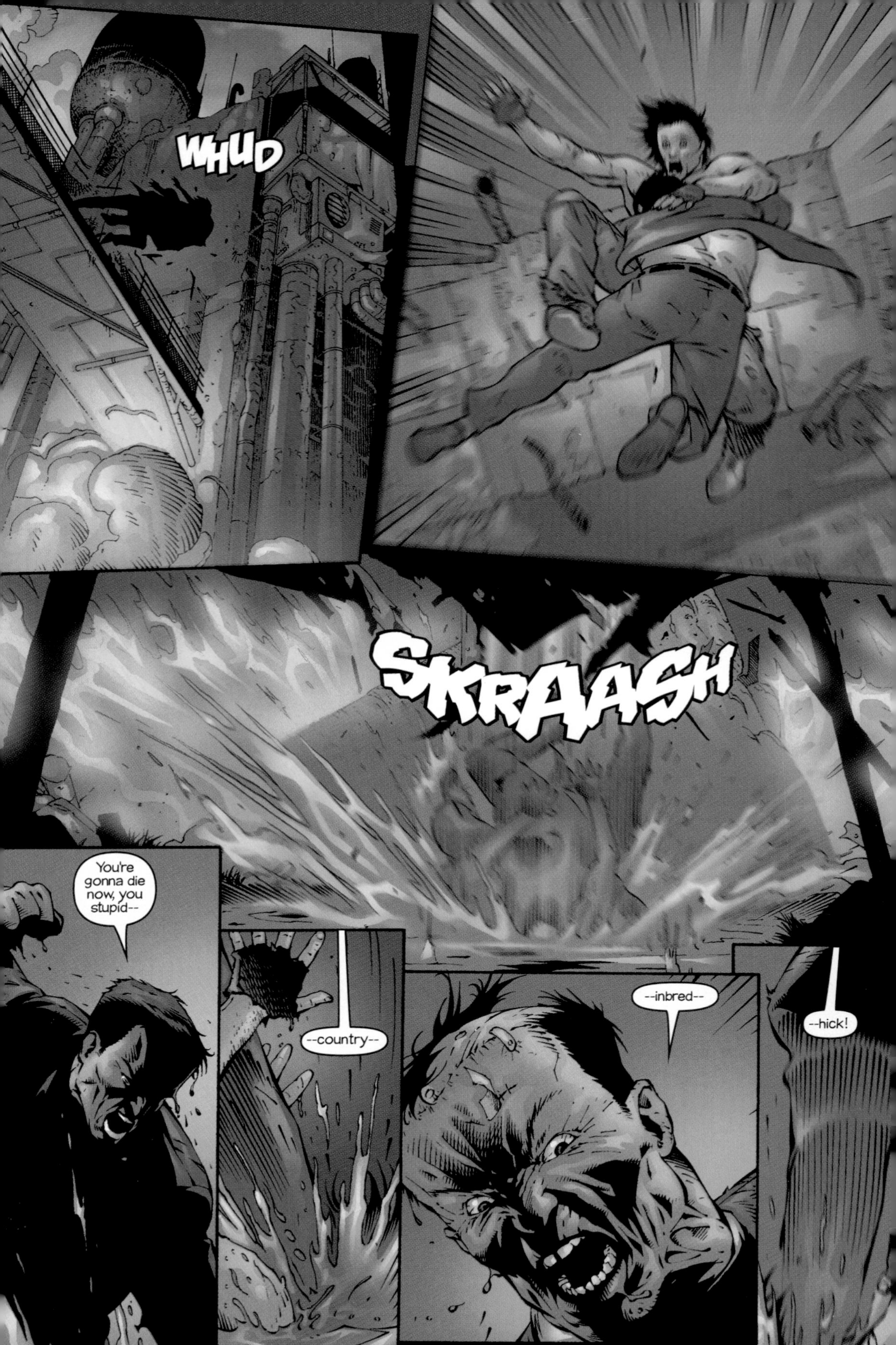
WHUD
SKRAASH
You're gonna die now, you stupid--
--country--
--inbred--
--hick!

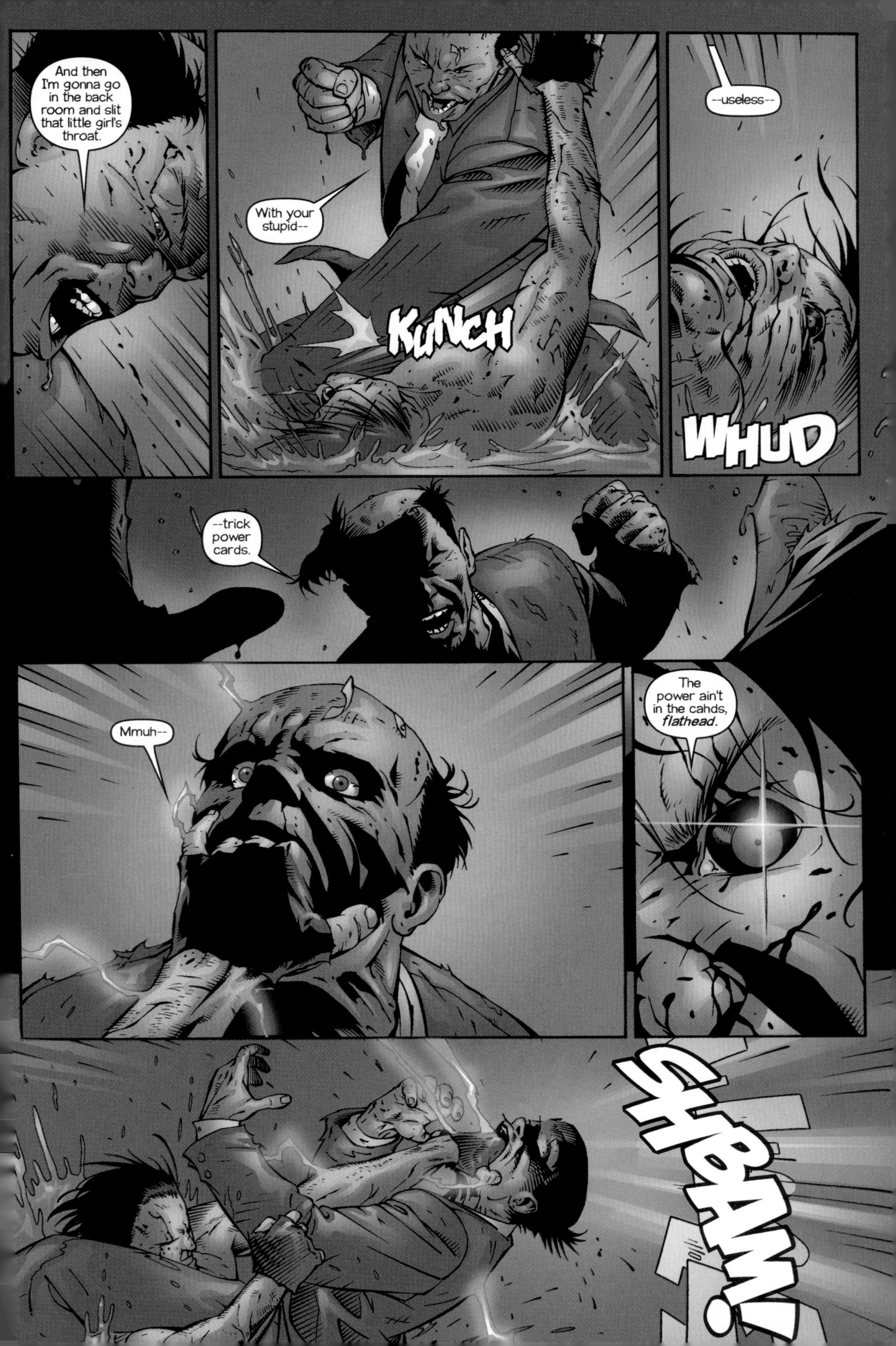
And then I'm gonna go in the back room and slit that little girl's throat.
With your stupid--
KUNCH
--useless--
WHUD
--trick power cards.
Mmuh--
The power ain't in the cahds, *flathead*.
SHBAM!

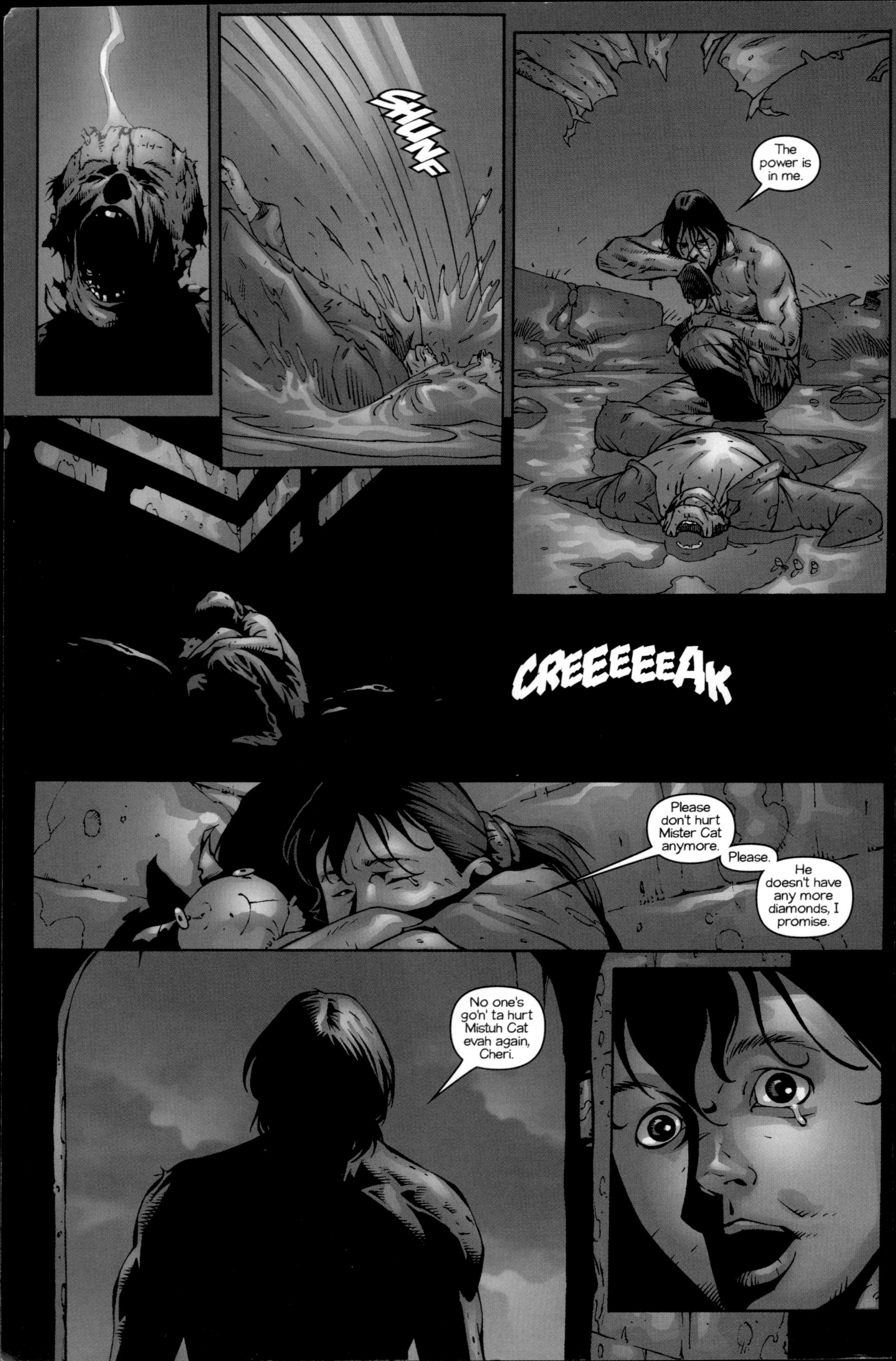

SHUNF
The power is in me.
CREEEEEEAK
Please don't hurt Mister Cat anymore.
Please.
He doesn't have any more diamonds, I promise.
No one's go'n' ta hurt Mistuh Cat evah again, Cheri.

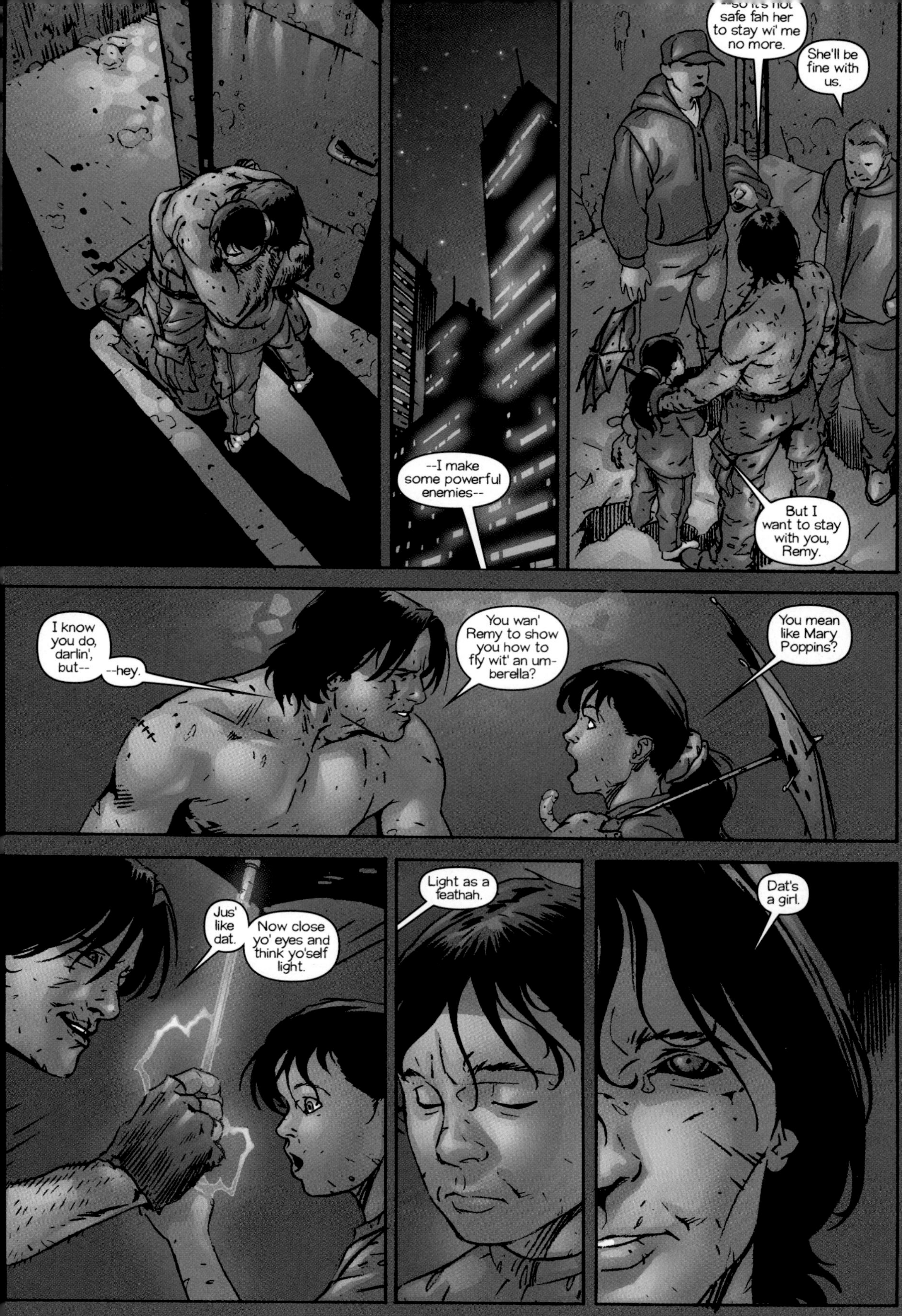
--I make some powerful enemies--
safe fah her to stay wi' me no more.
She'll be fine with us.
But I want to stay with you, Remy.
I know you do, darlin', but--
--hey.
You wan' Remy to show you how to fly wit' an um-berella?
You mean like Mary Poppins?
Jus' like dat.
Now close yo' eyes and think yo'self light.
Light as a feathah.
Dat's a girl.

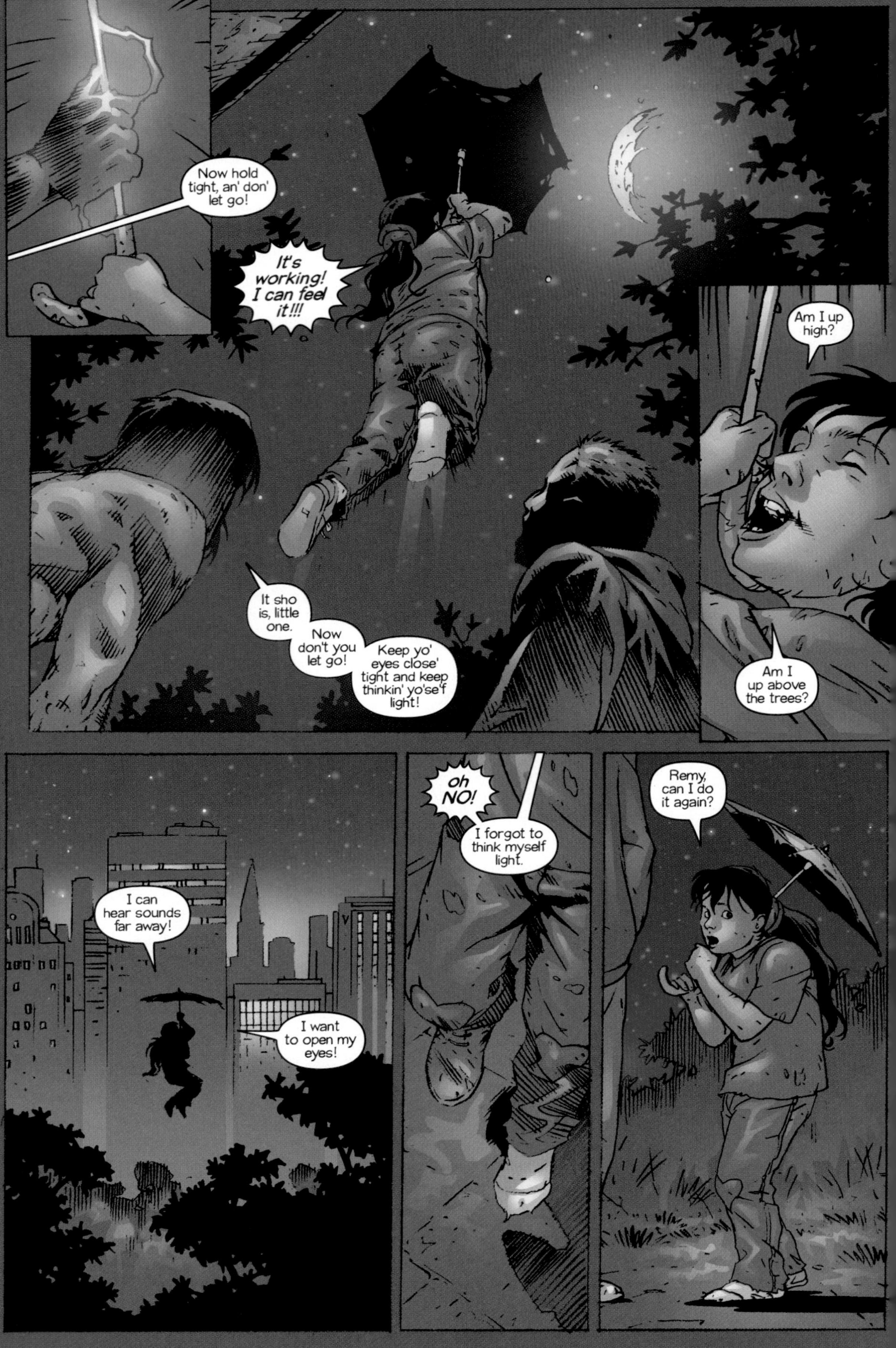
Now hold tight, an' don' let go!
It's working! I can feel it!!!
It sho is, little one.
Now don't you let go!
Keep yo' eyes close' tight and keep thinkin' yo'se'f light!
Am I up high?
Am I up above the trees?
I can hear sounds far away!
I want to open my eyes!
oh NO!
I forgot to think myself light.
Remy, can I do it again?

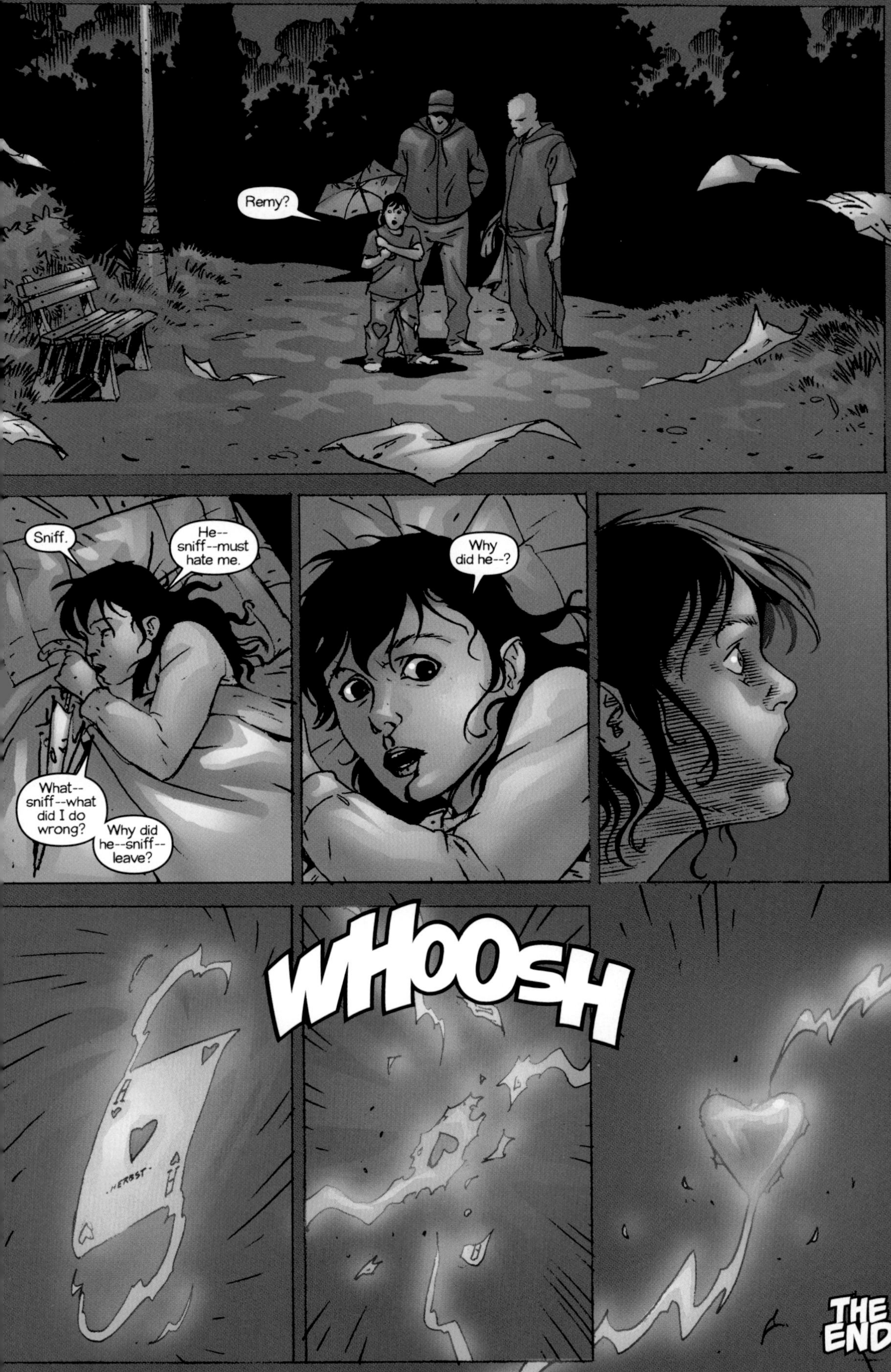
Remy?
Sniff.
He--sniff--must hate me.
What--sniff--what did I do wrong?
Why did he--sniff--leave?
Why did he--?
WHOOSH
THE END

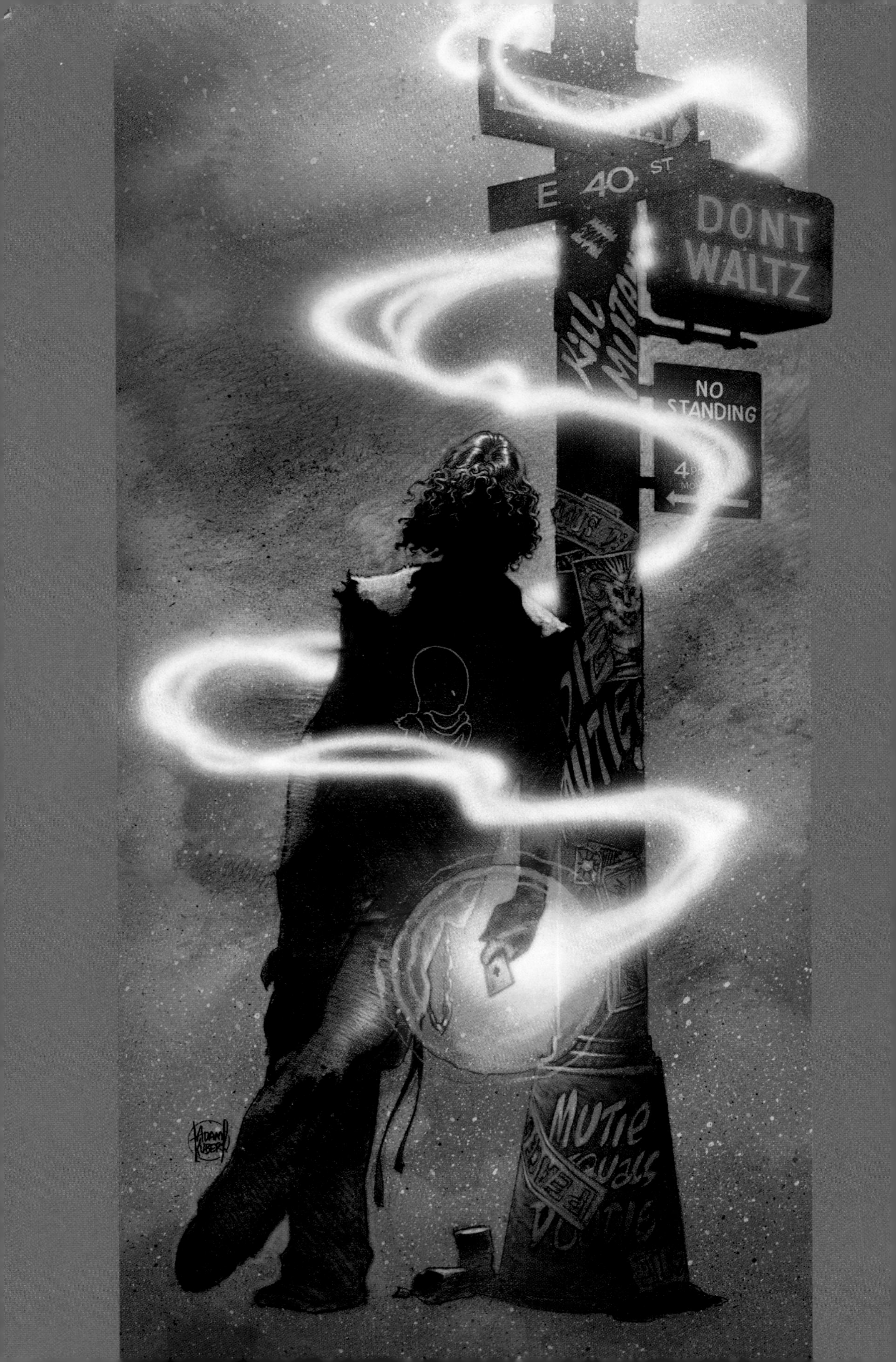
E 40 ST
DONT WALTZ
NO STANDING
MUTIE
ADAM KUBERT

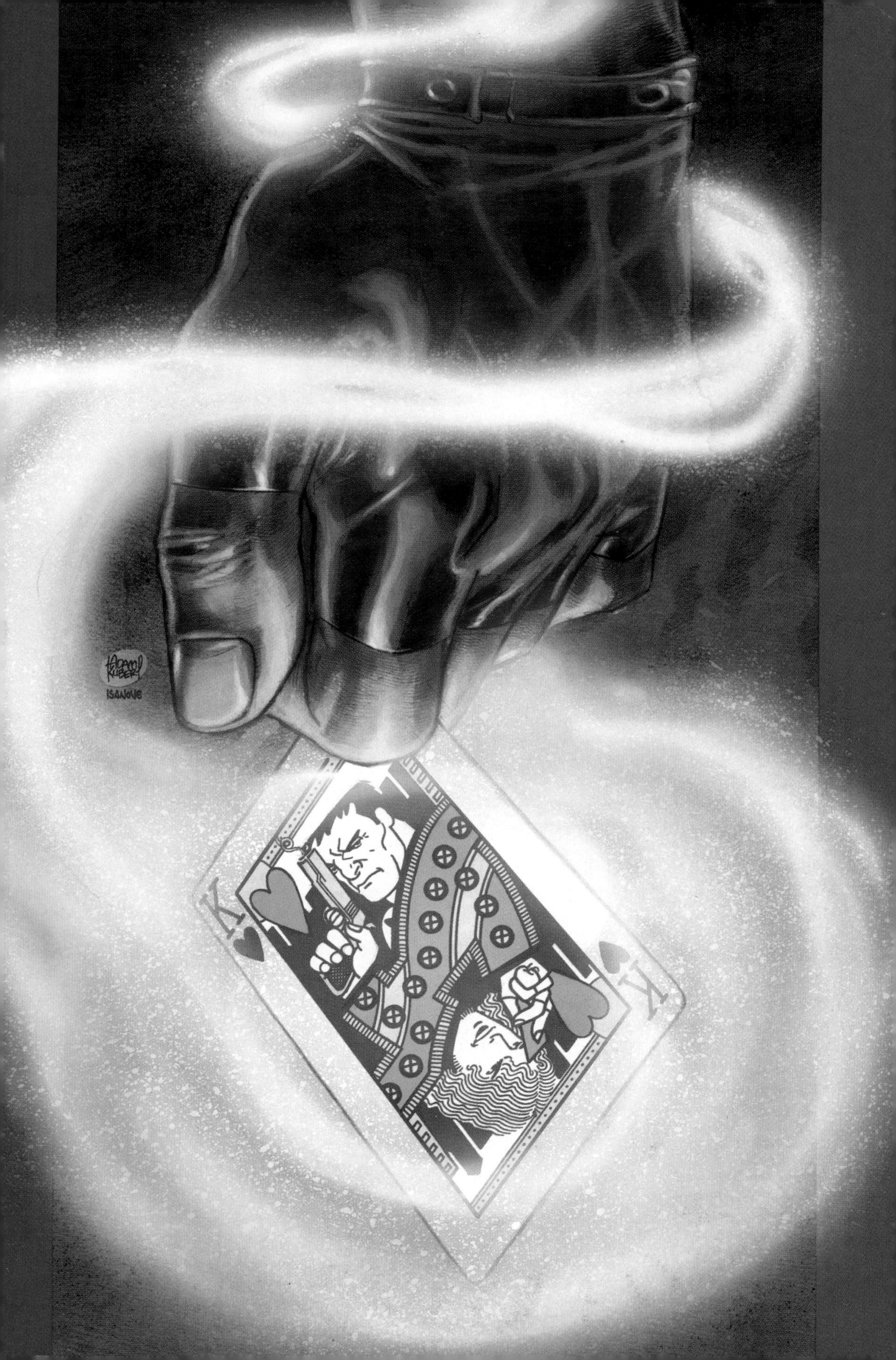

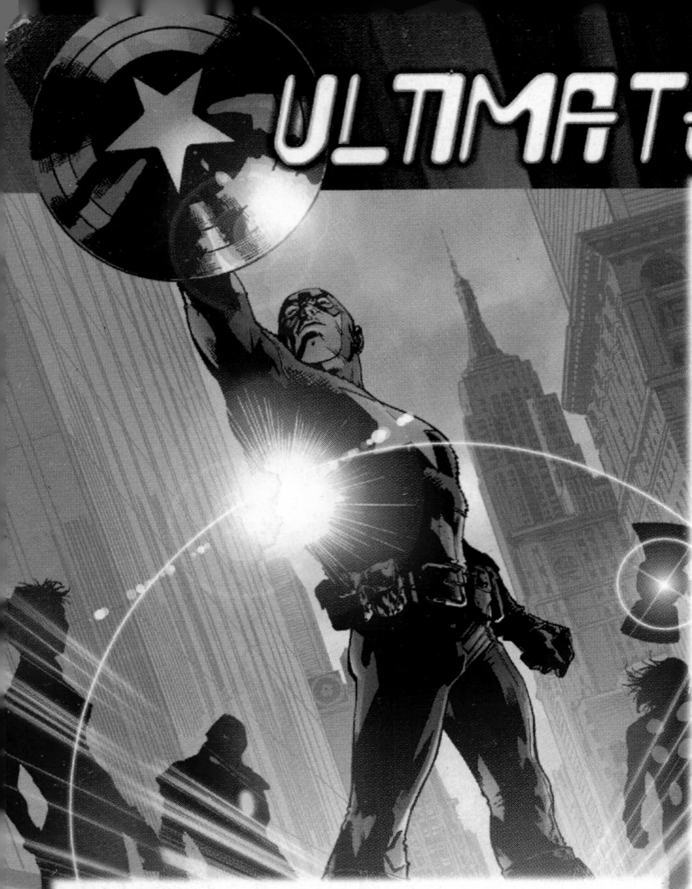
ULTIMATE SAVINGS!